The Right to Know

Initiative for Policy Dialogue at Columbia

Initiative for Policy Dialogue at Columbia

JOSEPH E. STIGLITZ, SERIES EDITOR

The Initiative for Policy Dialogue (IPD) at Columbia University brings together academics, policy makers, and practitioners from developed and developing countries to address the most pressing issues in economic policy today. IPD is an important part of Columbia's broad program on development and globalization. The Initiative for Policy Dialogue at Columbia: Challenges in Development and Globalization presents the latest academic thinking on a wide range of development topics and lays out alternative policy options and trade-offs. Written in a language accessible to policy makers and students alike, this series is unique in that it both shapes the academic research agenda and furthers the economic policy debate, facilitating a more democratic discussion of development policies.

The Right to Know: Transparency for an Open World is an important addition to this series. It attempts to present a balanced account of the debate over secrecy, including stories of efforts to create and enforce new standards of government transparency, as well as examples of legitimate instances in which secrecy may be better than disclosure. *The Right to Know* discusses the political struggles and significant public policy challenges engendered by disclosure policy. Our objective is to help decision makers and citizens better understand the range of policy options and to make difficult choices.

For more information about IPD and its upcoming books, visit www.policydialogue.org.

The Right to Know

Transparency for an Open World

Ann Florini, Editor

FOREWORD BY Joseph E. Stiglitz

Columbia University Press　New York

Columbia University Press
Publishers Since 1893
New York   Chichester, West Sussex
Copyright © 2007 Columbia University Press
All rights reserved

Library of Congress Cataloging-in-Publication Data
The right to know : transparency for an open world /
edited by Ann Florini.
p.   cm. — (Initiative for policy dialogue at Columbia)
Includes bibliographical references and index.
ISBN 978-0-231-14158-1 (cloth : alk. paper)
1. Transparency in government.
2. Freedom of information. I. Florini, Ann.
II. Title. III. Series.
JC598.R547 2007
352.8'8—dc22
2006036068

References to Internet Web sites (URLs) were accurate at
the time of writing. Neither the author nor Columbia
University Press is responsible for URLs that may have
expired or changed since the manuscript was prepared.

Contents

Foreword

There is growing international recognition of the importance of transparency for meaningful and effective democratic processes. How can citizens meaningfully express their voice about what the government is doing if they do not know what the government is doing? And how can they check government abuses? Indeed, what is probably the world's most effective anticorruption NGO, Transparency International, focuses its attention on transparency. As the old expression has it, "Sunshine is the strongest antiseptic."

Excessive secrecy has a corrosive effect on virtually all aspects of society and governance by undermining the quality of public decision making and preventing citizens from checking the abuses of public power. Societies, though, do not have to tolerate such secrecy from their governments. Although it is often a struggle, it is possible to make public institutions more transparent.

My own interest in the subject of transparency is a natural outgrowth of my theoretical work in the economics of information. For four decades, I have studied how imperfect information affects economic processes—how it can lead to abuses of market power and undermine the efficiency of the economy. I have studied closely how managers, for instance, may work to create asymmetries of information to allow them more discretion to benefit themselves at the expense of other stakeholders (including shareholders and workers). When managers abuse their positions, firms will be less efficient; returns on capital will be lower, making it more difficult to raise additional finance. Choice and competition provide an automatic, if only partial, check on abuses. And I have raised concerns about how, for instance, disclosure requirements may reduce the scope for these abuses and increase the efficiency of the economy.

Imperfections of information lead to analogous problems in the political sphere, with even more dire consequences. Choice and competition are typically more limited. Citizens must pay their taxes even if they feel the money is being wasted. Even in countries with democracies, contestability may be limited, and corrupt governments can get reelected. But information about what the government is doing, enabling citizens to scrutinize how their money is being spent, can make a difference. Government officials know this—which is why they often work hard to limit the information available.

For two hundred years, Sweden has had legislation promoting transparency. America's Freedom of Information Act, strengthened in response to the abuses under President Nixon, recognized the citizens' right to know what their government is doing, a marked contrast to the "official secrets acts" that had determined what information was available in other countries, where the presumption was that the citizens did not have the right to know. Democracies have hailed the importance of free speech and free press. But a free press with little or no information about what the government is doing cannot provide an effective check on government. Even as citizens see the right to know as a fundamental right, they have encountered a myriad of problems in implementation. IPD has played an important role in energizing a global movement for legislation supporting the right to know, and we are proud of that.

Most IPD task forces focus on economic issues to help developing countries explore policy alternatives. This book, however, addresses a topic crucial not only to economic development but also to governance in all societies and at all levels. Today, citizens and societies everywhere are grappling with the politics and policy dilemmas of transparency. This book is meant to help in that process.

Joseph E. Stiglitz

Introduction

The Battle Over Transparency

Ann Florini

The cliché is not quite right: information by itself is not power. But it is an essential first step in the exercise of political and economic power. Opening up flows of information changes who can do what. That is why there are few more important struggles in the world today than the battle over who gets to know what.

But the debate over transparency and access to information is more than a power struggle. It is also a war of ideas about what transparency is good for and when secrecy may better serve the public interest. This is no trivial or arcane debate. The arguments for and against transparency reflect fundamental issues about the nature of democracy, good governance, economic efficiency, and social justice, at levels ranging from villages to global institutions.

The debate is encapsulated in part in competing words: "transparency" and "the right to know" versus "privacy" and "national security." It is showing up in a host of skirmishes, in arenas ranging from the offices of municipal governments to corporate boardrooms to the halls of major international organizations. By and large, "transparency"—the term—has been winning the rhetorical debate, so much so that *Webster's* proclaimed it the "Word of the Year" for 2003. But the outcome of the fight for widespread access to information is yet to be decided.

Over the past few decades, citizens in all parts of the world have shown themselves to be increasingly unwilling to tolerate secretive decision making. As a result, India, South Africa, the UK, Japan, Mexico, and a host of other countries all have adopted major freedom of information laws; intergovernmental organizations such as the World Bank and the IMF have adopted sweeping new disclosure policies; and hundreds of major multinational corporations have adopted voluntary codes that require them to disclose a wide range of information about their environmental, labor, and other practices.

Citizens are insisting that governments, IGOs, and corporations should disclose more information on many grounds. Often, demands for greater transparency go with a push to crack down on corruption. The name of the leading anticorruption organization is Transparency International. And transparency is indeed a potent weapon in the anticorruption arsenal. An unfortunately large number of officials, and executives seem to need that bright light shining on them to deter them from turning public service into a means of private gain.

But the proponents of greater disclosure argue vociferously that transparency is far more than an instrument for cleaning up governments. It is a key component of public policy effectiveness and efficiency. Even the most competent and honest decision makers need feedback on how the policies they have set are working out in practice, feedback that is only possible when information flows freely in both directions.

And information access may provide a key to overcoming the disjunctures of globalization.[1] There is a huge disconnect between the global and regional scales at which problems increasingly need to be solved and rules made, and the national scope of political institutions. Examples abound, from highly integrated global capital markets to manufacturing systems to trade policies to public health. Without free access to information, people in one part of the world have little chance of even knowing about—much less having a say in—decisions made far away that affect them.

Beyond the pragmatic arguments for transparency, we find fundamental moral claims. One relates to democracy. As democratic norms become entrenched more widely around the world, it is becoming apparent that a broad right of access to information is fundamental to the functioning of a democratic society. The essence of representative democracy is informed consent, which requires that information about government practices and policies be disclosed. And in democracies, by definition, information about government belongs to the people, not the government.

A human rights argument combines pragmatic and moral claims, seeing access to information as both a fundamental human right and a necessary concomitant of the realization of all other rights. Those of course include the political and civil rights with which freedom of information has long been associated. As Article 19 of the Universal Declaration of Human Rights makes clear, the freedom to speak on public issues is meaningless without the freedom to be informed. Beyond this, advocates increasingly argue that information access is the right that makes possible the achievement of social and economic justice, "one that levers and supports the realization of rights to proper welfare support, clean environment, adequate housing, health care, or education," in the words of one recent book.[2]

Yet citizens seeking information—and governments wanting to open up—find themselves up against powerful forces: entrenched habits, protection of privilege, and fear of how newly released information might be used, or misused. Arguments against disclosure abound everywhere disclosure is sought.

Sometimes those arguments are sound. No reasonable person would demand that a government release information about troop movements in time of war, or require that corporations give away trade secrets essential to their business, or insist that individual citizens sacrifice their basic right to privacy.

But the boundaries of what constitutes legitimate secrecy are rarely obvious. No country wants its adversaries to have access to details about the design and potential weaknesses of its weapons— but soldiers whose lives may be threatened by those weaknesses would benefit greatly from having those weapons subjected to public scrutiny before they are needed. Proprietary business information may include data about potentially dangerous flaws in products sold to children, or about production processes that produce unacceptable toxic emissions. Individual privacy claims need to be weighed against the need of citizens to know whether their leaders are living lives of suspicious luxury on meager public-sector salaries.

And because information is related to power, reason is only part of the debate over how far disclosure should go and when secrecy should reign. The battles over the right to know versus the right to withhold also reflect bitter struggles over existing patterns of political and economic privilege.

This book contains numerous, wide-ranging stories from the battlefront: the grassroots campaigns waged in India under the slogan "The right to know is the right to live"; China's top-down effort to "informationize" its economy; the ongoing international NGO campaign to improve the disclosure policies of intergovernmental organizations such as the World Bank and the International Monetary Fund (IMF); the continuing tensions over whether security is best promoted by secrecy or by greater openness. These stories epitomize the enormous range of policy choices now facing national governments, international organizations, corporations, and citizens' groups. What laws should govern the rights of citizens to have access to government-held information, and how can those laws be meaningfully implemented? To what extent do international organizations, corporations, and citizens' groups have an obligation to reveal information, and to whom? Who is entitled to know what? And what good does disclosure do?

To start the book off, this introduction defines "transparency" and lays out the theoretical reasoning behind the claim that publicly useful information is generally underprovided. Then it provides the historical context, for the fight to know has a long and significant past. Finally, it lays out the plan of the rest of the book.

The Meaning and Purposes of Transparency

Although the word "transparency" is widely used, it is rarely well defined. There is no consensus on what the definition should be or how transparency should be measured. Such problems are not unique to the transparency phenomenon. For example, many political scientists have made valuable contributions to our understanding of domestic and international politics without being able to pinpoint precisely the meaning of so fundamental a concept as "power." But we do need a working definition, something good enough to make for coherent analysis. Of whom is information being demanded? What specific information is needed, and for what purposes?

One reason for the lack of precision is that the term is being used in so many different issue areas. In politics, it is widely used to refer to enabling citizens to gather information on the policies and behavior of their governments.[3] In economics, the Working Group on Transparency and Accountability of the Group of 22 defined it as "a process by which information about existing conditions, decisions and actions is made accessible, visible, and understandable."[4] In the security field, a United Nations group defined transparency as involving the systematic provision of information on specific aspects of military activities under informal or formal international arrangements.[5]

For the purposes of this book, it is most useful to employ a broad definition: "transparency" refers to the degree to which information is available to outsiders that enables them to have informed voice in decisions and/or to assess the decisions made by insiders.

Such a definition gets us beyond the technological focus common to discussions of the information age. Technological determinists assert that we are facing a future of living in a "transparent society" largely because technology is making it increasingly difficult for anyone to hide from scrutiny.[6] The technology is indeed impressive—private companies are now launching high-resolution imaging satellites and selling the resulting data to the general public, video cameras seem to be recording everything everywhere, and advances in miniaturization are making it increasingly difficult for people to know whether they are being observed by some minuscule monitor.[7]

But even the technological marvels now spreading around the world will not make transparency inevitable. Indeed, some of the same technologies that have fostered the information revolution are being used to control the resulting flow of information. Technology can certainly facilitate transparency, but whether it does so depends on a range of policy choices. And much of the world's progress toward greater transparency in recent decades has not required particularly sophisticated information technology.

Instead, the kind of transparency that allows outsiders to hold decision makers accountable and have informed say in decisions requires that decision makers release information, both proactively and in response to requests. The disclosures are not necessarily entirely voluntary, in the sense of being left completely to the discretion of the disclosers. In some cases, governments require corporations or individuals to release information, and in others, intergovernmental or nongovernmental organizations apply pressures that are not legally binding but are nonetheless powerful. Yet those requirements and pressures still leave substantial freedom of action to those who must decide whether, and to what degree, to comply.

And the holders of information often face incentives to keep information secret. Broadly speaking, transparency is valuable because it contributes to overcoming what social scientists call agency problems. In all governance situations, principals (such as citizens or shareholders) delegate responsibility to agents (such as a government or a corporate board) to make decisions on their behalf. Problems arise because the principals are never able to perfectly monitor their agents: they know less about the situation the agents face and the actions they take than the agents themselves do. So the agents may make misguided or self-serving decisions against the interests of their unknowing, unseeing bosses.

Why do these information asymmetries occur? To some extent, they are the unavoidable outgrowth of a useful division of labor. Insiders such as government officials and corporate managers are more informed than outsiders because the outsiders have delegated management to them. Outsiders delegate responsibility in this way partly because it is costly to become informed and make decisions. (The other reason is that deliberating and making decisions is more efficient with a smaller group.) If gathering and processing the information required to make decisions were a simple matter, then there would be less need for such representative governing institutions as corporate boards and parliaments. Principals cannot acquire the full range of information available to their agents without negating the efficiency advantage of having agents.

But this division of labor creates opportunities that agents/insiders can readily exploit by withholding so much information that accountability becomes difficult. Officials have strong motives for keeping others ignorant of their behavior. One is that secrecy provides some insulation against being accused of making a mistake. It is much easier for an official to deflect criticism if important information about the situation the official faced, the decision that was made, and who made it remains secret. A second incentive is that secrecy provides the opportunity for special interests to have greater sway. Relationships with special interests allow insiders to exchange favorable policies for personal gain (in the form of naked bribery, campaign contributions, or perks), but it is more difficult to maintain these profitable relationships when financial transactions and the decision-making process are transparent.

The History and Current State of Transparency

Demands for open flows of information have a long history in both politics and economics. Sweden claims pride of place as the first country to have a law granting its citizens access to government-held information, enacted in the late eighteenth century.[8] But other countries have grappled with the issue for a long time. One of the framers of the American Constitution, James Madison, wrote compellingly on the importance of information in a democracy:

> A popular Government, without popular information, or the means of acquiring it, is but prologue to a farce or a tragedy; or perhaps both. Knowledge will forever govern ignorance; and a people who mean to be their own governors must arm themselves with the power which knowledge gives.[9]

In the private sphere, corporations have found themselves facing demands for disclosure of financial data for almost as long as publicly held corporations have existed. Great Britain experimented with disclosure laws starting in the mid-1800s. In the United States, starting early in the 1900s, large numbers of small investors proved able to put substantial political pressure on the government to institute corporate disclosure standards that would protect them from deceit and insider dealings.

After World War II, with the expansion of governmental bureaucracies in many countries and the emergence of multinational corporations and large intergovernmental organizations came new concentrations of power able to withhold information from people whose lives they affected. At the same time, the Cold War led to the rise of a highly secretive national security complex in the traditional bastion of transparency, the United States.

Counterpressures to all this were limited, although there were some. One notable victory for transparency came in the form of the U.S. Freedom of Information Act, first passed in 1966 and strengthened in 1974. In the 1980s, transnational networks of civil society activists launched campaigns demanding information from intergovernmental organizations, particularly the World Bank. East and West negotiated some arms control agreements that included verification provisions that made the security establishments of the two sides increasingly transparent to each other.

But the real explosion of global demands for disclosure came in the 1990s. Early in that decade, only around a dozen countries had laws providing for public access to government-held information. These were largely the established democracies of the English-speaking world and Scandinavia. Ever since, however, adopting disclosure laws and policies has become something of an international fad. As of 2006, the total is on the order of 70 countries, with more adopting such laws all the time.[10] The new additions include countries with varying levels of democratic traditions and varying degrees of economic advancement. All found themselves pressed by the spread of democratic norms, the increasing strength of civil society organizations, and the rise of increasingly independent media around the world to agree to release vastly more information to their citizens than ever before.

At the same time, global economic integration led international investors (and the governments of capital-rich countries) to demand disclosures on corporate and national accounts in emerging economies, especially in the wake of the 1990s Asian crisis, which many blamed on excessive secrecy by Asian corporations and governments. International financial institutions—the World Bank and the International Monetary Fund—which are major promoters of economic integration, began demanding information from their member governments and then posting it on Web sites. Those institutions themselves faced intense pressure from activists around the world to open up their analyses and processes of decision making.

In the late 1990s, with the American economy soaring and economic crises plaguing markets in Asia, Russia, and Latin America, the American system of corporate disclosure—the rules governing accounting and auditing, the professionalism of auditors, the conventions of corporate governance that emphasized detailed and timely financial reporting to investors—was heralded as a model for the rest of the world. With the outbreak of corporate scandals just after the turn of the century, however, the adequacy of American-style corporate financial disclosure was again in doubt. When the twenty-first century began, Enron, then the seventh largest U.S. company, enjoyed an extraordinary reputation for innovation and success.[11] But shortly thereafter, its long-masked internal financial shenanigans came to light, leading to its collapse. The machinations of corporate insiders at such scandal-ridden firms not only deprived millions of shareholders (and employees) of savings and retirement benefits but also may have contributed substantially to the global meltdown of financial markets.[12]

The damage showed that the much-vaunted American model of disclosure-based corporate financial regulation had failed to keep up with the times. The U.S. Congress moved rapidly to patch up the regulatory framework, enacting the Sarbanes-Oxley Act. That law, among many other things, requires the chief executive officer and the chief financial officer of publicly traded firms to sign off on audit reports personally and tightens standards for what financial information must be publicly disclosed.[13]

As of this writing, the fallout continues. The two top Enron officials charged with the massive fraud that brought the company down were convicted on most charges in May 2006. Sarbanes-Oxley remains a bone of contention, with some in the business community complaining of arduous compliance costs.

The United States is also at the center of renewed debate over the relationship between secrecy and national security. Civil libertarians, transparency activists, and increasingly members of both political parties contend that the Bush administration has reversed long-standing trends toward greater openness in that country, even to the point of secretly reclassifying vast quantities of documents already in the public record.[14]

In short, early twenty-first century transparency is in a state of flux. The traditional proponent of transparency, the United States, is sending very mixed messages to the rest of the world. Nonetheless, dozens of countries are pushing ahead with new disclosure laws and regulations that apply not only to the public sector but increasingly to the private sector as well.

In Asia, even the one-party state in China has taken significant steps toward greater governmental disclosure, and India's revised national freedom of information law, passed in 2005, stands as one of the world's most comprehensive disclosure laws. Most Latin American countries have a right to information included in their constitution, although these generally have not been either implemented or enforced. But in 2004, the presidents and prime ministers of the Americas committed themselves to providing the legal framework for implementing the right to information.[15] More than half a dozen Central and South American countries have disclosure laws, and enabling legislation is being debated or considered in almost all countries in Central America and the Caribbean as well as South America, with the notable exceptions of Cuba and Venezuela.[16] The case is similar in Africa, where a number of countries include the right to information in their constitutions, and more than three years ago the Declaration of Principles on Freedom of Expression, reaffirming the African Charter on Human and People's Rights, provided a similar mandate to heads of state. However, only a handful of African countries, most notably South Africa, have passed or are even considering relevant legislation. And around the world, the efficacy of the whole panoply of laws, rules, and voluntary standards remains very much in question.

Plan of the Book

The chapters in this book paint a vivid portrait of how transparency has evolved over the past few decades, where the world now stands, and what issues are likely to be confronted in the ongoing struggle between secrecy and disclosure. They show that the transparency picture is quite mixed. Information access is certainly more widespread now than it was several decades ago, but we are far from living in a truly transparent world, and some trends, particularly in the security field, may point toward a more secretive future.

We begin with a series of detailed case studies of how and why information-access laws came into being in several countries and regions, of particular interest for the lessons they can teach the rest of the world. One such case study is India. Unlike nearly every other country's campaign for greater access to information access, spearheaded by middle-class professionals, India's drive was fueled from the grassroots up. Other actors—not least an impressively independent Supreme Court—have played vital roles. But Shekhar Singh shows that the chief lesson from India is how some of society's most marginalized voices can effectively demand the information they need to protect their most basic rights.

China presents a very different perspective, with the transparency trend driven from the top. Hanhua Zhou provides an insider's perspective on how the government's push to modernize its economy has led to reforms aimed at increasing openness at many levels, from village affairs to national legislation. Jamie Horsley gives us an outsider's take on why China is evolving as it is, and what special considerations arise when a nondemocratic regime attempts to ride the transparency tiger.

Ivan Szekeley's overview of Central and Eastern Europe pulls lessons from a region that has undergone a dramatic transformation in the past two decades. His chapter shows that the region presents in microcosm a whole slew of issues relevant to information access: democratization; the role of intergovernmental organizations; the role of business; the importance of learning from one country to another; the conflict with traditional conceptions of security; the special attention often given to information about the environment; and the difficulties of implementing laws on information disclosure, especially when those laws are not designed with implementation in mind.

Ayo Obe's chapter on Nigeria affords a cautionary tale about how difficult it can be to bring about passage of access to information legislation. Nigeria is a hard case for reasons common to many countries: pervasive corruption; the general lack of public outrage over that corruption in a country whose wealth is based on natural resources that most citizens do not feel they own; the colonial heritage of secrecy and ethnic divisions. Nonetheless, a small but active constituency is pushing hard for greater transparency.

The book then turns to several thematic chapters. Of course, the simple passage of a law does not guarantee public access to government information, as the chapter on implementation by Laura Neuman and Richard Calland makes clear. The successful implementation of a transparency law requires a number of supporting institutions: the bureaucratic apparatus to store information and process access requests, watchdog groups to pressure the government to keep its commitment to access, and legal institutions to uphold the access law. Without each of these, information access can easily be stifled even with the best laws. The chapter points to a number of examples drawn from Latin America, which is not otherwise covered in this book, but lessons on implementation apply across the board. South Africa's Promotion of Access to Information Act (POATIA), for example, has been recognized as the "gold standard" of freedom of information laws but has suffered serious problems of implementation. An NGO survey of South African government agencies found that 54 percent of agencies contacted were unaware of the act, 16 percent were aware of it but not implementing it, and only 30 percent were aware and implementing it.[17]

Richard Calland then examines whether and when disclosure should be required of private as well as public entities. In addition to the questions of financial disclosures, corporations are facing growing pressures to release other types of information. The "corporate social responsibility" movement is calling on them to improve their environmental and labor practices. Because the activists doubt that either national governments or international organizations will effectively regulate business behavior in these areas, they are conducting campaigns, aimed at consumers and investors, intended to pressure corporations into adopting and complying with codes of good conduct. To demonstrate compliance, corporations are pressured to release information on their practices. And because privatization is moving the provision of public goods into private hands, serious questions arise about when business-held information falls under the heading of proprietary secrets, and when the release of that information is essential for public accountability.

The transparency rules of intergovernmental organizations such as the World Bank, the IMF, and the World Trade Organization (WTO) have been among the most hotly contested issues in globalization debates in recent years. Critics have alleged that these institutions work too secretively, denying outside organizations and citizens the ability to weigh in on fundamental decisions about national and international economic and social policies. As Thomas Blanton's chapter shows, the intergovernmental organizations are caught between different modes of thinking: the diplomatic and central banking sectors whence they came, with heavy traditions of secrecy and confidentiality, and new expectations of openness that transparency proponents argue are more appropriate to their expanding roles in the growing global regulatory system.

Having looked at transparency practices at the national, regional, corporate, and intergovernmental levels, the book turns to two chapters that focus on issue areas. First, Vivek Ramkumar and Elena Petkova examine transparency as a tool of environmental governance. Over the past half century, environmental degradation has emerged as an issue of front-rank importance, but one where good decision making has proven particularly elusive. The extent of humanity's impact on the planet, due both to population growth and to increasingly intense use of natural resources, threatens to overwhelm the absorptive capacity of the natural environment. But because information revealing the extent of the problem is often not even collected, much less widely distributed, the effects are often ignored until after massive—perhaps irreparable—damage has already been done. Ramkumar and Petkova show how new regulatory approaches based on disclosure are leading the way toward a new paradigm of governance involving a high degree of citizen participation—which may prove useful for global problem solving across the board.

Alasdair Roberts tackles the crucial debate over whether secrecy or transparency best assures security. That debate took on new intensity after the events of September 11, 2001, particularly within the United States, where the government has cited national security concerns as the rationale for a number of rollbacks in public access. In the aftermath of the terrorist attacks, the Bush administration removed a variety of information from government Web sites, created new exemptions to the Freedom of Information Act, and extended classification authority to some domestic agencies such as the Department of Agriculture and the Environmental Protection Agency (EPA). A number of transparency gains made in the 1990s, such as the increased disclosure of information about risks to citizens from chemical plant accidents, have been threatened or lost. Outside the United States, however, September 11 has had relatively little impact on thinking about transparency. Although U.S. backtracking makes a handy excuse for those already opposed to opening up, it has not overwhelmed the movement for greater transparency around the world. Indeed, some dozen countries have adopted access to information laws since then.

Whither Transparency?

The book's conclusion by Ann Florini weaves together many of the various threads of the preceding chapters. Two major themes emerge. First, the trend toward transparency that has emerged in recent years provides no certain indicator of the future. Given that there is no technological inevitability to the spread of transparency, it remains unclear whether policy makers in both the public and private sectors will continue to favor increasing levels of disclosure. Indeed, in some cases, as the security chapter makes clear, the trend appears to be toward greater opacity. Nor is it clear whether the level of civil society demand for disclosure will create sufficient pressures to overcome the continued reluctance of many decision makers to open themselves to public scrutiny.

Second, transparency can be an effective, sometimes a transformative, tool serving the public interest. But merely demanding or disclosing information is not enough to ensure that openness achieves its intended goals. Policy makers and citizens alike have to do the hard work—designing intelligent policies, ensuring their implementation, and keeping up political pressures to ensure that private interests in preserving secrecy do not succeed. This book offers many lessons in how to achieve those goals.

NOTES

1. Ann Florini, *The Coming Democracy: New Rules for Running a New World* (Washington, DC: Island Press, 2003 and Brookings Institution Press, 2005).

2. Richard Calland and Alison Tilley, eds., *The Right to Know, the Right to Live: Access to Information and Socio-economic Justice* (Cape Town, South Africa: Open Democracy Advice Centre, 2002), v.

3. See, for example, the many references to transparency in the documents of the European Union, such as the Amsterdam Treaty. Information available from http://europa.edu.int/eur-lex/lex/en/treaties/treaties_other.htm.

4. International Monetary Fund, *Report of the Working Group on Transparency and Accountability* (Washington, DC: International Monetary Fund, 1998).

5. United Nations Experts Group, Report to the Secretary General, UN Document A/46/301, *Study on Ways and Means of Promoting Transparency in International Transfers of Conventional Arms* (New York: United Nations, 1991). One researcher found nearly a dozen definitions, all related to the

ease with which information flows among various actors. See Alexandru Grigorescu, "The Conceptualization and Measurement of Transparency," paper prepared for the Annual Meeting of the northeastern American Political Science Association and International Studies Association–Northeast, Albany, NY, 2000, 16–17.

6. David Brin, *The Transparent Society* (Reading, MA: Addison-Wesley, 1998).

7. Ann Florini and Yahya Dehqanzada, "Commercial Satellite Imagery Comes of Age," *Issues in Science and Technology* 16 (1) (1999): 45–52; Ann Florini, "The End of Secrecy," *Foreign Policy* 111 (1998): 50–63.

8. Gustaf Petren, "Access to Government-Held Information in Sweden," in Norman S. Marsh, ed., *Public Access to Government-Held Information: A Comparative Symposium*, 35–54 (London: Stevens & Son, 1987).

9. James Madison, Letter to W. T. Barry, August 4, 1822, in Philip R. Fendall, *Letters and Other Writings of James Madison Published by Order of Congress* (Philadelphia: Lippincott, 1865), III:276, available at www.jmu.edu/madison/center/main_pages/madison_archives/quotes/great/issues.htm.

10. See the biannual surveys of the state of freedom of information laws around the world conducted by David Banisar of Privacy International, at http://www.privacyinternational.org/article.shtml?cmd[347]=x-347-543400.

11. This discussion draws from Shang-Jin Wei and Heather Milkiewicz, "A Case of 'Enronitis'? Opaque Self-Dealing and the Global Financial Effect," Brookings Institution Policy Brief #118, 2003.

12. Shang-Jin Wei and Heather Milkiewicz, "A Global Crossing for Enronitis," *Brookings Review* 21 (2) (2003): 28–31.

13. http://frwebgate.access.gpo.gov/cgi-bin/getdoc.cgi?dbname=107_cong_reports&docid=f:hr610.107.pdf.

14. Mathew M. Aid, "Declassification in Reverse: The U.S. Intelligence Community's Secret Historical Document Reclassification Program," February 21, 2006, http://www.gwu.edu/~nsarchiv/NSAEBB/NSAEBB179/index.htm.

15. In January 2004, the heads of state in the Western Hemisphere met in Mexico to discuss poverty, trade, democracy, and development. At the conclusion of the Summit of the Americas, these 34 presidents proclaimed that "Access to information held by the state . . . is an indispensable condition for citizen participation and promotes effective respect for human rights." Declaration of Nuevo Leon, Summit of the Americas, Monterrey, Mexico, January 2004. The declaration further recommended that all states commit themselves to "providing the legal and regulatory framework and

the structures and conditions required to guarantee the right to access to information of our citizens." Cuban leader Fidel Castro was not invited. This description of the state of transparency in Africa and Latin America is courtesy of Laura Neuman and Richard Calland.

16. The Venezuelan government has tried to link hemispheric access to information provisions to more controversial freedom of press issues, most recently at the Organization of American States (OAS) General Assembly. Beyond these efforts, Venezuela has been silent on passage of a national law.

17. Alison Tilley and Victoria Mayer, "Access to Information Law and the Challenge of Effective Implementation: The South African Case," in Richard Calland and A. Tilley, eds., *The Right to Know, the Right to Live: Access to Information and Socio-Economic Justice* (Cape Town: Open Democracy Advice Center, 2002), 72–85; Freedominfo.org, *Public Servants Don't Know the Law, Aren't Implementing Transparency* (2002), http://www.freedominfo. org/reports/safrica2.htm.

PART ONE

National Stories

Chapter One

India

Grassroots Initiatives

Shekhar Singh

In India, as perhaps the world over, the battle for the right to information is a battle for political space. Many elements in the Indian society and system of governance make this a critical battle. For one, India is a robust democracy where political parties and candidates have to work very hard to influence voters. Increasingly, the people of India have been demanding better governance and are no longer willing to rely solely on elections to hold officials accountable. The right to information has given them an opportunity to call their government and its functionaries to account not only once every five years, when they cast their votes, but every day.

Also, transparency is an issue that cuts across all of the traditional areas of concern and action. The fact that the right to information (RTI) movement in India has recognized this and has consequently made a conscious effort to integrate with other movements has ensured that the campaign for increased transparency is diverse, creative, and strong.

Today many civil society groups are using the right to information in their struggles. The women's movement in the state of

Rajasthan, for example, has used it to demand that the women against whom atrocities have been committed are kept informed of the progress in their case and the details of various medico-legal and forensic reports. Many civil liberties and human rights groups across the country are now using the RTI to ensure transparency and accountability of the police and custodial institutions. Activists in the state of Maharashtra are exposing the use of influence in the transfer of government officials and in the leasing of public land to private parties.

The use of the RTI is becoming widespread among movements working with people displaced by dams and factories, those denied their share of food by the ration shop owner, communities affected by polluting industrial units, or forest dwellers evicted from their homes. In many cases, the information asked for is not provided appropriately, or at all. However, it is becoming increasingly difficult to outright deny to the people the information they seek. As movements and groups sharpen their questions and develop their skills, the government and other institutions are being forced to reveal more and more. Clearly, the notion of a right to information has become part of the language of sociopolitical discourse. The nature of the right is every day being defined by the actions of mass movements and of individuals, who are matching their own resolve to access information with the inherent hesitation of established systems of governance and influence to opening themselves for public scrutiny.

This chapter tells the story of how the common people of India, in villages and cities, have started demanding accountability of their bureaucracy and their elected representatives. The first part briefly traces the evolution of the notion of transparency in India. It then discusses in detail some of the various people's movements that typify the Indian experience, including the pioneering movements in the Indian states of Rajasthan, Delhi, and Maharashtra, and the focus on transparency in the environmental movement and in the movement for cleaner elections. Then it goes on to describe the process of formulating the right to information laws in India and ends with a discussion on contemporary issues and debates relating to transparency, including possible future directions.

The Evolution of the Notion of Transparency in India

Initial demands for transparency in the 1950s, after the installation of an independent Indian government, were heard in relation to corruption, to reports regarding disasters (especially railway accidents), and increasingly about human rights. Also, debates about transparency in public life were part of the debates among political parties and even among the ruling Congress Party, as the following passage will illustrate.

> Prime Minister Nehru has asked Congressmen not to close their eyes to the fact that a lot of "impurities" do exist in the Congress organisation from which even some of the "highest people in the party hierarchy are not immune." At the Congress Subjects Committee meeting at Satyamurthinagar (Avadi) on January 20 [1955], Mr. Nehru was intervening in the debate on the resolution moved by Mr. Morarji Desai on purity and strengthening the organisation. Referring to the point made earlier by Mr. Algurai Shastri that the resolution should not publicise the malpractices that had crept into the Congress, Mr. Nehru said this approach was completely wrong. "I have heard the speeches made by delegates. Mr. Algurai Shastri has said that in one paragraph of the resolution we have criticised ourselves and thereby put the noose round our necks which other people might use to drag us with. But this has no relation to the resolution. I say that the resolution is appropriate, full sixteen annas in the rupee. I say, and say it with a challenge, that the atmosphere in the Congress is not good and pure. After all what is the yardstick with which we are going to measure our work and ourselves? I have been President of the Congress and I know from personal experience that there is a lot of impurity in the Congress and even some of the biggest Congressmen are a party to it. Why should we hide these things? Are we to live behind purdah and wear a veil?[1]

Concurrently, various factors were making the Indian public increasingly restless to be included in the process of governance. For one, the rhetoric about independence and democracy, let loose after the British left, had started working. The general public had begun to believe that the government was theirs and that they had rights in relation to it. Even though there was little genuine empowerment, there was an increasing sense of empowerment. Along with this, education and literacy were spreading and more and more people could read and write. A new generation was coming up that had never known imperial rule and had, as a consequence, a healthy irreverence for those in authority. Besides, the domination of a single political party, the Congress Party, was waning, and alternate political formations were emerging and raising questions.

Perhaps most important was the spread of media. Apart from newspapers, the radio network rapidly grew to cover almost the whole country by the 1960s. Though the government controlled all the radio channels, at least their existence ensured that the horizons of the Indian public were significantly widened and they started getting interested in things happening hundreds, sometimes thousands, of miles away.

Equally important was the rapid growth of the Indian cinema—in Hindi and in many of the regional languages—facilitated by the electrification of most of India. The fact that many of the movies depicted social themes and highlighted social injustice and corruption in government further fueled the interest of the Indian masses in the political process.

The Chinese invasion of 1961 and the resultant collapse of the Indian defenses led to an unprecedented, and often strident, demand for transparency. The whole nation wanted to know what had gone wrong and who was responsible. During the 1960s there was also the escalation of "insurgencies" or civil unrest and armed rebellion in different parts of India. In the next twenty to thirty years, northeast India, especially Mizoram and Nagaland, West Bengal and adjoining areas, Punjab, Jammu and Kashmir, and parts of Andhra Pradesh were all affected. These resulted in the unleashing of a new level of police and military action and a consequent outcry against the violation of human rights, and in a renewed demand for transparency. There was also a spate of *habeas corpus* litigations. The "internal emergency," imposed in 1975, resulted in the suspension of many civil rights and liberties and the imposition of an oppressive regime with little scope for dissent. The formation of the People's Union for Civil Liberties and Democratic Rights (PUCLDR), in 1976, gave impetus to demands for various types of civil liberties and rights, including those of transparency. In the elections of 1977 the regime was defeated and the new government once again reinstated democratic processes. However, this government did not last long.

Meanwhile, in 1975, the Supreme Court ruled (*State of UP v. Raj Narain*) that "In a government of responsibility like ours where the agents of the public must be responsible for their conduct there can be but a few secrets. The people of this country have a right to know every public act, everything that is done in a public way by their public functionaries. They are entitled to know the particulars of every public transaction in all its bearings."

Then, again, in 1982 the Supreme Court of India, hearing a matter relating to the transfer of judges, held that the right to information was a fundamental right under the Indian Constitution. The judges stated that "The concept of an open Government is the direct emanation from the right to know which seems implicit in the right of free speech and expression guaranteed under Article 19(1)(a). Therefore, disclosures of information in regard to the functioning of Government must be the rule, and secrecy an exception justified only where the strictest requirement of public interest so demands. The approach of the Court must be to attenuate the area of secrecy as much as possible consistently with the requirement of public interest, bearing in mind all the time that disclosure also serves an important aspect of public interest" (*SP Gupta & others vs. The President of India and others*, 1982, AIR [SC] 149, 234). However, despite the progressive judgments and pronouncements by the Supreme Court of India, the government was unmoved and no serious effort was made to enact a transparency law.

In 1984, the disastrous gas leak in the Union Carbide plant in Bhopal led environmentalists to make renewed demands for transparency in environmental matters. Though at least two court cases were filed and some progressive judgments obtained (see section on the environment), not much else happened.

The year 1989 saw a change of government at the national level, as the ruling Congress Party once again lost the elections. The new ruling coalition promised to quickly bring in a right to information law, but the early collapse of this government and reported resistance by the bureaucracy resulted in status quo.

The early 1990s saw the emergence of a grassroots movement in the state of Rajasthan, spearheaded by the Mazdoor Kisan Shakti

Sangathan (MKSS).[2] This movement, described below, struggled to get a right to information law passed in Rajasthan and joined with other movements and activists to form a national platform called the National Campaign for People's Right to Information (NCPRI) in 1996.

In the early 2000s, another strong grassroots movement for transparency was initiated in the state of Maharashtra, led by the noted social activist Anna Hazare. Using Gandhian tactics, he not only forced the Maharashtra state government to repeal an earlier weak act and pass a much stronger right to information act but also ensured that the President of India assented to this new act, in contradiction to the stated Government of India policy. Movements have sprung up both in rural Maharashtra and in the cities of Mumbai (Bombay) and Pune, using the new Mahrashtra RTI act to expose corruption and bad governance.

Much before the first national act was passed, in December 2002, many states had already passed similar, and often better and stronger, acts. The states that had their own right to information act included Delhi, Assam, Karnataka, Rajasthan, Goa, Tamil Nadu, Maharashtra, and Madhya Pradesh.

People's Movements for Transparency

Perhaps the most critical component of the Indian journey toward operationalizing people's right to information has been the grassroots struggles for transparency. The fact that this journey has not been abandoned, despite numerous hurdles and setbacks, owes much to its being fueled by the commitment and the energy of those for whom the right to information is essential to survival, and to a life with dignity. The fact that the demand for transparency in public affairs had come most vocally from the grassroots, in both rural and urban areas, also makes the Indian experience somewhat different from experiences in most other parts of the world.

Transparency and Rural Livelihoods: The Story of MKSS

In 1990, Aruna Roy, Nikhil Dey, and Shankar Singh, three people from diverse backgrounds, together with a number of peasants and workers from villages around Devdungri in Rajsamand District of Rajasthan, formed the Mazdoor Kisan Shakti Sangathan (MKSS). A nongovernmental organization, in fact more correctly a grassroots people's movement, the MKSS consists of poor farmers and workers, men and women alike, many of whom have never been to school. Yet their organization raised the issue of RTI in such a potent manner that it changed the discourse on what had been seen for many years largely as an academic issue. When the MKSS was formed, its stated objective was to use modes of struggle and constructive action to change the lives of its primary constituents: the rural poor. In the period leading up to the formulation of this objective, the group had taken up issues of land redistribution and minimum wages, seen traditionally as the two basic issues of the rural landless poor.

During the hunger strikes organized by the MKSS in 1990 and 1991 to demand statutory minimum wages, the group began to realize the significance of the right to information. Workers demanding minimum wages were invariably told that there was no record of their having worked at all. The demand to examine the records was denied on the plea that these were secret government documents. But now the MKSS started demanding copies of the records of works done in the name of the people. This demand was accompanied by determined public action, which captured the imagination of the people and shocked a bureaucracy that had for years been using the cover of secrecy to avoid democratic accountability.

Thus, the real battle for transparency was destined to be fought in the villages of India, belying the expectations of many intellectuals. In retrospect, it was not, as many had thought, an issue too sophisticated to be grasped and operationalized by "illiterate" rural masses. It was not a concept that had to be refined in debates and seminars in the cities of India and then slowly disseminated to the rural areas. The energy for the full onslaught on political, bureaucratic, and other vested interests safeguarding the age-old tradition of secrecy finally came from the Indian "hinterland."

A decision by the MKSS in late 1994 to use the mode of village-based public hearings (jansunwais) to conduct social audits based on information gathered from the government revolutionized the use of RTI in India and energized the rural people. Using dramatic slogans like "hamara paisa-hamara hisaab" (our money, our accounts), the public hearings became platforms to publicly audit government spending. However, it took a forty-day *dharna* (sit-in) and the efforts of the poor people, struggling for their livelihoods and survival, to finally establish that the right to information was central to democratic activism.

The *Beawar* Dharna *(Sit-In)*

By December 1994, it had become clear that, given the powerful and entrenched opposition to the demand for information, there was a need for people's legal entitlement if information was to be accessed. Accordingly, the MKSS decided to broaden the struggle to include the demand for a right to information law. As a first step, it organised a *dharna,* preparing to sit in for a long period. Over a hundred villages provided wheat, hundreds of people agreed to give two to three days of their time, and a core group was formed to sustain the *dharna* for at least a month.

The location selected was the town of Beawar, with a population of about 100,000 people. Though an intense RTI campaign had been under way in the villages around Beawar for over two years, the townspeople knew little of this struggle. So when in April 1996, over 1,000 men and women marched into Beawar, bearing banners, shouting slogans, and singing songs, they drew attention. It was obvious that the marchers were from the rural hinterlands. The women, who made up more than half of the group, were dressed in colorful *lahengas* (long skirts), and most of the men wore traditional peasant dress. As the residents of Beawar watched with growing curiosity, the long procession snaked its way through the town, stopping for a moment to hand over a sheaf of papers to a representative of the state government. Then the visitors made their way to the town center, where they began setting up tents of flimsy material and making preparations for what would turn out to be a long stay. While Beawar was no stranger to agitations, this was unfolding into a rather extraordinary one.

What made this *dharna* really unusual was that instead of asking for the customary *roti, kapda,* and *makan* (food, clothing, and shelter), what the visitors wanted was, of all things, the right to information. What they had handed over to the government representative in Beawar was a memorandum asserting the people's right to information (RTI), with the specific demand for the right to obtain certified copies of details of development expenditures made in their villages.

And so it was that a simple demand for minimum wages became a fight for the right to information. Those who descended upon Beawar in April 1996 astutely timed the *dharna* with the campaign period of that year's national parliamentary elections. Citizens were offered a small glimmer of hope to break out of the vicious cycle of Indian politics, which forced them to choose among undeserving candidates. For a change, during that election campaign in Beawar, democracy was being debated and redefined.

Those on *dharna* began to drive home the point that by using the right to collectively and individually ask questions and demand answers, citizens could begin to shift power from the ruling elite to the people. It was a first step toward participatory governance, where the disadvantaged and the dispossessed could establish their right to livelihood and to effectively govern themselves. The poor started to see that they had to be involved in the RTI campaign because, as one of the slogans proclaimed, "the right to know (is) the right to live."

Jansunwais *or Public Hearings*

The *jansunwais* (public hearings) soon became a powerful and imaginative tool popularly used on a range of issues by different kinds of groups all over the country. These village-based public hearings provide an open platform where anyone can come and have their say on matters being examined. The jansunwais have acquired a kind of democratic legitimacy that agitations do not have. They are dramatic affairs where "information" and its analysis reveals the who, the how, and the why of various misdeeds and gives courage to the exploited to bring their predicament out into the open.

An elaborate preparation process precedes a jansunwai. For example, the details of expenditures made in the preceding couple of years in a *panchayat*[3] (covering a village or group of villages) are accessed from the government. These records are then examined and compiled into easily understandable tables with headings like date, item, expenditure, beneficiary (if any), and remarks (if any). A preliminary assessment (including discussion with villagers and field verification) is done to determine how authentic these records are.

Then the date, time, and location of the jansunwai are fixed and announced. During the jansunwai, the details of the purported expenditure are read out, one by one, and the people are asked to publicly authenticate the items listed and the expenditure incurred.

The first jansunwai in Kot Kirana panchayat (December 1994) was held in front of an incomplete building with no roof. As the list of purported expenses was being read out, an item on which 30,000 rupees had been spent the previous year in constructing the roof of a government office came up for verification. Everyone burst into spontaneous laughter, for the roofless building nearby was that very government office. In another case, the name of a villager was read out as the recipient of hire charges for his bullock cart. The agitated villager protested loudly, saying that he was never given any money and, in any case, he did not own a bullock cart. He added, for good measure, that if they still insisted that they had hired his bullock cart, then could they please return it to him, for he had never got it back. The muster rolls revealed a number of ghosts. A large number of people, long dead and gone, had been resurrected and shown to have worked as laborers. There were places where the same people were recorded as present and working on different sites on the same dates and at the same time.

The *jansunwais* uncovered not just ghosts of people, but even "ghost works." For example, in the case of Janawad panchayat (April 2001), the massive revelations of fraud in the jansunwai forced the government to order its own investigation. The resulting report admitted that more than 7 million rupees were defrauded in a six-year period, in a single panchayat. Given the fact that in Rajasthan alone there are 9,000 panchayats, the total amount defrauded in the state, if this case was typical, would run into billions of rupees annually. The report also revealed a complete breakdown of all supervisory and monitoring systems.

The jansunwais have also led to some breakthroughs in the even more complex area of accountability. In Kukerkhera panchayat (January 1998), the evening before the jansunwai was scheduled, the *sarpanch* (head of the panchayat) came to see the MKSS volunteers. She admitted to them that the previous year, she had pocketed 100,000 rupees of the panchayat money and offered to return half of it immediately and the remaining half in the next couple of months. She wanted to be saved the humiliation of being exposed in the public hearing. The matter was raised in the jansunwai the next day, and the villagers decided to accept her apology and to use the money that she was returning to build a school, especially as this money could be shown as the villagers' contribution and would attract a matching amount from the government. Eventually in 2000, perhaps as a result of such hearings, the Rajasthan Panchayati Raj Act was amended and social audits, where all the villagers publicly examine records and audit the work done in their area, were made mandatory.

The Impact

The use of the RTI to conduct social audits has acted as a deterrent to corrupt officials. For example, in 2004, much of the 6,000 million rupees sanctioned for drought relief in Rajasthan were actually spent on drought relief and not pocketed by corrupt politicians, contractors, and officials. However, apart from specific effects like this, the RTI campaign has also had a profound impact on the nature of governance and the interface between the government and the people.

One very important outcome of the RTI campaign in Rajasthan has been the enactment of a state RTI law. The RTI movement drafted it after open public discussions in seminar rooms and in street corner meetings in every part of the state. Though the law eventually passed by the legislature was a watered-down version, a far cry from the "people's draft," this process has led to a growing demand for public participation in law making, not just for the right to information but in all areas. The incorporation of mandatory social audits in the law has also opened up possibilities for creating the institutions required for participatory democracy. As the right to information begins to provide access to documents, a second generation of questions relating to accountability are being raised, and it is methods like public audits that will have to be found to provide some of the answers.

The RTI campaign in Rajasthan continues to be fashioned primarily by organizations working with the poor and by questions framed by the poor themselves. Public hearings have now spread to different parts of the state and are conducted by different organizations on not only local government expenditures but also the public distribution system, the health system, the watershed program, human rights violations, and land rights issues. In each of these areas the campaign has not only managed to raise issues related to corruption and the arbitrary exercise of power but also found a means of engaging with the government on issues of policy formulation and implementation. In fact, even NGOs and civil society groups have started placing the details of their accounts before the people of the area where they work.

Transparency and the Environmental Movement

One of the first organized movements in India to raise the issue of transparency was the environmental movement. Though the initial efforts centered on specific cases, these were quickly broadened to cover larger environmental concerns.

In the last twenty years, environmental laws have progressively allowed *locus standi* to individuals. All the major environmental laws enacted after 1984 have a provision that the people have a right to put the government on notice, usually of 60 days, by which time it must remove the cause of complaint or face a legal challenge. Many of the earlier laws have been amended to include such clauses. In addition, holding a public hearing has become increasingly accepted in the process of carrying out environmental impact assessments. Many types of data, especially relating to pollution levels, are now routinely and *suo moto* (without being asked for) made public. However, much of the sensitive information is still difficult to come by, especially where powerful commercial or business interests are involved. Two of the landmark cases fought for access to environmental information are described below.

The Sriram Food and Fertiliser Industry Case

In 1984, the leak of a deadly gas from the Union Carbide factory in Bhopal suddenly made environmentalists and the public in India aware of how little they knew about the chemical and nuclear industry in India and the disasters that were waiting to happen. There was, consequently, a spate of cases filed by various individuals in exercise of their right to litigate in the public interest.[4] In 1984, M. C. Mehta, a lawyer who subsequently became famous as a tireless campaigner for the environment, filed one such case in the Supreme Court of India. His "public interest" case asked the court to close down the

Sriram Food and Fertiliser Industry, located in the heart of Delhi, as it used and stored hazardous chemicals without maintaining the required safeguards, and therefore was a grave public hazard.

Unfortunately, before the Supreme Court could hear the case, an oleum gas leak occurred in the factory (in 1985). Though the gas that leaked was not highly toxic and there were no casualties, the spread of the gas in congested areas of Delhi caused widespread panic and throat, eye, and skin irritation. Consequently, the case was taken up for hearing on a priority basis.

During the hearing, it emerged that although the Delhi government had commissioned a study of the safety aspects of this industry and the findings had been submitted to the government some months before the leak, the findings were not made public and not even shared with the industry that was the subject of the study. This and other such absurdities made the then Chief Justice of India, who was heading the bench, remark in open court that he wished someone would take up the issue of the right to information.

Responding to these remarks, Kalpavriksh, one of the NGOs involved in the case, filed an intervention as a part of the ongoing case asking the court to lay down the right to information as a fundamental right. Essentially, the petition argued that the right to life, guaranteed by the Constitution of India as a fundamental right, implied a right to know if one's life was threatened (specifically due to possible leaks of toxic chemicals or other hazardous substances), for otherwise one could not fully exercise one's right to life. The right to life also gave the right to know who was threatening one's life and in what manner; what action, if any, the government was taking to remove the threat; and what the citizens could do to safeguard their lives.

Though the Supreme Court did not pass any final orders on this petition, its contents were mentioned many times during the hearing, and the court made clear from time to time that they were not happy with the aura of secrecy that surrounds the government and industry.

The Poona Cantonment Case

In 1986, the Bombay Environmental Action Group (BEAG) filed a case in the Bombay (now Mumbai) High Court, seeking specific information from the Poona Cantonment Board. They felt that some buildings in Poona (now Pune) Cantonment were being constructed in violation of the building bylaws. They repeatedly requested the Poona Cantonment Board to let them inspect the relevant building plans and related documents. However, no satisfactory replies were received from the board.

Consequently, the BEAG filed a Writ Petition in the Bombay High Court seeking such inspection. However, as this process took several months, some of the buildings under scrutiny were, in fact, completed before the case was heard. Though the BEAG could not prevent these structures from being built, they won a larger battle, as the High Court not only permitted inspection of the plans but also made some telling observations. In their order they said:

> Real democracy cannot be worked by men sitting at the top. It has to be worked from below by the people of every village and town. That sovereignty resides in and flows from the people. So said the Father of the nation in whose name we swear. Therefore, "who will watch the watchman," is the vexed question before our democracy. For this, people's participation at all levels is a must.[5]

The Supreme Court subsequently considerably widened this High Court judgment.

> We would also direct that any person residing within the area of a local authority or any social action group or interest group or pressure group shall be entitled to take inspection of any sanction granted, or plan approved, by such local authority in construction of buildings along with the related papers and documents, if such individual or social action group or interest group or pressure group wishes to take such inspection, except of course in cases where in the interest of security, such inspection cannot be permitted.[6]

Transparency and Development Projects

The social, environmental, and economic impacts of "development" projects, especially large dams, have been at the center of major debates for the last twenty-five years. Vigorous people's campaigns have contended that a majority of these megaprojects are neither economically viable nor environmentally sustainable, and that they have taken a heavy toll on rural populations that they have displaced or otherwise adversely affected. Recent estimates suggest that over 20 million people have been displaced since independence just by major dams, and most of them have not been properly rehabilitated, becoming even poorer and more disempowered than they were before "development" hit them.

These projects might never have been built in the first place if they had been fairly and comprehensively assessed prior to initiation. The right to information movement decided to start a series of public hearings around controversial state and national projects to bring the details out into the open. Consequently, the Narmada Bachao Andolan (Movement for Saving the Narmada River) decided to enforce transparency on the government in relation to the projects being planned for the future. One is the Maheshwar Project, on the Narmada River. In 2002, the NCPRI organized a public hearing around this project.

Concerned officers of the Madhya Pradesh government, people from the affected villages, people's representatives, and activists of the Narmada Bachao Andolan were invited to this jansunwai. Nearly a thousand people affected by this project were present. Representatives of many organizations of Bhopal and the state were also present.

During the public hearing, critical questions about the economic and social viability of the project were raised. Women who had allegedly been subjected to violence by the police spoke up. So did villagers who claimed that, despite assurances given by the government and the project proponents, they had not been compensated for the loss of their homes and their livelihoods. Other public hearings around development projects have since been held.

Transparency and Elections

The huge amount of money spent during elections, in violation of electoral laws, and the criminal background of some of the legislators and parliamentarians have often been seen as some of the factors inhibiting good governance in India. Recently, both the Election

Commission and the Supreme Court of India have recognized this problem. In March 2003, the Supreme Court passed an order making it mandatory for all candidates standing for either state or national elections to declare, on affidavit filed along with their nomination forms, their educational qualifications, their criminal record (if any), and their financial assets.

Elections to four state assemblies were held in December 2003. The RTI movement in India decided to widely disseminate information regarding electoral candidates, filed in pursuance of the Supreme Court order. The NCPRI took up this work in Rajasthan, in collaboration with the MKSS, and in Delhi, with the Centre for Equity Studies and Parivartan, an RTI group.

In both states, the transparency groups were first involved in trying to get the voter's lists authenticated so that all genuine voters were included and spurious names were deleted. In Rajasthan, the lists were read out in *gaon* (village) and ward *sabhas* (gatherings), allowing the local people to help identify fictitious voters and vouch for those genuine ones whose names had been left out.

In Delhi, a public hearing was held for such verification. In addition, copies of lists were sent to Resident Welfare Associations of the various colonies, which then helped in the verification process.

Once nominations were filed, copies of the affidavits filed by the various candidates were collected and their data analyzed. This analysis was then widely disseminated, and an interactive Web site was created where all these data and analyses were put up and comments and reactions invited from the people.

Transparency and Urban Municipal Governance: The Story of Parivartan

Nearly a third of India's population, about 300 million people, lives in urban areas. The urban population has grown at a rate much faster than the overall rate of growth, as there is a large amount of immigration from rural areas. Consequently, the municipal infrastructure in most cities is stretched to the limit, and there is not only a perpetual shortage of water and electricity but also inadequate transportation facilities and poor sanitation. The fact that India is a relatively poor country with serious financial constraints aggravates the situation.

However, it is also true that even those resources that are allocated for providing municipal services and infrastructure are often misappropriated or otherwise wasted. Therefore, things are much worse than they need to be, even with the current paucity of resources.

A group of Delhi citizens decided to use the newly enacted Delhi Right to Information (RTI) Act to attack the problem of waste and corruption. A young civil servant, Arvind Kejriwal, took the lead and formed a group called Parivartan. Parivartan started working in two resettlement[7] colonies in Delhi, New Seemapuri and Sundarnagri, focusing on the status of civic amenities and services provided by the Municipal Corporation of Delhi (MCD). In the process they discovered many problems with the functioning of the MCD in that area.

The Jansunwai

Consequently, in December 2002, Parivartan, along with the NCPRI and with the help of local NGOs and residents, organized a jansunwai on the amenities and facilities reportedly provided by the MCD. The jansunwai was attended by about a thousand people and presided over by a panel chaired by a retired judge of the Supreme Court of India. In the public hearing, the various contracts given for constructing civic amenities were read out and local residents testified as to whether or not the work was undertaken, and if it was, whether it was done fully or left incomplete.

Based on these public testimonies by the local people, it emerged that of the 13 million rupees officially spent on providing civic amenities in the area (and corresponding to 64 works and contracts), items or works worth about 7 million rupees did not physically exist. This figure did not include the amount in question on account of quality issues, like the quantity of cement used or the depth of bitumen on the road.

EFFECT OF THE JANSUNWAI ON THE LOCAL PEOPLE AND THEIR REACTION

The local people were understandably agitated when they realized that officials and contractors had pocketed the funds sanctioned for many sorely needed civic amenities. Their anger was aggravated by the fact that for years they had been pleading with the local officials to provide these amenities but were constantly told that the money was not available. The RTI campaign triggered a number of debates and discussions in the community. People were amazed at the size of the fraud and demanded a platform where they could raise their voices collectively.

The jansunwai made people realize for the first time that the government can be held accountable in full public gaze. They felt empowered and recognized their right and obligation to demand accountability from the government. Before the jansunwai, the public were in awe of the local government officials and political representatives. The hearing once and for all changed all this.

As a result of the public hearing, each block in Sundernagari has formed a *mohalla samiti* (local area committee), comprising representatives from each street in the block. The *samitis* monitor the execution of civil work and insist on making public the contents of each contract before it can be executed.

REACTION OF THE LOCAL BUREAUCRACY

Prior to the jansunwai, the local MCD engineers, though pretending to be cooperative, tried their best to ensure that information was not made available. They also refused to cooperate and alleged that false allegations were being made against their department.

After the jansunwai, a team of Parivartan workers and MCD engineers jointly inspected a number of sites. However, the engineers insisted on giving flimsy explanations for most of the deficiencies. Nevertheless, there was a marked difference in their attitude. The officials are now far more responsive and courteous in their dealings with the public, and whenever any person from Sundernagari or New Seemapuri calls them, they listen to the grievance, make an effort to redress it, and invariably make public the details of contracts. Whenever demanded by the public, the engineers themselves visit the site.

While Parivartan was holding street corner meetings in preparation for the jansunwai, the local MLA (Member of the Legislative Assembly)[8] started holding parallel meetings in the same area. He publicly criticized Parivartan and alleged that its representatives had demanded 300,000 rupees from him and, as he could not meet the demand, they were tarnishing his image. Slowly, these allegations started taking the shape of threats. Some people informed Parivartan that plans were afoot to get their workers kidnapped or hauled up by the police on some false charges. Some of the local supporters were pressured to disassociate themselves from Parivartan.

When Parivartan workers went to invite the local MLA to the jansunwai, he accused Parivartan of being an organization of touts who extort money from government officials. He also questioned its source of funding and warned them that he would not allow the jansunwai to take place in his area. Parivartan workers politely told him that holding a jansunwai was their democratic right, so it would be held. However, if he had any questions about the funding or workings of Parivartan, they would be happy to publicly answer them. Ultimately, he came to the jansunwai, accompanied by about forty of his supporters. He and his supporters repeatedly tried to disrupt the meeting but could not succeed.

Reportedly, after the jansunwai, a number of MLAs met the Chief Minister (CM)[9] and requested her to prevent such hearings from taking place in the future, as they could adversely affect the electoral prospects of the ruling political party. They also fed the CM wrong information about the jansunwai, alleging that it was attended by outsiders especially brought from neighboring states, and that the people who gave evidence were from opposition political parties. However, at a subsequent meeting of Parivartan representatives with the CM, these issues were cleared up and the CM reacted very positively. She promised an inquiry into the alleged discrepancies and also promised to study the recommendations for systemic changes made by Parivartan, and to implement those that were found feasible. Since then, the following five recommendations have been accepted by the MCD:

1. A board displaying basic information will be displayed at the site of every work.
2. The list of all completed works will be displayed on notice boards of all division offices for at least a month after completion.
3. The details of all ongoing works in an area will be pasted on the walls of the MCD store in that area.
4. The files containing old contracts will be placed in MCD stores, where the public can come and inspect them at any time.
5. The list of all works carried out by the MCD in an area in the previous year will be displayed on a prominent wall in that area.

THE REACTION OF LOCAL CONTRACTORS

Before the jansunwai, during site verifications and street corner meetings, Parivartan workers were threatened by some of the contractors with dire consequences if they pursued their inquiries. However, at the same time another contractor willingly confessed, on camera, how he had swindled money on various works he executed. He gave specific information on the deficiencies in the works and the amounts of bribes he paid in each case. He said that his motive for confessing was to get the unscrupulous officials sent behind bars, as they forced even the honest contractors to become corrupt!

In all the contracts for which copies were obtained before the jansunwai, the contractors appeared to be underbidding in order to get the contracts. A number of contracts were awarded at prices at which it would be impossible to carry out the work. This was possible only because the contractors already had an agreement with the supervising officials that they need not actually do the work but could submit false bills and share the earnings. However, since the jansunwai, the local engineer has confirmed that not only has there been a marked improvement in the quality of works being implemented but also underbidding has stopped.

Transparency and Arbitrary Governance:
RTI Activism in Maharashtra

RTI is also being effectively used to check arbitrary governance. The best examples come from Maharashtra, which has not only the most progressive RTI law but also a very active community of middle- and upper-middle class RTI activists. They maintain a very active e-mail list and discussion group (*HumJanenge*, meaning "we will know"), and are perpetually asking the government to explain its actions. The interesting thing about this Maharashtra model is that it is not very labor intensive and does not necessarily involve organizing large public meetings.

In December 2004, sixteen of the citizens who had successfully used the RTI Act for eliciting information were invited to display to the public, in Pune, their records relating to the requisitions for information successfully filed under the Maharashtra Right to Information Act (MRTI). The citizen users were also available for discussions with members of the public. Some of the issues taken up by these citizens are listed below:[10]

• In Pune, Major General SCN Jatar (retired), president of Nagrik Chetna Manch (an NGO), demanded the details of official cars used by the city's elected officials, like the mayor. He was shocked to learn that in 10 months, they spent 5 million rupees on their official cars. The mayor spent more than 700,000 rupees on the official cars between January and October 2003. Apparently the concerned officials had been going for joyrides and holidays at public expense.

• A local magistrate at one of the districts in Mumbai was transferred within a few months of assuming his position, despite the rules specifying a minimum tenure of three years. He was known to be a very honest and efficient officer and had become quite popular with the local people. Kewal Semlani demanded to know why he had been transferred out and whether the transfer was not a violation of the rules. Within a few days of the request for information being filed, the transfer orders were revoked.

• Shailesh Gandhi of Mumbai effectively used the act to elicit names of members of parliament, members of the legislative assembly, and ministers who recommended transfers of police officers in Mumbai. This was significant because the law says that if there is any request for the transfer of a police officer from any outside source, then unless the officer can prove that he was not behind that request, disciplinary action will be taken against him or her. Shailesh Gandhi finally received the information only after he approached the Lokayukta[11] in a second appeal. As he suspected, the information revealed that a large number of officials were in violation of the law but no action had been taken against them. Subsequent to this information becoming public, action has been initiated against a large number of the erring officials.

• Another query by Gandhi on the lease of land by the Bombay Municipal Corporation to the Royal Western India Turf Club (RWITC), a horse racing course in the heart of Mumbai (Bombay), revealed some curious facts. The first lease deed was signed in 1914 for a 60-year period. Another lease became effective in 1994 and remains in force up to 2013. But does this mean that no lease existed between the civic body of Mumbai and the Turf Club for two decades, after the first lease expired in 1974? And if so, what is the revenue lost by the people of Mumbai as a result, and who is responsible for this? Subsequently, Gandhi accessed information on a large number of leases and discovered that leases covering over 3 million square meters in the heart of Mumbai (where real estate is among the costliest in the world) had lapsed and no action had been taken.

• Sunetra Dolas, a 62-year-old grandmother living in Thane, Maharashtra, got two civic officials fined for withholding information. Dolas's fight began in July, when officials stonewalled her questions about the dubious constructions on a 3.5-acre plot given to a cooperative housing society in 1950 to provide houses for people belonging to certain disadvantaged groups. However, some of the members of the society began building houses for themselves on this land. Dolas made 32 applications seeking details of the area, type of buildings being built, and whether they had the required permits. The replies were very disappointing. The Municipal Corporation of Thane said that she was interfering in civic affairs and that they knew their job. The corporation also stated that this information could not be divulged, as it was a "state secret"! She was subsequently told by the corporation that they do not give the permits but some other department does. When she approached that department, they sent her back to the corporation. Finally, fed up with the runaround, she appealed, and her appeal was allowed. The two officers who were stonewalling her and giving her the runaround were fined 47,000 rupees.[12] They were also ordered to give her the information sought, which revealed that most of the constructions were illegal.

Transparency and the Right to Food

In India, as in many other countries of the South, access to food is one of the most pressing social problems. The Government of India, in order to ensure that the poor people get basic food at affordable rates, has run a public distribution system for many years. Poor families (below poverty line—BPL) and very poor families (*Antyodaya*) are each given a ration card. On the basis of this card, they can access rice, wheat, and kerosene oil at very subsidized rates (much below the market rates) from designated shops called ration shops and kerosene oil depots (KODs). The Government of India spends a whopping 150 billion rupees a year on distributing subsidized food. However, there are huge leakages in this system and a large proportion of this subsidy—calculated by some as 50 percent—does not reach the intended beneficiaries.

The government has a double-entry system where each beneficiary, when he/she goes to collect their grains/oil, has to get an entry made in their ration book, which they keep. The ration shop/KOD owner has to make a corresponding entry in the sale register he keeps and also issue a money receipt for the payment made by the beneficiary, which the beneficiary must sign. One of the common ways of siphoning off this subsidy is to make a false entry into the sales register and sell the ration/oil in the market for a much higher price. When the beneficiaries come to claim their share, they are told that there was no supply or that the supply has been exhausted. In some cases the shops remain closed so that the beneficiaries stop visiting after a while.

RTI activists in Delhi and in Rajasthan started using the RTI law to access information about the distribution of subsidized food, grains, and kerosene. Armed with this information, they organized public meetings to confront the shop owners and the officials with the rampant corruption in the system. A group called Satark Nagrik Sangathan (SNS)[13] was the first to organize a public hearing on ration shops and their malfunctioning in South Delhi. Parivartan, which was active in East Delhi, also took up this issue. Given below is one of the interesting case studies of using the right to information to procure one's basic right to food.

Triveni Shows the Way

Triveni is a poor woman from Delhi who has an Antyodaya[14] ration card, which entitles her to get wheat at 2 rupees per kilogram and rice at 3 per kilogram. The ration shopkeeper, however, always charged her 5 for wheat and 10 for rice. As the quality of the grain in the ration shop was poor and the price charged almost equal to the market price, Triveni stopped getting these items on her card. In February 2003 she learned for the first time, from a local NGO, that she was actually entitled to get rice and wheat at a much cheaper price. This shocked her, because she had never received grains at such cheap rates and no one had told her of her rights. She therefore filed an application under the Delhi Right to Information Act, asking for the details of rations issued to her per official records, and for copies of the cash memos purportedly issued to her. To her utter surprise, the official records showed that she had been issued, every month for the last many months, wheat at 2 rupees per kilogram and rice at 3 per kilogram. The cash memos showed thumb impressions under her name though she, being literate, always signed her name. As the thumb impressions were obviously fake, she now had foolproof evidence against the shopkeeper.

She therefore filed a complaint against him. However, the moment her complaint was received at the food department, the concerned shopkeeper learned of it, and he first offered her 20,000 rupees to withdraw it. Though her financial condition was very bad, she refused to accept the money. When this did not work, all the local shopkeepers started threatening her and terrorizing her. The ration dealers even threatened her family members and tried to get them to sign on a blank paper, but her family did not yield. Finally, on a Sunday, two inspectors from the food department came to her house and asked her to withdraw her complaint. Residents of the whole street gathered and protested the presence of the inspectors for an inquiry on Sunday. Seeing the public turning hostile, the inspectors left.

Later on, Triveni got a summons from the office of the deputy commissioner for food and supplies. When she appeared before him, he was quite sympathetic to the shopkeeper and hostile to her, as if she had committed a crime by making a complaint. He tried to persuade her to withdraw her complaint by saying that nothing worthwhile would come out of the case, as it would go on for years. But she insisted on continuing. Later, the Food Department also recorded the statement of her mother-in-law. Though no action has been taken yet by the Food Department against anyone, Triveni has started getting the correct quantity of rations at the right prices. The threats from the shopkeepers have also stopped.

Policies, Laws, and Institutional Structures

Efforts to enact a national law on the right to information have been going on for over a decade. In 1989, a noncongress government came to power at the center with Mr. V. P. Singh as the prime minister. Enacting a right to information law was a part of the electoral promises made by Singh's government. Yet the government came and went, albeit in under two years, without there being even the initial draft of the promised law. In conversations many years later, Singh revealed that though he had tried to get a suitable act drafted and introduced in Parliament, the bureaucracy had frustrated him at every step, and finally his government had fallen without any significant progress being made.

In 1996, a meeting was convened at the Gandhi Peace Foundation in New Delhi, where the National Campaign for People's Right to Information (NCPRI) was formed.[15] It had as members activists, journalists, lawyers, professionals, retired civil servants, and academics. One of the first tasks to which the NCPRI addressed itself was to draft a right to information law that could form the basis of the proposed national act.

The NCPRI and the Press Council of India formulated the initial draft, under the guidance of Justice P. B. Sawant, retired judge of the Supreme Court of India and Chairman of the Council. This draft was discussed at a meeting in 1996 attended by many concerned people, including representatives of the major political parties. The draft was then presented to the Government of India, which, as is its wont, set up another committee, under the chairmanship of the late Shri H. D. Shourie. This committee came up with a somewhat watered-down version of the act in 1997. The draft was further amended and introduced in Parliament in 2000 as the Freedom of Information Bill.

At this point, the bill was referred to a Select Committee of the Parliament, which invited comments from the public. The bill was passed by Parliament, with almost no amendments or changes, in December 2002. The process took nearly six years from the submission of the NCPRI/Press Council draft bill in 1996. Also, it is possible that the bill passed more because of prodding by the Supreme Court of India than because of any desire on the part of the government itself. Interestingly, until the elections and the advent of a new government in May 2004, even this weak act had not been notified and made operative.

Amending the RTI Act of 2002

Essentially, the four indicators of a strong transparency law can be seen to be *minimum exclusions, independent appeals, stringent penalties,* and *universal accessibility.* The 2002 act failed on all these counts. It excluded a large number of intelligence and security agencies, had no mechanism for independent appeals, prescribed no penalties for violation of the act, and restricted the access only to "citizens" and did not put a cap on the fees chargeable.

In May 2004, the United Progressive Alliance (UPA), led by the Congress Party, came to power at the national level, displacing the Bharatiya Janata Party (BJP)-led National Democratic Alliance government. The UPA government brought out a Common Minimum Programme (CMP), which promised, among other things, "to provide a government that is corruption-free, transparent and accountable at all times" and to make the Right to Information Act "more progressive, participatory and meaningful." The UPA government also set up a National Advisory Council (NAC) to monitor the implementation of the CMP. This council has leaders of various mass movements, including the right to information movement, as members.

In August 2004, the NCPRI formulated a set of suggested amendments to the 2002 Freedom of Information Act, designed to strengthen the act and make it more effective and based on extensive discussions with civil society groups working on transparency and other related issues. The suggested amendments were forwarded to the NAC, which endorsed most of them and forwarded them to the Prime Minister of India for further action.

Based on the recommendations of the NAC, the Government of India introduced a revised Right to Information Bill in Parliament on December 22, 2004. Although this RTI Bill was considerably stronger than the 2002 act, some of the critical clauses recommended by the NCPRI and endorsed by the NAC had been deleted or amended. Most significantly, the 2004 bill was applicable only to the central (federal) government, not to the states, and had almost no workable penalty provisions.

Consequently, there was a sharp reaction from the civil society groups and the government was forced to set up a group of ministers to review these changes and to refer the proposed act to a Standing Committee of the Parliament. Meanwhile, the NAC also met and expressed, in a letter to the Prime Minister, unanimous support for the original recommendations. Representatives of the NCPRI and of various other civil society groups, and other concerned citizens, sent in written submissions to the parliamentary committee and were invited to give oral evidence.

These efforts were mostly successful, and the committee and group of ministers recommended the restitution of most of the provisions that had been deleted, including applicability to states, and strengthened penalty provisions. The Right to Information Bill, as amended, was passed by both houses of the Indian Parliament in May 2005, received presidential assent on June 15, 2005, and came into force on October 13, 2005.

Thereafter, the focus shifted to implementation issues. As of this writing, government departments are either appointing no Public Information Officers (PIOs), as required under the law to receive requisitions, or appointing too many, so that people do not know which one to approach. Information is being routinely denied, forcing more and more people to appeal to the information commissions, where they exist. But in many states, information commissions have not been constituted or not given the facilities to become functional.

The civil society coalition behind the law has objected to the tendency of appointing serving and retired civil servants to the information commissions. These commissions are not only the final appellate authorities under the RTI Act but also responsible for overseeing its proper implementation. The NCPRI, in a hard-hitting press release on October 11, 2005, stated that:

> Being the appellate authority under the RTI Act, the Information Commission would be called upon to objectively adjudicate on disputes over access to information between the citizen and the government. The disputed information could often be about matters that were directly or indirectly under the charge of the retired civil servants, when they were in service. There would also be many occasions where the Commission would need to decide on releasing information that might embarrass the erstwhile colleagues and subordinates of such retired civil servants. In these circumstances, both being objective and appearing to be objective would be difficult.

> The Information Commission, through its orders and judgements, is expected to initiate a change in the mindset of the bureaucracy. Not only must the bureaucracy recognise and accept that the right to information is a fundamental right of the citizen, but they must also be prepared to justify their actions and decisions before the public. This is essential in a participatory democracy. Whether a Commission exclusively or overwhelmingly populated with former civil servants can provide such leadership is doubtful.

Perhaps because the process of getting the law passed was so participatory, there continues to be widespread concern and protest against all seeming weaknesses and deviations. There is some perceptible movement—age-old bureaucratic institutions are beginning to rub their eyes awake in response to the din.

Contemporary Issues and Debates

The Challenges Before the RTI Movements

The battle for transparency is not without ups and downs, nor without actual or imagined pitfalls. If transparency is really as potent a tool for people's empowerment as it is made out to be, it would be unrealistic to expect the state to willingly give up its stranglehold on information. Nor would the powerful interests who stand to get exposed allow this to happen without a fight. Consequently, many challenges confront the RTI movement.

Many skeptics, both well meaning and mischievous, continue to articulate their reservations about the right to information. For starters, it is argued that right to information laws will be misused to harass officials. Whatever the actual fears, the enunciated concern is that it is usually impossible for civil servants to work strictly within the law, as there are so many laws, many contradicting each other, and some outdated or inappropriate. The right to information would threaten many well-meaning officers who are trying to help the public by "bending" rules and laws. Another concern is that members of the public who have themselves violated the law might use the RTI against civil servants who try to book them.

There is also the fear that, once RTI catches on, the government will be inundated by requests and normal work will come to a standstill. However, the option of making most of the information, *suo moto,* available, especially through the Internet, also finds little support. Why make public something that has not been asked for?

There are the well-known concerns that excessive transparency can compromise national security and the strength of the state. Though the principle that certain matters, especially those concerning vital defense and security interests, need to be kept secret is generally accepted, the urge of the bureaucracy is to perpetually expand this list, while civil society pulls in the opposite direction. What needs to be excluded and what included is a matter of ongoing debate.

RTI is also seen to pose a threat to law and order and to promote civil strife and tension. Ironically, this thesis is based on the assumption that what people do not know does not hurt them. However, as they are made aware of the ways the government, the politicians, and certain commercial interests have been exploiting them, this is likely to create tensions and possibly result in violence.

Civil servants sometimes resent having to be answerable to the common man and woman. According to them, they are answerable to their bosses, to the government, and to the Legislative Assembly and Parliament. And the government is answerable to the people through the legislature and parliament. Why, then, should they be directly answerable to the people? A classic argument from representative democracy!

Perhaps the most unusual argument is that transparency will result in inaction, with civil servants refusing to make decisions or spend public resources, as they would constantly be in fear of prosecution. The fact that they can only be prosecuted if they do illegal and dishonest acts is lost sight of. Or is this a subtle acceptance of the fact that what motivates a lot of government action is illegal gratification, and once there is a real danger of being exposed, the main motivation to act disappears?

It is not only the civil servants who have to come to terms with RTI. Civil society groups and nongovernmental organizations also need to be transparent and publicly accountable. The public also has to learn how to use RTI. Though its use might not pose the sort of threat to peace and harmony that is suggested by certain sections of the bureaucracy, it often poses a threat to those using it to expose powerful interests. Recent experiences in India have shown that often applicants seeking to access sensitive information are subjected to threats and in some cases to physical violence.

Protecting RTI Activists

In September 2003, local leaders and ration shop owners attacked volunteers of Parivartan while they were helping people to access their ration records from a government office. The volunteers were severely beaten, and it was only after the intervention of senior officials that the volunteers, including four women, were evacuated by a police vehicle and driven to safety.

In November 2004, Santosh, a woman activist of Delhi working with people trying to get information about their subsidized rations, was attacked with a blade and her throat slit. Fortunately, she survived. This was not the first attack on her, and she had managed to escape an earlier attempt.

In June 2004, there was an attack on an RTI activist in Mahabaleshwar, near Mumbai (Bombay). The house of Balu Panchal, an environmentalist, was attacked and ransacked on World Environment Day and years of work reduced to ashes. Panchal had been campaigning against illegal felling of trees and against unauthorized construction, using RTI to access the incriminating information. This provoked the attack and the destruction of all the records that could have taken the case forward.

Therefore, to protect the seekers of information from harm, especially at the hands of those who run the risk of being exposed, is a major challenge before the RTI movement. Perhaps the immediate answer is to progressively make information available *suo moto*, in a manner (say, on the Web) such that anyone can access it without being identified.

Punishing the Guilty

To ensure that corruption (or other misdeeds) of officials, exposed using RTI, do not go unpunished is another major challenge. If no action is taken, it emboldens the corrupt officials and demoralizes the citizen. In fact, it makes things worse than before, for it removes fear from the mind of the official and hope from the mind of the citizen. There is the danger of sinking into even more profound cynicism, from "if only people knew" to "nothing happens, even when everyone knows."

Yet, RTI laws rarely, if ever, provide for speedy and effective prosecution of those who have been exposed. Therefore, the matter is left to the usual processes of the government and the courts. However, in India as in many other countries of the South, the courts and the related investigative agencies are horribly overburdened, and it takes years to get an investigation completed and much longer to get a conviction. Besides, having failed to prevent incriminating information from becoming public, the bureaucracy focuses on damage control and trying to prevent further action. The Kukurkheda story from Rajasthan and the experiences in Maharashtra and Delhi are cases in point.

In a jansunwai organized by the MKSS, in Kukurkheda panchayat, the sarpanch publicly accepted her guilt in a charge of corruption in public works to the tune of 100,000 rupees, and during the jansunwai itself returned the first installment of 50,000 rupees, which was deposited in the panchayat fund. The village community and the MKSS saw this as a major victory, although questions were raised whether mere refund of the amount misappropriated was adequate penalty and deterrence, or whether criminal charges should also have been registered.

Some days after the jansunwai, the Block Development Officer (BDO) called an informal meeting of sarpanches of the block, and they jointly persuaded the sarpanch of Kukurkheda to retract her confession and get back the money that she had returned. Subsequently, she illegally withdrew from the panchayat fund the 50,000 rupees she had repaid into it. Neither district nor block officials have taken any action against her.

By contrast, in Ajmer district, two sarpanches who had also returned misappropriated money detected during the jansunwai and refused to retract their confessions or reclaim the money had recovery orders and police complaints filed against them and were put behind bars.

In Delhi, after the public hearing in Sundernagari, in December 2002, various concerned people met the top political and administrative functionaries and demanded that the guilty be punished. A detailed report of discrepancies found in each contract was submitted to each of these government functionaries and the police were also contacted, but there was no response.

When all efforts failed, Parivartan filed a petition in May 2004, in the Delhi High Court, which then directed the Delhi police to investigate the allegations of corruption made by Parivartan and file a report before the metropolitan magistrate within six months. During the hearing, the Municipal Corporation of Delhi (against whom the charges had been made) said that they had already investigated the charges and found all of them baseless. However, the court observed that it was not proper for the "accused" to also be the jury and judge.

This order of the High Court caused panic among the concerned officials and contractors. Two of the engineers reportedly sank into severe depression, and many of the contractors refused to do any more work. In order to find a solution, the municipal councilor approached local activists and offered to ensure total transparency in the execution of all civil works carried out in the area. He said that he had directed the executive engineer to provide copies of estimates and sketches to the local NGOs before any work started. The public could inspect each work as soon as it was completed and any deficiencies would be immediately rectified. The contractors would be paid only after this was done. According to the councilor, the contractors and engineers were afraid of their works being subjected to a public postmortem in the form of a jansunwai, as this was often done long after the work had been completed and did not leave any scope for the rectification of faults. Meanwhile, the High Court case drags on. At the last hearing as of this writing, the Delhi Police had not yet collected evidence from the field, though nearly four years had passed since the work in question was allegedly executed.

What, then, are the options available to the individual or to civil society groups if no action is taken against government functionaries indicted in a public audit? Public audits of government authorities are a new phenomenon, and answers will perhaps emerge as more experience is gathered by diverse groups working in different regions on varied issues. However, recourse to some kind of organized peaceful protest seems inevitable if state authorities remain recalcitrant.

Future Directions

Having an RTI law enacted, even a good law, is only the beginning of the struggle. As already mentioned, the next important step is to ensure that the misdeeds discovered by the use of transparency laws are effectively and speedily investigated and punished. Along with this, a creative debate needs to be conducted on the legitimate limits to transparency. We must not let governments convince us that governance essentially involves secrecy. We must oppose the doctrine that national and individual security can only be ensured if the right to information is suspended or substantially inhibited. We must not only demonstrate that there is no good evidence in support of these contentions but also assert that public access to information is the bedrock of progressive democracy and, if this inhibits governance as we know it today, then it is governance that must change.

We live in an era of specialization. These are also times when knowledge, or at least information, is growing at a rate faster than ever before. But this rapid growth is also leading to more and more people knowing less and less of what is known. And the culture of specialization is resulting in information being packaged in ways that allow fewer and fewer people to understand it. If transparency is to be meaningful, that which is revealed must be understandable. Therefore, we have to evolve new methods of demystifying information and ensuring that all of humanity is in a position to comprehend the information and ideas that affect their lives.

The challenges are many, but there is also much energy across the country. Perhaps not since the concept of democracy itself was first mooted has any idea so caught the imagination of the people of India and so promised to revolutionize the way they will allow themselves to be governed.

NOTES

1. "Nehru Warns Partymen," *The Hindu*, January 21, 1955.

2. Loosely translated, the name means "coalition of workers and peasants."

3. *Panchayats* are local self-government institutions in most of rural India. The term *panchayat* is also used, as here, to cover the village or group of villages forming one unit of administration under the panchayat system.

4. "Public interest litigation" is an Indian phenomenon where individuals and groups who would ordinarily have no *locus standi* in a court of law because they are not an affected party are permitted to file cases that take up matters of "public interest," even if these matters do not directly affect the litigant.

5. Order of the Division Bench of the Bombay High Court, October 7, 1986, as quoted in the BEAG booklet on the case. *Bombay Environmental Action Group v. Pune Cantonment Board*, A. S. Writ Petition No. 2733 of 1986.

6. Order of the Supreme Court, October 11, 1986, ibid. *Bombay Environmental Action Group v. Pune Cantonment Board*, SLP (Civil) No. 11291 of 1986.

7. Resettlement colonies are so known because they are formed of people who had earlier "illegally" encroached on public land and were subsequently evicted and resettled by the government. These colonies are primarily populated by the very poor people who have emigrated from rural areas in search of livelihood.

8. Member of the Legislative Assembly, elected representative to the state legislature.

9. The elected head of the state government.

10. Prakash Kardaley, November 30, 2004, *RTI Experiences,* e-mail to Shekhar Singh.

11. The appellate authority under the Maharashtra Right to Information (MRTI) Act.

12. Over a thousand U.S. dollars—which would be more than two months' salary for a middle-level civil servant.

13. Loosely translated, this means "vigilant citizen's group."

14. A ration card, given to the poorest of the poor and entitling them to a fixed quantity of food grains every month at a subsidized rate, to be got from a designated ration shop.

15. The founding members were Ajit Bhattacharjea, Aruna Roy, Bharat Dogra, K. G. Kannabiran, M. P. Parmeshwaram, Prabhash Joshi, Prashant Bhushan, Renuka Mishra, S. R. Sankaran, and Shekhar Singh.

Chapter Two

Toward a More Open China?

Jamie P. Horsley

The People's Republic of China has joined the international move-ment toward greater government transparency, including making government records and decision making more accessible to its citi-zens.[1] While China is very much aware of and indeed has drawn les-sons from this international trend, the primary motivating force is domestic dynamics.

Transparency in China is in a transitional phase. Like many countries, China has a long tradition of government secrecy. The incremental progress toward greater information openness over the past twenty-five years was not triggered by a particular national crisis or scandal, as happened in the United States and Eastern Europe, although most changes in China during the late 1970s and early 1980s might well be attributed to a desire to prevent any repeat of the decade of lawlessness and destruction called the Great Proletar-ian Cultural Revolution of 1966–76. Instead, the transition toward greater transparency appears to have grown out of the confluence of an "open village affairs" movement that arose in the early 1980s, natural pressures from rapid economic development, momentum from the information technology revolution, and the demands of foreign trade and investment as reflected in China's 2001 commitments to the World Trade Organization.

China is planning for but does not yet have an information access law. General goals of greater governmental openness have been enunciated in national policy over more than a decade but have been carried out in a piecemeal fashion throughout the country. However, concepts such as the government's obligation to disclose information and the people's "right to know" are beginning to be translated into legal rights and obligations in experimental local legislation that should help institutionalize what the Chinese refer to as "open government information."

This chapter will discuss the development of open government information in China, as well as the prospects for further opening.

Introduction to the Chinese Context

China hosts the world's largest population, with approximately 1.3 billion people living in an area slightly smaller than the United States. The People's Republic of China was founded on October 1, 1949, as a "dictatorship of the people" led by the Communist Party of China (the Party), which retains a monopoly on political power today.

Following disastrous Party programs of collectivization and communization, and a chaotic decade of "Cultural Revolution" that left its economy and society in shambles, China adopted the "open door" policy in 1978 to increase foreign trade and selectively welcome foreign investment in the formerly closed country. Since that time, market reforms have gradually replaced central planning, reducing the number and economic contribution of state-owned enterprises, increasingly supporting private enterprise, and lifting price controls on all but a handful of commodities. Today, some 60 percent of industrial output is produced by nonstate enterprises, under what is termed a "socialist market economy." In 2002, the Party set a goal of turning China into a middle-income country with a "well off" population by 2020. Economic development remains the top priority.

These reforms, which have made China's one of the fastest growing economies in the world, with a 9.8 percent rate of growth in 2005, have been accompanied by enormous social change. The "iron rice bowl" of guaranteed employment and related social benefits for urban residents has been replaced with a market economy in which they must find or make their own jobs. Farmers are increasingly leaving the land to seek opportunities in the cities. Personal freedoms have expanded with the widespread loosening of social controls. Change has been supported by establishment of a rather sophisticated body of law adapted in many cases from successful models of other countries, although enforcement of these new laws remains problematic. Concepts of private property rights have gradually taken hold and were recognized in an amendment to China's constitution in March 2004. An accompanying amendment for the first time enshrined the notion of respecting and protecting human rights in China.

While economic growth has lifted hundreds of millions of Chinese out of poverty over the past few decades, this has occurred primarily in the industrial eastern part of the country. The government admits there are at least 85 million rural residents who live on less than US$75 per year and cannot afford quality food, education, and health care. Pressing problems such as sharp rural-urban and regional disparities, environmental degradation, and rampant corruption, which estimates value at some 3–5 percent of GDP,[2] are giving rise to increasing social unrest. Concern over instability prompted the current leadership to focus on better-balanced and sustainable development rather than growth for its own sake, as well as on new mechanisms to help better manage change.

Amid all this change, political reform has been modest. The Party, comprised of some 65 million members, or about 5 percent of the population, seeks to maintain tight control over policy formulation and implementation, and Party functionaries often concurrently hold government positions, creating what is commonly referred to as the Chinese "Party-state."

Under China's constitution, all power belongs to the people, and state power is exercised by them through the National People's Congress (NPC) and local people's congresses at the provincial, county, and township levels. The State Council, China's Cabinet appointed by the NPC, is the highest executive body, overseeing the central ministries and the work of local governments. The people's courts, also answerable to the NPC, are part of the administrative structure. The standing committees of the congresses, not the courts at the same level, interpret the national or local laws, for example. The constitution further specifies that the Communist Party of China is the sole political party in power. Other political parties and nongovernmental or civic groups and associations are tightly regulated and subject to official approval and registration.

The current constitutional structure provides for a four-tiered system of direct elections for deputies to people's congresses at the township and county levels, and indirect elections for the provincial and national people's congresses. The congresses at each level, rather than the populace at large, elect the government and judicial officials at the same level. Slates of candidates at all stages and all levels are largely controlled by the Party. The system as designed, lacking truly open, competitive, and direct elections, fosters vertical patron-client relations between the Party leaders at higher levels, who recommend the candidates for lower-level Party, congressional, government, and judicial positions, and horizontal accountability between local government and judicial officials on the one hand and the congress and Party organization at the same level that actually elected them on the other. Consequently, congressional deputies and government officials have felt little sense of accountability to the people they ostensibly represent, and the Chinese people have traditionally known little about their representatives and the matters they are handling, even though China's constitution calls on the people to "supervise" government work.

Change is occurring, however. Since the early 1980s, the Party has endorsed direct, competitive, and nonpartisan elections at the most local level of governance: in China's 660,000 villages, where some 700 million rural citizens live. While the Party recognizes that electing leaders at a very local level can foster greater trust and stability, it is hesitant to introduce that practice at higher, more formal political levels, where candidates are less well known, issues become more complex, and voters are more likely to organize around different issues, building pressure to permit competing political parties to represent their interests. Stimulated by successful experience with the village election model, however, the Party is permitting limited experiments with more competitive (but nonpartisan) congressional and direct governmental elections at the township and county levels, as well as promoting directly elected urban community councils. Elections within the Party itself are becoming more open and competitive. Party policy purportedly supports the strengthening of what it refers to as "socialist democracy," to better allow the people to make their will known and to supervise government—all under the leadership of the Party, however.

What explains these changes? To oversimplify, the Party leadership seems to recognize that, in order to maintain the Party's legitimacy, curb corruption, and address the complex issues of governance amid rapid development, the traditional model of governance must be adjusted. China's leaders acknowledge that a modernizing China requires a government that is efficient, law-abiding, and relatively open, one that facilitates, rather than controls, social and economic development and enjoys the trust of the people. To this end, the current leadership seeks to foster what the Party calls "political civilization," which encompasses development of the "rule of law" and of certain more democratic mechanisms to implement the constitutional right and duty of Chinese citizens to serve as "masters of their country" and "supervise" government. Such mechanisms include, importantly, greater access to government information.

Development of Government Transparency in China

From the Countryside to the City

The current emphasis within the Party and government on greater openness of information and of government affairs generally traces its origins to the collectivization and commune ideology of the Party, with its legacy of farmer participation at the commune (now the village) level and expectations of transparency, especially in local finances.[3] This tradition helped shape the more recent development of directly elected and self-governing villager committees and the related "open village affairs" program.[4]

Villagers spontaneously organized the first largely autonomous villager committees in 1980 to manage communal properties and agricultural production.[5] The dismantling of the rural communes following the Cultural Revolution (1966–76) left a vacuum in political, production, and community organization in China's vast and impoverished countryside below the township level, as well as a legacy of mistrust between farmers and Party cadres. Party leaders supported the advent of directly elected villager committees, hoping the system would promote stability and economic prosperity by allowing the people to choose leaders they trusted, by making those leaders directly accountable to their constituents, and by implementing a system of open village affairs, which emphasized financial disclosure on the part of the elected village leaders.

Despite unevenness of implementation, the village open affairs and self-governance program was very popular among the people and higher-level officials where it was implemented well. By the late 1990s, the "open village affairs" program was evolving into a broader "open government affairs" movement that was promoted in top-level Party and government policy documents.[6]

The adoption by the NPC in November 1998 of the permanent Organic Law on Villagers' Committees (the VC Law)[7] marked a significant advance in the institutionalization of more open governance at the village level. The VC Law requires directly elected villagers' committees (VCs) to implement the "four democracies": direct democratic election of VC members, democratic decision making through the villager assemblies comprised of all eligible voters, democratic management by the VCs, and democratic supervision by the villagers under new systems of "openness in village affairs." VCs must publish financial information, in particular, at least once every six months and guarantee the truthfulness of the information disclosed, as well as respond to inquiries from the villagers. Villagers refer to this disclosure system as the "Sunshine Project."[8]

In a March 1999 speech on villager self-rule, a vice premier described a growing rural concept of a "right to information" tied to economic development: "Following the deepening of rural reform and development of the market economy, farmers' thinking, concepts, and value orientation have undergone profound changes. Their sense of democracy and their sense of participating in the management of economic and social affairs have constantly increased. And more and more they want to have the right to information, dialogue, and decision-making. They long for direct participation in making decisions on major affairs in the village and the management of village affairs."[9]

Meanwhile, in the cities, urbanites were increasingly leaving the "iron rice bowl" of guaranteed employment by the government or state-owned enterprises and institutions, which had included em-

ployer-provided housing, schooling, medical treatment, and retirement benefits, to pursue entrepreneurship or work for the emerging private sector. As their numbers swelled, and as concepts of
property rights developed with the advent of private housing and
business ownership, the demand for greater information relating to
business and the economy as well as social services grew. Residents
and businesses, for example, needed information on urban development plans in order to make decisions about where to invest in a
new home or office building.[10] The development of China's stock
markets prompted the establishment of new information disclosure
standards systems to promote greater corporate transparency.[11]

In the year 2000, a detailed joint Party and State Council notice[12]
officially extended the open affairs program from the village to the
township, which is the most basic level of formal government in
China. The notice emphasized publicizing all financial affairs and
making it "convenient" for the people to supervise the work of township governments by providing more information and involving the
people more in decision-making. Townships were instructed to set
up public bulletin boards, much as was the practice in villages, and
adopt other means to regularly communicate with the public. The
notice further instructed the higher-level county governments to prepare for instituting "open government affairs" programs. By 2003,
even the higher-level municipal governments were directed to implement systems of open government affairs.[13]

Technological Stimulus

While the substantive notions of government transparency were
beginning to spread throughout the Chinese government, Chinese
universities and agencies were constructing a technical platform
that would support and further promote this transformation. In the
early 1980s, the Chinese government took the first steps to use new
information technologies such as computers and the Internet to
make information more accessible throughout government itself,
to strengthen the capacity to share information in support of gov-
ernment-directed industrialization and economic development,
and to make government more efficient. In December 1999, the
Party established a Leading Group on National Informatization to

set policy in this area. A State Council Information Office was subsequently set up to carry out "informatization" policies, and it was decided to develop a government "Intranet" to build a database and share information.

The initial emphasis of China's "E-government" program was on internal sharing of information among different agencies and vertically from the center to the localities to facilitate all kinds of government services and functions, including tax collection, foreign trade, and technological development, rather than providing greater information to the Chinese public. Through linking of databases, for example, tax authorities discovered that many companies that were registered with the industrial and commercial bureau had not registered with them to pay corporate income tax.[14] As the information database grew and technology advanced, this program established the technical platform for and a new norm of sharing more and more information. Central and local government agencies began making an ever-increasing amount of information about government functions and activities available and providing administrative services to the public over the Web. These new practices and changing attitudes toward the utility of a freer information flow spurred development of "open government affairs" programs.[15]

The rapid spread of Internet use, buttressed by the proliferation of Internet cafés for those without access to their own personal computers, extended the information revolution more and more to the ordinary citizen. As of mid-2006, roughly 130 million Chinese, or about 10 percent of the population, were using the Internet[16] to access all kinds of information, including some held by their government. Technology is clearly playing a large role in promoting the greater sharing of information in all sectors of government and society in China today.

WTO Commitments

China's accession agreements with the World Trade Organization (WTO) in December 2001 added impetus to the movement toward greater openness by requiring the country, as part of an international commitment with other member countries, to make trade-related rules and requirements transparent. China agreed to only enforce those laws, regulations, and other measures that have been published and are widely available; make those measures available to WTO members before they are enforced, absent emergency conditions; designate an official journal for the publication of relevant legal and policy documents; provide an opportunity to comment before measures are implemented; and establish one or more inquiry points where requesters can obtain information within thirty to forty-five days. Standard WTO rules do not generally require that its members establish inquiry points or provide a public comment period before a trade measure can be implemented. These commitments were specifically negotiated with China in order to compel changes in China's underlying legal system to facilitate greater transparency.[17]

China's leaders at all levels take these accession agreements seriously, conscious also that review mechanisms have been established under the WTO to monitor China's compliance. They have organized extensive training sessions throughout the country and study tours abroad to investigate means of implementing government transparency. WTO transparency obligations are constantly cited by Chinese reformers in support of efforts to promote greater information disclosure and open government. Implementation of these commitments is less than perfect,[18] but transparency at all levels of Chinese government is improving.

LEADERSHIP SUPPORT

Although the drive for greater transparency, especially in financial matters, most notably derived from China's farmers, they do not appear to have lobbied for change in any organized or well-articulated manner. Indeed, Chinese law and policy prohibit citizens from forming issue-oriented associations without official approval and do not provide clear channels for input into the policy process. The Chinese experience differs, then, from that of diverse countries like India, Peru, and Romania, where grassroots activism played an important and public role in bringing about access to information legislation.[19] Although social organizations, including business associations and consumer and environmental groups, may well be engaged in pressing for more openness, information on any such activities is not readily available. Instead, it appears that China's academic and political leadership at various levels has spearheaded the movement for greater information openness in and beyond China's villages.

As gleaned from Party and government policy statements and academic writings, the leadership's motivation to move toward greater openness turned on a combination of pragmatic goals: to involve a wider spectrum of the public in making increasingly complex policy decisions and laws to support China's drive for economic development, to curb rampant corruption with its negative economic and social consequences, to establish new mechanisms to ensure social stability and build trust in government, and to comply with China's transparency commitments in its 2001 WTO accession agreements.

The leader most associated with China's modern economic reform process, Deng Xiaoping, as early as 1984 endorsed the development of information resources to serve modernization.[20] His vision and support boosted China's embrace of information technology. "Informatization," the technological side of open information, is now a strategic priority in China's Tenth Five-Year Economic Plan (2002–07) and is recognized as key to achieving modernization.

Deng's successor, Jiang Zemin, developed leadership support of the "open government affairs" program, first introducing the concept officially in his report to the 15th National Party Congress in 1997.[21] He subsequently stressed the need to "keep the people informed" and strengthen "openness in government, factory and village affairs," as well as "citizens' participation in political affairs in an orderly manner," in his report to the 16th National Party Congress in November 2002.[22] Jiang and the Party thus set the necessary policy framework for greater access to government information and decision-making processes. State Council Premier Wen Jiabao, who is responsible for carrying out Party policy through government action, then called specifically, in his government work report to the annual meeting of the National People's Congress (NPC) in March 2004, to establish a system of "open government information" and to increase transparency of government work, in order to keep the people informed so they can exercise supervision over government work.[23] Thus, by the spring of 2004, China's government leaders were talking explicitly about the importance of institutionalizing open government information (OGI).

The Policy and Legal Framework for Greater Information Openness

Policy Framework

China's fundamental policy goal is social stability so the country can pursue rapid economic development. China has moved cautiously from a highly centralized, planned economy to a mixed economy that is replacing government mandates with more market-oriented mechanisms, while retaining a single-party political system. That system must find ways to accommodate increasingly divergent social, economic, and political demands and an increasingly assertive public opinion made even more influential through the spreading use of the Internet.

The Fourth Plenum of the 16th Party Central Committee in September 2004 called for Party members to improve their ability to run an increasingly complex nation, admitting in an unusually self-critical public statement that some of its own leaders lack quality, capability, integrity, and close ties to the people. The document warns that the "life and death of the Party" could hang in the balance if the Party's governing style does not become more responsive to the people.[24] It calls for supporting and improving open government affairs and systems to keep the people informed so they can better supervise government work. Moreover, the Party endorsed "open Party affairs," with greater transparency so that Party members can better understand and participate in internal Party work, themes that echo and should lend further support to transparency developments on the government side.

In March 2005, the Central Committee of the Communist Party and the State Council jointly issued a policy document (the "Joint Opinions") that for the first time placed the Party's support firmly behind institutionalizing the open government affairs program into a law-based system of "open government information."[25] This document recited the benefits of open government and outlined the basic principles of open information: 1) disclosure of all types of information concerning various administrative management and public services, except information involving state secrets, commercial secrets, or individual privacy; 2) disclosure upon the government's own ini-

tiative of matters that should be extensively known to and participated in by the public, as well as disclosure upon request; 3) timely
and satisfactory explanations in the event certain information cannot
be disclosed upon request; and 4) establishment of evaluation and
supervisions systems to ensure that government officials carried out
these principles. The Joint Opinions further called for the speedy
formulation of State Council Regulations on Open Government Information, while encouraging the localities to develop local rules to
establish a legal basis for open government affairs in the interim.

It is clear that a combination of economic and political factors is
driving the Party leadership toward recognition of the need to change
its style of governance and to promote greater transparency. Just as
financial oversight was the primary motivation for greater transparency in village affairs, so the economic imperative to permit the free
flow of information in order to realize sustainable economic development has been a driving force in developments at the national level.
The Chinese government has long been the primary source and ar-
chiver of all kinds of information relating to social, economic, and
political affairs. An oft-quoted statistic estimates that 80 percent of
all useful information in China is held by the government, and that
most of this information is not public.[26] Chinese scholars point out
that a monopoly on information leads to waste of and inefficient allocation of resources, corruption, and fraud, as well as policy-related
constraints. One example concerns 100 counties in Shanxi province
that applied for approval to build power plants utilizing their rich
coal reserves, only to discover after a year of wasted effort that the
existing power grid in the region could no longer accommodate any
more power plants.[27]

Despite the absence of national OGI legislation, a conducive policy framework is encouraging central government ministries to grant
greater public access to their files and share an ever-wider array of
information with the public, posting more and more information on
their official Web sites and implementing a recently introduced government spokesperson system. For example, the Ministry of Foreign
Affairs in 2004 announced new measures to open its archives and
declassified some 10,000 items from between 1949 and 1955, the
first batch of diplomatic files to be released since 1949.[28] The National
Auditing Office (NAO) decided in 2003 to make all its annual reports
public and for the first time released the entire text and posted it on

the NAO Web site. In the past, these reports had been submitted only to the State Council and the NPC.[29] In 2004, the NAO created a national "audit storm" with its public report that 41 ministries under the State Council had misappropriated as much as the equivalent of US$171.56 million, including the embarrassing news that the State General Administration of Sports had embezzled US$15.83 million from the country's 2008 Olympics special construction fund.[30]

Since its embarrassing initial cover-up of the Severe Acute Respiratory Syndrome (SARS) outbreak in early 2003, China is becoming more open in disclosing news about disasters, which typically have not been reported. Observers were surprised when China, not known for transparency regarding its military, reported a fatal submarine accident in May 2003, and the Chinese press covered a series of troubling mining tragedies in the autumn of 2004.[31] The State Council Information Office announced that government agencies would make more information accessible to the press and the public in 2005.[32] These are just a few examples of diverse areas in which the practice and culture of greater openness is expanding.

The Legal Framework for Information Access

While open government information is now endorsed as a policy matter, China still lacks national OGI legislation, and Chinese law does not provide clearly for information rights. Efforts to promote greater transparency under the "informatization" and "open government affairs" programs mentioned above have met with resistance from officials accustomed to preserving a shield of secrecy around themselves and their work. Despite high-level articulation of the importance of open government affairs, that program was never institutionalized in a uniform manner throughout the country. Without clear legal requirements, governments and local bureaucrats have been free to decide how and to what extent to publicize government information and operations. Indeed, existing legislation, such as the Law on Guarding State Secrets, the State Security Law, and the Archives Law, emphasizes secrecy, not disclosure of government-held information.

In recent years, however, the State Council and some local governments have undertaken to "legalize" the open government affairs program through OGI legislation. An important accomplishment of China's emerging OGI legal framework is that it establishes, for the first time in China's long and rich history, rights for the Chinese people to obtain government information and enforceable obligations on the government to disclose information.

Development of Basic Concepts

China's constitution does not specifically address information rights. However, certain constitutional principles do establish a legal basis for OGI and open governance. Article 2 stipulates the foundational principle that all power belongs to the people and that the people are to manage state affairs and economic, cultural, and social affairs through various channels and in various ways.[33] Article 3 makes the nominally elected congresses at all levels responsible to the people and subject to supervision by them. Article 27 requires state agencies and functionaries to maintain close ties to the people, heed their opinions, and accept their supervision, while Article 41 grants citizens the right to criticize and make suggestions regarding government agencies and their functionaries. These constitutional principles provide a framework for more participation by Chinese citizens in all kinds of decision making and other forms of supervising government. The citizens cannot exercise these rights without adequate information.

As the "open village affairs" program gained popularity and began to influence higher levels of administration at the grassroots level, economic pressure, including from increasingly significant foreign investors, prompted the central government to begin publishing more government documents and legislation. Before 1991, little government information was made public directly. It was primarily shared with lower-level government agencies and only on a need-to-know basis with others outside government.[34]

Spurred by the growing demand of foreign trading and investment partners and China's desire to rejoin the General Agreement on Tariffs and Trade, in March 1992 the State Council issued a directive to publish all national foreign trade and investment laws, regulations, and policies.[35] A 1992 United States–China market access document called on the Chinese government, in a section entitled "Transparency," to publish on a regular and prompt basis all legal and policy documents pertaining to trade matters.[36] Meanwhile, on the domestic front, China's 1993 consumer protection law was apparently the first Chinese legislation to enunciate a "right to know," stipulating that consumers enjoy the right to know and request accurate information about products or services that they buy, as well to know information about the protection of consumers' rights and interests.[37]

Other national legislation soon established additional principles of openness. A 1996 revision of the Statistics Law added the system of regularly publishing comprehensive statistics and the results of statistical investigations.[38] The Administrative Licensing Law (ALL), passed in August 2003 and effective July 1, 2004, stipulates that the government licensing and approval process shall be open, unless state secrets, commercial secrets, or individual privacy are involved.[39] Moreover, the ALL gives the public the right to inspect agency records relating to supervision of the implementation of licensed activities. The September 2003 Law on Environmental Impact Assessment promotes public participation in assessing the environmental impact of projects and establishes a system to share environmental impact assessment information with the public.[40] A local example is Shenyang Municipality's pioneering legislation on "public participation in environmental protection."[41] It stipulates that environmental information is a public resource and provides for "environmental information rights" as well as participation rights.

While additional examples could be cited, existing legislation provides at best a piecemeal approach to making government information more accessible, without detailed procedures and without any overarching legal framework that would ensure that administrative agencies would respect, and the people's courts would enforce, access rights. That is what a national "freedom of information" or "open government information" statute could provide.

Draft National OGI Legislation

Apart from the policy statements mentioned earlier on promoting openness in village and government affairs, no national legislation or detailed guidance was developed to support the "open govern-ment affairs" program. Seeking to institutionalize these concepts, deputies to the annual meeting of the National People's Congress filed proposals in 2001, 2002, and 2003 urging the drafting of a na-tional OGI law to satisfy the citizens' right to know, fulfill WTO com-mitments, help in legalizing government work, strengthen society's ability to supervise government, and realize the economic value of information resources.[42]

These legislative proposals led to inclusion of a draft OGI law in the five-year legislative plan of the Tenth NPC (2002–07), and may have prompted the State Council Information Office to task the Chinese Academy of Social Sciences (CASS), in May 2002, with re-searching and drafting legislation on open government information. CASS formed a research group headed by CASS law professor Zhou Hanhua, who conducted extensive research on information access laws around the world.

One of the group's first dilemmas was whether to draft a law or an administrative regulation. A law passed by the NPC could create new and enforceable rights, which local legislation cannot, and could cover the courts and the people's congresses as well as government agencies. However, drafting and deliberating national laws in the NPC takes a much longer time than formulating State Council regulations. In the interest of developing a nationwide legal basis for OGI as quickly as possible, the research group decided to take the regulatory route. Their experts' proposed draft of National Open Government Information Regulations (the "Draft National OGI Regulations") was submitted to the State Council in July 2002.[43] That draft, which has not been officially published, is still under-going internal consideration and substantial revision. As happened in other Asian countries such as South Korea and Japan, China in-stead proceeded to permit local experiments with open information systems to gain experience before introducing an OGI system on a nationwide basis.

Local Experimentation

Academics and government officials in the commercial city of Guangzhou (Canton) in China's southern Guangdong province were among the first to begin drafting local OGI legislation. Exposed early on to foreign trade and investment via nearby Hong Kong, Guangzhou had been an early proponent of, and had already developed detailed local rules on, the open government and E-government programs. Prompted to take additional concrete steps by an early 2002 central directive on further promoting "open government affairs," the Guangzhou Office of Legislative Affairs contracted with academics at Guangzhou's Zhongshan University and formed a working group in June 2002 to draft municipal-level provisions establishing a system of open government information (the "Guangzhou OGI Provisions").

The Guangzhou drafters say they did not have contact with the CASS research group in Beijing and came up with idea of OGI legislation on their own, prompted by their experience with village affairs transparency movements in Guangdong province and the "open government affairs" program in Guangzhou, as well as overseas research conducted by Guangzhou-based officials and academics in Great Britain and the United States. The Guangzhou OGI Provisions apparently were circulated for discussion at a nationwide administrative law conference in summer 2002. While much of the terminology and ideas are quite different, some of their language is the same as that in the Draft National OGI Regulations, so there appears to have been at least some cross-fertilization, probably at that point. In any event, the Guangzhou OGI Provisions, approved by the Guangzhou Municipal Government on October 30, 2002 and effective January 1, 2003,[44] made history by establishing unprecedented rights of access to government information in China.[45]

The government of Shantou municipality, located in one of Guangdong province's special economic zones, followed closely behind, as did the international commercial hub and special municipality of Shanghai, which adopted China's first provincial-level OGI legislation (the "Shanghai OGI Provisions") in January 2004.[46] In February 2004, the business center of Shenzhen in Guangdong province passed China's first "online OGI" provisions.[47] By the end of the year, more than 24 provincial and municipal-level governments had adopted OGI legislation, and the spread of local legislation continued throughout the country until an announcement in September 2006 that national Open Government Information Regulations might be issued by the end of that year.

New Information Rights

Breaking the deeply entrenched tradition of government secrecy, these local OGI provisions all establish a presumption that government-held information should be accessible, making nondisclosure the exception rather than the norm. They aim to protect the "right to know" of individuals and organizations—a right that does not appear in China's constitution and is not defined specifically as such in any national law to date—and establish two fundamental and, for China, novel ideas: that Chinese government agencies have an *obligation* to disseminate on their own initiative and disclose upon request most of the information that they hold, and that Chinese citizens have a *right* to access such information.

The Guangzhou OGI Provisions define individuals and organizations as "persons with the right to access," and government agencies and their functionaries as "persons with the obligation to make public." While the Shanghai OGI Provisions do not use those terms, they similarly provide that citizens, legal persons, and other organizations have the *right* to request information from government agencies, and conversely impose a legal *obligation* on the agencies to disclose all information not covered by a specified exemption.[48]

The local provisions further establish another new right, that of any person to access information concerning himself that is held by a government agency, as well as to request correction of any errors or inaccuracies in such information. For example, individuals have not to date had the right to review personnel files maintained on them, which might contain information on high school and university transcripts, work records, and employers' comments. But they have had to pay an annual fee to government agencies that maintain the files and for release of such files to prospective employers and others. In the past, companies could not sign a contract with a new employee without first obtaining the personnel file.[49] Accordingly, the right to request access to one's personnel file is important for confirming and correcting information as citizens seek to change jobs and as China begins to establish a consumer credit information system.

The local OGI provisions all specify a nonexhaustive list of broad categories of information that must be disseminated on the government's own initiative, a useful device in a country without a developed concept of "public record" information and where government is not accustomed to sharing information. In addition to development plans, municipal rules and regulations, budgets and actual expenditures, and data about each government agency, these provisions require publication of information on issues of particular public concern, such as epidemics (like the 2003 SARS outbreak), natural disasters, and other emergencies, and land use plans and approval documents relating to rural land requisition and urban redevelopment involving demolition of existing structures and relocation of residents. The sometimes forcible expropriation of land and homes of farmers and urban residents due to rapid development has led to protests, litigation, and a general public outcry for more transparency and what Westerners might refer to as procedural due process. Making the land use planning and development process subject to mandatory public disclosure, together with providing opportunities for the affected public to express their views, should help regularize this often controversial process.

Under these OGI provisions, citizens are also given the right to request information from government agencies that has not already been disseminated, which they have never enjoyed before. Information required to be disclosed affirmatively is generally published in periodic local government gazettes, in local media, and on the local government Web site, as well as made available at the agency itself for ease of public access. Under most local OGI provisions, each government agency is to compile and update a catalogue of information that it holds, as well as a guide on how to access it. Most OGI localities have already developed standardized request forms and user guides.

Exceptions to the Rule of Access

The local OGI provisions follow international practice in establishing categories of information that are exempted from the disclosure obligation, including private information about individuals, commercial secrets, state secrets, and information regarding matters still under deliberation. One goal of international legislation in this area is to specify with as much precision as possible the scope of necessary exceptions to the rule of openness, so as to prevent them from becoming huge loopholes for government nondisclosure. In China, the concept of a "commercial secret" has been under development for several years, although the precise contours are not yet well defined.[50] However, notions of individual privacy and the protection of personal data, nowhere clearly expressed in law, remain to be fleshed out,[51] and the most troublesome exemption is that for "state secrets."

Invocation of the overly broad Law on Protecting State Secrets, adopted in 1988,[52] can still basically eviscerate the disclosure mandate of all OGI legislation in China. This law defines "state secrets" as "matters that affect the security and interests of the state." This definition is illustrated with broad categories of information, including secrets concerning "important policy decisions on state affairs," "economic and social development," science and technology, and criminal investigations, as well as the more conventional areas of national defense and diplomatic affairs. Public health information— including information about diseases not yet listed by the Ministry of Public Health as a contagion that should be announced to the public—is, for example, apparently treated as a state secret under existing implementing regulations. Chinese officials and scholars have called for revision of the law to more clearly distinguish between what should be kept confidential and what can and should be disclosed. Although work on a comprehensive revision is under way, a revised State Secrets Law is not yet on the NPC legislative plan. Pending national action, local governments and requesters will be challenged to find ways to narrow its reach.

Open Decision Making

A major innovation of many local OGI provisions, not included in the Draft National OGI Regulations, is the stipulation that certain decisions should be announced during the drafting process for public input before they are finalized and implemented. These stipulations seek to further institutionalize mechanisms for greater public participation endorsed by the Party and authorized by the Legislation Law of the People's Republic of China.[53] These mechanisms include publication by people's congresses and government agencies of draft legislation and policies to solicit public input in writing, as well as holding public hearings on selected legislation or administrative rules deemed to affect "vital" public interests.

Following a trend set by the Guangzhou OGI Provisions, for example, the Shanghai OGI Provisions require the advance publication for comment of draft decisions, municipal rules, and plans that affect the "major interests" of Shanghai residents or have a "major social influence." Indeed, the Shanghai Government Legislative Affairs Office adopted a public participation procedure in formulating the Shanghai OGI Provisions themselves. It published a draft for comment in two local newspapers and on the official Shanghai government Web site, and consulted various legal scholars, government officials, foreign experts, enterprises, and nongovernmental organizations. This was the first time the government had sought public input on a draft regulation prior to adoption, although the Shanghai Municipal People's Congress had published several draft laws for comment and occasionally held hearings on them in the recent past. Shanghai and other local governments that include such a requirement in their OGI legislation are breaking additional new ground in terms of institutionalizing public participation and open government generally.

Implementing Open Government Information Systems

A major challenge of OGI legislation is to make it workable, to ensure that citizens actually use the law and that government agencies actually provide required and requested information.[54] The pioneering Guangzhou OGI Provisions, for example, went into effect amid great fanfare on January 1, 2003. But those provisions were entirely ignored by government officials, media, and citizens when the SARS crisis that apparently started in or around Guangzhou first became public in February 2003.[55] Even in the United States, where the media and citizens groups are more accustomed to pressing the government for information, it took years for people to begin to recognize the usefulness and effectiveness of the Freedom of Information Act (FOIA) in opening government files to the public.

Shanghai has done a particularly impressive job of spreading the word about the new OGI system. Citywide, fifteen municipal agencies felt to be particularly closely related to the interests of the public, including education, urban planning, social security, and labor, were selected for special training to get their information access systems established by the date the Shanghai OGI Provisions went into effect.[56] Outreach programs to potential users included business associations, lawyers groups, social organizations engaged in issues such as environmental and consumer protection, urban community councils, universities and scholars, the media, and other groups, as well as government officials unaccustomed to the practice of openness. One wealthy district in Shanghai has incorporated training residents on how to access government information over the Internet into the community-based citywide program to put "one million families online."

In the first month after the provisions took effect, the Shanghai government reported that 21.64 million people searched for information on their Web site, and various government agencies received 63,600 phone inquiries. The fifteen key agencies reported 989 requests for government information, to which 947 replies had been sent by month's end. Within five months, 12 administrative reconsideration cases had been filed with different government agencies, plus four lawsuits. Media also reported that the city of Wuhan, whose OGI provisions went into effect July 1, 2004, had ordered reconsideration of a request for information from the labor bureau by a laid-off worker that had been denied in August. These private enforcement actions indicate that at least some segments of the population in Shanghai and Wuhan are familiar with and using the new OGI legislation.

Most of the local OGI provisions stipulate administrative penalties for government officials who do not disclose required information or otherwise violate requirements and call for periodic investigations by local supervision agencies and government legislative affairs offices. Shanghai went a step further in requiring annual reports on what information was disseminated, statistics on disclosure requests and the types of information that were either disclosed or denied based on an exemption, statistics on any lawsuits or complaints received, major problems, and plans for improvement. Adopted from U.S. practice, this mechanism essentially incorporates OGI implementation into the performance reports of each agency and helps ensure they will pay at least minimal attention to carrying out the new system so they have something to report.

Another way to help ensure implementation is to give citizens effective administrative and judicial remedies to compel agencies to make government information public. Under the local OGI provisions and current Chinese law, residents are afforded only the traditional remedies of administrative complaint or administrative reconsideration by the agency that handled the information request in the first place, administrative litigation in the courts over specific government action or inaction, and civil suits for compensation in the event a violation of the provisions results in direct economic loss. Despite the initial positive result in the Wuhan case cited above, many Chinese scholars believe that the administrative remedies are unlikely to provide neutral relief in many of these cases, and administrative litigation is available under existing law only in cases of infringement of personal or property rights.[57] Whether the people's courts will accept cases involving new "information rights" created by municipal or provincial level governments and not endorsed by a national law passed by the NPC, and how they will enforce the local OGI provisions, thus remain to be tested. Observers note that China's courts are not truly independent and have little latitude to interpret legislation. However, the Shanghai courts set a positive example by accepting jurisdiction over the first known lawsuit under local OGI provisions in China. That lawsuit was filed in June 2004, just a little over one month after the Shanghai OGI Provisions came into effect.[58] Although the plaintiff ultimately lost her case on a technicality, the court made some positive findings, such as that the OGI Provisions did apply to information created before they went into effect, and criticized the government agency that refused to disclose the requested information for not having followed required procedures such as providing an explanation for its refusal. To avoid the shortfalls of the existing legal system, local governments might experiment with new institutions such as an independent information commission with adjudicatory powers, whose decisions could still be appealed to the courts, as has been done in the state of Connecticut[59] and, more recently, in Mexico.[60] However, the Chinese observe that such commissions are relatively expensive to maintain and would be yet another innovation to manage as they work to introduce the unprecedented OGI system. Another possible approach would be to establish an independent OGI office authorized to provide professional but nonbinding advisory opinions to both requesters and government agencies, as is done in the state of New York,[61] or an ombudsman system as is adopted in some other countries. Shanghai's mayor promised to establish a neutral body to handle

OGI complaints,[62] and the filing of the first lawsuit in Shanghai led to consideration of forming an expert committee to advise on issues relating to OGI implementation.

Contemporary Challenges

Prospects for National OGI Legislation

China's local OGI provisions are important first steps on the road to a national open government information law that will empower citizens to participate more actively in the management of their own lives and country. China's leaders appear to accept that a free flow of information can foster better economic decision making, curb corruption, build trust in government, and thus contribute to economic development and overall social and political stability. Just how free and open that flow should be has not yet been settled, however.

In the wake of widespread criticism of the Chinese government's secretive handling of the 2003 SARS crisis, which drove home the point that China is enmeshed in a global world that demands greater transparency, State Council Premier Wen Jiabao and other Chinese leaders and academics called for greater information openness.[63] Many observers predicted that the central government would move quickly to adopt national OGI legislation.[64] Although the State Council did act to promulgate national regulations on handling public health emergencies that called for timely, accurate, and comprehensive sharing of information with society,[65] deliberation on national OGI regulations was postponed, possibly to give local experiments—such as those in Guangzhou and Shanghai—time to work out the many challenging issues of regulation and enforcement in this uncharted territory.

Nonetheless, open government information has become a national policy, as reflected in government statements such as Premier Wen Jiabao's report to the NPC annual meeting in March 2004 and the Joint Opinions issued by the Party and the State Council in March 2005 that endorsed explicitly the legalization of the open government affairs program.[66] The State Council's ten-year program to implement "administration in accordance with the law," announced soon after the close of the 2004 NPC meeting, includes OGI as an important component.[67] That program talks, importantly, of the public's *right* to request open government information and calls on government agencies to facilitate that process.

The concept of a "right to know" first appeared in scholarly literature in the early 1990s, and is now frequently cited in scholarly articles, media reports and even policy documents. It was mentioned in an important Party document issued by the Fourth Plenum of the 16th Party Congress Central Committee in September 2004 as one of the Chinese people's "democratic rights" that need to be protected, as well as in the March 2005 Joint Opinions.[68] The right to know was also listed as one of the civil and political rights China is protecting as part of its human rights program in China's "white paper" on Progress in China's Human Rights Cause in 2003,[69] released by the State Council Information Office on March 30, 2004.

High-level policy statements are important, and promulgation of a State Council regulation establishing a nationwide OGI system would certainly expand and standardize the implementation of OGI systems throughout China. However, only when information rights are granted status under national law will they be clearly entitled to legal protection throughout China and by the people's courts. The drafting of a national OGI law, which has been placed on the NPC legislative agenda for the current session running through 2007, will be critical to ensuring the successful development of open government information in China. Such a law should also spur necessary work on related legislation, such as revising the State Secrets Law, drafting a privacy or personal information protection law, and expanding the scope of administrative and judicial relief explicitly to cover information rights.

Just as local experimentation often precedes central action, it is not unusual for China first to adopt administrative regulations at the State Council or ministry level, to gain experience while the supreme lawmaking body, the NPC, mulls over more comprehensive legislation. This approach is apparently being followed in the case of China's national OGI legislation.

Openness with Chinese Characteristics

The development of open government information in China over the past quarter century is noteworthy in several respects.

First, China is moving toward greater openness without having first undergone a democratic transition, even though information access is commonly associated with democratic values. Motivated primarily by the desire to ensure stability and continued economic growth at home, China's authoritarian leaders seem to accept that more open information benefits economic and social development. But they see it as a double-edged sword. While loosening the reins on day-to-day governance and encouraging a more open style of governance with "supervision" by the people and the media, the Party still attempts to retain tight control over information flows and media reportage, issuing directives prohibiting or limiting reporting on corruption scandals, farmer protests, and other sensitive news from time to time. Current Party General Secretary Hu Jintao, heralded as a populist who "puts the people first," has acquiesced in, if not led, a crackdown on free speech and the increasingly daring Chinese press. Since widespread unrest in the cities and the countryside since 2004 in particular, officials have detained, demoted, or arrested scores of prominent academics, writers, journalists, lawyers, peasant activists, and whistleblowers who are perceived to criticize the Party or the government or who otherwise champion the causes of disaffected petitioners.[70] Those targeted are frequently accused of revealing state secrets. Eighty-two journalists and Internet "campaigners" are in Chinese prisons, more than any other country, according to the Committee to Protect Journalists.[71] The actual implementation of the open government information policy clearly tests the "liberalism" originally attributed to the Hu Jintao–Wen Jiabao government.

It can be a struggle for citizens in well-established democracies like the United States to obtain information from reluctant government officials. Information disclosure in a single-party state like China is likely to be even more of a challenge, subject to strong political, even more than legal, constraints, although Party officials may well point to the "state secrets" or other exemptions from disclosure under OGI legislation to justify withholding politically sensitive information. The first OGI lawsuit filed in Shanghai is a good example of the problem. The requester sought access to seemingly innocuous real estate records from 1946 to 1968. While complicated legal issues delayed the court in reaching a resolution, officials reportedly feared the requester's motive was to seek documentary evidence to redress confiscation of real estate taken during the excesses of the Cultural

Revolution (1966–76), during which many citizens lost property. Using information access laws to open up past wounds, which in China could include those dating back to the original Communist revolution, various political and economic campaigns since then, and the more recent 1989 Tiananmen Square actions, is a phenomenon encountered in transitional countries around the world. The perceived threat to political stability may seem even greater in a country ruled by unelected leaders, and is undoubtedly part of the calculus behind the cautious approach to adopting such legislation in China.

A second notable aspect of China's growing government transparency as compared with other international experiences is the relative absence of organized nongovernmental or civil society input in the process. While the current OGI program in China can be traced to the grassroots self-governance movement for China's 700 million farmers, the dynamic of its evolution seems to have been interaction between a generalized social and economic demand (probably made much more specific at times in certain localities) and leadership acquiescence and support. Well-placed and influential academics, local officials, and other individuals who represent widely shared views may be active behind the scenes in promoting this process, but the articulation of the need for and development of OGI in China has had a definite elitist rather than a popular flavor. As civil society begins to develop and become more independent and active in China's restrictive political-legal environment, and as it begins to realize the benefits of recent developments in open information, it may begin to get more involved in pressing for greater information access. Whether and how an emerging civil society in China might contribute to promoting open government information will be issues worth watching.

Third, the Chinese leadership's early embrace of the technology that makes possible development of an "information society" to support economic development allowed creation of a technical platform that has facilitated China's gradual move toward openness. Promoters of more open government information may well have used the leadership's fascination with technical and "scientific" programs to support economic development not only to lay the technical foundation for but also to introduce new practices of sharing information to advance the much broader development of OGI policies and practices.

Fourth, while domestic concerns and developments can explain the impetus that has led to greater information transparency in China, international pressure and experience have also been brought to bear. China's transparency commitments in its 2001 accession to the WTO are taken seriously by the leadership and used as an argument by OGI promoters in support of the need for OGI legislation. Drafters at the national and local levels are all looking to learn from international experience, through research programs, international conferences, and soliciting the input of foreign practitioners and legal scholars.

Fifth, the spread of transparency in China has been incremental, based on a variety of complementary developments and experimentation conducted in different localities and within different bureaucracies with the approval of the center, as opposed to a distinct national reaction triggered by political crisis or scandal. Nevertheless, it is striking how quickly China's nascent OGI movement is growing at provincial, municipal, and lower levels to create new rights and impose new obligations with consequences for noncompliant government officials. From a handful of OGI provisions in place at the beginning of 2004, by mid-2006, the number exceeded 30 at just the provincial and municipal levels, not counting all the counterparts at lower government and agency levels.

It is unclear to what extent local legislation can actually create new rights that will be enforced by the people's courts, or to what extent the people, not accustomed to having the right to request all kinds of information from their government, and the government bureaucrats guarding the agency files will actually implement this important new system. While statistics and the filing of lawsuits and administrative actions indicate that Shanghai and Wuhan residents seem to be learning about and utilizing their new OGI system, officials in Changchun, the capital of northeast China's Jilin province, attribute the low number of visitors to the Changchun Archives Administration to search for information since local OGI legislation went into effect September 30, 2004, to unfamiliarity with the new system.[72]

Nonetheless, these new OGI systems are introducing new practices of openness and attempting to change attitudes and the way citizens relate to their government, and vice versa. Local governments are adopting slogans like "transparent government," "service-oriented government," "accountable government" and "law-abiding government" to describe how they see their role vis-à-vis society. One example of the new attitudes being promoted is the licensing law that took effect July 1, 2004,[73] which many Chinese see as truly revolutionary. That law seeks to restrain the exercise of administrative power by restricting the number of government agencies that have authority to regulate activity through licensing and introduces the concept that government should intervene only where individual initiative or the market cannot adequately do so. Transparency requirements permit citizens to monitor implementation of the licensing system. As one Chinese official describes the impact of the Administrative Licensing Law, in the past, Chinese viewed law as a means to control the people; now law is also being used to control government behavior.[74]

Can a nondemocratic China achieve true freedom of information and accountable government? In democracies, citizens can use the electoral process to bring pressure to bear even on unelected bureaucrats. More direct pressure can be applied through an independent judicial system that has the authority to enforce government compliance with the law. In China, in contrast, the Party ultimately controls the government personnel system and the courts. Although Chinese citizens can sue government agencies for abusive acts or failure to act as required under the 1989 Administrative Litigation Law, that law's coverage is narrowly drawn, and courts are frequently reluctant to accept cases that involve untested rights—since they are only supposed to apply and not interpret the law—or politically sensitive issues.[75] Thus, Chinese citizens basically lack the means to compel government compliance with newly emerging rights of information.

While Chinese officials do not have to account to the people in regularly scheduled and competitive elections and are still infrequently held liable in the courts for their actions or inaction, they nonetheless clearly understand that their credibility and the legitimacy of their leadership depend in large part on being responsive to the concerns and needs of their people. No government official welcomes public scrutiny of his or her decisions. Yet the promoters of OGI include government and Party officials, as well as scholars well versed in international practice. Many officials sincerely believe these mechanisms will help them do a better job, will help China develop on a sounder basis, and will help ensure social stability in these times of rapid change. Apart from matters of great political sensitivity, serious implementation of open government information systems could prove an important mechanism to help ensure that government becomes more responsive, if not strictly accountable, to the people. In that sense, putting in place new systems of open government information to permit citizens to exercise their nascent "right to know" can be a democratizing force in China. Whatever the end result, it is undeniable that a new culture of openness is being fostered in China today, with the cautious acquiescence and support of the Communist Party. Translating that culture into written law can only reinforce this positive trend.

NOTES

1. Thomas Blanton, "The Right to Know is Gaining Around the World," *International Herald Tribune*, October 11, 2003; Thomas Blanton, "The World's Right to Know," *Foreign Policy* 131 (2002): 50; Ann Florini, "The End of Secrecy," *Foreign Policy* 111 (1998): 50.

2. FriedlNet.com, "China's Corruption Crackdown" (2003), http://www.friedlnet.com/news/03031602.html.

3. Zhou Hanhua, ed., *Wo Guo Zhengwu Gongkai De Shijian Yu Tansuo (My Country's Experience with and Consideration of Open Government Affairs)* (Beijing: China Law Publishers, 2003), 89, 95–97.

4. See, in this volume, the chapter by Zhou Hanhua; Jamie P. Horsley, "The Democratization of Chinese Governance Through Public Participation and Open Government Information," in Renmin University School of International Studies, The Carter Center, Sun Yat-sen University, Jilin University, Association of Chinese Political Scientists in the United States and the Association of Chinese Professors in Social Sciences in the United States, *Political Civilization and Modernization in China*, Vol. 3: *The Political Context of China's Transformation* (Beijing: Renmin University, 2004), 569.

5. In the Guangxi Zhuang Autonomous Region, Sichuan and Hebei provinces. See Jamie P. Horsley, "A Legal Perspective on the Development of Electoral Democracy in China: The Case of Village Elections," and sources cited therein, in C. Stephen Hsu, ed., *Understanding China's Legal System*, (New York: New York University Press, 2003), 295 ff.

6. The Communiqué of the Fifth Plenum of the 15th Party Congress in October 2000 encouraged openness in "government affairs" and "factory affairs" as well as "village affairs," thus officially expanding the scope of the "openness" program beyond the village. "Communiqué of the Fifth Plenum of the Fifteenth Central Committee of the CPC" (*People's Daily*, 2000), http://www.people.com.cn/GB/channel1/10/20001012/268296/html (Chinese), http://english.peopledaily.com.cn/200010/11/eng20001011_52364. html (English).

7. Article 2, "Zhonghua renmin gongheguo cunmin weiyuanhui zuzhi fa" (Organic Law on Villager Committees of the People's Republic of China), adopted and effective November 4, 1998. Chinese text available from http://law.chinalawinfo.com/newlaw2002/SLC/SLC.asp?DB=ch1&Gid=21056; an informal English translation available from http://www.lawinfochina.com/index.asp.

8. Zhou Hanhua, ed., *Wo Guo Zhengwu Gongkai De Shijian Yu Tansuo*, 83.

9. Jiang Chunyung, "Ba cunmin zizhi zhejian rang jiuyi nongmin dangjia zuozhu de dashi banhao" (*People's Daily*, 1999), http://www.univillage.org/czht10.htm. See in English, Jiang Chunyung, "Do Well Matter of Primary Importance Which Allows 900 Million Peasants to Become Masters of Their Own Affairs," *People's Daily*, March 3, 1999. Translated in FBIS Article ID: FTS19990318000285, Document Number: FBIS-CHI-1999–0318.

10. "Zhengfu xinxi bu gongkai shimin ke qisu" (If Government Information Is Not Open, City Residents May Sue the Government), quoting Li Li, Director of the Guangzhou Municipal Government Office of Legislative Affairs (March 4, 2003), http://www.southcn.com/news/gdnews/gdtodayimportant/200303040378.htm; Xinhua News Agency, "China Strives to Promote Transparent Government" (2004), http://english.people.com. cn/200411/30/eng20041130_165654.html.

11. China Securities Regulatory Commission, "Information Disclosure and Corporate Governance in China" (2000), http://www.oecd.org/dataoecd/6/60/1931117.pdf.

12. Circular *Zhongfaban* 25 (December 6, 2000), issued by the General Office under the CCP Central Committee and State Council General Office on "Implementing in an All-Around Manner the System of Opening Government Affairs to the Public by Organs of State Power in Towns and Townships throughout the Nation," in Chinese. Translated in FBIS Article ID: CPP20010105000097, Chinese text of "Zhonggong zhongyang bangongting, Guowuyuan bangongting guanyu zai quanguo xiangzhen zhengfu jiguan quanmian tuixing zhengwu gongkai zhidu de tongzhi" (De-

cember 25, 2000), http://www.cass.net.cn/chinese/s04_nfs/policy.files/17. htm?te=2.

13. "Wu Guanzheng Stresses at the National Teleconference on Openness in Government Affairs the Need to Advance Openness of Government Affairs in Depth and Earnestly Safeguard the Fundamental Interests of the Broadest Masses of the People," Xinhua Domestic Service, September 25, 2003. Translated into English by World News Connection, FBIS Document Number FBIS-CHI-2003–0925, AFS Document Number CPP20030925000144; short article on the speech, in Chinese, "Shenru tuijin zhengwu gongkai qieshi weihu hao zuiguangda renmin de genben liy," http://www.buaa.edu/cn/html/jijianjiancha/jiaoyu/ckz134.htm.

14. "Zhengfu xinxi gongxiang wuda ganga" (Five Big Embarrassments in Government Information Sharing), Hunan Information Industry Association, http://www.hniia.cn/xxhlt/200410210142.htm.

15. See, e.g., in this volume, chapter by Zhou Hanhua; Zhou Hanhua, "Zhongguo de zhengfu xinxihua ji qi mianlin de shijian wenti" (Government Informatization in China and the Practical Problems It Faces) (2004), http://www.iolaw.org.cn/paper10.asp.

16. David Barboza, "The Rise of Baidu (That's Chinese for Google)," *The New York Times*, September 17, 2006."

17. See summary in United States General Accounting Office, *World Trade Organization: Analysis of China's Commitments to Other Members* (Washington, DC: United States General Accounting Office, 2002), 9, 47–49.

18. See, e.g., "China's WTO Implementation: An Assessment of China's Third Year of WTO Membership," Written Testimony by the U.S.–China Business Council, *Federal Register*, 69 (145) (2004): 45369–70.

19. See, in this volume, chapter by Shekhar Singh discussing the work of the Mazdoor Kisan Shakti Sangathan (MKSS); United Nations Development Programme, "Right to Information: Practical Guidance Note" (2004), 16–17, http://www.undp.org/oslocentre/docs04/RighttoInformation.pdf.

20. See above, note 14.

21. Jiang Zemin, "Hold High the Great Banner of Deng Xiaoping Theory for an All-Round Advancement for the Cause of Building Socialism with Chinese Characteristics to the 21st Century" (1997). See Section VI, Reforming the Political Structure and Strengthening Democracy and the Legal System. Available from http://xcb.ysu.edu.cn/jdzz/jzm/gjqz.htm (Chinese), http://www.fas.org/news/china/1997/970912-prc.htm (English).

22. Jiang Zemin, "Quanmian jianshe xiaokang shehui, kaichuang zhongguo tese shehui zhuyi shiye xin jumian" (Build a Well-off Society

in an All-Around Way and Create a New Situation in Building Socialism with Chinese Characteristics) (2002). See Part V, Political Development and Restructuring. Available from http://big5china.com.cn/chinese/2002/Nov/233867.htm (Chinese), http://english.peopledaily.com.cn/200211/18/eng20021118_106983.shtml (English).

23. Wen Jiabao, "Report on the Work of the Government" (2004). See Section III, Government Self-Improvement. http://www.peopledaily.com.cn/GB/shizheng/1024/2394441.html; official English translation available at http://www.chinadaily.com.cn/english/doc/2004-03/16/content_315302.htm.

24. "Chinese Communist Party Publishes Key Policy Document on Governance Capability" (*People's Daily*, 2004), http://english.peopledaily.com.cn/200409/26/print20040926_158378.html; and links to other sections of the policy document.

25. "Zhonggong zhongyang bangongting, Guowuyuan bangongting guanyu jinyibu tuixing zhengwu gongkai de yijian" (Opinions of the General Office of the Central Committee of the Chinese Communist Party and of the State Council on Further Promoting Open Government Affairs). March 24, 2005, available in Chinese at: http://news.xinhuanet.com/newscenter/2005-04/26/content_2877607.htm.

26. Li Jin, "Cong Henan Pingxing teda sharen'an kan gongmin de zhiqingquan wenti," *Criminal Law Review*; citation of the 80 percent figure in a study by Sun Yunchuan and Gao Jiubing, 1999. "Zhengfu wangshang xinxi ciliao huanjing guanli yanjiu," Tushuguan zazhi, http://www.iolaw.org.cn/paper10.asp. See also Zhou Hanhua, "Women weishenma xuyao zhengfu xinxi gongkai zhidu"(Why We Need an Open Government Information System) (2002), http://chinese.mediachina.net/index_news_view.jsp?id=53801.

27. "China Strives to Promote Transparent Government," *Xinhua News Agency*, November 30, 2004.

28. "China Declassifies First Diplomatic Files" (Xinhuanet, January 2004), http://news.xinhuanet.com/english/2004-01/19/content_1283797.htm. "Waijiaobu dang'anguan kaifang dang'an zanxing banfa," http://www.fmprc.gov.cn/chn/wjb/zzjg/dag/jdkf/t143266.htm.

29. "Auditing Reports to Open to Public," *China Daily*, July 5, 2003.

30. "Premier Welcomes Audit Report on Government Departments," *People's Daily*, July 5, 2004.

31. Robert Marquand, "New Openness in China Disaster," *The Christian Science Monitor*, November 29, 2004; Anthony Kuhn, "Chinese Submarine Accident Kills All 70 Aboard," *Los Angeles Times*, May 2, 2003; "Accidents

Reporting Shows a More Open Government" (Xinhua News Agency, 2004), http://www.china.org.cn/english/government/114996.htm.

32. "State to Speed Up Public Info Flow" (*China Daily*, 2004), http://www.chinadaily.com.cn/english/doc/2004-12/28/content_404046.htm.

33. Constitution of the People's Republic of China, adopted and promulgated on December 4, 1982 by the Fifth Session of the Fifth National People's Congress, as revised as of March 22, 2004, is available in Chinese from http://news.xinhuanet.com/newscenter/2004-03/15/content_1367387.htm, and in English translation (with amendments through 2004 at the end) from http://english.peopledaily.com.cn/constitution/constitution.html.

34. Zhou Wei, "Zhongguo gonggong xinxi gongkai falu zhidu de tedian, wenti yu fazhan" (The Special Characteristics, Issues and Development of China's Legal System for Open Public Information), *Journal of Administrative Law* 4 (2002): 2.

35. Ibid.; see "Guanyu chongshen zhiding, fabu quanguoxing duiwai jingmao fagui, zhengce youguan guiding de tongzhi" (Notice on Reaffirming the Provisions on Formulation and Publication of Nationally Applicable Foreign Trade and Investment-Related Laws, Regulations, and Policies), issued by the General Office of the State Council on March 26, 1992, http://www.law-lib.com/lawhtm/1992/8471.htm.

36. "Memorandum of Understanding Between the Government of the United States of America and the Government of People's Republic of China Concerning Market Access," signed October 10, 1992, http://170.110.214.18/tcc/data/commerce_html/TCC_2/PRCMarket.html.

37. Article 8, "Zhonghua renmin gongheguo xiaofeizhe quanyi baohufa" (Law of the People's Republic of China on Protecting Consumers' Rights and Interests). Chinese version available from http://www.eguo.com/channel/xiaofei/f/fg/1.htm; English version available from http://en.ec.com/cn/pubnews/2004_03_29/200875/1005146.jsp.

38. Zhou Wei, "Zhongguo gonggong xinxi gongkai falu zhidu de tedian, wenti yu fazhan," 3.

39. "Zhonghua renmin gongheguo xuke fa," adopted September 27, 2003 and effective September 1, 2004. Chinese text available from http://www.law-lib.com/law/law_view.asp?ed=79264.

40. "Zhonghua renmin gongheguo huanjing yingxiang pingjia fa," adopted by the National People's Congress Standing Committee on October 28, 2002 and effective September 1, 2003. Available from http://www.sepa.gov.cn/eic/649645345759821824/20021204/1036227.shtml.

41. See testimony of Brian Rohan of the American Bar Association and translation of the Draft Shenyang Municipal Measures on Public Participation in Environmental Protection at Congressional-Executive Commission on China, http://www.cecc.gov/pages/roundtables/012703/index.php. Chinese text available from Shenyang's Central Business District: http://www.cbd.gov.cn/channel/kejiao/0007/a002/news_paper/200282821647.stm.

42. "Guangyu zhiding 'Xingzheng jiguan zhengfu xinxi gongkai fa' de yi'an" (Proposed Bill Relating to Formulating an Open Government Information Law) (2002), National People's Congress (NPC), http://www.npcnews.com.cn/gb/paper289/1/class028900005/hwz204867.htm; "Lianghui daibiao ti'an: zhiding, Zhengfu xinxi gongkai fa" (Deputies Propose Bill on Open Government Information Law) (March 20, 2003), http://www.chinabbc.com.cn/news/news.asp?newsid=2004121314262&classid=106103.

43. See, in this volume, chapter by Zhou Hanhua. See also Zhou Hanhua, ed., *Zhengfu Xinxi Gongkai Tiaoli Zhuanja Jianyigao (Proposed Scholars' Draft of Open Government Information Regulations)* (China Law Publishers, 2003). The Scholars' Draft sets as its legislative purpose the protection of the public's exercise of the "right to know" and of public participation in the management of state and social affairs, promotion of the flow of government information, and supervision of government agencies in the exercise of their powers in accordance with the law. It creates the presumption of information access, with nondisclosure being the exception, and gives all natural persons (thus apparently covering foreigners), legal persons, and other organizations the right to obtain or access government information, except as otherwise provided by that regulation or other law. Substantially in accord with local legislation passed to date, the Scholars' Draft lists seven exemptions from disclosure that, with the exception of the exemption for "state secrets," which under current law is overly broad, conform generally to international practice.

44. Liu Heng, *Zhengfu Xinxi Gongkai Zhidu (The System of Open Government Information)*, 192–93 (China Social Science Publishing House, 2004).

45. "Guangzhoushi zhengfu xinxi gongkai guiding" (Open Government Information Provisions of Guangzhou Municipality) (2003), http://www/gz.gov.cn/egov/sqgk/200309170002.asp. See also Jamie Horsley, "China's Pioneering Foray Into Open Government," *The China Business Review* (2003), 40. Text also available from http://www.freedominfo.org/news/guangzhou (posted July 2003, together with an English translation by the author).

46. "Shanghaishi zhengfu xinxi gongkai guiding" (Open Government Information Provisions of Shanghai Municipality), http://www.chinacourt.

org/flwk/show1.php?file_id=91244. See also Jamie Horsley, "Shanghai Advances the Cause of Open Government Information in China" (2004), http://www.freedominfo.org/news/shanghai/index.htm (with an English translation by The China Law Center, Yale Law School).

47. "Shenzhenshi zhengfu xinxi wangshang gongkai banfa" (Measures of Shenzhen Municipality for Online Open Government Information) (2004), http://www.chinacourt.org/flwk/show1.php?file_id=92369. The Shenzhen Measures, which went into effect April 1, 2004, require government agencies to disseminate and post online, on their own initiative, some 35 categories of information, but do not provide a mechanism for requesting information that is not disseminated.

48. The Guangzhou OGI Provisions specifically apply to foreigners requesting information, but other local OGI provisions are typically limited to Chinese citizens and organizations. Nonetheless, some localities such as Shanghai have announced that foreign individuals, legal persons, organizations, and news media will in practice be given equal access to government information.

49. "Resistance Rises Against Personnel Files," (*Shanghai Daily*, 2003), http://www.cbiz.cn/NEWS/showarticle.asp?id=1772.

50. Article 10(3) of the Law of the People's Republic of China Against Unfair Competition defines "commercial secrets" broadly to mean "technical information or operating information that is not known by the public, can bring about economic benefits to the rightsholder, has practical utility and about which the rightsholder has adopted secrecy measures." "Zhonghua renmin gongheguo fan buzhengdang jingzheng fa," adopted September 2, 1992 and effective December 1, 1993. Available from http://news.xinhuanet.com/legal/2003-01/21/content_700654.htm, and in English, with membership, from http://www.ccpit-patent.com.cn/references/Law_Against_Unfair_Competition_China.htm.

51. Although privacy rights have been asserted in some cases, there is no law clearly establishing such rights. Instead, the constitution, Article 38, protects "personal dignity," and Article 40 protects the freedom and privacy of correspondence. Article 101 of the General Principles of Civil Law protects the right of reputation, without defining the concept. Recently, regulations on the use of computers and the Internet have prohibited damaging "privacy," again without defining the term. See Yingxi Fu-Tomlinson, "Personal Data Protection in China," *The China Business Review* 29 (4) (2002): 36.

52. Adopted September 5, 1988, effective May 1, 1989. English translation available from http://www.humanrights-china.org/zt/03102410/2003

12003112694228.htm; text of Chinese original, "Zhonghua renmin gong-heguo baoshou guojia mimifa." http://news.xinhuanet.com/legal/2003-01/21/content_699624.htm.

53. "Lifa Fa" (The Legislation Law), adopted by the National People's Congress March 15, 2000, effective July 1, 2000. Available in Chinese from http://www.china.org/cn/chinese/SFKSZN-c/82314.htm , and in English from http://www.novexcn.com/legislat_law.00.html.

54. See, in this volume, chapter by Laura Neuman and Richard Calland on the discussion of the importance of implementation.

55. News of the spread of the strange new disease that came to be known as SARS first spread on panicked rumors reported around February 8, 2003. When the Guangzhou Municipal Government and the Guangzhou Public Health Bureau held separate press conferences on February 11, apparently no one mentioned or asked about the applicability of the Guangzhou OGI Provisions. See "More Information Please: Epidemic Tests Government's Resolve," *Beijing Today*, February 28, 2002.

56. See Shanghai's government Web site, the top right-hand corner of which is devoted to open government information: http://www.shanghai.gov.cn.

57. "Zhonghua renmin gongheguo xingzheng susong fa" (Administrative Litigation Law of the People's Republic of China) (2003); available in Chinese from http://www.molss.gov.cn/correlate/xzssF.htm, and in English from http://www.jc-lawyer.com/english/ArticleShow.asp?ArticleID=845.

58. "Lawsuit Over Access to Housing Archives," *China Daily*, July 5, 2004.

59. See the homepage of the Connecticut State Freedom of Information Commission, http://www.state.ct.us/foi.

60. Mexico's Ley Federal de Transparencia y Acceso a la Informacion Publica Gubernamental, adopted April 30, 2002, establishes an independent Federal Institute of Access to Public Information to oversee the government's information management and declassification practices, and to promote the right of citizens to obtain government information. See Kate Doyle, "Mexico's New Freedom of Information Law" (2002), http://www.gwu.edu/~nsarchiv/NSAEBB/NSAEBB68/index.html.

61. See the homepage of the New York State Committee on Open Government within the New York Department of State, http://www.dos.state.ny.us/coog/coogwww.html.

62. "Han Zheng zai 'Shizhang rexian' yu shimin gonghua zhengfu xinxi gongkai" (2004), http://www.shanghai.gov.cn/shanghai/node2314/node2315/node4411/userobject21ai83745.html.

63. Sun Yafei, *Feidian: Jiasu xinxi gongkai bufa (SARS: Increasing the Pace of Information Openness)* (*Nanfang Zhoumo*, 2003), http:www.nanfangdaily. com.cn/zm/20030501/xw/ttzs/200304300462.asp. See also "SARS: A Valuable Lesson for Chinese Gov't to Learn," *People's Daily Online* (English version), June 8, 2003, http://english.people.com.cn/200306/08/eng20030608_117858.shtml.

64. See above, n. 63.

65. "Wen Jiabao qianshu guowuyuan ling gongbu shixing, Tufa gonggong weisheng shijian yingji tiaoli" (Wen Jaibao Signs State Council Order to Publish and Implement "Regulations on Emergency Response to Public Health Incidents") (Xinhua New Agency, 2003), http://news.xinhuanet.com/newscenter/2003-05/12/content_866362.htm.

66. See above, n. 23 and n. 25.

67. "Quanmian tuijin yifa xingzheng shishi gangyao" (State Council Outline on Implementing the Comprehensive Promotion of Administration in Accordance with the Law), adopted and effective March 22, 2004. See paragraph 10. Available from http://news.xinhuanet.com/zhengfu/2004-04/21/content_1431232.htm. For an English-language article generally describing this outline, see "Guideline to Build Law-Based Government Publicized" (Xinhua News Agency, 2004), http://www.china.org.cn/english/government/93677.htm.

68. See above, n. 23 and n. 25.

69. *People's Daily*, "2003 nian zhongguo renquan shiye de jinzhan (quanwen)." Available in Chinese from http://www.people.com.cn/GB/shizheng/1026/2418866.html and in English from http://english.peopledaily.com.cn/whitepaper/hr2004/hr2004(2).html.

70. Jonathan Watts, "Writer Held as China Turns on Intellectuals," *The Guardian*, December 22, 2004; Joseph Kahn, "China's 'Haves' Stir the 'Have Nots' to Violence," *New York Times*, December31, 2004; Edward Cody, "China Condemns Whistle-Blower: Official Denounced for Posting Letter Alleging Corruption in Communist Party," *Washington Post*, August 16, 2004.

71.ABC News Online (Reuters), "China Releases Journalists, Charges Two More," October 23, 2006, http://www.abc.net.au/news/newsitems/200610/s1771660.htm.

72. "Changchun Opens Government Information," *China Daily*, November 23, 2004.

73. See above, n. 39.

74. Anonymous, personal communication, July 2004.

75. The Administrative Litigation Law is cited above, n. 57.

Chapter Three

Open Government in China

Practice and Problems

Hanhua Zhou

This chapter is an introduction to the emergence of open government in China, where rapidly changing attitudes and practices have attracted widespread attention in the international community over the past several years. The first part offers an overview of current practices, with emphases on village affairs, legislation, government informatization, and "The Regulations on the Freedom of Information" that are currently being formulated. The second part analyzes why those practices have arisen. The third part discusses various problems facing the practice of open government in China.

The Practice of Open Government in China

China is applying the concept of openness in a wide range of areas, from village affairs to factory and school affairs, legislation, trials, procuratorial matters, policing, taxation, and so on. Almost all areas of social life have been touched. This chapter focuses on village affairs, legislation, government "informatization," and the formulation of "The Regulations on the Freedom of Information," a set of issues intended to provide a general understanding of China's system of open government.

Open Village Affairs

In the late 1970s, China's national economic reform began with rural reforms. At the same time, movement toward greater transparency began in the rural areas, led by farmers, and kicked off the move toward greater openness throughout the country. The phenomenon went through four stages of development.

The first stage: self-motivated practice. This was the period from 1982, when the villagers' autonomy system was incorporated into China's Constitution, to 1987, when "The Law on the Organization of Villagers' Commissions" (for trial) was enacted. During this time, major changes were under way in rural areas: reform of political structures, the abolition of the commune system, and the establishment of villagers' autonomous commissions. A small number of villages that carried out reform earlier than others introduced the practice of open village affairs. In this stage, the organizers were Party branches and the commissions of the villagers. The terminologies, contents, and procedures of the practice differed from village to village. Nonetheless, "The Law on the Organization of the Villagers' Commissions" gave a legal foundation and provided a strong boost to opening up village affairs by providing that "The villagers' commissions shall periodically publicize the accounts on incomes and expenditures on public affairs and public utilities and subject them to the supervision of the villagers and the economic bodies of the villages."

The second stage: standardization. This was the period from 1988, when "The Law on the Organization of the Villagers' Commissions" was enforced on a trial basis, to 1994, when the Central Committee of the Communist Party convened a special meeting on the construction of grassroots organizations in the rural areas. Along with broader implementation of "The Law on the Organization of Villagers' Commissions" in the rural areas, twenty-four provinces, autonomous regions, and municipalities directly under the central government set forth new local regulations. Most of these stipulated that the villagers' commissions should publicize in a timely fashion their expenditures and the costs of the villages' public utilities. The Central Government, the State Council, and the Ministry of Civil Affairs placed more emphasis on the construction of village organizations and forcefully promoted the standardization of openness in village affairs. More importantly, the Central Government issued "The Notice on Enhancing the Construction of Grassroots Organizations in the Rural Areas" in October 1994, raising, for the first time, the problem of duly "constructing the system of open village affairs."

By the end of this stage, the practice of open village affairs had extended from some specific villages to all villages of some counties. Leadership was now passed to the Party Committee of the Counties, the County Governments, and the Department of Civil Affairs of the Counties by the village party branches and commissions. The contents, timing, procedures, and forms of village-level openness became largely standardized.

The third stage: rapid development. This consisted of the period from 1995, when the Ministry of Civil Affairs held a National Meeting for the Exchange of Experiences on the Work of Villager Autonomy, to April 1998, when the General Office of the Central Committee of the Party and the General Office of the State Council issued "The Notice on Universalizing the System of Open Village Affairs and Democratic Administration in the Rural Areas." The Ministry of Civil Affairs honored 31 "Model Counties for Villager Autonomy," 16 "Best Towns and Townships," 150 "Town Stars," and 200 "Model Village Commissions," and thus started in the rural areas a vigorous campaign of developing the villagers' autonomy. In April 1997, the Central Commission for Discipline Inspection and the Ministry of Supervision convened "The Forum on Open Village Affairs and Democratic Administration" in Baodi, Tianjin, which reached a consensus that the practice of open village affairs was an important part of and an efficient way to build honest and clean governments in the rural areas. This gave a strong boost to the work on open village affairs.

During this stage, the scope of open village affairs extended to the provincial level and the leadership had become the provincial Party Committees, the provincial governments, the provincial committees of discipline inspection, and other relevant departments. The localities enhanced the standardized and systemized administrative regulations, systems, and file management.

The fourth stage: great advancement. This was the period after 1998, when the amended "Law on the Organization of the Villagers' Commissions" was put into force. The Communist Party set forth a "Decision on Some Major Issues in the Agricultural and Rural Works," which stressed that "democratic supervision at village level shall be carried out in an overall way. All major issues and affairs of common concern shall be publicized to the villagers. The emphasis of open village affairs shall be placed on open financial affairs." The amended "Law on the Organization of Villagers' Commissions" provided even clearer stipulations for the system of village openness and further clarified its contents, timing, requesting, public observation and legal liabilities, etc. On this basis, at the end of 2000, the General Office of the Central Committee of the Party and the General Office of the State Council set forth another document, aiming at promoting nationally the practice of open political affairs at the level of towns and townships.

As of this writing, the practice of village openness has spread throughout the country and a network of laws, regulations, and systems has taken shape. All relevant government departments helped to put this system into operation, and it has spurred the development of other practices of open government in China.

At the village level, openness has three components: financial, autonomous, and political. The financial component covers revenues, expenditures, property status, debts and financial claims, contract performance, etc. The autonomous component includes economic construction, public undertakings, farmer's burden, terms of office of the village cadres, etc. Political affairs mainly involve family planning, homestead approval, land expropriation by the state, disaster relief and relief distribution, etc.

Open Legislation

In China, transparency in legislation was originally understood to mean public access to final laws, regulations, and statutes. But this is not enough. Meaningful openness in legislation needs to include the disclosure of legislation drafts and processes, allowing citizens to raise inquiries and make comments and suggestions.

Like the trends in village-level openness, the movement toward greater transparency in the legislative process went through several stages. In the first stage, from 1949 to the early 1980s, there was essentially no openness. Only final legislation was published, whereas the legislation process, indeed all legal work, remained secret. High school students being recruited by law departments were told the work was "confidential." Legislation work was deemed more confidential. Draft laws and regulations and other legislative documents were all kept secret, and people engaged in legislation were not allowed to publish articles. Public discussion of draft laws and regulations was not permitted.

There were occasional exemptions for particularly important draft laws and regulations. For instance, the 1954 Draft of the Constitution of the People's Republic of China and the 1982 Amendments to the Constitution of the People's Republic of China were both published in newspapers for public discussion.

The period from the late 1980s to the end of the 1990s saw a gradual opening up, as economic reform led to demands for political restructuring. Standard procedures emerged for the disclosure of final legislation, and the legislative process became progressively more transparent. In April 1989, the 7th National People's Congress enacted new regulations declaring that the meetings of the National People's Congress would be held publicly with space for public attendance, that news conferences would be held, and that the drafts of some major laws would be published for the purpose of soliciting public opinions. From the mid-1980s to the end of the 1990s, the Standing Committee of the National People's Congress published ten legal drafts for public discussion, and the local authorities also published the drafts of some local regulations for public discussion. In 1998, Shenzhen took the lead to institute a public hearing system. In 1999, the Standing Committee of the People's Congress of Guangdong province followed suit and initiated a public hearing system, thus injecting new energy into the practice of open legislation and yielding satisfying results.

The third stage, since 2000, has been a period of systematization and standardization. In March 2000, the 9th National People's Congress passed a "Legislation Law," providing that "Legislation shall give full expression to the people's will, give full scope to social democracy, and ensure the people's participation in the activities of legislation through multiple channels." The law also provides the channels for public participation via written submissions, forums, hearings, and publishing of legal drafts for public discussion, etc. After the promulgation and enforcement of this law, the State Council issued successive regulations on the formulation of administrative regulations and on procedures for formulating statutes. And the People's Congresses of the provinces, autonomous regions, municipalities directly under the Central Government, and big cities also set forth their own regulations on local legislation, with more detailed provisions on public participation in legislative activities and rules on legislative hearings. At the same time, a public hearing system was adopted nationwide. In short, along with the deepening of economic reforms and the development of democratic politics, the legislative process became systematically more transparent, via the following methods:

1. Forums in which the drafting units, legislative agencies, or other institutions invite relevant experts and ordinary citizens from relevant state organs, social organizations, enterprises, and institutes to hold discussions and give opinions on the necessity, practicability, and contents of bills.
2. Written submissions by relevant state organs, social organizations, enterprises, institutes, and experts commenting on draft legislation.
3. Public discussions of particularly important laws, regulations, and statutes of vital interest to the citizenry that are publicized in newspapers. This is the most transparent and equitable method, but the huge amount of work involved means that it is only used for truly major issues such as the Constitution, the Law on the Organization of the Villagers' Commission, and the Marriage Law.
4. Hearings. The first Chinese law that had a provision for a hearing system was "The Law on Administrative Punishment," passed in March 1996 at the Fourth Session of the 8th National People's Congress, followed the next year by "The Price Law." In March 2000, the 9th People's Congress passed a "Legislation Law," which for the first time incorporated provisions for hearings into legislative procedures.
5. Argumentation. Argumentation differs from a forum or a hearing. It mainly concerns very special and technical problems in some bills. Relevant experts are asked to carry out research and make scientific and pragmatic recommendations.

6. Public hearings, in which relevant agencies, social organizations, the press, and ordinary citizens are allowed to be present and listen to the legislative agencies discuss or deliberate on a bill. The earliest Chinese law that provided for public hearings was "The Deliberation Regulations of the National People's Congress," passed in April 1989 at the Second Meeting of the 7th National People's Congress. The 3rd Clause under Article 18 provided: "Public seats shall be established at all the meetings of the Congress, and specific methods shall be provided separately." The majority of local People's Congresses and their Standing Committees also set forth provisions for hearing systems in their Deliberation Regulations. But by and large, hearings only came into widespread use in the late 1990s.

7. Opinion collection through the Internet. This is a brand new form of open legislation that has emerged because of the wide use of the Internet in recent years. The Internet is used in two ways. One is to publicize draft bills that are also being published in the press and collect responses. For instance, when the draft amendments to the Marriage Law were published in newspapers, they were also put on the Web site of the National People's Congress to collect public comments and opinions. The second is to feature draft rules and regulations only on the Internet, as is done by some departments under the State Council and some local authorities. For instance, since August 2001, the city of Chongqing has put the drafts of all local rules and regulations on the "Chongqing Web site for Open Government," with the purpose of soliciting opinions from the citizenry.

Government "Informatization"

Although the development of the Chinese economy is still at an early stage, the government is paying close attention to the global information revolution and is maneuvering to ensure that the Chinese economy and society become "informationized"—that is, fully engaged in and able to take advantage of the physical and institutional transformations of that revolution. The Tenth Five-Year Plan explicitly stated that "informatization" was a key strategic component of the drive for modernization. To that end, the government has energetically developed the information industry, promoted the wiring of government, and standardized Internet management.

During its institutional reform in 1998, the State Council decided to establish a new Ministry of the Information Industry. In December 1999, it was decided that the Leading Group for the Work of National Informatization would be formed, with Vice-Premier Wu Bangguo as the head. To strengthen the leadership, the State Council reorganized the Leading Group on National Informatization in August 2001, and Premier Zhu Rongji himself became its head. Meanwhile, the Informatization Office of the State Council was established.

With such strong support by the Central Government, the information industry and basic information facilities developed dramatically. By 2002, the share of the information industry in China's GDP had risen to 5.7 percent, from 2.3 percent in 1997. China had the world's largest number of telephone users (with over 85 percent of its villages connected) and the second-largest number of Internet users, and ranked third in global electronic and information product manufacturing.[1] China introduced deep reforms of the telecommunication industry to eliminate monopolies and introduce competition, including separating government functions from enterprise management, separating the postal service from telecommunications, and regrouping the telecommunication sector.

With this technological and institutional infrastructure in place, and with substantial cuts in charges for telecommunications services, information technologies are being used more and more widely. According to statistics from the Information Center of China Internet, released in January 2003, 20.83 million computers are connected to the Internet, and Internet users have reached 59.1 million.[2]

All this has laid a solid basis for extending the information revolution into the processes of governance. Actually, as early as in the 1970s, the Chinese government used computers to handle statistics and data on earthquakes, weather, power, etc. In the 1970s and 1980s, the government launched a number of projects to automate economic information flows. But the most significant change was Internet use after 1997, including the highly functional local networks and government Web sites that link various government departments.

On January 22, 1999, with China Communication and the State Economic and Trade Commission taking the lead, the information departments of more than 40 Ministries and State Commissions met to kick off the "Government Internet Project," aimed at promoting "informatization" of both the central and local governments. By the end of 2002, a total of 179,544 domain names were registered in China, of which 7,796, or 4.3 percent, had a .gov suffix.

To promote the development of e-government, in July 2002, the Leading Group for the Work of National Informatization set out specific "Guidance for the Construction of E-Government." It laid out specific achievements to be made in the Tenth Five-Year Plan in terms of the government Internet platform, business systems, databases, information sharing, information security systems, and systems of regulation and standardization of e-government.

In this tide of government "informatization," e-government took its initial shape. Built separately by the financial, taxation, customs, foreign trade, and technological departments, there are 108 computer information systems that boast nationwide coverage. With the General Administration of the Customs of the People's Republic of China taking the lead, 12 State Ministries and Commissions jointly developed the Port Management System. Through the system, all administrative procedures, including the formalities of import and export, can be handled directly online with the customs, inspection, industrial and commercial, and taxation authorities—an enormous change from the former system, in which enterprises had to go to all the separate sectors to finish the procedures for an item of import or export business. On June 15, 2001, the Bureau of Industry and Commerce in Beijing released regulations on joint examination and approval of the enterprises, laying down the principle that "the organ undertaking the registration shall inform all the other relevant organs to conduct and finish joint examination and approval within the specified time limit." An application for opening an enterprise only needs to be filed with the industrial and commercial agency. The latter will pass along the basic information to all other relevant agencies through the Internet. The agencies will conduct and finish the examination and approval within the specified time limit. And the industrial and commercial agency will be, in return, informed of the result of the examination, also through the Internet. The reform made the process significantly more convenient for the applicants and greatly reduced the waste of time and the opportunities for corruption.

To manage this rapid transformation, China has successively enacted a series of laws and regulations to enhance Internet management and information security.[3]

The Formulation of the "Regulations on the Openness of Government Information"

In the context of the fast development of open government and government informatization, the Leading Group on National Informatization, a high-level decision-making body headed by the Premier of the State Council, held its second meeting, passed the Tenth Five-Year Program on Informatization and the guidance on the development of e-government, and elevated the establishment of a legal system in that development to an important position. The drafting of the Regulations on Open Government Information, on the protection of private data and on information security, is at the top of the near-term agenda. Under the direct leadership of the Informatization Office of the State Council, the Draft Regulations on Electronic Signature and the Draft Regulations on the Openness of Government Information emerged.[4]

The Draft Regulations on the Openness of Government Information fully absorbed experiences from the laws of other countries and incorporated the following legal principles:

1. The Principle of Right. As in most information access systems around the world, access to government information is a right of the citizens, not merely a convenience for government operations. This is aimed at ensuring that transparency regulations have binding force.
2. The Principle of Openness. In the long history of Chinese administration, "not open" has been the guiding principle. Information was provided only in exceptional cases or as a favor. This spirit has seriously obstructed efforts to make government more transparent. It is necessary to make clear to personnel in the state agencies that transparency is the norm for government. This principle will also be crucial to the resolution of difficult cases in the future.

3. The Principle of Balancing of Interests. The Constitution of the People's Republic of China entitles citizens to enjoy the rights granted by the Constitution and other laws and regulations, and obliges citizens to perform the duties stipulated in the Constitution and other laws and regulations. When enjoying his or her legal freedom, rights and interests, a citizen shall not harm the legal freedom, rights, and interests of the nation, society, collectives, and other citizens. Because it is always possible that the right to know may conflict with other rights, such as privacy, or other interests, this principle is included in the draft regulations.

4. The Principle of Gratis. With the advent of the information society and the rising value of economic information, government agencies increasingly make money from the information under their control. To prevent agencies from raking in money inappropriately and driving up the costs of public access to government documents, government agencies must be forbidden to profit from the information they control. However, to reduce the burden of the agencies and prevent unreasonable requests, it is necessary for the requesters to bear the cost of searching, copying, and delivery.

5. The Principle of Free Use. The principle of free use, or the principle of marketization, means that, after acquiring government information, the requester may reprocess or otherwise commercially exploit it in a market-oriented way, and the government agencies shall not impose any prohibition or restriction and shall not claim any copyright or other kinds of protection. By definitely setting forth the principle of free use, the regulations are designed to motivate people's enthusiasm for exploiting and making full use of government information. It is also aimed at eliminating the negative influence of various kinds of unjustified rules, increasing the state agencies' sense of public service, and reducing the cost of public access to government information, thus promoting the development of the entire information industry and the information service industry in particular.

6. The Principle of Relief. The principle of relief means that, when a requester deems that his or her right to know is prejudiced, or a third party deems that his or her right of privacy

or business secrecy is prejudiced, he or she may apply for administrative review or file a lawsuit. According to the provisions in China's Law of Administrative Litigation, the concerned party may only file an administrative lawsuit against the specific act that constitutes an infringement upon his or her personal rights or property rights. This does not specifically include the right to know the truth. Similarly, although China's Law of Administrative Review provides that the concerned party may apply for an administrative review against any administrative act that constitutes an infringement upon any of his or her rights inclusive of personal rights and property rights, it was indefinite, from a legal perspective, whether this included the right to know the truth, because there was no definite provision on the right to know the truth in any Chinese laws and regulations. In practice, few applications for administrative review were filed against an infringement of the right to know the truth. The principle of relief is clearly set forth in the regulations. This will not only fill the loophole in the current legal system but also clarify the applicable scope of the Law of Administrative Review and the Law of Administrative Litigation, thus providing a strong guarantee for the right to know the truth.

The biggest problem in creating a system of transparent government is how to reasonably define what should be open and what should be kept secret to prevent national security and other public interests from being harmed. For this reason, the regulations stipulate seven exceptions:

1. national secrets according to the Law on the Protection of State Secrets;
2. information that shall not be made public according to the stipulations of other laws;
3. purely internal rules and affairs of the government organs that have no relations with the public;
4. business secrets of enterprises or other information provided by the enterprises to the government on the precondition of keeping it confidential;
5. personally identifiable information, but with the following exceptions:

a. personal information that can be made public according to the provisions of the laws and regulations;

b. personal information that must be publicized for the purpose of protecting the life, health, or property of the people;

c. personal information related to the obligations of public servants in the performance of their duty;

d. personal information that the person concerned agrees to make public;

6. information on the research, discussions, suggestions, or deliberations inside or among the government agencies during the process of policy making, the disclosure of which might adversely affect the process of decision making or cause chaos in the society;

7. information related to the enforcement of criminal law, the disclosure of which might adversely affect the investigation of the crime, the indictment, the trial, the enforcement of the penalty, or the right of the defendant to be tried equitably.

Except the above seven categories, all other government information shall be opened to the public.

The Causes of the Development of the System of Open Government in China

The rapid development of government transparency in China has profound social and economic origins. Perhaps most important, the development of an information society and economy demands the free flow of government information. Across the world, governments are the biggest information holders and controllers. Due to the influence of prolonged feudal rule, government opacity has long been a serious problem in China. The result is the formidable waste of the resource of its information. Some 80 percent of China's useful information is in government hands and most of that remains undisclosed, with severe consequences for economic development. Unblocking the flow could create huge benefits, as China's top leaders have clearly recognized.

Moreover, governmental transparency is essential to the right of the people to be masters of their own affairs. According to the Constitution of the People's Republic of China, China is a socialist people's democracy, and all power belongs to the people. They may exercise their power by electing the People's Congresses at all levels and, according to the laws, manage the state affairs and economic, cultural, and social undertakings through multiple forms and channels. The People's Congresses are responsible for the people and are subject to the people's supervision. All the state agencies and working staffs shall rely on and keep close relations with the people; they must frequently listen to the people's views and opinions, accept the people's supervision, and work hard to serve the people. Article 41 of the Constitution also stipulates that a citizen has the right to raise criticism and suggestions about the work of any state agency or working staff, and has the right to file a complaint, charge, or report to relevant organs on any illegal malpractice or nonperformance of duty by any state agency or working staff. In practice, for the people to exercise the power of managing state affairs and social affairs in any real sense, the precondition is to know the truth. If people have no idea about how the government work is proceeding, undoubtedly they cannot effectively supervise it. In recent years, citizens are attaching more and more importance to their own right to know the truth.

Third, governmental transparency is a basic World Trade Organization (WTO) requirement. The principle is honored in almost all WTO documents. WTO rules require the disclosure of generally applicable rules, regulations, bylaws, decisions, and intergovernmental agreements. Given the broad connections between trade and other parts of the economy, this strongly influences transparency across the board. Under its agreement with the WTO, China must accept the review of other WTO members in each of the first eight years after its entry into the organization. The review will cover the transparency of trade policy. The establishment of the open government information system will help China to satisfy the WTO requirements.

Fourth, governmental transparency will help to eradicate corruption, which has become a headache for both the Party and government leaders in China. Its roots are deep and complex, but two factors have clearly contributed: unchecked concentration of power and lack of transparency in the use of power. Thus, a constraint mechanism must be set up to prevent abuse of power, and the exercise of power must be subjected to the people's supervision. The open government information system will help to reveal the state organs' functions and powers, work procedures and results, time limits, and supervision methods to the public, suffocating the back-door practices from which corruption stems. It will also help to contain the abuse of power by granting the people not just information access but also the right to relief, as a personal right to supervision of the administrative powers and the judicial power's supervision of the administrative power are also developed.

Fifth, the openness of government information will facilitate the standardization necessary for a well-functioning market economy. Lack of credit, the chaotic market order, and the high costs for business transactions are the major factors restricting China's economic development. In dealing with such phenomena as the forgery of diplomas, counterfeit property rights certificates, falsification of government documents, contract fraud, stock speculation, and so on, there are basically two types of solutions. One is to intensify control and punishment, i.e., "crack down." This demands a great deal of government input, and the results are usually not satisfactory. The alternative, less expensive, and more effective solution is to increase governmental transparency.

Sixth, governmental transparency is conducive to the maintenance of social stability, which is of utmost importance to China's reform and economic development. Presently, at the grassroots level, some cadres do not have good relations or even have sharp contradictions with the masses, in part because the state organs and their staffs fail to work in a democratic and transparent way. Some even use their power for selfish purposes, to the serious disservice of the people. Governmental transparency can improve relations between the Party and the masses and increase public trust in the government. The experiences of government agencies in other countries demonstrate that transparency is the best and least expensive solution to this problem. Theoretically, a dynamic system in an open environment is stable when the system has the capacity for self-organization. A closed system without such a capacity cannot enjoy durable stability. In the information age, such self-organization depends upon the free flow of information. Without it, even a minor rumor can lead to turmoil in the whole society. Therefore, governmental transparency is an important measure to strengthen the psychological endurance of the public, and thus, preserve social stability.

Seventh, governmental transparency is a prerequisite for promoting the rule of law and reforming government management. Administering the country according to law is an objective requirement as well as a guarantee for the development of a socialist market economy, the construction of a socialist democracy, and the maintenance of lasting peace and stability. Rule of law is the fundamental strategy. In order to translate the rule of law into reality and build up a state of socialist rule of law, government agencies and their staffs at various levels must function according to law and sincerely defend the legal rights and interests of the public. At present, some government agencies or staffs do not observe laws in their performance of functions and duties. Especially at the grassroots level, the awareness of laws and policies remains weak. By setting up the system of open government information, making the public acquainted with the working methods and procedures of the government agencies, and subjecting administrative acts to the supervision of the masses, the concept of rule of law will be strengthened among the government organs and staffs.

Traditionally, administration according to law implied that government powers and functions should be exercised strictly in compliance with the stipulations of the laws, including the procedures, steps, time limits, and working methods. That approach was oriented to the planned economy system. But it did not work well, with information decentralized and not effectively shared among government organs or made available to high-level decision makers. Now, however, because the extension of administrative functions is unavoidable, the emphasis is on transparency and public participation. This poses a challenge for information management, administrative procedures, and policy making with regard to information technology. These changes to the traditional manner of government administration will substantially improve the efficiency of the management of government information.

Major Problems Facing the System of Open Government in China

In spite of the great headway made toward open government in China, there are still many obstacles and difficulties.[5]

First is the absence of an authoritative institution that could co-ordinate the policies on open information. At present, there is little coordination or consistency among the many efforts to bring about greater openness.[6] At the village level and the township level, the co-ordinating department is the department of civil affairs, in coopera-tion with the department of discipline inspection and other relevant departments. But at other levels, the coordinating departments and the leadership are much more complex. The departments of legal affairs, personnel, civil affairs, and supervision are all engaged. Ad-ditionally, the management of information security and the enforce-ment of relevant laws involves departments from the State Commis-sion of Encryption Management, the Ministry of Public Security, the Ministry of State Security, the Ministry of the Information Industry, and the National Administration for the Protection of State Secrets to the Information Office of the State Council. These ministries rarely coordinate or learn from one another's experiences, adding substan-tially to the cost of increasing transparency and making it difficult to get beyond the exploratory stage of reform.[7]

Second is the absence of a unified "Law on Open Government Information." Specific provisions have appeared in many Chinese laws and regulations. For instance, "The Archive Law" has provi-sions on the management and openness of government archives; "The Law on the Protection of State Secrets" has provisions on the secrecy of government information; "The Law Against Unfair Com-petition" has provisions on the protection of business secrets; "The Statistics Law" has provisions on the management and openness of government statistics, and so on. Because there is no unified law to standardize and clarify provisions on relevant problems, there is no cooperation and coordination among the departments and localities in the process of reform. Some reform measures have been delayed or suspended as a result. For example, the Credit Registration and Consultation System under the People's Bank of China (the central bank) possesses China's largest database on capital and credit. But due to the absence of relevant laws and regulations, its information cannot be open to the public. This has directly affected the estab-lishment of China's credit system, which is so urgently needed in the development of the market economy. If this situation continues after China's entry into the WTO, the practices of some sectors and localities will not conform with the WTO principle of transparency.

It has become imperative to pass a unified law on open government information so as to meet WTO requirements.

Third, overall, the concept of governmental transparency in China remains one of opening up to the public information on the procedures and results of government activities. How and what to open are decided by the government; the public is only a passive beneficiary. If the government does not open the systems or documents that should be accessible, the public can do nothing about it. It is now essential to start building on the achievements to date and undertake thorough reform of both the system and the concept. Outmoded conventions and customs that are not suitable for the market economy and information society must be gotten rid of and all obstacles hindering the free flow of government information must be removed, so as to guarantee the freedom of the public to acquire and utilize government information.[8] As mentioned above, this will require confronting the reality that many government agencies and staff are profiting from their control of information and will not readily cede that control.[9] Today, in some Internet services provided by some government organs, even the access to some new laws and regulations is not free of charge. Maybe, someday, we will shamefully find that the Chinese people could acquire gratis the latest foreign laws and regulations and foreign government information through the Internet, but have no access to Chinese laws and regulations and our own government information because of its hefty price. The result will be information monopoly and blockage in the information society.

Fourth, it is necessary to modify the State Secrets Law and other relevant laws. As mentioned above, the most important thing is to properly handle the relations between "open" and "not open." Otherwise, transparency might adversely affect the vital interests or national security of the state. In China, the prevailing secret law was legislated ten years ago. In view of the classification, declassification, punishment for secret leakage, relief measures, etc., the system has lagged far behind the requirements of the actual situation, with some information that should be defined as or kept secret available, while other information that should be open still hidden. This has constrained the openness of government information. And some leakage of state secrets has done serious harm to the state interest. To ensure the coordinated development between the state secrecy system and the open government system in China, the modification of the current State Secrets Law is essential.[10]

The experiences of other countries make clear that there are always some exceptions in the practice of open government. Sweden's Law on the Freedom to Publish provides seven exceptions. The United States's Law on Freedom of Information provides nine exceptions. Among all the exceptions, classified documents are only one kind of them. Because China lacks a legal definition of exceptions, the scope of "secret" is defined much more widely than necessary, and nonsecret documents are also kept away from the public. The failure to correctly distinguish nonsecrets from secrets is among the most important factors contributing to the blockade of government information. Only when there is a reasonable definition of and a clear distinction between what may be opened and what may not be opened can there be a sound foundation for the realization of open government information.

In defining the scope of open information, coordination between the State Secrets Law and criminal law is also a problem. According to the law, state secrets fall into three categories: top secret, secret, and confidential. On each classified document, the competent agency must indicate its classification. A document without an indication of classification does not constitute a state secret and its disclosure does not constitute a leak. However, according to Article III of the Criminal Law, any stealing, inquiring, collecting, or buying of state secrets or intelligence for the purpose of illegally providing them to foreign institutions, organizations, or personnel constitutes a crime, and any leakage of state secrets constitutes a crime. But what kind of information constitutes intelligence? There is no provision in Chinese law. This creates a problem: a document without an indication of its classification could also be treated as "intelligence" in the later judgment and its disclosure could also constitute a crime.[11] If the provision is not clarified and the law is not coordinated with the State Secrets Law, along with the expanded openness of information, it will become the major factor restricting the development of governmental transparency.

Another noteworthy problem is the relationship between government information and archives. In other countries, archives are governed by the law on the freedom of information. All the archives that do not fall within the scope of exceptions can be treated the same as other government documents and can be disclosed to the public. In China, government information is divided into archives and nonarchives. Archives are governed by the Archive Law, but no law applies to nonarchives. According to Article 19 of the Archive Law, "Generally, the archives kept by the State can be disclosed to the society after the expiration of thirty years as of the formation of the archives. In the cases of economic, scientific, technological, cultural, and other relevant archives, the period could be shorter than thirty years; while in the cases of the archives that involve state security or other vital interests which are not suitable for disclosure upon the expiration of thirty years, the period shall be longer than thirty years. The specific period shall be decided by the competent archive management agency of the State." In other words, the Archive Law has restricted disclosure of the archived government information to the public. In principle, the nonarchived documents are also kept for thirty years before they can be disclosed to the public. Therefore, the Archive Law, which should facilitate openness in government, actually impedes it. Legislation on open government needs to address the problem of its relations with the Archive Law. Otherwise, the law could only be applicable to nonarchive documents and thus be limited.

Fifth, it is necessary to grant the public the right to inquire about government information. At present, openness depends on the willingness of government agencies to post in their offices the working systems and procedures, print and issue work manuals, set up bulletin boards, hold propaganda meetings, put government information on the Internet, and so on. These measures have played an important role in informing people about the government's work and defending their legal rights and interests, but this approach has serious limitations. Especially as the economy and society become less dominated by the government, it will become more and more apparent that there exists no smooth avenue for the public to learn about the government system.

Within the WTO framework, establishing an information inquiry point has become an important means to effect government transparency, by setting up a procedural right for applicants entitling them to acquire information under certain conditions. To some extent, this offsets the lack of open channels at the present stage, gains experience, and creates conditions for the overall launching of the system of open government at a later time. It is necessary to study a series of problems including the costs, charging of fees, reduction of and exemption from charges, mechanism building, application procedures, and reform of working methods and devise solutions to bring about a breakthrough in open government.

Sixth, the Internet needs to be fully utilized in the construction of open government. Public access to government information imposes costs for storing information and providing it to the public. Before the Internet, those costs were large enough that the public had to share in them. Some people were even unable to acquire government information because of economic reasons.

The advent of the Internet completely reversed the situation, drastically reducing the costs and making information management and storage much more convenient for government agencies. It is obvious from looking at some government Web sites that the Internet has not been used to full advantage. Some government sites are actually commercial sites or sites on special fields, showing a dislocation of roles. Some government sites simply repeat content already published by the press. Some carry very limited content and are rarely updated.

Government Web sites should be characterized by the accuracy, all-inclusiveness, timeliness, and authoritativeness of the information published on them. Thus, the public could gain access to government information in the most efficient way. To begin this process, some standards should be set and the public invited to evaluate government Web sites. Over the longer term, thorough studies are needed on the new problems caused by such utilization of the Internet, including the new challenges posed for information storage by the rapid update of technology, the assortment and definition of information, the openness and security of information, the pluralization of information resources, and so on.

NOTES

1. Wu Jichuan, "Follow the Guidelines of the 16th Congress of the Party and Promote the Fast Development of the Information Industry in China," *Research on Soft-Science of Telecommunication* 1 (2002): 2.

2. "Statistics on the Internet Development in China, January 2003," China Internet Information Center, http://www.cnnic.net.cn/download/2003/10/10/170932.pdf.

3. To enhance legislation in the telecommunications area, in 2001, the Chinese Ministry of the Information Industry formed a leadership group for the drafting of the telecommunications law, a working group, and an expert consultative commission. On October 10, 2001, the framework draft for the telecommunications law was finished. It made provisions, in a systematic way, on such problems as the security of the telecommunications network, information security, telecommunications supervision, etc., and is therefore of great significance.

4. In the process, many municipal governments, such as Guangzhou, Hangzhou, Chengdu, Shengzhen, Kunming, Wuhan, etc., as well as provincial governments, such as Hubei, Shanghai, etc., have been promulgating local bylaws on the openness of government information. The general structure and major stipulations of these bylaws have been influenced more or less by the draft of the Regulation on the Openness of Government Information. Therefore, they are not discussed them in detail here.

5. A recent case is very reflective of the problem. According to the report by *South China Weekend* on October 12, 2000, the Editorial Department of *The Tribune on Rural Development* under the Agricultural and Industrial Commission of the Party Committee of Jiangxi Province published a booklet entitled "The Working Manual on the Reduction of the Farmers' Burden," in the form of an additional issue in 2000. Within half a month, 12,000 copies of the booklet were sold across 11 areas of Jiangxi Province. Almost all the buyers were farmers. On August 11, the Editorial Department suddenly received a notice that sale of the booklets must be stopped immediately and those purchased must be reclaimed. Accordingly, relevant departments exerted every effort to recall the booklets according to the registered addresses of the buyers. Even some local agencies of public security received the order to take back the booklets household by household without a single exception. Their slogan was "The (negative) effects must be cleared up wherever the booklets are sold." By the end of August, 11,000 copies of the booklet were sent back to Nancang and stored in a warehouse, waiting to be destroyed. What is most inconceivable is that the booklet is in no sense an illegal publication, only a compilation of the Party's rural policies.

6. Over a period of time, public access to government information has been called "openness of government affairs," "publicization," "two openness and one supervision," "e-government," "the system of publicizing the working

system," "freedom of information," "open government information," "open administration," and so on. Sometimes these different names refer to different contents, resulting in different practices in implementation.

7. Guangzhou was the first municipal government in China to adopt local legislation on the Openness of Government Information, which was implemented January 1, 2003. However, during the outbreak of SARS around the same time, the bylaw was not publicized and the people could not get any information from relevant government agencies.

8. In another instance, despite the efforts by the Central Government to promote the informatization of the national economy and the project of "online government," neither could be done effectively due to the lack of relevant laws and regulations. Similar cases are innumerable.

9. According to Clause 1 of Article 5 of China's Copyright Law, the protection of copyright does not apply to "laws, regulations, and resolutions, decisions and decrees of the state agencies, and other documents which are of the nature of legislative, administrative and judicial documents, and other official translations." In compliance with this provision, almost all government documents are to be open to the free use of the public. Of course, the concrete implications of the provision in the copyright law need to be clarified further. It is yet to be determined whether all the government information and archives are covered. Additionally, as has been seen with the provisions in some other laws and regulations, the spirit of encouraging the free use of government information, which is cherished in the copyright law, is not followed and supported in a consistent way. For instance, it is expressly provided in "The Regulations on the Management of the Compilation, Edition and Publishing of Laws," which was promulgated by the State Council in 1990, that compilation of laws can only be undertaken by the authority; nongovernmental organizations can not compile laws for their internal uses. The protection provided in the regulations on the compilation of laws is much more forceful than the protection provided by the copyright law on works under copyright. It has, in fact, made the authority the sole supplier of the compilation of laws. I can understand the original intention of trying to guarantee the high quality of the compilation of laws, but cannot help doubting its effectiveness and rationality.

10. In terms of legislative strategy, because formulating a special law on public access to government information will be inevitably confronted with many difficulties, it might be a good alternative to modify the relevant existing laws, including the Secret Law, for the purpose of further guaranteeing the people's right to know the truth.

11. According to Article 5 and Article 7 of "The Explanations on Some Questions in Regard of the Applicable Laws in the Trial of the Cases of Stealing, Inquiring, Purchasing and Illegally Providing State Secrets and Intelligence to Foreigners," if the concerned party steals, inquires about, purchases, or illegally provides information to foreigners when he is aware or should have been aware that the item, although without indication of classification, is of great concern to the state security and state interest, a punishment shall be imposed according to Article 111 of the Criminal Law. In the trial of such cases, it shall be determined by the State Department of Secrecy whether the concerned items are state secrets and what kind of classification they fall within. These two articles imply that materials or information without indication of classification could also become secrets or intelligence in a later determination.

Chapter Four

Central and Eastern Europe

Starting from Scratch

Ivan Szekely

For decades, the countries of Central and Eastern Europe were shut off from the mainstream of democratic development. Since the end of communist or state-socialist political systems in 1989 and thereafter, the region has seen a flurry of efforts to make up for the lost years, developing new legal and institutional frameworks apace in an attempt to transform whole societies rapidly into functioning democracies. Some of the most essential efforts focus on transparency and accountability of the public sector. From a starting point of almost complete governmental opacity, the region presents in microcosm the whole array of issues that can arise in the struggle to achieve greater transparency.

The region includes the overlapping areas of Central Europe (a concept derived from prewar German political and economic influence), Eastern Europe (generally considered as a group of former communist satellite countries), and southeastern Europe ("the Balkans"), as well as the Baltic countries, which were part of the Soviet Union itself. This analysis will concentrate primarily on Hungary, Bulgaria, Romania, Slovakia, and Ukraine, countries with a range of experiences with regard to the speed and means by which change has been achieved.

Of course, not every issue is of equal importance in every country. It is not surprising that, given their great differences in economic situation and political stability, the newly democratic countries have reached different stages of development with regard to transparency and accountability, and thus represent a broad range of possible policy responses to the problems of creating transparency that all of them face. In countries with a strong, centralized political authority and a presidential system, such as Belarus and Ukraine, the core issues are freedom of the press, freedom of expression, and access to government-held information. In countries with a balanced political spectrum, such as Slovakia and Hungary, a tendency to overpoliticize is a core problem: that is, almost every event related to transparency (or any other aspect of information rights and practice) has a political context in terms of day-to-day party politics.

But the Soviet-type monopoly of information handling had characteristic features that spanned the region, just as the demand for public access to information and the processes toward transparency in the new democracies of Central and Eastern Europe share key characteristics. These processes can offer general and relevant lessons to other countries—the practices and innovative solutions introduced may be of use even to the highly developed Western democracies and especially to other emerging democracies.

The Common Heritage

While the Western political ideal is based on the autonomous, self-determining citizen and the transparent, accountable state, the communist ideal was based on the self-determining party-state leadership and the transparent, accountable citizen. For decades, information handling was a party-state monopoly. In these countries the provision and the content of information were subordinated to centralized political will. Data, statistics, and trends in society were hidden and/or falsified according to party interests, and only a select few had access to reliable information. Society was governed partly by secret decisions and orders, so even the rules that established rights and duties were not accessible for those concerned. Collective rights were overemphasized at the expense of individual rights; informational rights were neither granted nor respected. Information was provided in a paternalistic manner; the very notion of "information" was mixed up with "propaganda." Not surprisingly, the general public had no trust in the truthfulness and correctness of information.

Even before the fall of the communist regimes, the countries of the region did have two rather peculiar sorts of transparency, best described as "reimported public sphere" and secondary (alternative) public sphere. Both were considered equally unwelcome and were repressed to a certain degree by the regimes.

For a number of decades, the broadcasts of Radio Free Europe and Radio Liberty played a crucial role in the reimportation of the missing public sphere. These radio stations gathered news and commentaries relating to the Iron Curtain countries (based on the analyses of official communiqués, the reports of dissidents and tourists, secret service materials, and the information provided by citizens) and broadcast them back to these countries in the local language. The joke about the members of the Central Committee still being in session when Radio Free Europe had already reported what resolutions they had adopted reflected public perceptions of the radio station's effectiveness and rapid reaction.

The secondary (alternative) public sphere was associated with the underground movements and the democratic opposition, which had become very well organized by the time the democratic changes came. These activities typically included the preparation, dissemination, and discussion of the so-called "samizdat" publications (government-suppressed literature). While officially prohibiting it, the regime in many ways tolerated the existence of this practice, regarding it as an important source of information for its own purposes, in consideration of the fact that the samizdat publications often provided a platform for prominent intellectuals to make their critical comments.

But these relatively minor sources notwithstanding, by and large the communist legacy was a pernicious one for transparency. The traditional opposition between state and society, historically characteristic of countries of the region, can still be observed, manifested in the lack of public trust in institutions and information alike.

Key Issues Facing the Region

This heritage of almost complete opacity left all the countries in the region needing to introduce quickly a series of transparency-related policies and institutions to address a wide range of information issues. Perhaps the most visible major issue in the region is the role of the press (including print, electronic, and online media). The problem is twofold: first, how to transform the centralized, party-directed, censored media into a competitive free press, and second, how to avoid a new centralization of power and content in the hands of the commercial media. An additional issue is ensuring quality and reliability of information in the new press as a prerequisite of real transparency.

The mass privatization, or reprivatization, that has taken place in several newly democratic countries raises two transparency-related concerns. One is the transparency of the privatization process itself. The other is the privatization of public information and documents that thereby become inaccessible, despite new legislation guaranteeing access to public information.[1] Even the change in the form of ownership can result in limitations on access. The transformation of the national news agencies into state-owned corporations provides opportunities for these corporations to make formerly free services available only for paying users.[2]

The new international connections, commitments, and obligations have a controversial role in the transparency process. On the one hand, the international community expects the new democracies to enact and implement laws guaranteeing individual rights and freedoms, including free access to public information and the protection of information privacy. On the other hand, the new alliance with NATO and the informal dependence on U.S. support force these countries to restrict access to public information, to extend secrecy legislation, and to cooperate in antiterrorist measures, all of which implies the curtailment of newly granted informational rights.[3]

The ongoing waves of legislation and regulation in the region include many new provisions that have directly or indirectly affected the legal framework around transparency. But some of the provisions contradict others, with the result that decision making on requests for information is left open to arbitrary consideration and often restrictive interpretation. In addition, there are not enough independent judges, prosecutors, and lawyers with sufficient training and experience in related cases.

As the countries of the region attempt to modernize public administration, many governmental offices have established public relations and press departments. But information intended to enhance the public image of an organization is not necessarily objective and complete.

Another key transparency-related issue is regulation of the new business sector in the areas of fair competition and business-citizen relationships. Across the region, the level of regulation, along with the quality of business ethics, varies tremendously, but in general it is lower than in established democracies and market economies. In the more developed, newly democratic countries these problems have led to innovative solutions regarding the borderline between legitimate business secrets and information of public interest, especially in areas where state and business sectors have a common interface, such as privatization and concession.

The Initial Enthusiasm

When the communist regimes first fell, there was a surge of awareness of the transparency issue that lasted for a couple of years. In the more liberal new democracies, it was moderate and appeared only in certain areas; in the countries of strong central authority, it was comprehensive and powerful.[4] In countries where the legal guarantees of public information were still lacking, the formal and informal struggle for transparency was launched, leading to a new wave of legislation around the turn of the millennium, although it did not always bring substantial changes. It has now become apparent that the laws passed in the early years of the new political system—riding the initial surge of interest—played a positive role; they exerted a lasting influence both on the emergence of the democratic institutions and on public opinion.

In the turbulent period of the collapse of the old regimes, the archives of the secret police monitoring internal opposition and dissidents were opened. In East Germany the population raided the local offices of the Stasi.[5] According to the well-known Russian dissident Boris Pustintsev,[6] people walking into the abandoned archives of the Party's branch offices were met with the sight of documents lying all over the floor. In a live television broadcast in Hungary, a guilt-ridden secret agent talked about the content of classified documents he himself helped to smuggle out and publish.

In countries where power was transferred peacefully in a negotiated and institutionalized framework, such as Hungary and Bulgaria, the entire process took place under the glare of public scrutiny. New political parties formed amid loud propaganda, accompanied by heated public debates and the enthusiastic support of the participants. Since the development of legitimate and independent political parties had not been possible under the communist regimes, the situation necessitated the introduction of "imported" institutions of transparency, the "transition" laws and the rulings of the constitutional court. All this was accompanied by the dismantling of the previous regime's institutions dealing with classified information, including the police and the secret services, in terms of both structure and staff.

As the initial euphoria faded and the countries buckled down to the task of creating and implementing workable governance structures, the same institutions were reorganized, recovering not only their legality but also part of their legitimacy, supporting the new political structures and institutions. Pustintsev, again, best summed up the situation in the countries that retained or rebuilt a strongly centralized administration, by remarking that the doors of the archives had now been fitted with new locks, symbolically as well as physically.

The scenario of an initial move toward greater transparency followed by a relapse was also observed in the media, where the ownership changes were accompanied by organizational restructuring and the consolidation of the journalists' system of contacts and priority of sources. In Romania, for example, efforts in the early 1990s to introduce a more liberal, Western type of journalistic practice went sour when the media groups came under Romanian ownership, into the hands of private proprietors who reverted to the traditions of communist propaganda. In addition to hindering the objective dissemination of information of public interest, this also encouraged corruption among journalists and led to the practice of feeding distorted information to the public.[7] On top of all this, a certain withdrawal from politics was observed among the general public, accompanied by the tabloid papers' rising popularity and the experience that the majority of the people were more interested in obtaining practical information necessary for their personal betterment than in political engagement.

New Laws, New Institutions

The legal framework of freedom of information, along with the notion and the institutional infrastructure for a transparent and accountable public sector in general, only began to emerge in the region at the end of the 1980s, parallel with the processes of the democratic political transition. However, the policies, rights, and institutional structures related to transparency were established at a different pace and with different results in the various countries. The differences mirrored the pace and process of the democratic changes, the unique historical opportunities and constellations, the level of civilian involvement, and quite often the dedicated work of prominent personalities. Transparency-related reforms occurred in two waves. The first wave emerged in the early 1990s, that is, amid the turbulent circumstances of political and institutional changes, while the second wave evolved a decade later, in the period of consolidation of the new system.

Hungary was among the first to build a legal and institutional system and the accompanying practice of treating transparency and free access to public information not as a separate entity but as an organic element of the new and comprehensive system of information rights. The Hungarian model, like the early models in several other countries, drew a dichotomy between state and nonstate information, signaling that the prime objective of the new system was to break the state's monopoly on information. The model defines two fundamental categories of information/data: personal data and data of public interest. There is one fundamental rule for each category: the right of self-determination in the former and openness in the latter.

The Hungarian Constitution declares both fundamental rules as fundamental rights. The basics of implementing them are laid down in the combined Data Protection and Freedom of Information Act,[8] while the most important exceptions are contained in the sector-specific acts and the Secrecy Act,[9] with the sanctions listed in the Penal Code. The Penal Code addresses not only the traditional category of the disclosure of state secrets but also the disclosure of business secrets, along with illegitimate data handling, which prohibited not only the abuse of personal data but also the keeping secret or forging of data of public interest. After the mid-1990s, sector-specific laws on handling/controlling information were passed by Parliament,[10] along with legal regulations specifying exceptions to the fundamental rules, including the Secrecy Act that replaced the old regulation devised by the communist regime. Around this time, the first Parliamentary Commissioner for Data Protection and Freedom of Information (DP-FOI Commissioner) was elected.[11]

Ukraine passed its law on transparency in the first wave, in 1992.[12] Government agencies are obliged to inform the public about their activities and resolutions, and citizens are, in principle, entitled to demand access to any official document, and agencies must respond within ten days. The fundamental right to public information was enacted in the Constitution of 1996. The Ukrainian Secrecy Act, along with the list of state secrets,[13] was enacted in the mid-1990s. However, no sector-specific laws have been established, nor have the rules and regulations pertaining to the handling and controlling of information been harmonized; only an additional decree[14] was issued in 1997 about the dissemination of public information. The ultimately democratic outcome of the heavily contested presidential elections in 2004–2005 may offer an opportunity to improve the implementation of the existing law and to introduce significant amendments.[15]

Romania, along with Slovakia and Bulgaria, represents the more recent wave in legislation. The Romanian access law[16] was enacted in 2001. It contains all the fundamental elements of a modern FOIA, although by defining a rather broad range of exceptions, it exempts many areas from the rules of free access; at the same time, it obliges government agencies to publish detailed information on their activities. Rather peculiarly, it assigns a separate agency to deal with the media, the "materialization" of the citizens' access to information. Such articles usually form part of laws on media. According to this, only accredited journalists are allowed to take part in the press conferences of official bodies, and the accreditation can be withdrawn at any time. A separate independent supervisor has not been elected to control the implementation of transparency, although the general ombudsman may act in information-related complaints.

The *Slovakian* Parliament enacted a series of relevant laws in the "second wave." First was the 1998 act on access to information on the environment,[17] which gave journalists, civil organizations, and ordinary citizens practical experience in obtaining official information. (In *Bulgaria,* the law on protection of the environment [1991] played a similar role as the first legislation providing for an individual right to information without the need to prove a legal interest.) Then came a broad law on information[18] in 2000. Like its Hungarian counterpart, the Slovakian act ties the range of actors obliged to give access to information to certain public functions, thus extending the obligation to private organizations if they are involved in those functions. Enacted in 2001, the Slovakian Secrecy Act,[19] like those of other recently established democracies, reflects the conditions of NATO accession.

Bulgaria's law on access to information (APIA),[20] enacted in 2000, also links the obligation to give access to information to various public functions, but tops it off with the criterion of the use of public money. Since the law makes no provision for administrative appeal and there is no independent supervisory body, a court procedure is the only option available to rejected applicants. One of the rules of mandatory automatic provision of information requires the ministries to maintain a Web site and publish information electronically. Legislation on the protection of information and on secrecy was promulgated two years after the enactment of the APIA, which made the latter more difficult to implement, as the administrators easily got lost in the tangle of applicable rules and regulations. At the same time, the secrecy act enacted the four-grade classification system in line with the NATO requirements and is in contradiction with the APIA regulations in several places.

Movements and Driving Forces

In the first phase, it was primarily theoretical experts and reform-minded leaders of the new political regimes who were behind the creation of the laws and institutions concerned with information. In the second phase, at the end of the 1990s and around the turn of the millennium, it was the various civil organizations that needed political and professional support. We may say that the first phase was more "elitist" and the second phase more "plebeian," although the national differences were also significant.

In Hungary in the 1980s, that is, well before the change of regime, a multidisciplinary panel of experts began to gather and to analyze the available Western laws, studies, and practical experience in the area of individual information rights, with regard to both data protection and freedom of information. By the time the communist regime fell, the concept of a new information-legal regime had already been established; moreover, the draft of the later combined data protection and freedom of information bill had been completed. One panel member became the influential president of the newly established Constitutional Court (László Sólyom, who also became President of the Republic in July 2005) and reinforced the realm of information legislation with a number of milestone decisions.[21] The most important legal rules were created and the institution of the DP-FOI Commissioner set up by the middle of the decade. With this historical advantage, Hungary became a model country of the new information rights and shared its experiences with other countries in the region. At the same time, this situation substituted for the development of civil movements fighting for the enforcement of these rights, which is represented by just a handful of NGOs at present.

A team of lawyers in Bulgaria drafted an FOI bill in 1992, but their work was never continued. In this country, the most important player in the effort to guarantee free access to public information is a civil organization, the Access to Information Programme (AIP).[22] It was established in 1996 by lawyers, sociologists, economists, political scientists, and journalists to launch a public debate on access to information and to keep the issue continuously on the agenda.

The operation of the forces supporting the early passage of the Ukrainian Law on Information is not known to the wider public; however, it may be assumed that the Chernobyl disaster and the issue of access to environmental information have made public opinion, as well as legislation, more sensitive, as in a number of other countries in the region. In contrast to the Bulgarian AIP, the Kharkiv

Group for Human Rights Protection (KHPG)[23] did not choose to specialize in this specific problem area but is fighting for the enforcement of a wide range of human rights, the discontinuation of governmental secrecy, and the documentation and disclosure to the public of breaches of rights. Its activities in the latter area contribute indirectly to the enhancement of transparency, and the promotion of freedom of expression has become one of its prime activities in recent years.[24]

The Romanian Academic Society (SAR), a group of influential intellectuals, has decided to lead the movement "from above," with professional scientific analyses, well-positioned legislative proposals, and political lobbying that reflects a clear assessment of the situation. In Slovakia, a group of 11 civil society organizations that came together under the rubric Citizen's Initiative and eventually grew into a coalition of 122 NGOs launched a campaign that led to the passage of an information access law and ensured that the law conformed to international norms. They used a number of tools and methods: political lobbying, wide-ranging media campaigns, the publication of articles and speeches, the broadcasting of interviews with the members of Citizen's Initiative; they designed a visual logo for the campaign, sent out some 50,000 postcards to be forwarded to the President of the National Council demanding the passage of the law, and prepared radio and television commercials.

As noted earlier, in the ex-communist countries the institutions of democracy and transparency could not evolve organically; therefore these institutions had to be "imported," especially in the first years of the new political system. At the same time, Western democracies wanted to *export* these institutions.[25] Consequently, international influences played and still play a significant role in establishing institutions of transparency, as demonstrated not only in "elitist" but also in "plebeian" movements. An obvious source of this influence was the practical aid of international nongovernmental organizations that extended beyond supporting the civil sector; another source was the cooperation among national NGOs that evolved at a later stage.

There existed—mainly informal—expectations of openness on the part of democratic countries and intergovernmental organizations; however, at the time of the disintegration of the closed political and military block of the CEE countries, the possibility for foreign analysts to obtain formerly secret economic and political information outweighed the need for citizens of new democracies to have access to information of public interest. The newly established formal connections, especially after September 2001, have had even more controversial effects on transparency and, generally, on the implementation of information rights: the expectations of Western-type openness and the mandatory restrictions on access to information and documents had an influence at the same time.

Do People Use the New Laws?

Experience around the world has shown that the laws, institutions, and policies devised to guarantee transparency constitute a necessary but insufficient precondition for implementation and for the practice and socialization of accessing information. This applies strongly to the case of the CEE countries, where the eagerness to achieve rapid integration with the democratic international community can easily produce shop window legislation and unenforceable laws—a dangerous prospect. Laws that have no real impact can disillusion the domestic advocates of transparency and pull the wool over the eyes of foreign bureaucrats who require that states meet certain formal criteria. The FOIA in Bosnia,[26] for example, is one of the finest pieces of legislation in this area, yet it exerts a minimal influence on the practical implementation of transparency.

The most important questions are: How well do the administrators know their obligations to give information? How well do the citizens know their rights to information and the means and institutions to enforce these rights? Do they use these rights, means, and institutions? How good a service do the administrators provide to those applying for information?

In the countries studied, three types of organizations conduct surveys and analyses to measure and evaluate the various aspects of transparency and accountability: the official, independent guardians supervising access to information, the NGOs, and the international watchdog organizations. Since in several countries the agency that *de facto* supervises the access to information is an NGO and some of the international organizations active in this area also belong to the civil sphere, the nongovernmental sector plays a primary part.

Hungary's DP-FOI Commissioner keeps a record of the number of applications turned down, along with the grounds on which access was refused. The annual reporting of these data is mandatory under the law. However, the commissioner also asks the data controllers to provide information about the number of applications they have complied with.[27] These data should be treated with strong reservations. The standard of discipline in reporting is unsatisfactory even among the organizations in the public sphere. Even more importantly, the methodology of defining what qualifies as data to be reported is unclear.

In Bulgaria, the AIP conducts regular surveys among the organizations (state and local self-government bodies, the mass media, and other entities financed from the state budget) that are obliged to release information. Its findings are then published in an annual report,[28] along with a brief account of the legal procedures it has filed. In 2002 the empirical study[29] covered approximately 300 public administration organizations and their local branches and 100 local governments. It addressed the question of the infrastructure for receiving and assessing applications and the mandatory publication of public information. From the statistics of the AIP's own legal aid service, we know that the number of rejections without explanation is exceedingly high.

In Ukraine, it is not just the access to information that is clogged: its survey and supervision are equally difficult. The KHPG continuously collects and evaluates the rather small number of cases related to access—or nonaccess, more likely—to information. An analysis entitled "Freedom of Access to Governmental Information"[30] provides a summary of its activities between 1994 and 2001. The report reveals that, after an initial opening up, the trend has been toward closing down information flows. Since 2000, the KHPG has kept track of decrees, rulings, and other legal documents that are known to exist, but the content of which is kept secret. Classified as "For service use only" or "Not for printing" or "Not for publishing," these documents seem to have increased in number throughout 2002.[31] Oddly, the steepest increase came during the preparation of the president's decree on the additional measures for guaranteeing transparency of the activities of state agencies.[32]

In Romania, the team of experts delegated by the Romanian Academic Society (SAR) has compiled a long list of quantitative and qualitative analyses on access to information. Their survey[33] conducted in the summer of 2003 aimed to find out how much of the taxpayers' money the government organizations had been spending on publishing their own information and on promoting their image, and how exactly they had spent it. The team concluded that the public institutions have no clear strategy and the information regarding the sums spent on publishing information is not as readily accessible as it should be.

In addition to gathering and analyzing objective data, there are other ways of monitoring the rights of access to information. The Slovakian civil initiative called Citizen's Shopping is both interesting and innovative. The basic idea is that public administrators in agencies that are obliged to provide information themselves are asked to turn to other public institutions and ask for information and access to public documents as private citizens, concealing their true position. The experience of how they are served and treated and whether their application is granted or rejected will provide them with useful information for discharging their duties in their own organization.

The project launched by the Open Society Justice Initiative under the title "Monitoring Access to Information" has a much more ambitious goal: it wishes to standardize a Freedom of Information Monitoring Methodology for evaluating access to information legislation and practice in selected countries. The pilot project covers five countries, three of which are in CEE: Macedonia, Armenia, Bulgaria, South Africa, and Peru. It is hoped that the eventual results will help not only to pinpoint problems but also to reveal the roots of those problems and develop possible solutions.[34]

These experiments have shown that we do not have one simple indicator for measuring the practical implementation of the access to information: the combined, well-tuned, and context-sensitive application of empirical and theoretical approaches and quantitative and qualitative methods is needed to draw conclusions of general validity. Comparative evaluations about the different countries should also be treated with care: even in the case of a group of countries undergoing a similar informational regime change, the national differences may be considerable. Another lesson of the series of studies is that the freedom of information and all the other elements of transparency should not be regarded as an ideal state that can be attained through a proper political course; it is more like a permanent process, in which the demands, the circumstances, and the conditions perpetually change—especially in a region where each country has a dynamically changing society in a state of transition.

Problems in Implementation

Despite the evident achievements, both the broad spectrum of surveys—analytical studies, quantitative surveys, registries, databases, interviews, institutional inventories, case studies—and the practical, day-to-day experience reveal a range of problems in the implementation of new laws on transparency.

The practice of accessing information of public interest in the countries studied is colored not only by deep-rooted social and political traditions of blocking information but also by the traditional style of government. In the case of some countries, Hungary included, the Prussian tradition of state administration based on administrative secrecy, which had characterized the prewar period, continued to exert an influence. This was followed by four decades of Soviet-type state administration, not generally described as open and citizen-friendly. These traditions matter in terms of both the mentality and the culturally transmitted behavior pattern of the civil servants working in the public administration of the new democracies.[35]

On the face of it, for example, Ukraine seems to follow a similar legislative course in this area as Hungary; however, the law has barely been implemented. Ukraine's public servants are not at all familiar with the rules regulating access to information and even less willing to apply them. There is no independent supervisor of the implementation of the rights to information, and no culture in public administration acknowledging the citizens' right to information as a fundamental (although not always implemented) element. Similarly, the liberal critics of the Romanian law maintain that its implementation is not satisfactory and that the secondary values of transparency in general are not realized sufficiently, specifying the peculiar features of public administration and social culture in Romania as the main causes.

According to its annual assessment for 2002, the Slovakian civil organization Citizen and Democracy Association[36] claims that, thanks to the law, fundamental public information has become available, although the authorities often withhold information relating to the business sector, including information regarding privatization.

A relatively large percentage of the population has heard of the act, but the official bodies' inclination to give access to data varies (according to the report, this inclination is considerably improved when the applicant is accompanied by a lawyer), and this could hinder its broader application.

Even now, more than a decade after the change of regime, questions of access to the documents of the KGB, Stasi, and other former secret services pose a problem. Most of the countries concerned have passed legislation concerning the status of these documents. However, the main problem is posed not by the nature of the legal solution used but by its poor enforceability. The successor organizations of Securitate, the communist secret service in Romania, do not transfer the documents in their possession, while in Poland the special organization set up to handle such documents did not have a head for a long time. In Hungary, despite the operation of an independent institution, there is still a great deal of uncertainty concerning the contents, authenticity, and completeness of the documents, which creates the possibility of political blackmail. Experiences show that there is no satisfactory solution to these problems, other than the passage of time, perhaps. The younger generations are no longer interested; however, the issue is still on the agenda in public life.

Another current problem is the cost of public information—both its official and black market price. The black market price (that is, the price of information obtained through bribery) is not common knowledge; Romanian analyses estimate[37] that it costs 50 to 200 U.S. dollars to obtain a piece of information. This is, however, not only a Romanian phenomenon; a number of Western sources reported the possibility of the issuance and even theft of government documents for money, primarily in the successor states of the Soviet Union.

Addressing the Problems

Who has a mandate and efficient means to address these problems? In a public administration tradition and in a social and cultural milieu such as is present throughout Central and Eastern Europe, where the requirement of transparency is a new element in the history of data management, the institutions charged with supervising the implementation of the law have a prominent role to play. Of all the countries in the region, only Hungary, Slovenia, Estonia, and Latvia have a specially appointed body for this. In the countries that have designated the institution of general Ombudsman (People's Advocate, Public Mediator), such as Romania or Bulgaria, the person in charge investigates the complaints related to the rights of access to information and the rules of controlling information to a limited degree. In Albania it is the express duty of the Ombudsman to supervise the implementation of the—otherwise almost completely ignored—law.

Interestingly, in several of the new democracies the same official supervises both the protection of personal data and the freedom of information (in Hungary, the Parliamentary Commissioner for Data Protection and Freedom of Information; in Estonia, the Data Protection Inspectorate; and in Latvia, the Data Inspectorate). Besides the obvious economic considerations that may warrant such an arrangement, the joint interpretation of the two rights can have some other significant advantages, for example, ensuring consistent positions on the borderlines between the two informational rights.

The Hungarian Parliament elected its first Commissioner in the summer of 1995. His office has accomplished pioneering work, and the Commissioner himself has considerably enhanced his professional reputation. In general, his powers are "weak," such as those associated with an Ombudsman: he possesses broad investigative powers but can only make formally nonbinding recommendations. Nevertheless, in the majority of the cases, the data controllers follow his recommendations even if they disagree with his arguments.[38]

In Bulgaria, the Public Mediator does little more than respond to individual complaints that arise when government agencies refuse to disclose information of public interest. Broad supervision of access to information is instead carried out by an NGO, the AIP. In addition to legal counseling, writing draft proposals, and lobbying, it fulfills functions traditionally associated with supervising, such as informally investigating individual cases, filing court procedures, conducting comprehensive surveys and analyses, and collecting and registering cases associated with access to information. In the last few years, in particular, since the passage of the access legislation, it has also undertaken educational activities for both civil servants and citizens, and the number and importance of lawsuits instituted by or with the participation of the AIP is increasingly significant, as is the professional support given to similar organizations in other countries.

However, the Bulgarian success story also raises questions: how far the activities of an NGO could extend, to what extent it may take over state functions, and whether state administration and society will ever reach a stage of development where they will be able to carry on such initiatives independently, so that the AIP could remain a true civil critic and actor of the system.

The Ukrainian KHPG discharges similar functions (collecting and analyzing cases, issuing newsletters and other publications in a critical voice, filing court procedures, etc.), under much worse conditions but with the same commitment. The KHPG is fighting for the observation of a broad range of human rights; its work associated with transparency is closely related to the freedom of press and the freedom of expression. The legal experts and other professionals cooperating with the KHPG have produced numerous research papers on the qualitative study and critical assessment of the elements of transparency. Their activities even include the preparation of a draft containing the missing elements of the existing legal framework. V. Rechitsky has drawn up a document entitled "A Model Draft of the Ukrainian Law 'On Public Oversight of the State Activities,'" which covers, among other things, the institution of public debates, the supervisory role of the Parliament, the limiting of the administration's information monopoly, and—a legal novelty—the investigative powers of human rights organizations. The same author has prepared the draft of the "International Convention on Protection of Intellectual Freedom," a major initiative that may seem idealistic to Western readers, yet is a thoroughly understandable response to the abuses in Ukraine.[39] KHPG, along with other human rights organizations such as the Ukrainian Helsinki Committee, has been closely monitoring the almost revolutionary circumstances of the 2004 presidential elections and publicizing reports about violations of legal and ethical norms on elections and access to information.[40]

Perhaps the most important lesson is that where there is an efficient official supervisor, the civil sphere fighting for transparency is weak, while in countries with either weak supervision or no supervision at all, civil society organizations take over the missing function.

Hungary and Bulgaria exemplify the two models. In Hungary, the high esteem the Commissioner enjoys fills NGOs with complacency, even if they criticize his activities sometimes, while in Bulgaria the AIP is forced to take over several government functions that are absent— which in turn gives comfort to the government. The ideal combination would be to have an efficiently functioning independent supervisor and strong civil control at the same time, since their respective roles, legitimization, styles, and practice are different and complementary.

In addition to the independent supervisory institutions and the civil society organizations, there are other important institutions and factors that affect the transparency landscape.

International cooperation has significant and well-established channels of influence. One is official exchanges of experiences, primarily by means of international forums and mutual visits of the independent supervisory agencies. What is missing, however, is an exchange of experiences among those obliged to supply information, something that could be initiated by the independent controllers or the NGOs monitoring the observance of access rights.

Another influence is professional and financial assistance rendered by international NGOs. ARTICLE 19, a British-based civil organization fighting for freedom of expression and the free flow of information in partnership with local organizations in more than thirty countries, plays a particularly active role in the CEE region.[41] It takes part in the preparations for and debates of draft legislation, bringing the players of the access area together, inviting foreign experts, and compiling reports. Furthermore, as happened during the legislative debates of the Bulgarian APIA, it even promotes the passage and execution of legal rules corresponding to the international norms by lobbying, convincing local politicians,[42] and publishing its positions. The Open Society Institute (OSI) is also active in this area through its various programs and coinstitutions.[43] For OSI, the issues of access to information plays a significant role primarily in the identification of anticorruption policies, the transparency of the funding of elections and parties,[44] the EU Accession Monitoring Program (EUMAP[45]), the monitoring project of the Justice Initiative already mentioned above, and the research conducted as part of the International Policy Fellowship.

A further typical form of international cooperation is visits of individual experts. Experts and activists from countries where sufficient useful information has been gathered in the area of access to information visit other countries in the region, have their legal rules and reports translated, deliver lectures, and consult not only with the representatives of the civil sector but also with members of parliament and civil servants. In the last few years, Hungary has been particularly active in sharing its experiences, and most recently, second-wave countries have seen increasing cooperation.

A positive development of the past few years is that the friendships and work-related relationships that have evolved and the ever more frequent practice of professional assistance have overcome what had been reluctance among local Central and Eastern European civil organizations to establish closer links with other local or regional civil organizations, because they had seen them as rivals, given that they maintain themselves from the same Western professional and financial support. One sign of cooperation is the development of the Freedom of Information Advocates Network and Web site,[46] which aims to help NGOs with campaigning, advocacy, and fund raising through exchange of information, ideas, and strategies, and by providing a forum for collaboration and to facilitate the forming of coalitions of NGOs to address FOI issues at a regional or global level.

The most important institutional platform of the democratic changes was the media, which came complete with their traditional infrastructure. The campaigns launched by the civilian organizations, which produced a broad social consensus, generally enjoyed the support of the media. However, the role of the media in fighting for transparency has not always been positive.

While KHPG gives regular accounts of assaults sustained by journalists—threats issued, the beatings, disappearances, and bribes offered; the censorship exercised by the authorities; criminal proceedings instituted against newspapers, radio stations, and television channels; police searches in editorial offices; and other atrocities—the whole of the Ukrainian press was not KHPG's partner in its campaigns. As critically stated in KHPG's newsletter,[47] journalism in the Ukraine is not yet mature enough for the consistent application of freedom of speech, while self-censorship and the concealment of politically compromising cases are on the rise. The public protests and the scandals around the presidential elections in late 2004 have polarized not only the political forces but the media as well.

According to the evaluation of A. Mungiu-Pippidi, head of SAR,[48] the media in Romania did not support the campaign for freedom of information because they have become complicit in a range of largely dishonest information-related activities. There is a thriving black market for information, including blackmail with information and blackmailing for information. These practices have become so widespread that any legal and institutional regimes that would clear up the area of access to information would threaten lucrative opportunities for journalists of this kind.

In contrast, the campaign in Slovakia relied on cooperation with the press, and this cooperation is also the basis of the civil monitoring of implementation. Through their good contacts, journalists easily locate information sources. However, the response time of public administration is disappointingly slow, and they may therefore lose their initial interest. In addition, their behavior may provoke suspicion in civil servants who do not have a very high opinion of journalism as a profession. The Citizen and Democracy Foundation (CDF) conducted surveys that led to the discovery that either the Slovakian journalists were unfamiliar with the law on access to information or, if they were familiar with it, they hardly used it at all in their work. This is in accord with the Hungarian experience: although the Hungarian journalists know the DP-FOIA well (or at least have heard its name), and although they often threaten to use it, in practice they very rarely rely on it to obtain information in their daily work.

In short, throughout the region media support for passage and implementation of access to information laws is spotty at best. One reason for this apparent disinterest is that the formal procedure is far too slow for the purposes of a daily paper; therefore, it can only be of use to investigative journalists. The other reason is that in the journalistic society, the value of information *available to all* is much smaller than the value of information obtained from exclusive sources, through personal contacts, or even by illegal means.

Lessons Learned

The developments of transparency and access to public information have brought about a number of lessons to learn for the new democracies of Central and Eastern Europe, not only within the individual countries but also among them. Some of these lessons may prove or have proved to be useful for the new democracies of other regions around the world, as well as for the traditional, well-functioning democratic countries.

The most important conclusion for the new democracies is that both the supply of and the demand for transparency and accountability can be difficult to maintain once the euphoria of the change of regime has faded. It is thus desirable to move quickly in constructing the system of access to information and to make the best of the opportunities arising from the restructuring of the legal system and state administration.

In drafting their legislation, most countries profited greatly from international models. There are exemplary model cases and arguments that are generally applicable and may be used in all countries with modern access legislation in spite of the differences in their internal laws. Yet it was not possible to simply incorporate certain provisions into the existing legal system by copying and pasting.

The enactment of access to information laws is a major accomplishment but is not sufficient in itself. The best method for ensuring appropriate accessibility of public information is the institution of an independent information commissioner. That role may also be assumed by a respected and professionally prepared civil society organization, but this does not exempt the state from the obligation of setting up an official institution. It is best if the commissioner is elected or appointed, with adequate resources at his disposal, simultaneously with the coming into force of the legislation. At the same time, the commissioner should encourage the adoption of the necessary secondary norms and specific practical measures. It may seem simpler to leave the interpretation of the law to the judiciary. This, however, requires the development of a cadre of highly qualified lawyers with expertise in the area, a more demanding feat than the creation of the institution of the independent commissioner, at least initially.

The new democracies are encumbered with heavy political struggles and efforts should therefore be made to depoliticize and to popularize the notion and practice of transparency as far as possible. If people see access to public information as some kind of abstract law that is worth nothing in practice, a shop window measure of the government in power or a tool in political struggles, its socialization does not stand a chance. Where information means nothing more than sensation, scandal, and a possibility to discredit your opponent, a distorted picture will evolve of transparency in society, and the fight for access to information will be limited to activists and politicians who have vested interests in its application.

What the new democracies all have in common is an interconnection between the demand for freedom on the one hand and the demand for transparency, the chance to discover their past, on the other. Both approaches to achieving greater transparency in the CEE countries—reforms introduced from above and civil society activism—can play a role in the creation of public access to information. Overpoliticization is a common peril: public information issues may become an area of political infighting. Another common feature is the central role of the media. Then there is the danger that the initial openness will gradually evaporate with the consolidation of the new institutional system, as the traditions of administrative secrecy revive. In these countries the continuous monitoring of public access to information and the establishment of independent supervisory bodies are crucially important. But most important of all is that the demand for openness and the idea of putting the institutions of transparency to good use be broadly embraced in an environment where the traditions of such mentality had been lacking.

For the layman, the simple question whether life has improved in consequence of greater transparency during the period of democratic transition remains unanswered. In all likelihood, greater transparency has complicated the lives of people holding high office, people who attempted to exploit the situation after the democratic transition, and people who tried to preserve and convert their earlier influence. Similarly, the new developments hardly made life easier for business monopolies trying to exploit the legal gaps and deficiencies of the newly emerging market economy, nor did they help the black marketers of the information scene and, therefore, a narrow segment of the press. By contrast, the media as a whole—despite certain objectionable symptoms in their daily practice and the apparent lack of interest of the majority of journalists—have found it considerably easier to access public information already because of the mere existence of access laws and the growing willingness of government bodies to disclose it. The maneuvering space of the political opposition broadened; it could better obtain and publicize information and documents relating to the activities of the ruling government, which was one of the essential preconditions of the emergence of a more balanced political arena. In addition, making the life of the weaker side, the individual, the citizen, easier, transparency has also encouraged a better division of informational power. In the more developed new CEE democracies, the demand for and the concepts of access to public information have grown roots in public opinion to a considerable degree. It is to be hoped that in the long run this process will lead to embedding of the practices of information rights.

The phenomena described above can be felt to a different extent in the various countries, just as the transparency situation has reached different stages of development there. But throughout the region, freer access to public information has apparently been instrumental in fostering democratic development, encouraging the discovery of the past, working toward both the emergence of an informed public and the limitation of bureaucratic power, and fighting corruption. In other words, it has been an efficient, if not omnipotent, medicine to cure the symptoms of the all-pervasive secrecy inherited from the political past.

NOTES

1. See, in this volume, the chapter by Richard Calland.

2. The Hungarian DP-FOI Commissioner in a 2004 statement (352/A/2004-3) pointed out the contradiction between the constitutional right to have access to information of public interest and the provision of the law that states that the national news agency, MTI, within its public service activity, cannot be forced to provide free services. The Commissioner's argument stressed that MTI holds a quasi-monopolistic position in the area of news services and is being financed, at least partly, from the state budget.

3. See, in this volume, the chapter by Alasdair Roberts.

4. For an analysis of the Ukrainian situation, see Yevgeniy Zakharov and Irina Rapp, "Freedom of Access to Government Information," in Kharkiv Group for Human Rights Protection, *Freedom of Expression in Ukraine 2001* (Kharkiv: Kharkiv Group for Human Rights Protection, 2002).

5. The popularly known abbreviated name of the secret police in former East Germany.

6. At present he is head of the St. Petersburg–based NGO "Citizens' Watch."

7. Alina Mungiu-Pippidi, "Coalition for Transparency—The Passage of the Freedom of Information Act in Romania Case Study" (2001), http://www.sar.org.ro/files_h/docs/advocacy_foia/7_case_study.pdf.

8. Act. No. LXIII of 1992 on protection of personal data and disclosure of data of public interest.

9. Act No. LXV of 1995 on state secrets and office secrets.

10. For example, the Direct Marketing Act (Act CXIX of 1995 on the use of name and address data serving the purposes of research and direct marketing), the Identification Act (Act No. XX of 1996 on the identification codes and methods superseding the personal identification number), or the Medical Data Act (Act No. XLVII of 1997 on the handling and protection of medical and related data).

11. László Majtényi, professor of law.

12. Law on Information, 1992.

13. Law on State Secrets, 1994 and "List of Information That Belongs to State Secrets," 1995.

14. "On the Order of Dissemination of Information on Public Bodies and Local Government Activity by Mass Media," Statute of September 23, 1997, No. 539/97.

15. See ARTICLE 19's assessmentof the Ukrainian Election Law and its implementation in the 2004 Presidential Election, October 27, 2004, http://www.article19.org.

16. Law No. 544/2001 on free access to information of public interest.

17. Act No. 171/1998 Coll. on access to information on the environment.

18. Act No. 211/2000 Coll. on free access to information.

19. Act No. 100/1996 Coll.

20. Access to Public Information Act.

21. For instance, with his decision frequently quoted internationally, on the anticonstitutional nature of the universal personal identifier (Decision No. 15/1991 AB).

22. http://www.aip-bg.org/index_eng.htm.

23. http://www.khpg.org/en.

24. Zinoviy Antoniuk, "Open Letter on Non-Transparent and Criminal Activities of Power" (2004); Vsevolod Rechitsky, "Comment of the KHPG on the Political Reform in Ukraine" (2004). Both available from http://www.khpg.org/en/index.php?r=a2b3c1d1oe11.

25. Alexandru Grigorescu qualifies these ambitions in the area of transparency as "unsuccessful norm transmission" (see "European Institutions

and Unsuccessful Norm Transmission: The Case of Transparency," *International Politics* 39 [4] [2002]). It should be noted, however, that imported formal norms generally remain unfamiliar among attributes of internal law, and that the introduction of these norms is a necessary but by no means sufficient condition of implementing and socializing the rules of transparency. In addition, the interests of the West and the international organizations are rather controversial in the area of substantial exporting of these norms.

26. Office of the High Representative and EU Special Representative, "Freedom of Access to Information Act for the Federation of Bosnia and Herzegovina" (2001); http://www.ohr.int/ohr-dept/media-d/med-recon/freedom/default.asp?content_id=7269.

27. In an abbreviated form, these reports are also published in English; both versions available from http://www.obh.hu.

28. Alexander Kashamov, et al., "The Current Situation of the Access to Public Information in Bulgaria 2001" (Access to Information Programme, 2002), http://www.aip-bg.org/all.htm.

29. Access to Information Program (AIP), "Report on Access to Public Information in Bulgaria 2002"; whole survey published in *The Year of the Rational Ignorance,* Access to Information Program (AIP), 2002.

30. Zakharov and Rapp, "Freedom of Access to Government Information."

31. See Kharkiv Group for Human Rights Protection, "Freedom of Expression in Ukraine" (2001, 2002), http://www.khpg.org, respectively.

32. President's Decree No. 683 of August 1, 2002.

33. Cristian Ghinea, "Transparency for an Independent Media: How Do Public Institutions Spend the Money for Publicity? Case Study based on the Freedom of Information Act," http://www.sar.org.ro/.

34. Discussed in detail in this volume; see the chapter by Laura Neuman and Richard Calland. See also "Transparency and Silence" (Open Society Justice Initiative, 2006), http://www.justiceinitiative.org.

35. See the chapter by Laura Neuman and Richard Calland.

36. http://www.foiadvocates.net/members/cda.php.

37. See Mungiu-Pippidi, "Coalition for Transparency."

38. See the "Annual Reports of the Parliamentary Commissioner for Data Protection and Freedom of Information," http://abiweb.obh.hu/dpc/index.htm.

39. Vsevolod Rechitsky, "International Convention on Protection of Intellectual Freedom: A Draft" (Ukraine: Kharkiv Group for Human Rights Protection, 2002), http://khpg.org/en/index.php?id=1085224381.

40. See, for example, Kharkiv Group for Human Rights Protection, "Constitutional and Legal Analysis of the Political Situation in Ukraine (on 25 November 2004)" (2004); http://www.khpg.org/index. php?id=1126181130.

41. http://www.article19.org.

42. In September 1999, five international experts addressed a letter to the National Assembly stating their common position on the necessary amendments of the bill, and were given audience by the Chairman of the Human Rights Committee of the National Assembly.

43. http://www.soros.org/initiatives/regions/central-eastern_europe.

44. See, for example, *Monitoring Election Campaign Finance: A Handbook for NGOs* (Open Society Institute, 2005).

45. http://www.eumap.org.

46. The FOI Advocates Network was established in 2002, on September 28 (known as the International "Right to Know" Day); see http://www. foiadvocates.net.

47. "Ukrainian Mass Media Are Not Prepared for the Freedom of Speech," *Prava Ludyny* 7 (2000), http://www.khpg.org/en/index.php?r =a2b3c1d7e7. See also Zakharov's analyses in *Freedom of Expression in Ukraine 2001*.

48. See Mungiu-Pippidi, "Coalition for Transparency."

Chapter Five

The Challenging Case of Nigeria

Ayo Obe

In my village, Enugwu-Uku, whenever anything was to be done, the *ekwe* [a wooden drum] would be beaten by the designated person. When it is beaten, people know that there is something to be done, and that people should come to the village square for information. To the extent that people were to be affected by actions to be taken, they had to be involved in the decision, there was nothing like just ordering them.

—Nicholas Peter-Okoye, describing the situation in precolonial Igboland

The idea that members of a community should be involved in informed decision making was not unknown in precolonial times, as the above quote shows. But nineteenth-century European colonizers brought a different approach—one of government secrecy—to ruling the peoples of the area that came to be known as Nigeria.

Dismantling that apparatus and making government open is raising a number of challenges for today's Nigerians. This chapter examines how different aspects of Nigeria's history and political and socioeconomic makeup encapsulate several of the factors that make attaining and sustaining a viable transparency regime particularly difficult in many countries. These range from the effects of colonial cobbling together of numerous ethnic groups and a colonial heritage of secrecy to the corrosive and corrupting effect of long years of unaccountable military dictatorship against a background of increasing economic dependence on income from petroleum resources. It is in this challenging environment that a campaign for greater transparency is being waged.

Background

In many ways, Nigeria—from arid deserts in the far north to petroleum-rich mangrove swamps on the Atlantic coast—is a microcosm of Africa itself. A former British colony with an inherited colonial administrative infrastructure, the country has several ethnic groups with diverse cultures, the competition among which is barely contained within unwritten conventions dictated by *realpolitik* and written constitutional requirements to "reflect the federal character" of the country in public and private life. Although it returned to civilian rule in May 1999, Nigeria has spent most of its post-independence years under military dictatorship. And since the early 1970s, an economy based on agriculture and an infant industrial sector has dwindled into dependence on a petroleum industry (that is itself heavily dependent on overseas-based multinational oil corporations) for over 90 percent of its income.

Nigeria's experience of access to information therefore illustrates a number of factors that have militated against and may continue to militate against an orderly transition from a system where governments hoard information to one where they release information, of which citizens make effective use to challenge and to change government actions and policies.

Military Rule/Civilian Rule: From Idealistic Revolution to Corrupt Kleptocracy

One major factor that has shaped Nigeria's access to information experience is the fact that twenty-nine of the country's forty-four years since independence have been spent under military dictatorship. Although most of Nigeria's military rulers have been careful to describe this as "an aberration," its length and depth has been such as to make civilian rule seem like the aberration. The signs are that having gained a hold on the country's oil wealth, Nigeria's soldiers will not easily relinquish their grip, as their shadow hangs over even the country's most recent return to civilian rule. While Nigeria's last but one military dictator died in the course of attempting to "succeed himself" as a civilian president,[1] the winner of the presidential elections that heralded the return to civilian rule in 1999, General Olusegun Obasanjo, had previously ruled the country as a military dictator.[2] The leading contestants in the 2003 presidential elections were both former military dictators,[3] and as of this writing, Nigerians are faced with the prospect of yet another former military dictator joining the contest for the 2007 presidential elections.[4] Although, following the failure of attempts to amend the Constitution to provide for tenure elongation, President Obasanjo will not himself be a candidate, a leading member of his party has expressed the view that only a former "military man" should succeed him.[5]

The original coup makers of 1966 may have had idealistic motives for what they termed their "revolution," but by 1979, when Obasanjo handed power to elected civilians, easy access to the wealth from the oil industry, shielded from public scrutiny by civil service traditions and military autocracy, had thoroughly perverted whatever idealism there had been. Even "corrective" military regimes, by arbitrarily sacking and retiring numerous public officers without due process,[6] only ended up teaching the survivors to ensure their own future financial security by fair means or foul.

The four-year civilian interregnum of 1979 to 1983 came with a hugely expensive system: nineteen states,[7] each with its own executive and legislature, a bicameral national legislature, and a federal executive headed by a president, as well as an army of federal and state appointees. The increased numbers of those with access to the nation's treasuries meant even more pressure to conceal what was being done with its oil income. During this period an estimated US$5–7 billion illicitly left the country for overseas bank accounts.

The introduction of a Structural Adjustment Programme by the 1985–1993 military dictatorship of General Ibrahim Babangida caused a plunge in living standards for all salaried workers, with a consequent leap in corruption as those in a position to do so recouped their losses by extorting money from anybody whose misfortune it was to have to transact business with government. For Babangida, oil wealth was both the path and the prize, particularly when such income increased following the first Gulf War. The Nigerian people barely knew enough to realize that they were being robbed. Although, as described below, questions were raised by *Financial Times* journalist William Keeling, as he was not a Nigerian, the problem was easily dealt with by his deportation. Babangida therefore had both the funds and the freedom to continue to "settle" his critics, and this—coupled with his eight-year "transition to civil rule" program, during which he continually changed the rules, the goalposts, and the players—led to his being described as a ruler who had both corrupted democracy[8] and democratized corruption.

The Resource Curse

The next factor is petroleum, discovered in the Niger Delta in 1956. Income from oil had increased to such an extent in the wake of the 1973 Arab-Israeli war[9] that the then military ruler, General Yakubu Gowon, declared that his problem was not finding money, but how to spend it: a problem "solved" by distributing it among those with access to power—mainly unelected military dictators or their chosen civilian successors.[10] Despite increased demands for resource control by the peoples on whose land or off whose shores the oil is mined, the general perception—of not only the rulers but, crucially for the prospects of accountability, also the ruled—is that the money the government realizes from this mineral wealth does not come from taxpaying voters, and thus not from anyone to whom account must be rendered. Rather, the money accrues from rents and joint venture proceeds paid or earned by huge foreign corporations or government agencies. This sense of lack of ownership means conditions that might foster demands for openness and accountability about government spending failed to develop, and the income from that mineral wealth has virtually disappeared in a cloud of secrecy, waste, and theft. For the most part, it is impossible to say where the billions of dollars earned from oil since 1970 have all gone. There is no reconciling the lack of development on the ground and the steep dive in living standards with the huge amounts received, while the per capita gross national product is less in real terms today than it was at independence in 1960.[11]

The unhappy coincidence that oil revenues began to constitute a major part of the country's income at the same time that it was under the grip of military rule had adverse effects for democracy and human rights as well as, of course, transparency and good governance, since the fatal combination of dictatorial authority and stupendous oil wealth proved a lure too powerful to resist. Nigeria was subjected to either broken promises to relinquish power or plots and schemes to seize or retain control by direct or indirect means.

Ethnic Diversity

The next crucial factor that interplays with the first two to further obscure transparency in Nigeria is ethnicity. The country is an artificial colonial creation, which officially came into existence in 1914. Borrowing Winston Churchill's description of India, a leading Nigerian politician[12] said that Nigeria was not a nation, but "a mere geographical expression": that there were no Nigerians as such, rather, a myriad of ethnic groups.[13] One solution to this diversity was the federal system of government. However, the existence of so many different nationalities and ethnic groups meant that not only was there competition and conflict among them, but loyalty to one's particular group often superseded any commitment to the national project. Apart from competition among the different ethnic groups for their "share" of the oil wealth, this created a climate in which issues such as transparency, openness, and the converse qualities of corruption and secrecy were viewed and judged through ethnic-tinted glasses, so that any attempt to call treasury looters to account was usually drowned in a welter of accusations of selective tribal witch hunting.

The Civil Service: Colonial Traditions of Secrecy and Self-Preservation

Another factor is Nigeria's inheritance of the colonial government's culture of blanket official secrecy encapsulated in a series of Official Secrets Acts, which was enthusiastically embraced by postindependence rulers and their civil servants. Although all Nigeria's Constitutions since independence in 1960 have paid lip service to the right to "receive and impart ideas and information without interference"[14] within the context of a right to freedom of expression, what is given with one hand is held back by the other. Section 39(3) of the 1999 Constitution for example, preserves laws that are:

> reasonably justifiable in a democratic society—
>
> (a) for the purpose of preventing the disclosure of information received in confidence, maintaining the authority and independence of courts . . .
>
> (b) imposing restrictions upon persons holding office under the Government of the Federation or of a State, members of the armed forces of the Federation or members of the Nigeria Police Force or other Government security services or agencies established by law.

This ambivalence reflects Nigeria's history as a former British colony. Not only did the colonial government not recognize any duty to make information generally available to the colonized people,[15] it had its own tradition of secrecy, characterized by Official Secrets Acts dating back to 1911. Independent Nigeria in turn passed its own Official Secrets Act in 1962,[16] which prohibits the transmission of "any classified matter," defined in so nebulous a fashion[17] that it is hardly surprising that almost any government document can be stamped "Secret" for one reason or another.[18] It is these habits of secrecy that have held sway rather than constitutional provisions and international and regional agreements,[19] by which Nigeria purported to guarantee freedom of information and which it took no concrete steps to actualize.

While one might hope to find some safeguard or counterpart to the civil service culture of secrecy in civil service traditions of loyal patriotism, the corrosive effect of years of military dictatorship all but destroyed the latter. And, as noted above, arbitrary attempts at reform through wholesale sackings and forced retirements in which the innocent were punished along with the guilty taught that there was neither security for a public servant's old age nor safety in honesty and probity.

Corruption and Lack of Accountability

These factors combined to bring about a high rate of corruption,[20] and even after the return to expensive[21] civilian rule in 1979, this had to be added to the already debilitating combination of a collapse in oil prices and an increasing debt profile. This reversed the nation's economic fortunes to such an extent that by 1986 the country was groaning under a Structural Adjustment Program, which decimated the middle class and caused an explosion in corruption without any economic improvement.

Certainly structural adjustment policies created havoc and poverty across the continent, as many African countries were buried beneath mountains of debt. Yet Nigeria ought to have been shielded to some extent from the harsh international economic climate and the even harsher World Bank/IMF solutions by its position as the eighth-largest exporter of petroleum in the world. But since the early 1970s and Gowon's infamous description of the surplus oil revenue as a problem, Nigeria's rulers had preferred to treat oil revenue not as necessary resources from which to meet the rising expectations and minimum requirements of an increasing population, but as a surplus to be deployed in the quest for political power or distributed for private enjoyment. As a result, Nigeria sank lower on all indices measuring the quality of life, while the determination of public officials (whose salaries remained fixed while inflation rocketed) to maintain their standard of living ensured that it performed execrably on issues of accountability, for example, moving from bottom to second from bottom on the Transparency International Corruption Perceptions Index with monotonous and depressing regularity.

The 1999 return to civilian rule under the leadership of a president who in the years since 1979—when he had voluntarily relinquished power to an elected civilian government—had not only founded the African Leadership Forum at which problems and solutions in governance issues were dissected and studied but also been on Transparency International's board, did not produce much improvement in this position. Although Obasanjo recognized corruption as a critical issue and, at his inauguration on May 29, 1999, promised to make its eradication a cornerstone of his administration, nearly six years later, Nigeria did little more than exchange its "gold" medal in corruption for "silver" and "bronze"[22] until 2005 when it moved slightly higher—into sixth place.

Challenging Secrecy

The struggle to control oil wealth, colonial traditions of civil service secrecy, long years of unaccountable military rule—particularly as dictators sought to silence opposition in order to remain in power and continue to bleed the nation dry—and the protective ethnic cordon thrown around any erring member all combined to create a climate of corruption that has been extremely unfavorable to ideas of transparency or free access to information. Despite this, the campaign by Nigerians for specific legislation guaranteeing their right to access public information dates back to 1992. At the same time, a combination of political competition at home and pressures from outside has begun to open aspects of government to public scrutiny.

Yet it was not corruption as such that led to the first demands for access to government information. Even Babangida had insufficient resources to fill the mouth of every critic with enough honey to shut them up. In any case, the cost of settling powerful critics meant fewer resources for other government duties. The unfortunate result in the case of the Nigeria Police Force was that the police were forced to "live off the land" through a combination of extortion and bribes.[23] Coupled with a return to and increase in coercion and oppression as Babangida struggled to hold on to power, this increased human rights abuses enormously. Nigeria's first human rights organizations[24] were formed at this time, and it was from this burgeoning civil society that the first demands for a systematic right of access to government information came.

At the same time, other seeds of nonpartisan responses to government were being sown. As the succession of one military dictator after another saw increased human rights violations and corrupt looting of the nation's oil income, newspapers and magazines that were independent of both government and vested political interests began to provide Nigerians with criticism and comment that could not simply be dismissed as the ranting of frustrated politicians.

The Human Rights Momentum

When pastoral visits revealed that most of those in Nigerian prisons were still awaiting trial, in some cases for over ten years for vague offenses like "wandering," for which the maximum punishment would have been a sentence of a few months,[25] the Civil Liberties Organisation (CLO), Nigeria's first indigenous human rights group, was founded in 1987 to provide systematic assistance to those who lacked means to secure the enforcement of the fundamental rights guaranteed by the unsuspended parts of the 1979 Constitution. Although the CLO obtained the release of many of these prisoners through court actions to enforce fundamental rights, it was clear that the problem was both deep and widespread. Sympathetic prison warders might unofficially disclose details of detainees, but any attempt to obtain a clear overall picture was met with the wall of official secrecy.

The haphazard nature of the system into which such unfortunates were thrown meant severe overcrowding in all Nigerian prisons, while the fate of those who had no friend or relative to bring them additional food and supplies was grim. Between the overcrowding and poor nutritional status of many prisoners, it is hardly surprising that disease was rife or that there was a high rate of mortality. But again, the CLO's attempt to get facts and figures upon which to build a campaign for better treatment for prisoners was frustrated by the refusal of prison authorities to release details of prison deaths. In the event, the CLO was able to circumvent prison secrecy by gaining access to the mortuary records, where long and deeply disturbing lists showed that by far the greatest number of corpses came from nearby prisons, with disease and sickness aggravated by poor nutritional status being the primary causes of death.

Any attempt to get nationwide statistics would obviously require details of the number and location of prisons, lock-ups, and other detention facilities in the country. But this was classified information: a matter of national security! And while the CLO believed that prison conditions were, rather, a matter of national disgrace, it was also clear that no useful official information would be released, or indeed, because of the Official Secrets Act, *could* (lawfully) be released.

As the 1990s commenced, the Babangida regime became more and more repressive. Public criticism of the failure to return the country to democratic civilian rule heightened. The State Security Service detention cells, so ostentatiously emptied when Babangida had seized power in 1985, began to fill up again. Because there was little that critics, apart from the failed coup plotters of April 1990, could be actually charged with, the junta resorted to administrative detention into which the courts had no jurisdiction to inquire, creating another wall of secrecy that human rights activists needed to breach.

Campaigning for FOI Laws Under Military Dictatorship: A Specific Campaign for Access to Information

The first calls for freedom of information legislation arose therefore because it was clear to human rights activists that they could not do their work properly without access to government records and information. So in 1992 the CLO began seeking ways to scale the government wall of secrecy. Because journalists were facing the same problems, it was natural for the CLO and the Nigeria Union of Journalists (NUJ) to collaborate on the issue. It soon became clear that there was room for an NGO specifically devoted to the rights of journalists and freedom of the press,[26] and this led to the formation of Media Rights Agenda (MRA), which prepared a consultation paper on access to publicly held information.

Although the massive corruption of the Babangida junta was a matter of public concern because it was clear that oil money was being used to buy off critics or to secure the loyalty of those who could assist in repressing the people, this was the first time that specific remedies for the problem had been considered. FOI legislation was conceived along with an Ethics in Government Act as part of a twin structure designed to make government honest and accountable. However, the latter proved stillborn.

Preparation of a Draft FOI Law

In 1992, when it was agreed that MRA should spearhead the drive for freedom of information legislation, it was anticipated that Babangida would at last hand power over to a democratic civilian government, and then the climate for the establishment of a more open government would be more sympathetic. In the event, the Babangida transition was aborted when, after successful elections at the state level and for the National Assembly, the presidential election results that would have completed the process were cancelled in June 1992. After a brief attempt to install a selected civilian head of state, Nigeria was plunged into an even deeper abyss of corruption and human rights abuse when the Abacha regime seized power in November 1992, although—like Babangida's 1985 seizure of power—the coup was sugar-coated at first.

Despite the now much less favorable climate, the three organizations pressed ahead and produced a draft FOI bill based on consultations among themselves, suggestions made in questionnaires administered to practicing journalists, and the experiences of other countries. The MRA then spearheaded a series of workshops, conferences, and seminars to bring in more stakeholders, widen the circle of consultation, and refine the draft.

The next step was to press for enactment. But rather than present the bill to the Constituent Assembly, which Abacha had set up to frame a new constitution for Nigeria, since the three organizations had condemned it as lacking credibility, they instead sent the bill to the Federal Ministries of Justice and Information. It was always recognized that the chances of enactment under the Abacha dictatorship were slim, but because the Minister of Justice, Dr. Olu Onagoruwa, had been an activist of sorts and always shown sympathy for human rights issues, the committee met with him to press the issue. However, the Constituent Assembly departed from Abacha's script when it passed a resolution demanding the end of military rule by January 1996. This washed away the remnants of the regime's sugar-coating with a new wave of repressiveness. Onagoruwa's influence within the dictatorship (such as it was) evaporated, and with it any chance of his pushing the enactment of the bill as a military government decree.

In any case, shortly after the Constituent Assembly vote, the phantom coup plot that led to the jailing of several serving and retired soldiers, including Olusegun Obasanjo as well as civilians, burst on the national scene. Among the victims was the CLO's own Executive Director, Abdul Oroh,[27] who, as a professional journalist, had been an energetic advocate of FOI legislation. Oroh was released after a year in detention toward the end of 1996. By then it had become clear that Abacha too had no genuine intention of relinquishing power, but had determined to succeed himself as a civilian president.[28] For the civil society groups involved in pressing for freedom of information, the struggle to end military rule took precedence.

A Shift from Human Rights to Accountability

In June 1998, however, Abacha died of a heart attack amid an increasing wave of civil dissent. The regime of General Abdulsalami Abubakar, which took over, recognized that it had no choice but to return the country to civilian rule without delay. Elections were therefore held for various levels of government between December 1998 and February 1999.[29] This provided an opportunity to revive the FOI issue, and to review draft FOI legislation with which to meet the incoming civilian administration. A March 1999 conference organized by MRA with participants from both inside and outside Nigeria discussed the draft bill prepared by MRA, the CLO, and the NUJ; with the draft then further revised in the light of the conference's recommendations, civil society was ready to hit the ground running with the return to civil rule.

The focus of the campaign had changed. Abubakar had gradually released all Abacha's political prisoners, and relaxed restrictions on freedom of expression and other civil and political freedoms. But the revelation of the staggering amounts allegedly stolen by the Abacha family meant that transparency concerns shifted from human rights to corruption and lack of accountability.

Campaigning for FOI Legislation Under Civilian Rule

Civil Society: A Proactive Approach

Obasanjo's declaration of an all-out war on corruption at his inauguration on May 29, 1999 therefore caught and reflected the national mood of disgust at the extent of government corruption, particularly when placed against the increasing poverty of most citizens. Civil society organizations felt that their draft FOI legislation fitted perfectly with Obasanjo's objectives. Their position was that rather than pre-serve the climate of secrecy in which corruption could flourish and then pick off only some of the wrongdoers whose crimes might or might not be punished at the end of a very long day, it would be more effective to make the right to receive and impart information real. An FOI law would provide the necessary "disinfectant of sunshine" that would not only deter much would-be corrupt activity but also make the detection of any that remained a great deal easier.

MRA therefore sent the newly revised draft bill to President Obasanjo a few days after his inauguration, both to express support for his declared commitment to fighting corruption and to ask him to present the draft to the National Assembly as an Executive Bill along with his proposed anticorruption legislation. Such support would have been extremely helpful since, as in many other legisla-tive systems, bills sponsored by the executive stand the best chance of being enacted.[30] Similar letters were addressed to the Ministers of Justice and of Information, but the president declined to present the FOI bill and instead advised MRA to send the draft directly to the Na-tional Assembly.[31] Meanwhile, several months later the Ministry of Justice got around to advising MRA to "properly channel your cause through the Federal Ministry of Information which is the relevant governmental body that regulates the practice and dissemination of information. Your case will be duly considered if it originates from the relevant Ministry."[32]

Obasanjo: Reaction and Control

Unlike civil society's proactive approach, the solution proposed by President Obasanjo to the tide of corruption then threatening to en-gulf Nigeria was reactive. He established a completely new anticor-ruption machinery in the form of an Independent Corrupt Practices Commission (ICPC). While few new offenses were actually created, the accompanying legislation gave the commission sweeping pow-ers with which it could delve into a person's life, financial affairs, telephone conversations, correspondence, etc. in order to determine whether corrupt activity or enrichment was taking place.

By the end of the Obasanjo administration's first term in office in 2003 however, there had been announcements of investigations and arrests, workshops and seminars, slogans and campaigns, but no convictions. The constitutionality of the law was challenged by the few who were actually charged with offenses.[33] Most people, however, soon perceived the commission as a weapon with which the executive branch of the federal government was undermining and threatening political opponents in both the federal legislature and the state governments, rather than redressing widespread corruption within the executive branch.

Activists expressed outrage over the selectively blind presidential eye that was turned to repeated calls to investigate allegations of corruption against one of his predecessors, Ibrahim Babangida, which they considered particularly glaring. As with other cases that he had not himself initiated, the president's response was to demand that complainants bring him proof. And yet he controlled the entire machinery of state, the police, and security services, as well as the ICPC, with its extensive powers.

The saga of the Okigbo Panel report underlined continuing government determination to keep a tight hold on information that it did not want in the public domain. In 1994, the Abacha regime had set up a Panel of Inquiry under Pius Okigbo, to probe how the windfall from the increase in oil prices caused by the 1991 Gulf War had been spent. A summary of the panel's report revealed that the Babangida regime had conspired with top officials of the Central Bank and squandered the entire fortune on unproductive or dubious projects. Out of the US$12.4 billion Gulf War windfall, US$12.2 billion had been disbursed, leaving a balance of only US$206.037 million. The money was frittered away through "Dedicated Accounts" that were not accessible to auditors. No further action was taken by the Abacha regime, and the full details of the report were not publicized.

Almost immediately after Obasanjo was reelected in 2003, jostling for position in the 2007 elections commenced. To the consternation of many, Babangida emerged as a key contender for the distant contest. His record in office therefore became a legitimate subject of concern, and The Punch newspaper sought to obtain a copy of the Okigbo report. It could not be found anywhere. In November, the newspaper reported that it had conducted a two-month-long search in all relevant quarters, including the office of the Secretary to the Government of the Federation (SGF), the Department of National Archives, and the Federal Ministry of Information. None could provide a clue as to the whereabouts of the report, even though the current SGF had been a member of the Okigbo panel.

The SGF's office responded that it was searching, claiming: "The report is not lost. It is with the Federal Government." When journalists asked Obasanjo about the report, he claimed to have contacted Okigbo's widow for a copy. But Mrs. Okigbo denied this. She had not spoken to the president, nor had she any copy of the report. The president's spokesperson thereupon denied that Obasanjo would have had any cause to contact Mrs. Okigbo, maintaining that the report was with the government. But *The Punch* was passed from one section of government to another in its continued efforts to secure the report—rounded off by the assertion that "those who had authority to see the report had access to it."

As the newspaper noted in an editorial published on November 18, 2003, the Okigbo Panel Report was one of a long line of reports in which public figures had been indicted, without anything being done:

> Not a few Nigerians implicated by these probes still walk tall in the streets as free men, while some of them are holding or eyeing sensitive public offices. The non-availability of a document of such profound importance as the Okigbo Panel report is a tell tale clue on the contempt with which officialdom holds the anti-corruption campaign. It is tragic that probes in the country scarcely lead to punishment for culprits or the furtherance of justice and transparency in public life. The fate of past probes and the reports therefrom confirm the painful fact that inquiries have become tools used to divert public attention from official corruption, ineptitude and other crimes, or to intimidate and blackmail political opponents.

For Nigerians, the Gulf War oil windfall highlighted once again the fact that as far as those in government were concerned, not only would there never be any "surplus" for the Nigerian people to enjoy however much oil prices might increase, but the vanished surplus was likely to be applied to maintain in office those who had little concept of government beyond personal profit, thus perpetuating the vicious cycle.

Legislative Advocacy: Lobbying for FOI Legislation

After receiving the president's discouraging July 1999 letter, MRA immediately set about introducing the FOI bill at the National Assembly. Copies of the draft were distributed to some of the legislators, and one of them, Tony Anyanwu, agreed to act as sponsor of the FOI bill. Anyanwu secured cross-party support from a further twenty-four members who volunteered to be cosponsors of the bill, which was then sent to the legal drafting department of the National Assembly.

Copies of the bill were sent to all 469 members of the National Assembly, and although only one response was received, it was an important one. Jerry Ugokwe replied that he was himself planning to present his own FOI bill to the House, as he had become interested in the subject when he found himself able to access public documents under the American Freedom of Information Act during his studies in the United States. As his draft was more or less a wholesale lifting of the U.S. legislation with expressions and references to institutions and procedures that had no place in the Nigerian system of law or government, harmonization of the two drafts meant that the civil society version survived largely intact. With this, the bill was gazetted[34] and had its first reading in the House on February 22, 2000: the first civil society bill to be presented to the National Assembly.

At first there was speedy progress, with the House Information Committee undertaking a study tour of the United States and the United Kingdom in order, as they put it, to see how freedom of information legislation functioned in more advanced democracies before submitting a report on July 25.[35] Even the executive appeared to be coming around as the third reading approached, when the Minister of Information made the first public declaration of support for the FOI bill by any member of the executive branch: "No state, especially a democratic state, can achieve any meaningful development if the citizens do not have access to information about matters that affect their everyday life. It is indeed fundamental in any democratic governance."

Although coming at that late stage, such support tended only to recall Dr. Johnson's warning on patronage,[36] in retrospect this belated embrace by the executive presaged stagnation and ultimate failure as the entire project fell victim to external politics which, despite spirited efforts by a coalition of groups and organizations interested in FOI legislation—particularly in the run-up to the 2003 general elections—failed to secure the bill's all-important third reading in the House, let alone begin its passage through the Senate. Members who had previously appeared supportive now seemed either indifferent to its enactment, or worse, determined to prevent it from proceeding further.[37] They complained that there had been no public hearing, and although when the National Assembly continued to delay because of an alleged "lack of money," MRA raised funds for what turned out to be a well-attended public hearing, no further progress was made.

A Renewed and Continuing Campaign for FOI Legislation

Although the subject failed to catch on as an election issue, the new session saw the FOI coalition renewing its energy and commitment to the passage of the legislation. The coalition was expanded to include the National Human Rights Commission, which undertook extensive advocacy with different government departments to sensitize them to the importance of FOI legislation and to answer some of their concerns.

The new House of Representatives sworn in in June 2003 had as one of its new members Abdul Oroh, the former journalist who had been Executive Director of the Civil Liberties Organization and a key advocate of FOI legislation from the human rights side of the national discourse. Now he was a key mover in the renewed drive for the enactment of the FOI bill, and at the time of writing, the bill had successfully completed its passage through the House of Representatives and by February 2005, had had its second reading before the Senate. Dissatisfied with the report of its Information Committee, the Senate set up an *ad hoc* committee to study the House version of the bill. Indications are that the report of that committee has recommended adoption of the House bill, but proposes that the National Human Rights Committee should act as the implementation body, rather than a new one being set up. It remains possible that the legislation will be enacted before the end of the life of the legislature in 2007.

Executive Ambivalence

There is therefore reason for optimism regarding the prospects for the FOI bill's passage through the National Assembly. The question facing advocates of the bill after that is the attitude of the executive. At the outset, disturbing signs suggested that despite rhetoric about fighting corruption, the presidency was in reality lukewarm, if not actually opposed, to the enactment of any genuine freedom of information law in Nigeria. As the third reading in the House of Representatives approached, President Obasanjo gave interviews in which he claimed (wrongly) that the FOI bill was mostly imported from foreign countries and failed to take account of Nigeria's "peculiar local situation."[38] Obasanjo also complained at the lack of restriction on release of information to non-Nigerians, claiming (again, wrongly) that allowing noncitizens access to information "is not done anywhere else in the world." In an attempt to cut this objection off at the pass, the bill was amended so that only Nigerian citizens have the right to access information, although in practice, there is no limitation on what citizens can do with such information once they have obtained it.[39] While the president would be spared the embarrassment of having to reject the bill if it failed in the National Assembly, his consent is required before a bill can become law, and a presidential veto can only be overcome by a two-thirds majority. With the issue of tenure elongation finally buried, it remains to be seen whether the president will wish to leave free access to public information as part of his legacy to Nigerians or whether reluctance to let control of information slip into the public domain will prevail.

That there may be a genuine desire to run an open and transparent administration has been suggested by the way the presidency has been releasing information about government income and expenditure. But only selected information has been revealed, and that in a manner suggestive of a desire to give the *appearance* rather than the reality of open government or to achieve specific political aims.

Lessons Learned

It is difficult at this stage—with no legislation yet in place—to offer any final thoughts on lessons learned. The present campaign is to have FOI legislation enacted in Nigeria, and it has not yet been won. While indications from the Senate appear favorable, the experience during the 1999–2003 session of the National Assembly, when previously supportive or neutral members withdrew their support or even became actively hostile, shows that nothing should be taken for granted. Having one of the prime motivators of the FOI legislation as a member of the National Assembly has proved important, but the question of attitude of the executive will have to be faced sooner or later, since not only is presidential consent required to complete the legislative process, it is ultimately the executive that must implement the act.

Given that even President Obasanjo, who was formerly a trustee of Transparency International, has shown so little interest in promoting access to information, the civil society campaign is beginning to look elsewhere for levers. Of course, organizations such as Transparency International, whose regular placing of Nigeria at the bottom of its Corruption Perception Index causes the executive serious embarrassment, will be important. But with President Obasanjo's emergence as Chairperson of the African Union, coupled with Nigeria's declaration of an intention to submit itself for evaluation under the Peer Review Mechanism of the New Economic Partnership for African Development (NEPAD), the FOI coalition had an even more potent lever of persuasion, as the existence of FOI legislation in Nigeria would allow the country to present a more desirable profile for review.

Prospects for the Future

At present, only the Evidence Act in Nigeria gives the public access to government documents, and it is limited to the context of ongoing litigation. But even if the obstacles to the enactment of the FOI bill can be overcome, that will not be the end of the story. Indeed, there are already signs that the passage of any such legislation will only expose more of the problems that citizens of the Nigerian state and others like it face in their quest for a truly transparent and open government. The tools by which a FOI regime can be made effective will still remain in the hands of the executive. And while the Obasanjo administration has established some pro-transparency bodies and mechanisms that play well on the national and international stages, experience has shown that any departure from the presidentially approved script can result in the crippling of such initiatives. For example, the administration established a Human Rights Violations Investigation Commission (the Oputa Panel) in 1999, but when public pressure extended the period into which it was to inquire beyond 1983, back to 1966—thereby encompassing the period during which President Obasanjo ruled as military dictator—the administration simply starved it of funds. The Ford Foundation eventually provided funds for the Oputa Panel to work, but its report has remained in the cooler since it was submitted to the federal government. Civil society organizations decided to publish its Executive Summary in January 2005.

It is true that since the return to civilian rule in 1999 quite a few windows (or perhaps one should say "peepholes") have been opened on aspects of the Nigerian government in its attempt to appear genuinely open. The federal government has, for example, been publishing the amounts paid to state governments for themselves and their local governments, is participating in the Extractive Industries Transparency Initiative, and publishes details of large foreign exchange purchases. Some state governments have also made a show of publishing their own audited accounts.

But the light thrown on some selected areas also serves to highlight those where no voluntary disclosure has been made. For example, when the federal government started releasing details of the amounts paid to state governments for themselves and their local governments in paid advertisements, some state governors protested: "There is no justification whatsoever for the Federal Government to continue to publish the monthly statutory allocations to states and local governments whereas Nigerians do not even know how much the Presidency receives."[40]

The openness about the money paid to other tiers of government is not matched by disclosures about the amount paid to the federal government, even though this is by far the lion's share of federally collected revenue. Although the protests were met with advice to consult the audited accounts submitted to the National Assembly,[41] even legislators find it difficult to obtain the information they need to carry out their duties. Moreover, given that such information as they were able to glean resulted in a May 2004 report of the House Committee on Public Accounts that was a damning indictment of the waste and corruption within the federal government, many dismiss the much-touted openness as one-sided.

No figures are published about how much each of the federal government's many ministries, parastatals, departments, units, and other agencies receive. An "impenetrable fog"[42] shrouds the accounts, and the public can only speculate about the billions allegedly spent on federal roads, the National Electric Power Authority, and the oil refineries with not only no discernible improvement, but in many cases, visible deterioration.

The proposed FOI legislation will certainly provide more rights than the Evidence Act. But although the FOI bill requires public institutions to keep records, it is here that the potential for the most sabotage lies. At present, there is hardly any systematic approach to keeping records and statistics. The population of the country itself is a matter of projection or guesswork. Some junior government officials survive on the income they get from being encouraged to "find" files that are otherwise "lost." As one commentator observed, one has to engage in "virtual espionage" to secure even the most basic information.[43]

Doubts about the extent of the Obasanjo administration's commitment to openness solidified in 2003. At the beginning of that year, Vincent Azie, the acting Auditor-General, published an interim audit report for 2001. Many thought that at last, here was the first sign that the federal government was serious about the quest for accountability in government and, consequently, about the fight against corruption. Rather than generalizations about corruption and misappropriation of government funds and property, the report gave specific facts and figures about how government money was being misspent, misapplied, and misappropriated. By making open its insistence on compliance with the rules and regulations regarding expenditure, the report began creating a climate of accountability in government circles.

The report was particularly welcomed because previous reports—insofar as the public was aware that the nation's accounts had been audited at all—would come out several years after the funds to which they related had been spent, and the major actors possibly long since departed from office. This one covered 2001 and the actions of people appointed and still working under the Obasanjo administration. The interim report was thus hailed, with several newspaper opinions and editorials commending Mr. Azie's actions and calling for his confirmation as substantive Auditor-General.

But what newspaper editors and citizens' groups received with astonishment and delight caused shock and consternation elsewhere. The Minister of Information berated Azie for releasing the interim report before the queries that it raised had been answered, an approach that activists contended would be appropriate for a private firm but not for the government. Having refused to submit Azie's name to the Senate for confirmation, the executive wrote to him terminating his appointment as acting Auditor-General of the Federation on the excuse that an acting appointment could not be held for more than six months. Nothing further has been heard about the audit report for 2001, or indeed, for any year since, and Azie has retired.

Notwithstanding the evident conviction of some key members of President Obasanjo's team about the need for transparency in their individual spheres of government, doubts persist about the genuineness of the overall commitment of the federal government to relinquishing control over information. For example, while Nigeria has subscribed to the global initiative for transparency in the extractive industries and established a Nigerian Extractive Industries Transparency Initiative (NEITI) in February 2004, of the twenty-eight-person National Stakeholders Working Group set up to oversee its implementation, fully half are federal government employees. The publicity about this Working Group being "composed of individuals from Civil Society, Media, Government, Indigenous, National, and Multi-National companies"[44] implies that civil society is a major player, but in fact there are just two civil society representatives and only one from the media out of the twenty-eight. As a result, there is some feeling that the Nigerian end of the initiative exists because of pressures from external interests, and that its purpose is to satisfy them. Nonetheless, the first report made available by the appointed auditor revealed considerable discrepancies between the figures produced by the government's representative in the industry, the Nigerian National Petroleum Corporation (NNPC), and those of the oil companies. State governments have also made good use of the figures to challenge the failure of the NNPC to pay all monies due to the Federation Account (which would then be distributed among the federal, state, and local governments according to a fixed formula).

Attitudes and Habits

Freedom of information legislation, if it is to be effective when passed, will require a sea change in attitude on the part of government. At a crucial moment during the journey of the FOI bill through the House of Representatives—which was presenting itself as a champion of open government—even a member of the House was refused access to information about how the Speaker was spending its budget. The executive branch has also demonstrated a deeply ingrained resistance to the release of information to ordinary members of the public on demand.

For example, Section 140(1) of the 1999 Constitution provides: "A person elected to the office of President shall not begin to perform the functions of that office until he has declared his assets as prescribed in the Constitution." Relying on this provision, MRA and the Human Rights Law Service (HURILAWS) wrote to the Code of Conduct Bureau pointing out that Obasanjo ought not to have been sworn in as president until he had made the relevant declaration. Receiving the reply that the president had indeed declared his assets before a Commissioner for Oaths, the two organizations requested a copy of the declaration. But the bureau responded that there was no law requiring the president to make a public declaration of his assets, unless the National Assembly were to prescribe it. Upon receiving details of this correspondence, the National Assembly claimed (among other reasons) that it was bound by the Official Secrets Act and could not make a law that derogated from it. Yet the Official Secrets Act itself is deemed to be an act of the National Assembly, and since it was not entrenched in the Constitution[45] there was nothing to prevent the National Assembly making a law that declarations of assets should be made public, or available to the public. In fact, in 1999 only one of the hundreds of public officers who took office made the declaration of his assets public: the Governor of Katsina State. Meanwhile, when a U.S. estate agent's Web site revealed then Governor Abubakar Audu of Kogi State as the owner of a multimillion-dollar mansion in the United States, the value of the property naturally prompted speculation about how and when he had acquired it. If after becoming governor, from what funds, given that even a governor's salary was insufficient to provide for such a purchase? If before, had he mentioned it on his Declaration of Assets form? The Code of Conduct Bureau refused to disclose whether the property had been declared by the governor on assuming office. Even when Audu was not reelected in the April 2003 election and therefore lost his constitutional immunity on May 29, the Code of Conduct Bureau continued to protect his secrets.

But attitudes outside government also present obstacles to the establishment of open government in Nigeria. The campaign for the enactment of FOI legislation has not been a grassroots effort. While proponents of the legislation have mounted a sustained campaign to overcome executive resistance to enactment, the inability of federal and state governments and law enforcement agencies to secure conviction or punishment in even well-exposed cases of wrongdoing has created apathy and cynicism over whether such legislation will bring about much change in the culture of impunity and/or immunity. Although the Economic and Financial Crimes Commission (EFCC), originally established to combat Internet scams and the advance fee frauds that had made it difficult for genuine Nigerian businesses to operate abroad, secured some high-profile convictions,[46] it too suffered from the perception that it was being used against political opponents, or—before the tenure elongation issue was finally laid to rest—those who had indicated an interest in the yet-to-be-confirmed-vacant presidency in 2007.[47]

Much will depend on civil society if FOI legislation is to be transformed from a privilege for the elite few to a tool of real accountability in the hands of many. But civil society's use of government information remains patchy, and in all but a few cases Nigerian NGOs have been unable or unwilling to take the benefits of free access to information to communities directly affected. The expressway from Lagos to Benin becomes nigh impassable despite billions voted in annual budgets for road maintenance; a newspaper columnist finds a wide gap between claims on the Web site of the Jigawa state government and the reality on the ground—yet beyond generalized complaining, little is done.[48]

Indeed, the extent to which civil society has the will or the capacity to make effective use of such information is open to question. Although the civil society representatives involved in the NEITI, for example, have established a wider support group of civil society organizations in furtherance of a "grassroots approach," there are internal concerns about the lack of commitment and political will to make the best use of even what may be a less-than-perfect system for transparency within the petroleum industry.

Similar fears exist, although to a lesser extent, for the anticipated more comprehensive freedom of information legislation. The slightly higher expectations stem from the fact that—unlike the extractive industries initiative—the FOI bill results from a local initiative, and it is therefore hoped that civil society and the media will make more use of it. Also, while the FOI bill makes it a criminal offense to withhold or destroy information properly requested by members of the public, criminal offenses under the legislation proposed in support of the extractive industries initiative are only for giving false information to the government;[49] the only requirement on the NEITI itself is to publish the auditor's report on the income from the industries. This situation is likely to create more sense of ownership of the FOI bill among Nigerians than among members of the NEITI.

While stories of the MKSS in India are repeated to spur FOI advocates on to victory (see the chapter by Shekhar Singh in this volume), replication on Nigerian soil is as yet rare. There are a few instances of grassroots campaigns, such as that conducted by the Justice Development and Peace Commission of the [Roman] Catholic Secretariat, which—with its publication of the details of the payments to state and local governments as revealed by the Federal Ministry of Finance and its "People's Parley," by which it calls officials to render public account of their stewardship—is trying to create a demand for accountability.

A great deal remains to be done, however. While it is important to require government and its organs to rise to the challenge of making information available to citizens, it is equally important to empower citizens to make use of that information.

The Military-Civilian Continuum

As noted above, military dictators who presided over the dissipation and disappearance of Nigeria's oil income continue to cast a long shadow over current attempts to build a democratic government and a functioning and effective transparency regime. The current head of state, Obasanjo, is a product of the military-in-government establishment, which has continued to gain power since 1966. The underlying authoritarian nature of government has not changed simply because the key actors now wear *agbada*[50] instead of khaki. Despite its multiplicity of media outlets—many of them independent—Nigeria remains an illiberal, closed society with an extremely fragile democracy. Tightly controlled or brazenly rigged elections are a microcosm of the true condition of all the apparatus necessary for a properly and freely functioning democracy, in the legislature, the judiciary, and the rule of law: the form and appearance are there, but the substance is lacking.

In this militarized political culture, the unsupportive reaction of the Obasanjo administration to the idea of fighting corruption by throwing open everything about government should not be surprising. Putting the fight into the hands of the ICPC or the EFCC, which decide what *they* want to investigate and whom *they* intend to prosecute, leaves the executive in absolute control. Given the numbers of former military officers and others who have benefited from their stay in power to win office in the present "democratic" system, it may be optimistic to expect any sudden change. Although in an age of globalization, a government in a country like Nigeria may be unable to prevent all its secrets from being revealed in more open countries, it would be naïve to imagine that openness of such countries within their own borders necessarily translates into openness about their dealings with other countries. Moreover, huge amounts of information are not in the international public domain. Oil companies, for example, may face pressure in their home countries and as a result of the global Extractive Industries Transparency Initiative, of which the NEITI is a part, to reveal exactly how much they pay to governments in oil-producing countries. But what records would they have of those with direct access to Nigeria's oil fields and oil wealth?

Even if the considerable hurdles on the road to the enactment of FOI legislation can be overcome, implementation will remain very much an open question. The civil service is more than practiced at not producing information that the powers-that-be have determined should remain hidden. A letter written to Obasanjo in April 1990 by the man who had served him and his assassinated predecessor, Murtala Muhammed, as Secretary to the Federal Military Government (SFMG), Allison Ayida, underscores the point. General Obasanjo had published a book of recollections of his 1976–79 military administration under the title *Not My Will*. In a letter dated April 1, 1990, written in response to some of the comments in the book, former SFMG Ayida exposed the civil service capacity for "not finding" documents that might embarrass those in power, even—as in this case—for fellow members of the ruling Supreme Military Council:

> When the white paper on the Adeosun Indigenisation Panel report was drafted . . . you gave me the draft white paper and report for my comment . . . your specific instructions included, "where a Nigerian had acquired the bulk of the shares in any enterprises outside Schedule I, the shares should be confiscated" and forfeited to the Federal Government and the names of the "moneybags" publicized. Apparently, you had not studied Volume III of the report where names of such shareholders were listed. When I drew your attention to the pages where your name appeared, you readily agreed that the panel's recommendations should be rejected. . . . When eventually the council memorandum was circulated, we agreed that Volume III should not be circulated or published but that you should mention that any member interested in the particulars of those who "cornered" the indigenisation shares, should see the SFMG. Several members [of the Supreme Military Council] contacted me for the list but no member saw the list of names![51]

Challenges for the Future

Perhaps the most important lessons will be learned only if and when the Access to Public Information—the FOI—bill has become law in Nigeria. Obvious logistical hurdles are likely to present themselves during implementation. But beyond these lies the battle to inspire the people to use FOI as a tool in their own emancipation. In a country where few are seen to have been punished for breaches of the law, FOI legislation cannot succeed against a civil service determined to resist it and with the citizenry not confident that they are entitled to demand accountability from their governments or that there will be any positive outcome from fledgling attempts to do so.

The challenge before Nigerians in general and civil society in particular, however, is to begin to practice using and disseminating information. Even before FOI legislation is enacted, civil society organizations need to cultivate the habit of requesting information from government, accessing whatever information is disseminated by government—and using it.

NOTES

1. General Sani Abacha, who had been adopted by each of the then five registered political parties as their presidential candidate for the forthcoming elections, died on June 6, 1998, before the elections could be held.

2. General Olusegun Obasanjo, who ruled from February 1976 to October 1979, was elected President and took office in May 1999.

3. General—now President—Obasanjo and General Buhari, whose action challenging the result of the 2003 presidential elections failed by a 4–1 majority, but with the results from the president's home state, Ogun State, being annulled.

4. General Ibrahim Babangida, who ruled from August 1985 to August 1993.

5. Senator David Mark, former military governor of Niger State, report in *The Punch*, Saturday, June 3, 2006.

6. Or indeed, any process at all: a bald announcement on the national news was often the first time many public officers heard that they were no longer in service.

7. Now thirty-six States and one Federal Capital Territory.

8. He commenced a transition to civil rule program, but continually changed the rules and postponed the handover until his cancellation of the presidential election of June 12, 1993 led to civil protests that forced him to make what he called the "personal sacrifice" of "stepping aside."

9. Together with the fourfold increase in the price of oil by the Organization of Petroleum Exporting Countries (OPEC) to levels which—in real terms—have not been seen again, even thirty years later.

10. Leaders of the National Party of Nigeria, NPN, which held power under President Shehu Shagari from 1979 to 1983, often said that there were "only two parties in Nigeria: the NPN and the Army." General Ibrahim Babangida, who ruled Nigeria from 1985 to 1993, bluntly declared that while the armed forces might not know who was going to succeed them, they definitely knew who was *not* going to succeed them. And one leading member of the present ruling People's Democratic Party (PDP) has warned that it is current President Obasanjo who will "choose his successor."

11. http://www.climatelaw.org/media/gas.flaring/report/section1. For information on the Nigerian economy, see http://www.cia.gov/cia/publications/factbook/geos/ni.html#Econ.

12. Chief Obafemi Awolowo, "Leader of the Yoruba," Premier of the Western Region from 1954 to 1959, Vice Chairman of the Federal Executive Council, and Federal Minister of Finance from 1966 to 1970.

13. Nigerians can claim anything from 250 to 450 ethnic groups, but most expert opinion agrees that there are approximately 45 to 60 main groups.

14. Section 24(1) 1960 Constitution; Section 25(1) 1963 Constitution; Section 36(1) Constitution of the Federal Republic of Nigeria 1979; and Section 39(1) 1999 Constitution.

15. Despite romantic notions back "Home" about "the white man's burden," the purpose of the British colonial empire was primarily extractive; the amalgamation of 1914 came about because although the northern part of the country had to be occupied (to keep the French out in accordance with the 1884 Berlin carve-up, if for no other reason), the costs of administering it outweighed the income, while the income from the southern part exceeded the costs of administration.

16. Official Secrets Act, Chapter 335, Laws of the Federation of Nigeria 1990.

17. Section 9(1) of the Official Secrets Act [Cap. 335] defines classified matter as "any information or thing which, under *any system of security classification* from time to time in use by or by any branch of the government, is not to be disclosed to the public and of which the disclosure to the public would be prejudicial to the security of Nigeria."

18. For example, the Federal Ministry of Justice might decide to stamp as "Secret" papers that it was also filing in court, even though under the

Evidence Act, such filed papers thereby became public documents of which members of the public could (in theory) obtain certified true copies.

19. At their meeting in Barbados in 1980, Commonwealth Law Ministers declared: "public participation in the democratic and governmental process is at its most meaningful when citizens had adequate access to official information."

Article 9 Clause 1 of the African Charter on Human and People's Rights makes the following provision: "Every individual shall have the right to receive information." Nigeria passed the African Charter on Human and Peoples' Rights (Ratification and Enforcement) Act in March 1983, but without any enforcement mechanism.

As recently as March 2003, Nigeria signed the African Union Convention on Preventing and Combating Corruption, which *inter alia* guarantees access to information.

20. Just the reintroduction of elected legislatures at the federal and state levels alone meant that there were quite simply many more people who now had access to the national cake, and it was unofficially estimated by Western diplomats that between US$5 billion and US$7 billion was transferred abroad by corrupt politicians during the four-year period that Shagari was in power (1979–1983).

21. At independence in 1960, Nigeria had inherited the parliamentary system of government, in which the executive was picked from the elected members of parliament. Military dictatorship, of course, had no legislators to pay, but in 1979 Nigeria adopted the presidential system of government, where the executive was a separate expense, while the increase from three Regions to nineteen (and presently thirty-six) states would in itself have represented a massive expenditure, quite apart from the fact that each state also had its own separate legislature and executive to pay for.

22. Out of 133 countries surveyed by Transparency International, Nigeria ranked 132 on the Corruption Perception Index for 2003 with a score of 1.4 out of 10; just one point and one place above bottom-ranked Bangladesh. In 2004, Nigeria ranked third from the bottom, above Bangladesh and Haiti.

23. E.g., by arresting people for spurious reasons and releasing them only when they paid "bail," extraction of bribes for every service provided to detainees, accepting money from civil creditors to detain civil debtors until payment was completed, and extortion at road blocks, etc.

24. The Civil Liberties Organisation (of which the writer was President from 1995 to 2003) was the first, formed in October 1987. The following year, the Committee for the Defence of Human Rights was formed.

25. In a country with extremely poor communications and low levels of literacy, arrested people who could not contact relations to "bail" them out from the police station could simply disappear—especially against a background of poor record keeping. Those who had traveled from one part of the country to another were particularly vulnerable. Once forgotten inside the system, they often remained there.

26. The NUJ was primarily a trade union for journalists, while the CLO was a membership organization with members drawn from all walks of life, concerned with the full range of civil and political human rights guaranteed by the Nigerian Constitution, the African Charter of Human and People's Rights, and other regional and international instruments.

27. Oroh was arrested and detained without trial in July 1995 under Decree 2, after the human rights community had held a press conference in which it stated its belief that there had been no coup plot.

28. The five registered political parties had all adopted Abacha as their sole presidential candidate, even though he was not a member of any of them.

29. Formal handover was on May 29, 1999.

30. Letter dated June 10, 1999 from MRA to President Olusegun Obasanjo.

31. Letter dated July 19, 1999 from Mr. Ojo A. Taiwo, personal assistant to President Obasanjo, to MRA.

32. Letter dated January 20, 2000 (not received until March 29, 2000) from Mrs. Christie Ekweonu on behalf of the Minister of Justice to MRA.

33. Under Nigeria's federal constitution, prosecution of most criminal offenses fell within the competence of the states, rather than the federal government, while provisions that allowed tapping of telephones, inspection of mail, or access to bank records appeared to conflict with constitutional guarantees of the right to privacy.

34. Federal Government Official Gazette No. 91, Vol. 86.

35. The major result of the tour was that the committee recommended that the actual cost of making the information available should be borne by the applicant except in certain special cases, instead of being either free or subsidized, as the original civil society draft had proposed. FOI legislation had not come into force in the UK at that time.

36. "Is not a Patron . . . one who looks unconcerned on a man struggling for life in the water, and, when he has reached ground, encumbers him with help?"

37. "Campaigning for Access to Information in Nigeria: A Report of the Legislative Advocacy Programme for the Enactment of a Freedom of Information Act," *Media Rights Agenda* (June 2003):33.

38. Although this was a criticism that might have been leveled at Rep. Jerry Ugokwe's original bill, this was not the case with the civil society-produced bill then passing through the House.

39. There are some concerns on the part of civil society that applicants for information may be required to demonstrate their citizenship before being given the information they seek.

40. "Governor Ahmed Makarfi of Kaduna State," *ThisDay on Sunday*, June 28, 2004, http://www.thisdayonline.com/archive.php.

41. This advice from presidential spokesperson Femi Fani-Kayode was disingenuous, to say the least, as audited accounts were published well after the money had been received and spent, whereas what the state and local governments were getting was made public as or even before it was paid. Moreover, Nigerians had seen how Acting Auditor-General Vincent Azie was treated when he published an interim report on federal government income and expenditure.

42. "Editorial: A Graft War Yet to Begin," *ThisDay on Sunday*, June 28, 2004, http://www.thisdayonline.com/archive.php.

43. "Odia Ofeimun: Proposal Made to the National Assembly for a Freedom of Information Act," *The Guardian*, December 8, 2003.

44. EITI Nigeria Group Update of Activities, October 11, 2004; NEITI Advertisement for Independent Auditor in *The Punch*, December 20, 2004.

45. I.e., the Constitution did not contain any provision that the Official Secrets Act could only be amended in the manner provided for amending the Constitution itself—that is, by a two-thirds majority in each house of the National Assembly and a two-thirds majority in two-thirds of the State Houses of Assembly.

46. Most notably, former Inspector-General of Police Tafa Balogun was suddenly retired and eventually convicted on fifty-eight counts of unlawful enrichment in 2005.

47. Former Military Administrator of Borno and Lagos States, Colonel Buba Marwa, had commenced the wide-ranging visits to different parts of the country and sectors of society that are the herald of a presidential bid, when he was arrested in December 2005 by the EFCC over his role in the siphoning abroad of funds by the Abacha government. After being held for questioning for several days, he was released without charge in January 2006. But nothing more was heard of his presidential ambitions until the defeat of tenure elongation meant that there would, after all, be a vacancy in the presidency in 2007.

48. When the outcry over the condition of roads in the southeast became deafening, Olisa Agbakoba (founding President of the CLO) made specific attempts to find out why CCC Ltd. had been awarded the contract to repair the Onitsha-Owerri road, rather than the well-known companies that were building roads in Abuja and elsewhere. He discovered through the Internet that CCC was a Middle Eastern company, brand new in Nigeria, with no local presence beyond an Abuja office. But as he himself asked: How did local advocacy challenge government's decision to make that award?

49. The proposed Extractive Industries Bill only requires the audited report on the total monies paid to the federal government from the extractive industries to be made available to the general public.

50. Indigenous civilian clothes.

51. It should be noted that it was in no way illegal for public officers to have purchased shares.

PART TWO

Themes

Chapter Six

Making the Law Work

The Challenges of Implementation

Laura Neuman and Richard Calland

Prologue: Unearthing the Goblet

Carlton Davis is Jamaica's Cabinet Secretary, the country's most senior public servant. In July 1993, on one of his first days on the
job, he took a walk around his new domain and discovered a room
full of papers. There were piles and piles of documents. Rooting
around, coughing with the dust, he moved one particularly large
tower only to discover beneath it a silver goblet. Polishing it with
the sleeve of his jacket, he read to his amazement that it was a
special commemorative Olympic trophy that had been awarded
to the successful Jamaican athletics relay team decades before. It
was a national treasure, yet it had been literally buried in papers.
What other nuggets of history or critical information were lost in
the chaos of unorganized and discarded documents? A scientist by
training, he understood the value of learning from the past and the

importance of good documentation to make this possible, and was greatly concerned by what he had found. Looking back now, Davis traces his commitment to access to information to that moment. He recognizes the value of access as a human right and the role information can play in engaging citizens. But equally so, as a leader in Jamaica's quest for modernization in public service and more efficient governance, he believes that a well-implemented access to information law is an instrument that governments can use to learn from past successes and mistakes.

Introduction

Davis is one of a new breed of public servants determined to challenge a culture of secrecy, whose commitment will determine whether the host of legal and institutional changes described throughout this book lead to significant and lasting transformation in the relationship between those in power and the citizens they serve. Although there is now widespread international recognition of the importance of establishing effective information regimes, there has not been equivalent emphasis laid on the obstacles facing governments and citizens in responding to the challenge of implementing transparency law and policy. This demands leadership, resources, and the personal conviction of "transparency champions."

The actions of governments in the implementation phase are often related to the original motive or purpose for supporting a transparency law, and the manner in which the law was passed. When the law was passed as part of an integrated policy or to meet an inherent need or civil society demand, there has tended to be greater commitment to implementation. So for some governments like Jamaica's, it is the desire for efficiency and modernization that drives them to pass access to information (ATI) laws. For others, it is the need to rebuild trust with citizens through the sharing of information and creation of new political space, such as in Bolivia, which has initiated transparency mechanisms while waiting for the passage of enabling legislation, or in South Africa during its democratic transition. A commitment to the establishment of a new order based on human rights spurs the creation of a new access to information regime. In Sinaloa, Mexico, the governor passed a comprehensive access to information law because he wanted his citizens to have faith in the state government and therefore begin paying their taxes. In all of these cases, generally there has been a greater emphasis on implementation so that the benefits of the law are realized.

But where a government has passed the law to satisfy an international financial institution as a "condition" for loan or debt relief or to join an intergovernmental organization, regional trade group, or common market, its true commitment to full implementation may be in question. For example, in both Nicaragua and Honduras, the executive branch included the passage of an access to information law as one of the conditions to receive debt relief under the Highly Indebted Poor Countries Program of the World Bank and IMF. Until recently, both countries had suffered from a lack of enthusiasm from other sectors, most prominently the legislative branch, and passage of the law remains elusive.

Whatever the underlying reason for establishing a transparency regime, after a decade of proliferation of access to information laws, with around seventy countries now enjoying a legislated right to information, it is clear that the stimulus of both a supply of information and a demand is the key to meeting the policy objectives. This supply-demand intersection is a fundamental part of our hypothesis for effective implementation and use of the law. This chapter will focus on the government side of the equation—the "supply side"—where there is a new body of knowledge arising from the legislative explosion of the past decade. Examples from Latin America, the Caribbean, and South Africa will highlight the recent lessons learned.

Notwithstanding the emphasis on the "supply side," ensuring the success of an ATI law is a matter of co-responsibility. Not all the burden lies with government: citizens, civil society and community organizations, media, and the private sector must take responsibility for monitoring government efforts and using the law. Without an adequately developed "demand side," the law is likely to wither on the vine. In other words, the demand and supply sides must match, and where they intersect will determine the quality of the transparency regime.

Great focus continues to be placed on passing access to information laws; model laws have been widely distributed, with specific versions for Africa and most recently Latin America and the Caribbean,[1] and many countries around the world have heeded the call to enact them. Nevertheless, experience has proven that passing the law is the easier task. Successful implementation of an open information regime is often the most challenging and energy-consuming part for government. And yet, without effective implementation, an access to information law—however well drafted—will fail to meet the public policy objectives of transparency.

Diagnosing the Implementation Challenge

Although the sheer number of civil servants engaged in the application of an access to information law may be immense—from all ministries and more than 200 agencies in Jamaica to approximately 100,000 public authorities in the United Kingdom that are mandated to apply the law—until recently little attention has been paid to the theory and practice of implementation.

In 2003, the Open Society Institute (OSI)'s Justice Initiative recognized the need to assess the success of implementation efforts and advance good implementation practices.[2] In five countries a pilot monitoring study was conducted. In each country, four different types of people—non-governmental organization representative, journalists, ordinary individual citizens, and "excluded person" (defined as someone who because of their social or economic circumstances faces serious obstacles to engagement, for example illiteracy, disability, or poverty)—submitted a total of approximately 100 requests to 18 different government agencies. The same request was made to each agency twice, by a different requester, in order to test whether the agency responded differently according to the type of person. In addition, there were three distinct classes of requests submitted, as determined by the pilot study organizers: routine, difficult, and sensitive.

The results illuminate the challenges of implementing transparency legislation, and coincide with the firsthand experiences of many implementers and users. Of the 496 requests for information filed in the five countries during the monitoring period, a total of 35.7 percent, or just over one in three requests, received the information sought. Approximately half of the requests (49.6 percent) received the information or written refusals within the time periods established in the respective laws.[3] This is clearly progress toward transparency. As the report noted, "the five monitored countries are all introducing new standards of government transparency, while undergoing democratic transitions. In this context, both outcomes—compliance with international FOI [Freedom of Information] standards in almost 50 percent of the cases, and the provision of information in response to 35 percent of requests—can be seen as a solid basis for building greater openness."[4]

Unfortunately, the OSI report also records that over one third of requests met with complete silence from the authorities. In terms of these "mute refusals," as the survey refers to them, South Africa fared the worst, with 63 percent of the properly submitted requests completely ignored. As the country report on South Africa comments, "These results are of particular concern given that South Africa's FOI law, the 2000 Promotion of Access to Information Act (PAIA), the first of its kind in Africa, has been hailed as a model for other African countries."[5] Though the South African law may be the best drafted and most comprehensive among the five test countries, in terms of compliance with international standards and best practice, only 23 percent of requests were successful, compared with 34 percent for Macedonia, which had no legal right to access information, Armenia with 41 percent, and the best performing, Peru, with 42 percent. The OSI report on South Africa noted that "a common feature of the bodies which performed well in the monitoring was that they had made a serious commitment to implementing the law and believed in its potential."

Implementation of an access to information law is complex, and common challenges may include difficulty in adjusting the mindset of the bureaucracy and people who hold the information; a lack of capacity in relation to record keeping and record making; insufficient resources and infrastructure; inadequate staffing in terms of training, specialization, and seniority; and a lack of capacity building or incentive systems. The OSI monitoring exercise helps illustrate that even the best laws can be rendered meaningless when the myriad of implementation challenges are not addressed.

Enabling legislation for the right to information should be seen as a three-phase process: passage, implementation, and enforcement of the access to information law, the "transparency triangle." All three elements are crucial and interrelated, but experience indicates that the implementation phase is paramount and serves as the base of the triangle. Without full and effective implementation, the right to information becomes just another example of the "hyperinflation" of new laws that serve no one.[6] While many of the chapters in this book describe struggles to pass laws, the focus in this chapter is on what happens after the bill is signed.

Setting the Stage

The successful implementation of an access to information regime depends on a variety of factors, both technical and political. The more technical aspects are discussed in detail below, but in realizing implementation of the right to information, three additional points are crucial: the degree of societal involvement in the demand for and drafting of the legislation, alternative approaches taken by the government, and embedding provisions for implementation into the law.

Instituting a New Information Regime: The Process

In terms of legitimacy, sustained monitoring, and usage, the process through which the new access to information law is conceived and promulgated is critical. As discussed above, governments may choose to provide this right to information for a variety of reasons: a new constitution is drafted; a new administration or a faltering ruler is seeking methods to raise their image in response to a government scandal, corruption, or public health crisis; to meet provisions for acceptance to multilateral organizations; or to comply with international treaties and agreements. But when civil society has played a significant role in advocating for the law and lobbying around the key provisions, the information regime has tended to truly flourish, thus overcoming the "check the box" syndrome. In countries such as South Africa, Bulgaria, India, Mexico, Peru, and Jamaica, widespread civil society campaigns or well-publicized efforts from highly influential civil society groupings augmented and encouraged the government efforts to pass enabling legislation. While implementation still has proved to be a challenge, in each case, civil society organizations that emerged from the campaigns for the law are monitoring and testing the system and urging greater government compliance. Through the campaign for a legislated right to information, organizations became vested in the law's success, there was more significant buy-in from society, and in turn the laws have enjoyed greater credibility and use.

In Jamaica, for example, a diverse group from civil society worked together to seek amendments to the proposed law and to fight for more robust legislation. This coalition included such strange bedfellows as human rights and democracy non-governmental organizations (NGOs), journalists' associations, prominent media owners, private sector representatives, and the Civil Service Association.[7] Many of these same actors have remained engaged in monitoring the government's implementation efforts and in using the law, and as a special Parliamentary Committee considered additional changes to the legislation in 2006, the civil society monitoring efforts were the only statistics on implementation available for consideration.

In South Africa, the Open Democracy Campaign Group, which from 1995 to 2000 pushed for a strong law to give effect to the right to access information enshrined in the country's new 1996 constitution, included human rights NGOs, church organizations, environmental pressure groups, and the powerful trade union umbrella body COSATU.[8] These advocacy efforts translated into a constituency willing and eager to use the new instrument and prepared to monitor government's implementation and enforcement performance.

In countries where civil society was not engaged in the debate, the right to information has atrophied and the law has never been fully implemented. Belize passed its Freedom of Information law in 1994, one of the first countries in Latin America and the Caribbean to do so. It was accomplished with little public or parliamentary debate and no civil society involvement. For the past decade the law has been used only a handful of times, and rarely with success. When asked, NGO leaders indicated minimal knowledge of the law and little faith in its ability to promote greater transparency.[9]

In the worst cases, when there is no participatory process, laws are passed that are contrary to the principles of openness and limit freedom of information and expression, as in both Zimbabwe and Paraguay.[10] In contrast, Peru presently enjoys a comprehensive access to information law that was drafted with a wide sector of civil society involvement, support from the ombudsman's office, and extensive consultations with the armed forces. However, the right to information was not new to Peru. In response to the collapse of the Fujimori dictatorship and the pervasive allegations of government corruption, in 2000, the interim president, Valentine Paniagua, issued a presidential decree supporting a right to public information held by the executive. Laudable in its purpose, this unilateral decree was not fully applied or utilized. Although the newly passed legislation does not greatly expand on the decree, the manner in which it was promulgated, with civil society advocacy and debate, has led to increased legitimacy, implementation, and use.

Civil society alone may not be sufficient to ensure full implementation of an access to information law. However, where there are strong advocates, government and information holders' failure to comply is more often noticed and challenged. Thus, committed civil society organizations serve as a counterbalance to faltering implementation efforts. Through continued use of the law and monitoring, implementation problems may be highlighted and the government obligated to assign greater emphasis and resources to resolve obstacles. Without civil society engagement, administrators could simply allow the right to fade away from neglect and disregard.

Vanguard Steps

Like Peru's former president Paniagua, other government leaders are increasingly seeking means to demonstrate their commitment to transparency without waiting for completion of the law-making and implementation phases. If the process of passing the law includes consensus building and sufficient time for effective implementation is afforded, it potentially could be years before anyone could exercise his or her right to information. Moreover, in some contexts the fragmentation, weakness, or skepticism of the legislature has blocked the passage of a comprehensive law. Thus, in an attempt to satisfy citizen desire for more immediate results and to learn critical implementation lessons earlier, executives are experimenting with tools other than legislation, such as Supreme Decrees and voluntary openness strategies.

For example, in Peru, Argentina, and Bolivia, supreme decrees that carry the weight of law were issued to promote transparency. Such decrees can be accomplished quickly, demonstrate government commitment and political will, begin the process of shifting the culture of secrecy, provide implementation experience, and serve as a platform for the more extensive legislation. But there are also strik-ing disadvantages. First, supreme decrees apply exclusively to the executive, leaving aside the other branches of government and the private sector. Moreover, they often serve as a pseudo-panacea mini-mally satisfying the call for openness, but potentially slowing down the passage of a comprehensive right to information law. As they do not engage the legislature, they are rarely, if ever, accompanied by a budget for implementation. Compared with any other legislation that addresses information availability or disclosure, supreme de-crees always will be the lowest on the totem pole, and their objectives will often be frustrated by older secrecy provisions that override the decree. Moreover, supreme decrees are rarely produced in an inclu-sive process of drafting and consultation, and thus provide less op-portunity for building legitimacy and buy-in. Finally, if not effectively implemented, a supreme decree, like a law, can raise unrequited ex-pectations and delegitimize positive government efforts.

In Bolivia, the passage of a Supreme Decree for Transparency and Access to Information has proved particularly detrimental. Following its issuance in January 2004, which provided a right of access to a limited class of documents, media representatives and some civil society groups strongly rejected the effort. Failure to con-sult with these relevant stakeholders and poorly drafted exemptions provided sufficient fuel for key groups to publicly denounce the de-cree. Since its initial announcement, there have been few efforts to systematically implement its provisions, and even fewer examples of its use. This damaging experience has caused some sectors, most strikingly members of the media workers' union, to distrust further access to information initiatives, including proposed comprehensive legislation. The decree in Bolivia became so distracting that the only issue under discussion was its reform or rescission, as the media refused to support the consideration of a comprehensive law until the other point was resolved. Four years (and three presidents) later, the media workers' union remains skeptical of any effort regarding access to information.

In Argentina, the Supreme Decree for Transparency, issued by President Kirchner in February 2004, initially enjoyed greater public support. In contrast to the Bolivia case, it was issued in response to more than five years of civil society demand for the right to informa-tion. In the wake of the 2002 economic collapse and presidential resignations, fearful and disorganized members of the Lower House passed the draft access to information law. As the political parties regrouped and regained some legitimacy, they no longer saw the need for such a threatening piece of legislation and blocked its final passage in the Senate. The only recourse was a supreme decree. However, as with the Peru example, the decree has not satisfied the need for a law, and civil society groups continue their campaign.[11]

Short of a legally binding tool, governments are increasingly considering pilot projects as a vanguard to an access to information law. Voluntary Openness Strategies (VOS) and Codes for Transparency, such as the United Kingdom's Publication Schema, can begin the transformation from a culture of secrecy to one of openness and be a platform for the more comprehensive right to information legislation. Focusing the VOS on a few key pilot ministries and agencies that agree to provide an extensive range of information to citizens can help prepare for effective implementation of a transparency law, when ultimately passed. These pilot bodies have the opportunity to develop best practices and to become "islands of transparency."

Other pilot projects could include release of certain classes of documents across the government, or release of all information related to a particular theme. In India, the Ford Foundation agreed to fund a "model district" where intensive focus is placed on one district to "address all micro-issues and nuances involved in implementation" and demonstrate what is possible.[12] The World Bank, in response to activist demands, appears prepared to begin such a pilot project with a one-year experimental public release of key documents simultaneously with their submission to the board.[13] These pilot projects may satisfy some user demand while concurrently preparing governmental bodies for the more extensive rollout of transparency measures.

Drafting the Law: Taking Account of the Implementation Challenge

Finally, when writing an access to information law, it is important to consider the processes and procedures necessary for its effective implementation and full enforcement. It is easy to become overly preoccupied with the exemptions section, to the exclusion of other key provisions. While national security exceptions may be more interesting and controversial than the implementation procedures, they are often much less important in determining the bill's overall effectiveness in promoting real transparency. In Peru, there were months of productive meetings between the Press Council and the armed forces to negotiate and agree on the national security exemptions. However, this same energy was not invested in designing the archival system or appeals process.

Focusing exclusively on the exemptions is misguided. In reality, if governments are determined to withhold information for whatever reason, they will do so regardless of the exactness with which the exceptions to access are written in the law. Thus, more emphasis must be given to the procedures for legal challenge when and if the exemptions are used to shield information. Issues such as mandatory publication of certain information, time limits for completion of information requests, administrative duty to assist the requester, costs for requests and copying, sanctions for failure to comply, reporting requirements, and appeals procedures must receive much greater attention. These practicalities ultimately will determine the value and usability of such a law for ordinary citizens.

For example, there needs to be greater detail in the law or regulations on the procedures for implementing and applying the legislation. In countries such as South Africa, where civil servants are accustomed to following laws with great deference, it proved critical to provide for all the implementation mechanisms within the law and limit discretion. Moreover, with greater exactitude in the law, it is easier to hold government departments to account for failure to properly implement it. In other words, it is easier to demand and get adequate implementation of systems and procedures where the law is clear and specific, with sufficient level of detail, than where it is vague or too general.

Two additional legislation-drafting issues deserve brief mention. First, principles for good record making and records management may be included within the access to information law, particularly when countries lack specific archiving legislation to guide the public administrators. The specifics can be detailed through regulations, but it is helpful to have clear statements of purpose related to information systems as part of the access to information mandate.

Second, the primacy of the ATI law must be clearly stated within the law's text. There is often other extant legislation that deals with information—whether it is on archiving, official secrets, the armed forces, banking, or public administration. Canvassing the multitude of laws that speak to the issue of information would be difficult and time-consuming for both the requester and the civil servant who must respond. Arguably, if a public servant were expected to review each potential law and article related to the subject matter of each request, the response time would be enormous and the result likely to be a denial. To eliminate conflict of laws, promote full implementation, and reduce confusion among stakeholders, it is critical that the access to information law is the overriding legislation. The ATI law should clearly state that it governs all requests and capture all exceptions to release.

The state of Sinaloa, Mexico has one of the most advanced and modern access to information laws in the region. Passed before the federal law, it has been in effect since April 2002. During the initial period of application, the government has identified the failure to explicitly state the primacy of the law as one of its major flaws. Because of the problems and delays encountered, such as confusion and opportunity to subvert the objectives of openness, the implementers are already requesting an amendment or modification to clearly state that in questions of information, the access to information law will govern. The same has proven true in Jamaica, where the Information Officers have joined civil society efforts to amend the Access to Information Act to unquestionably apply as supreme over all requests.

Implementation of the Law

Robust implementation is very difficult to achieve, and thus far insufficient attention has been paid to the multitude of obstacles and potential solutions. As the British minister responsible for its Freedom of Information law argued the year before it came into effect, "Implementation has been beset by three problems. . . . A lack of leadership. Inadequate support for those who are administering access requests. And a failure to realize that Freedom of Information implementation is not an event: it is a process which demands long-term commitment."[14]

The Politics of Implementation

Effective implementation demands political commitment from the top, both to ensure that the necessary resources are allocated and to overcome entrenched mindsets of opacity. The resource demands are significant, particularly in societies where a culture of secrecy has dominated the past and where there are no processes already in place to facilitate the archiving and retrieval of documents.

Most governments are accustomed to working in a secretive fashion. The notion of transparency is invariably far beyond the range of experience and mind-set of most public bureaucrats. Therefore, a fundamental mind shift is necessary, prefaced with political will for a change in approach. The mind-set of opacity is common; it seems that in general, bureaucrats have developed an ingrained sense of ownership about the records for which they are responsible. Releasing them to the public is akin to ceding control and, therefore, power.

Moreover, comprehensive information regimes can take an enormous amount of energy and resources. Daily, governments are faced with a myriad of priorities and the reality that there are not enough resources in the national reserves to meet all demands. In a recent study of efforts to implement the new law in Great Britain, the Constitutional Affairs Committee received a submission from the local government association stating "that resources are the single most important issue in FOI compliance."[15] It went on to explain, "By far the largest issue for local authorities is the lack of resources. They do not have the time, money, or personnel to easily organize information on a corporate basis in order to allow ready retrieval for FOI purposes." In the United States, recent efforts to improve the functioning of the Freedom of Information Act have not been accompanied with additional resources, leading many advocates to question the intention and increasing the potential for their failure.

Thus, once the access to information law is passed, some governments claim credit for the passage but fail to follow through to ensure that the law will succeed in practice. Others, realizing the enormity of the tasks necessary to implement the law, fail to commit the appropriate resources or simply lose interest. Still others that have demonstrated the requisite political will may find it difficult to sustain. The indicators of political will vary from country to country, but some might include the government's preparedness to underpin the right to information in the constitution (as in South Africa and perhaps Bolivia), the government's willingness to accept and encourage citizen participation in the process of writing the law, or the provision of sufficient and continued resource allocations. Whatever the specific method, political will must be signaled clearly and from the very top, if the task of entrenching a new culture of openness is to survive beyond the implementation challenges and for the long term.

In Jamaica, Bolivia, Mali, and Nicaragua, we have had the privilege to lead implementation workshops for senior public servants. In these retreats of department directors, permanent secretaries, and information officers, we asked what would be necessary to ensure adequate implementation. The resounding answer in each country was resource allocation and political will. Interestingly, when asked what would be a demonstration of political will, the civil servants responded, "resource allocation." Unfortunately, in these and many other countries with new information regimes, national and ministerial budgets are not prepared with clear line items for access to information, thus mandating implementers to find monies from other pots, or take on additional responsibilities and costs without an increase in resources. As leading scholar Alasdair Roberts noted in his recent research, "The budget for central guidance of the British FOI implementation effort exceeded the budget of the Jamaican Access to Information Unit (with its staff of four); the government's Archives and Records Department; the other parts of the Prime Minister's Office; and the Jamaican Houses of Parliament—combined."[16]

A major part of the fight for financial resources entails determining the specific needs. This is not a simple task. However, in general, costs for a new information regime include three categories: startup, ongoing, and exceptional. Start-up costs may include a study of the extant archiving and record-keeping system, development of a new archiving system, preliminary training of civil servants, equipment purchases for processing requests, like photocopiers and printers; and expenses related to hiring and setting up a new coordinating unit for information. Ongoing costs would include annual salaries and benefits for information officers, ongoing training related to record keeping and the law, promotional and awareness-raising activities, overhead and rental for related offices, equipment maintenance fees, paper, and other costs related to provision of documents. The exceptional category may cover items such as extraordinary litigation costs or large seminars.

In practice, many of the resources applied toward the needs of an access to information regime are drawn from existing budgeted items. For instance, rather than hire a new staff person, the administration gives already employed civil servants additional responsibilities; computers are used for more than one purpose; or overhead costs are not broken down. Specific cost information is available in only a few countries in the Western Hemisphere, and generally only in those like Mexico, where there is a separate line item in the overall federal budget. However, there are some cost figures that can guide the discussion. For example, in Mexico the first annual budget for the Federal Institute for Access to Information was US$25 million. This provides the "Rolls Royce" version of access to information, such as a brand new building, staff of over 150, and an advanced Internet-based system that would make major corporations jealous. In Mexico, the government expends approximately 0.033 percent of GDP on their access to information regime. Other countries have much more limited expenditures, such as the estimated U.S. 0.0007 percent of GDP or Canada's 0.004 percent.

The political fight for resources is easier to wage when the benefits are quantified, for example, in terms of money saved from reduced corruption. In Buenos Aires a transparency pilot project was initiated in the public hospitals whereby procurements for medical items, such as needles, bandages, surgical gloves, and plastic items were made public. The result was a savings of 50 percent, merely through the publication of contract bids. A similar exercise was conducted for Mexico's largest public university, with a like outcome due to greater transparency. This does not even take into account the benefit of increased foreign investment or increased confidence in government—not to mention greater efficiency in administration. In Mali, a recent internal organization of records of government employees and people receiving government salary demonstrated more than 1,000 "ghost employees" benefiting from government payroll without doing any work. In Uganda, when the amount of monies destined for local schools was made public, the percentage that reached the schools went from an estimated less than 20 percent to more than 80 percent.

Nevertheless, in light of increasing social demands and worsening economies, governments continue to face the political dilemma of servicing the needs of the access to information regime over other programming, and articulating the overall benefit (versus cost) of good governance.

WHO LEADS THE EFFORTS

The choice of agency or individual to implement the new access to information regime is a political decision that may determine whether the law succeeds. Nominating a lead implementer with sufficient seniority, respect, and power will provide the foundational message to other parts of the administration, public service, and civil society that the government is serious in its efforts. As the Canadian Information Officer stated in his annual report to Parliament, the person charged with implementing the access to information must be sufficiently senior that he or she is confident in making the difficult decisions and must carry the weight to encourage others in promoting the objectives of transparency through the release of information. "Good policies . . . need champions if they are to be effectively implemented."[17] In identifying leaders, it is important to cultivate these "champions" at key nodal points in government. The political leadership of people such as Jamaican Carlton Davis or Mignone Vega, Director for Communications for the Presidency of Nicaragua, has assured that implementation efforts of a law or voluntary strategy continue, even in the face of political and logistical obstacles. Placing the key implementer in the ministry of the president or prime minister, as in Jamaica and Nicaragua, increases the likelihood of political support and acquiescence by the other ministries. On the other hand, when implementation is spread across line function ministries, as is the case in South Africa, there is a possibility that peer ministries will ignore directives and that implementation efforts will wane.

In South Africa, the initial impetus for an access to information regime came from the Deputy President's office just one year after the transition to democracy in early 1995, when then Deputy President Thabo Mbeki appointed a task force to produce a white paper on access to information. The task force was high level, including one of Mbeki's most trusted lieutenants and one of the country's most highly regarded human rights scholars. Though its report attracted much attention, as the process of finalizing the law became protracted, the energy of the group dissipated. Ultimately, responsibility for the final passage of the law was transferred to the Ministry of Justice, one of the busiest departments of government and one that has proved singularly ill-equipped to master the challenge of implementation. Political leadership has been conspicuous by its absence. At a meeting between the then Minister of Justice Penual Maduna and a group of visiting deputies from Armenia in January 2003, the minister appeared ill-briefed on the implementation of the law and informed his visitors that his department was fully complying and had not been the subject of any appeals. This was inaccurate. Not only have there been several appeals against refusal, but his department was at the time the subject of two pieces of litigation under the act. This absence of leadership in implementation, seen also in Belize and Trinidad and Tobago, has led to inconsistent implementation and compliance with the law.

PUBLIC SERVANTS: ON THE FRONT LINE

Public servants are on the front line of implementation. These critical stakeholders must be engaged early and strategically in the process of establishing and implementing the law. Ultimately, this constituency will be responsible for making the law meaningful for users—and have the power to either facilitate the process or create unnecessary roadblocks.

Civil servants, as the face of government, have grown accustomed to being blamed for all range of problems and citizens' grievances; although they have no control over policy decisions, they are tasked with implementation. Moreover, public functionaries often must contend with contradictory roles and responsibilities and competing interests. An access to information law can add to the dissonance, as coordinators "on occasion, experience an uncomfortable conflict between their responsibilities under the access to information act and their career prospects within their institution."[18]

However, as developing democracies seek to professionalize public service, tools such as access to information can support this objective. In Bolivia during a recent workshop on access to information implementation, the civil servants identified an access to information law as a means of protecting themselves from arbitrary decision making by politicians and a way to diminish untoward political pressures. These more senior public functionaries also listed such benefits as increasing efficiency, reducing bureaucracy, and identifying and eliminating bottlenecks.

In Jamaica, the civil service association recognized the opportunity the access to information law provided to enhance customer service and more clearly demonstrate who was responsible for poor policy choices, i.e., the political masters. Thus, Mr. Wayne Jones, the President of the Civil Service Association, accepted a lead role in promoting the passage and implementation of a comprehensive access to information law. The union's stance also has led to greater buy-in from the relevant front line workers.

Government System Building: Developing the Supply Side

Governments must establish the internal systems and processes to generate and provide information and training of civil servants to ensure understanding and compliance—the mechanics of the supply side.

RECORD KEEPING AND ARCHIVING

If there are no records to be found, or they are so unorganized that locating them becomes an insurmountable obstacle, the best access to information law is meaningless. In order to respond to requests, an adequate information management system must be designed and established. This is not an easy task.[19]

Many countries that have recently passed ATI laws, such as Mexico and Peru, have rather precarious record-keeping traditions. In countries with previously authoritarian governments, such as South Africa, many records have been lost or deliberately destroyed. Government officials in Argentina tell of their difficulty in receiving documents necessary to complete their work, often due to inadequate record keeping and organization systems. In 2002, an analysis was undertaken by the Anticorruption Office (AO) of Argentina to determine the prevalence of civil servants receiving multiple paychecks. The AO found that the greatest obstacle to assessing and stopping this illegal practice that was costing the country millions of dollars was the lack of a functioning database and systematized records.[20] It proved nearly impossible to get the most basic information on the number of positions and the names of those employed in them.

Governments generate millions of tons of paper each year. In some countries, a lack of record-keeping processes and space constraints have translated into huge bonfires of critical documents. Until a few years ago, Bolivia burned most of the more than 192 tons of paper that the executive branch generated each year. In other countries, such as Jamaica, where there has been a long history of secrecy but emphasis on document retention (both passed down from the British colonial rule that ended 40 years ago), "the practice of retaining all records created contributed to the congestion in the system, as dormant and obsolete records were shelved with current files, further compounding the problem of timely retrieval."[21]

In many places, until the advent of access to information regimes, national archivists and record keepers had been considered more akin to untrained secretaries than to degreed professionals, and were not provided the resources or respect necessary to fulfill their mandate. As one records manager stated, "Traditionally, record-keeping in the Jamaican public service has been an arcane and often overlooked field. Records management continues to be perceived as a low-level administrative/clerical function, largely focused on the management of public records at the end of their life cycle (i.e. the disposition phase)."[22]

In fact, in many government agencies, the secretary was responsible for filing and maintaining all critical documents. However, as computers have become more commonplace, secretarial staff have been reduced, further depleting record-keeping resources.[23] A recent report of the United States Interagency Committee on Government Information addressed the need to improve accountability for records management. The report highlighted the "low priority assigned to information and records management" and recommended that "agencies must have an expectation that their actions have important positive or negative consequences, and there needs to be an effective mechanism for evaluating agency actions."[24] The committee suggested that appropriate incentives be established for proper management and protection of records as "valuable Government assets."

Perhaps more damaging to the establishment and maintenance of files is the widespread misconception by civil servants and elected officials that the documents they generate belong to them. We have heard this view from Argentina to Bolivia to Jamaica and Belize, all the way to the U.S. state of Georgia. Thus, when leaving their post or retiring, they take the files home with them—and they are forever lost to the archiving system.

Even when past documents are available, the task of ordering them is monumental, and potentially unrealizable. In terms of human and financial resources, the start-up costs can become astronomical for the organization of hundreds of years of documents. Rather than allow this to become an insurmountable obstacle to the government's willingness to pass the law, some advocates pragmatically suggest that in the initial stages of an information regime, governments ignore past documents and establish an archiving system for future information. In terms of citizen needs, often the contemporary documents such as budgets, policy decisions related to education and health, and information on crime and justice are of greatest value. Governments concerned with scarce resource allocation, such as Nicaragua, have considered focusing their record-keeping reforms on current and future generated documents, and then, over time, ordering the vast quantity of historical information.

Electronic documents have created a new set of problems and needs for record keeping and archiving. A comparative study of the implementation of access to information laws in the Commonwealth of Australia, New South Wales, Queensland, and New Zealand found that "across all four jurisdictions, we encountered concern bordering on alarm at the implications of the growth of email. We encountered few examples of systematic filing and destruction of email, nor of any central protocols for how emails should be stored."[25] As the modern trend of electronic communication and documentation continues, record-keeping systems will need to respond.

Part of this process of organizing and identifying records involves the creation of "road maps" of the documents that exist. This is as important for the holders of information as it is for the potential requesters. Without knowing what records there are and where they are located, an implementation regime seems unlikely to be anything other than frustrating for both holders and requesters. Six months after the Jamaican law came into effect, senior civil servants stated that one of the greatest advantages of the law, thus far, was their own increased knowledge of government and the records that various agencies hold. For this reason, many modern ATI laws such as the South African, Mexican, Trinidadian, and Jamaican include provisions mandating the creation of such "road maps."

Record keeping—the management of documents on a daily basis—is inextricably linked to the archiving of historical or critical information. Unfortunately, in some countries the archival laws are inconsistent with modern record-keeping systems (particularly in relation to electronic records) or conflict with access to information laws. In Jamaica, for example, the archivist has discretion whether to release documents, and the decision is not based on public interest or principles of transparency. Thus, there also exists a need to ensure consistency within the record management policies. As the U.S. electronic records policy working group has pointed out, "To be accountable for information and records management requirements, agencies must have a clear understanding of what needs to be done and how to do it. . . . If agencies are provided with a clear set of standards that are made understandable through the educational opportunities and there are effective mechanisms for evaluating agency actions, the odds for a successful outcome are significantly improved."[26]

RECORD MAKING

There is no value in a right to access to information if no reliable document exists. Record-making standards also must develop and mature. One Bolivian public administration expert commented that most of the documents presently generated by his government are trash, created simply to satisfy some administrative requirement with no clear understanding by the public servant of its use or importance: "That which is certain is that the public entities generate and accumulate incalculable volumes of information that for the most part have no utility from the perspective of efficacy, efficiency, and economy of its operations."[27]

On the other end of the spectrum, as governments become aware of the depth and breadth of information that is open to the public, there is sometimes a backlash to information generation. Fear of embarrassment or mistakes may portend the rise of "cell phone governance." Important policy decisions are made at lunches, made via telephone, or simply not recorded. An Arkansas appeals court recently ruled that the Fort Smith board of directors and city administrator violated the state's freedom of information act and open meetings provisions when a decision to purchase property was made via telephone. The court found that telephone conversations are a "meeting" under the terms of the act, holding that "It is obvious that [the board's] actions resulted in a consensus being reached on a given issue, thus rendering the formal meeting held before the public a mere charade. . . . By no reasonable construction can the FOIA be read to permit governmental decision-makers to engage in secret deal-making."[28]

As this practice becomes more common, access to information laws will need to respond with more detailed provisions for record making. Similar to the rule-making procedures in the United States and the Financial Management and Accountability Act of 1997 in Australia, to curtail the deleterious effects of cell phone governance, policy makers must be mandated to keep records that, at a minimum, detail who made a decision, when, and why, and list the relevant sources used.[29]

AUTOMATIC PUBLICATION

The best approach for dealing with vast amounts of information is simply to make as many records as possible automatically and unconditionally available. This limits the need for government decision making and is therefore less of a drain on resources. Moreover, it is clearly better for the "demand side," as proactive disclosure reduces the number of requests and delay in information receipt. Indeed, the best implementation model is not only to categorize as much information as possible as automatically disclosable but also to publish the information at the point the record is created. This is what in the freedom of information lexicon is known as the "right to know" (RTK) approach. Information and communication technologies makes this easier and cheaper. In Peru, for example, during the transitional authority in 2001 when greater transparency was a watchword of the interim government, the Department of Finance led the way with a Web site-based approach to transparency, publishing huge volumes of information. A focus on automatic publication through the Internet has continued, with the National Office of Anticorruption tasked with monitoring the development of public body Web sites and periodically issuing reports. The most recent report, the sixth of the series, found that all government ministries were in compliance with the automatic publication provisions of the access to information law, and 37.3 percent of the decentralized public agencies were in full compliance. In comparison, in the municipalities there was only 2.1 percent complete compliance.[30]

Clearly, using government Web sites is an important way of adopting an RTK approach, but there are dangers too. It should not be seen as a panacea, especially in the developing world, where few people have access to the Internet.[31] Moreover, with the changing technologies, even the most current advances may quickly become outdated. Thus, any electronic record-keeping or publication scheme should be seen as a companion to hard copies and traditional publication, rather than as a substitute. Finally, one must be vigilant that governments not interpret automatic publication requirements as license to make whole databases or reams of documents available without organization and consideration—making it impossible for interested people to understand and use.

INTERNAL SYSTEMS

Internal Procedures (the "Internal Law"). It is crucial that governments develop—and users understand—clear guidelines for the civil servants charged with implementing the law. To ensure consistency and efficiency in implementation, the guidelines should cover records management, assessment of requests for information, provision of documents, and interpretation of the law.

For users, applying to access the record of the internal system is one way of discovering the extent to which a government agency is taking the implementation issue seriously.[32] Things to look for would be training and the development of a manual for line managers and information officers and/or their units, and internal rules relating to good practice and important procedural matters such as compliance with time limits. Also, there should be a thorough internal system for recording requests, such as an electronic database that can itself by subjected to public and parliamentary scrutiny.

Given its history and role in the oppression perpetrated by the apartheid state, it is somewhat surprising and ironic that of the twenty-six national government departments in South Africa, the Department of Defence has shown the greatest commitment to implementing the law properly. A Johannesburg-based NGO, the South African History Archive (SAHA), already had discovered that Defence was performing surprisingly well when, in contrast to other departments, it dealt with many of the requests SAHA submitted efficiently and courteously. SAHA's diagnosis accorded with that of the OSI study and ODAC (Open Democracy Advice Centre)'s own assessment. The Department of Defence had put in place a number of specific steps to implement the act that could be emulated in other agencies, including:

- a manual and implementation plan;
- a register of all requests;
- human resource allocation to the Promotion of Access to Information Act (PAIA) even though there is no special budget;
- designation of the CEO as the Information Officer and all division chiefs as Deputy Information Officers, with assistants handling PAIA requests;
- establishment of a PAIA subcommittee that deals with major issues—e.g., disclosing information on arms procurement contracts, sensitive information, and large-volume requests;
- provincial departments sending the requests to the head office to process.

In contrast, bodies performing badly either had not instituted systems or had systems that were not functioning.[33]

Information Officers and Training. In addition to internal systems, there is a need for line managers responsible for implementation and responding to requests. Most modern ATI laws create information officers or similar positions. In Canada, access to information coordinators has been the backbone of implementation and administration efforts. Similarly, the Mexican, Peruvian, and draft Bolivian and Nicaraguan access to information acts call for the establishment of designated information units or officers in each public body to serve as the front line respondents assisting applicants.

One obvious indicator of the strength of implementation is whether such officials have in fact been appointed and whether they have received specialist training.[34] A comparative study of four commonwealth jurisdictions found that "there was universal agreement that a significant investment had to be made in training," which should "encompass both general staff (at all levels) and FOI coordinators/specialists (where such existed)."[35] Moreover, training should not end when the law goes into effect. Staff changes, lessons learned, and amendments to internal policies and procedures dictate the need for continual training of information officers and other relevant civil servants.

The public needs to know whom to contact and how to reach them. Most modern ATI laws include such requirements. The South African law, for example, requires government to have the name and contact details of the information and deputy information officers listed in all telephone directories.

These information officers can work together, through the establishment of networks or working groups, to share best practices and lessons learned. In Jamaica, the information officers meet periodically and serve as a mutual support system. Such networks also serve to demonstrate the value and professionalism of the position.

Implementation Plan: The Value of Strategic Planning and Consensus Building. If governments are wise, they will consult with the potential user community when they draw up their implementation plan. One of the causes for optimism in the Jamaican case is that despite its government's historical culture of secrecy, the access to information implementation unit carried out a consultancy exercise with civil society in August 2002, soon after the law was passed, and again in March 2003.[36] This process enabled government officials to share, in a positive and confidential setting, their own concerns with colleagues across government and individuals from civil society, and afforded the latter group an opportunity to develop a better understanding of the obstacles facing civil servants and to hold them to account.

The first workshop asked the simple question: What needs to happen to effectively implement the new access to information law? The workshop identified a lack of political will and resources—human and financial—as the chief obstacles to effective implementation. The second workshop focused on prioritizing key activities. It found that some aspects, such as the appointment and training of access to information officers and passage of the necessary regulations to operationalize the act, had been neglected. These sessions of shared experiences and problem solving allowed government to take the necessary decision to postpone implementation with less fear of civil society reprisal.

As the Jamaica example demonstrates, it is often managerial weaknesses rather than flagging political will that slows implementation or creates the greatest obstacles. The delay in putting the Jamaica law into effect had much more to do with lack of preparedness than government fear. In Great Britain, Parliament heard evidence from government departments that a failure to share best practice across sectors led to delays and inconsistent messages.[37] Identifying key managerial or logistical weaknesses, sharing lessons learned, and providing consistent guidance will allow administrators to apply resources more wisely, in a focused and efficient manner.

Specialized ATI Implementation Oversight and Coordination Units. Specialized units and oversight bodies have proven critical to ensuring full implementation and compliance with the law. "Without a continuous oversight body, government efforts are dispersed and diluted with no clarity in responsibilities or guidelines and reduced ability to conduct long-term planning and to promote best practices, thus costing governments more in terms of human and financial resources."[38] Moreover, when there is no implementation monitoring and coordinating body, users are forced to navigate the systems on their own and public servants are burdened with additional responsibilities, but often must handle them with less training and resources.[39]

For that reason, countries such as Mexico, Jamaica, and Canada have established access to information units or oversight commissions responsible for assisting and monitoring implementation, raising awareness about the new right to information, and providing a clear focal point for all efforts. A designated specialist unit, such as the Mexican Federal Institute for Access to Information (IFAI) or the Jamaican Access to Information Unit, allows the government to provide a uniform and focused response to problems and demonstrates clear commitment. In contrast, in Peru, each ministry or agency is to have a designated access to information person, but there is no federal coordinating body. In the United States, agencies set their own policy, creating a patchwork system and uneven implementation of the law that provides users vastly different experiences across government. In South Africa, no special unit has been established to oversee implementation; the responsibility for the ATI law has been simply added to the long list of responsibilities ordinarily carried by the director-general (permanent secretary) of each line function ministry or agency.

The IFAI has a mandate emanating from the access to information law, whereas the Jamaica unit was created spontaneously as a means for addressing all implementation issues. As the IFAI is authorized by statute, it is a "legal" body and has enjoyed a budget sufficient to meet its objectives and tasks. This has not been the case for Jamaica, where the ATI Unit has been dependent on monies from the Information Minister in the Office of the Prime Minister, and its existence depends on the good will of the minister.

Experience has demonstrated that specialized coordination units are necessary beyond the implementation phase, particularly for education, training, and monitoring. In Trinidad and Tobago, the Freedom of Information Act went into force on February 20, 2001. Shortly thereafter, a Freedom of Information (FOI) Unit was established to provide technical and legal guidance to government bodies, raise citizen awareness of the new law, and monitor and report on implementation efforts. The Cabinet initially authorized the FOI Unit for one year and then extended it until September 30, 2003, when the unit was disbanded. Even before its termination, the size of the staff was being reduced. Although there have been no quantitative studies to determine the effect of the unit's discontinuance, some statistics serve to indicate its importance and continued need. In the period of August–November 2001, when the FOI Unit was active in training civil servants and educating citizens, there were 37 requests for information and 88 quarterly reports received from government, representing 55 percent of all agencies mandated to submit reports. For the same period in 2002, when the unit was still engaged, there were 63 requests for in-formation and 32 reports received, representing 20 percent of all agencies. By November 2003, when the contract of the last member of the unit expired, there had been only 6 information requests, and a mere 8 percent of all agencies were still complying with the reporting requirements.

Civil Servant Sanctions and Incentives. Political will within a democratic framework and managerial effectiveness within a bureaucracy both re-quire clear incentives for action and disincentives for inaction. In all access to information laws in Latin America and the Caribbean, as well as in South Africa, sanctions exist for any public servant who destroys, alters, or damages documents or provides exempt documents contrary to the provisions of the law. What is less common are explicit disincen-tives (sanctions) for those who fail to meet implementation deadlines, delay provision of documents to requesters, or create unwarranted dif-ficulties for users. The draft Bolivian law has added sanctions for these "process" and implementation-related failures, as well as for document-ed related illegal actions. The Canadian government, as it considers amendments to its twenty-year law, has recommended adding penalties for failure to respect deadlines. In Great Britain, senior managers were named to lead the implementation effort and oversee the efforts of the FOI officers. Months before the law was to go into full effect, the British Parliament heard that "many FOI officers were having difficulty get-ting senior managers to take the requirements of FOI implementation seriously . . . One explanation has been that the penalties for non-com-pliance are not clear."[40]

But rewards for good behavior are just as important. In Canada, the Treasury Board, which is responsible for ensuring continued implementation of the federal access to information law, has begun a system of public awards and certificates for exemplary civil ser-vants. Additional incentives would include pay raises based on per-formance evaluations that contain specific implementation criteria, promotions, and bonuses.

Phased-in Effectiveness of Law. The establishment of processes and the necessary mind shift from the culture of secrecy to openness takes an enormous amount of time and energy. The pressure on governments to implement access to information laws quickly is unfortunate. In Jamaica,

Mexico, Peru, and South Africa, the governments gave themselves one year or less to put the law into effect. In each case, they soon discovered the many obstacles. Although most of these countries pushed through the implementation in the prescribed time, many of the necessary procedural details had not been resolved. In Jamaica, the government was forced to postpone the date the law would come into effect three times and amended the enabling legislation to allow for phased commencement.

Given that a stumbling start may undermine a law's legitimacy, longer lead times for implementation are preferable. The time period must be long enough to build public-sector capacity and inform citizens of their rights, but not so long as to reduce momentum or make the government appear to be faltering in the commitment to transparency, as occurred during the UK's five-year implementation period. During this phase, government will generally focus on establishing procedures, passing regulations, and preparing or updating record management.

But government leaders and civil society groups need to ensure that a longer lead time is not used for mass record destruction. In Japan, a "surge in the destruction of documents eligible for disclosure under the Freedom of Information Law by 10 central government offices" was reported in the lead up to the law coming into effect. The report claims that, for example, "the agriculture ministry scrapped 233 tons of documents in fiscal 2000, a 20-fold increase on the 11 tons destroyed in fiscal 1999."[41]

A potentially successful model for implementation is a phased-in system whereby the law becomes effective first in a few key ministries and agencies and then is phased in over a specified period of time until all of government is online. This approach creates models that can be more easily amended or altered to address emerging problems, before they overwhelm the entire information system. As Maurice Frankel of the Campaign for the Freedom of Information in Great Britain told a Constitutional Affairs Committee reporting on Britain's progress toward implementation, "I think [the big bang approach] is bad verging on potentially catastrophic . . . central government could have done this much earlier, had a lot of experience . . . and could have dealt with a lot of the problems which are going to come up relatively easily. Instead of that, every single authority in every sector is confronting the same problem simultaneously with no opportunity to learn from anybody."[42]

During the initial phase, responsible civil servants should meet regularly to discuss systems capability and lessons learned, and ensure that these are widely shared and applied by the next set of agencies in which the law goes into effect. The government should capitalize on this time to complete and approve any necessary regulations and internal policies. And interested NGOs and citizens should become more familiar with the law's value and defects, make requests, learn how to effectively monitor government implementation efforts, and engage positively with the first-round implementers.

A potential disadvantage to the phased-in approach is that governments may choose to put nonessential ministries or unimportant agencies in the first round of implementation, thus sending a signal that they are not serious about transparency. Alternatively, they may find that citizens are making more requests than expected or soliciting the most sensitive and embarrassing information. This reality check could cause the government to delay further implementation. Moreover, citizens may become frustrated as requests are transferred to government entities not yet in effect. Therefore, in a phased-in approach, we encourage timelines for each phase to be established as part of the enacting legislation or regulations, clear rules relating to transfer of requests to "non-phased in" bodies, and intense public education explaining the approach.

Sustaining the Demand Side

Although the focus of this chapter is the "supply side," without an equivalent demand for information, government will inevitably stop directing human and financial resources toward the implementation and administration of an access to information regime. Thus, the response from civil society needs to be energetic, committed, and long term. Through recent experience, we have seen that strong campaigns have formed around the issue of passage of the law, only to disintegrate during the implementation and usage phase. Without a demand for information and vigorous monitoring of government implementation and enforcement efforts, the hard-won right to information can quickly atrophy.

Thus, notwithstanding the distinct obstacles to effective usage in South Africa exposed by the OSI study (see above), demand for access to information through the law remains and is led by the ODAC, alongside other NGOs such as SAHA and the Treatment Action Campaign (TAC). For example, painstaking effort by the field-workers of the ODAC has shown how ATI can make a material difference in the lives of poor people. In Kouga, in rural Western Cape, despite a ministerial decision to allocate resources, the municipality had "borrowed" for another area the forty houses that had been earmarked for one community. Pressing for access to the minutes from the meeting at which the decision was made by the municipality led to a reversal of the decision. In Emkhandwini in remote Kwa-Zulu Natal, the villages wanted clean water; they were tired of the five-mile trek to collect it from the nearest town. The municipality was arrogant: the villages had no right to any information about water access. ODAC pressed the District Council, and it was revealed that there was a plan: to phase in piped water over five years, with a weekly delivery by truck of a large barrel of clean water in the interim. It was a good plan; the villagers were content. ATI, properly implemented, can be good for government as well as citizens. By corollary, secrecy, as the Emkhandwini case shows, is harmful to both.[43]

Conclusion

The challenges that face countries wanting to implement access to information policies include a lack of education and awareness, a lack of capacity, a lack of political will, and a culture of bureaucratic secrecy. As this list demonstrates and this chapter asserts, although there are technical aspects to good implementation, it is not simply a question of getting the mechanics right. Adjusting the mind-set—changing, as they say in Spanish, the *mentalidad* (the mentality)—is a far more important and challenging priority for policy makers and activists alike. The obstacles are immense and the pitfalls many, but the rewards equally monumental. But as our own understanding of the theory and practice of good implementation grows, so the capacity to diagnose implementation problems increases immeasurably. Properly implemented, an access to information law can change the rules of the game not just for civil society but also for government, and serve to enhance democratic politics.

1. See Article 19 Model Law and Socius Peru 2003, British Council.

2. One of the authors, Richard Calland, participated in the development, testing, and refinement of the methodology. The Open Democracy Advice Centre, Cape Town, coordinated the South African part of the survey in 2003, and in 2004 coordinated the African regional portion that includes six countries: South Africa, Mozambique, Kenya, Senegal, Nigeria, and Ghana. The five countries included in the pilot study were South Africa, Macedonia, Bulgaria, Peru, and Armenia. The pilot study was refined and in 2004 the first full study was conducted in sixteen countries. At the time of writing, the findings were not yet available.

3. Macedonia, which did not have an ATI law, applied a twenty-day time limit for the purpose of the exercise, above the international average of fifteen days.

4. Open Society Institute, Justice Initiative, "Access to Information Tool: Overview 2003," unpublished paper.

5. Open Society Institute, Justice Initiative, "Access to Information in the Republic of South Africa, Access to Information Tool: South Africa 2003," www.opendemocracy.org.za.

6. In the authors' work in Bolivia, we often heard of the failure to implement well-drafted laws. Moreover, one scholar suggested that his country, Ecuador, counts more than 800,000 laws, as none are removed from the books. According to him, only a small percentage of these laws are implemented and enforced.

7. For a more detailed account on the passage of the law in Jamaica, see Laura Neuman, "The Carter Center Access to Information Project: Jamaica Case Study," in Laura Neuman, ed., *Access to Information: A Key to Democracy* (Atlanta, GA: The Carter Center, 2002).

8. For a more detailed account of the campaign, see Mukelani Dimba, "A Landmark Law Opens Up Post-Apartheid South Africa" (2002), http://www.freedominfo.org/reports/safrica1.htm.

9. The authors of this paper visited Belize in 2003 and had the opportunity to meet with civil society leaders, media representatives, and members of government and opposition parties to discuss the Freedom of Information Act of Belize.

10. For a more detailed account of the Zimbabwe situation, see Article 19/MISA-Zimbabwe, "The Access to Information and Protection of Privacy Act: Two Years On," 2004.

11. See America for the Sanction of Access to Information Law in Argentina, a campaign led by Poder Ciudadano and other leading Argentine NGOs such as el Centro de Estudios Legales y Sociales and el Centro de Implementacion de Politicas Publicas para la Equidad y el Crecimiento, as well as media and environmental NGOs, which called on interested actors throughout the region to send letters to the Argentine Senate requesting the passage of the access to information law. More information regarding the campaign is available from http://www.poderciudadano.org, or in English from http://www.redinter.org/InfoRID/22538.

12. Yashwantrao Chavan Academy of Development Administration (YASHADA), Action Research Project; see "Prune Newsline," *The Indian Express,* December 15, 2004.

13. IFTI Watch Update, "World Bank Poised for Breakthrough on Disclosing Draft Documents" (2004), http://www.freedominfo.org/ifti/worldbank/20040528.htm.

14. House of Commons Constitutional Affairs Committee, "Freedom of Information Act 2000—Progress Towards Implementation," vol. 1, November 30, 2004, quoting Lord Falconer of Thornton, speech to Campaign for Freedom of Information, March 1, 2004. Available from The Department of Constitutional Affairs, http://www.dca.gov.uk/foi/bkgrndact.htm#top.

15. House of Commons Constitutional Affairs Committee, "Freedom of Information Act 2000—Progress Towards Implementation," vol. 1, November 30, 2004. Available from The Department of Constitutional Affairs, http://www.dca.gov.uk/foi/bkgrndact.htm#top.

16. Alasdair Roberts, *Blacked Out: Government Secrecy in the Information Age* (New York: Cambridge University Press, 2006).

17. Office of the Information Commissioner of Canada, *Annual Report Information Commissioner 2001–2002* (2002). See Chapter I: Performance Overview.

18. Office of the Information Commissioner of Canada, *Annual Report Information Commissioner 2000–2001* (2001). See Chapter III: v) Recognizing, Fostering, and Protecting the Coordinators.

19. "Good recordkeeping is a pre-requisite for the successful administration of the Access to Information Act as well as a central component of good governance." See Office of the Information Commissioner of Canada, *Annual Report Information Commissioner 2002–2003* (2003). See Chapter II: Addressing the Crises in Information Management.

20. Nestor Baragli, "Acceso a la Información y la Lucha Contra Corrupción" (Access to Information and the Fight Against Corruption), in *La*

Promoción de Democracia a Través del Acceso a la Información: Bolivia (The Promotion of Democracy Through Access to Information: Bolivia) (Atlanta, GA: The Carter Center, 2004).

21. H. Rumbolt, "Challenges and Successes in Implementing the Access to Information Act in Jamaica," in Laura Neuman, ed., *Access to Information: Building a Culture of Transparency* (Atlanta, GA: The Carter Center, 2006).

22. Emerson St. G. Bryan, "The Records and Information Management Profession: The View from Within the Jamaican Public Service," *ACARM Newsletter* 33 (2002).

23. Interview with Robert Bohanan, United States Archivist, May 2004.

24. Electronic Records Policy Working Group (Michael Kurtz, Chair), *Recommendations for the Effective Management of Government Information on the Internet and Other Electronic Records* (2004).

25. Edward Adams and Andrew Ecclestone, *Implementation of the Freedom of Information Act 2000, Study Visit to Australia and New Zealand.* Report submitted to Department of Constitutional Affairs, United Kingdom, 2003.

26. Electronic Records Policy Working Group, *Recommendations*.

27. Antonio Birbuet Díaz, "Public Administration and Access to Information in Bolivia," in Laura Neuman ed., *The Promotion of Democracy Through Access to Information: Bolivia* (Atlanta, GA: The Carter Center, 2004).

28. *Harris vs. City of Fort Smith*, Arkansas Court of Appeals, 2004.

29. Financial Management and Accountability Act of 1997.

30. Comisión Nacional Anticorrucpción, *Informe No.6: Monitoreo a Portales de Transparencia de la Administración Pública* (Lima: Comisión Nacional Anticorrupción, 2004).

31. Although the Peruvian report documents government compliance, it does not provide any data on the number of users or "hits."

32. At the time of writing, the Open Democracy Advice Centre, South Africa, is awaiting the response to Right to Information requests made to all government departments and other important public sector entities (around 100 in total) for access to their internal policy documents relating to the implementation of the South African law (PAIA).

33. Open Society Institute, Justice Initiative, "Access to Information in the Republic of South Africa, Access to Information Tool: South Africa 2003," www.opendemocracy.org.za.

34. ARTICLE 19, "Principles on Freedom of Information Legislation, Principle 3, Promotion of Open Government Sresses the Importance of Training Inside Government Bodies" (London: ARTICLE 19, 1999). See also ARTICLE 19, Chapter 4, "Raising Awareness and Educating the Pub-

lic and Duty-holders about the FOIA Rights and Obligations in Promoting Practical Access to Democracy—A Survey of Freedom of Information in Central and Eastern Europe" (London: ARTICLE 19, October 2002).

35. Adams and Ecclestone, *Implementation.*

36. The authors facilitated this process as a part of the Carter Center's Access to Information Project.

37. House of Commons Constitutional Affairs Committee, "Freedom of Information Act 2000—Progress Towards Implementation," vol. 1, November 30, 2004. Available from The Department of Constitutional Affairs, http://www.dca.gov.uk.foi/bkgrndact.htm#top.

38. Laura Neuman, "Mechanisms for Monitoring and Enforcing the Right to Information Around the World," in Laura Neuman ed., *Access to Information: Building a Culture of Secrecy* (Atlanta, GA: The Carter Center, 2006).

39. Ibid.

40. House of Commons Constitutional Affairs Committee, "Freedom of Information Act 2000—Progress Towards Implementation," vol. 1, November 30, 2004. Available from The Department of Constitutional Affairs, http://www.dca.gov.uk.foi/bkgrndact.htm#top.

41. "Leap in Records Scrapped Prior to FOI," *Yomiuri Shimbun,* 2004. Available in English from http://foia.blogspot.com/2004/12/japan-leap-in-records-scrapped-prior.html and in Japanese from http://www.yomiuri.co.jp/newse/20041209woo1.htm.

42. House of Commons Constitutional Affairs Committee, "Freedom of Information Act 2000—Progress Towards Implementation," vol. 1, November 30, 2004. Available from The Department of Constitutional Affairs, http://www.dca.gov.uk.foi/bkgrndact.htm#top.

43. Open Democracy Advice Centre, "Five Years On: The Right to Know in South Africa" (Cape Town, April 2006).

Chapter Seven

Prizing Open
the Profit-Making World

Richard Calland

Transparency is now a generally accepted norm for the democratic state, understood to be essential for democracy, of significant instrumental value in enhancing efficiency in public administration, and crucial to the effective exercise of other rights.[1] There has been a huge amount of activity and progress in recent years, with government action matching civil society activism to promote the right to know. More than fifty laws creating some sort of legal right to access public information have been passed since 1995.[2]

This focus on the public sector leaves out large, and growing, amounts of relevant and important information held by private entities. For while the case for transparency in the public sphere has been successfully made and in many places implemented, public power has seeped into a new range of institutions and bodies. Because of the massive trend toward privatization, goods and services once provided by the state, or at least considered to be state responsibilities, are now provided by private firms under various arrangements with governments. As Roberts notes, in the last quarter of the twentieth century "authority has flowed out of the now-familiar bureaucracy and into a new array of quasi-governmental and private bodies. The relocation of authority has provoked another doctrinal crisis: the old system of administrative controls, built to suit a world in which public power was located within government departments and agencies, no longer seems to fit contemporary realities."[3] Like archaeologists who finally locate the buried tomb of Egyptian King Rameses II but, when they prize open the door, find that the riches within have been long since looted, advocates for government transparency will now find that much public information has been spirited away into the hands of the private sector.

In addition, there is growing awareness that the public effects of many private sector activities (e.g., environmental effects) warrant public scrutiny, and disclosure is increasingly seen as a potentially effective regulatory tool. Many corporations have begun to operate voluntary disclosure regimes in response to civil society demands and the "corporate social responsibility" (CSR) context. Yet disclosure of private-sector information is haphazard at best, with little consensus on what business should be required to disclose. This presents a significant challenge to the advocates for transparency, from both an instrumental and a philosophical, human rights–based perspective.

These two issues—privatization and the trend toward disclosure of environmental, labor, and other information in the CSR context—raise powerful questions. Should corporations that are playing quasi-public roles and providing public goods and services be held to the same standards of public transparency and accountability as their public sector brethren? Does voluntary disclosure of environmental and other social impact information adequately fill the existing regulatory gap, or should such disclosures be standardized and made mandatory? Who decides, and on what basis?

This chapter addresses these questions in turn. It lays out the history of and reasoning behind corporate secrecy and describes the trends that have occasionally pushed for greater openness. It then takes in turn the concerns raised by privatization and by civil society demands for greater corporate social responsibility. It explores the rapidly changing legal regimes concerning corporate transparency in many parts of the world, with special attention to the case of South Africa, one of the few countries that specifically extends its right-to-know law to cover the private sector.

The (Old) Case for Corporate Secrecy and the Shift Toward Disclosure

Corporations are bureaucracies, and as such are prone to adopt a culture of secrecy, as often a matter of subconscious impulse as deliberate strategy or policy. As Max Weber argued in his classic essay on bureaucracy, a preoccupation with secrecy is an inherent characteristic. As Weber also notes, secrecy has tended to be regarded by managers and directors as a major power resource in maintaining a competitive advantage over rival organizations.[4] As more farsighted corporations have come to recognize, however, this may be a counterproductive approach. While the control of information may be the *sine qua non* of twentieth-century corporations, as J. K. Galbraith asserted, the modern view is more likely to see disclosure as good for *competition* rather than for *the competition*. Secrecy is the friend of unfair or uneven market access; in contrast, openness supports the search for fair and competitive markets.

The old case for corporate secrecy is built mainly on the dated model for the profit-making world generally. The private sector makes profits, along the way creating jobs and wealth as well as providing goods and services people want, and governments regulate corporate activities to protect workers, communities, shareholders, and the environment. Corporate law, at least in the Anglo-Saxon world, explicitly forbids corporations to pursue anything else but their own self-interest: "Corporate social responsibility is illegal—at least when it is genuine."[5] But the model is breaking down. Not only was it never very effective at reining in corporations, as a long line of corporate scandals, most recently at Enron and Worldcom, shows, but it is even less effective in the current era of new globalization, where corporations can "shop" for the least onerous regulations and many governments lack the capacity to enforce regulation.

Disclosure in the private sector raises many of the same questions as it does in the public sector. To further the debate on for-profit transparency, it is important to recognize the legitimate concerns of business and the origins of its traditional preference for secrecy over openness. There are also reasonable concerns about cost and the potential damage to reputation that disclosure might cause. And it is important to recognize that secrecy may serve not only the narrow self-interest of the corporation but also, indirectly perhaps, the interests of society. Some degree of corporate secrecy is necessary to protect concerns touching the general interest: incentives for innovation, the functioning of the market, the integrity of the decision-making process, and personal privacy.[6]

Mary Graham, in her book *Democracy by Disclosure*, characterizes the case for secrecy—or the conflict between competing values and interests, as she puts it—in a similar way, but with important sense of nuance. As with public/government information, there is a spectrum. Some information should clearly be withheld: releasing information about a planned police raid on an organized crime syndicate beforehand would incontrovertibly not be in the public interest. Equally, at the other end of the spectrum, many pieces of information clearly should be provided because no possible or conceivable harm to the public interest could be contemplated.

Thus, the real debate, as with public information, is in the middle ground—the gray areas of information. Corporations have long considered information of this sort as proprietary: "This is a private company, therefore, ipso facto, this information is mine/ours and not yours. I have no duty to disclose it." This attitude can be traced back to the history of corporations and later developments in jurisprudence that encouraged a culture of secrecy by "humanizing" the corporation.

Early corporations of the commercial sort—such as the Dutch East India Company—were formed under legal frameworks by state governments to undertake tasks that appeared too risky or too expensive for individuals or governments. Corporations were therefore created as an extension of the government, chartered by the monarch (and later the state) to "promote the general welfare." Corporations were given privileges such as limited liability because their sole purpose was to improve civic life through such enterprises as building highways and postal service. In short, the public, through its elected representatives in government, created corporations and granted them special legal status. Limited liability proved to be especially important; the role of the for-profit world expanded drastically as a result.[7]

Subsequently, not only was the corporation's original purpose abandoned, but the constraints that once operated on these entities were forsaken as well when they won "human rights" in a U.S.

Supreme Court ruling in 1886.[8] In contrast, government has never been afforded the same "legal personality." Making the legal case against governmental secrecy has, therefore, been far easier. In the case of public access to information, laws have sought to deal with the question of where to place the "transparency line" by first identifying categories of exempt records and second, in the better laws, balancing them with what is known as a "public interest override provision." Public interest overrides declare that if the harm that would be done to the public interest by withholding the information is greater than the harm contemplated by the exemption that justifies withholding the information, then the information should be disclosed.

Conceptually and legally, a similar approach could apply to corporations. Access laws that cover state information are subject to exemptions that capture the public interest in keeping some things secret. If a law were to cover private entities in similar fashion (such as the South African access to information [ATI] law, which is discussed in more detail below), it too could contain exemptions to public disclosure. There are legitimate reasons for keeping some information secret, and this need can be articulated and protected in law. But this is not because the company is a privately owned entity, but because there is a public interest to be protected in permitting the withholding of information.

Because laws dealing with access to information have not generally been extended to cover private entities (see below), there is no guidance as to how to deal with the range of information that they hold and control. But this does not mean that there is no spectrum. Few, if any, would argue against the most obvious legitimate secret of a corporation, namely, its trade secrets. Should Coca-Cola be required to disclose its original recipe? No. To do so would be to totally undermine the impetus and incentive for entrepreneurial endeavor and for the necessary investments in capital that are required to develop new products. But as Graham points out, trade secrets represent a relatively small cluster of data at one end of the spectrum.[9] Personal privacy would occupy a similar location: no one could sensibly or legitimately suggest that the personal health data of an individual employee, his or her HIV status for example, should be disclosed publicly. At the other end, Graham asserts, lies another cluster of data that lies indisputably in the public domain—

basic financial information required by federal and state laws and health, safety, and environmental data required under traditional regulatory regimes.

This reflects the major shift toward transparency that has stealthily but steadily occurred over the past 100 years. Invariably these positive developments have been provoked by a crisis or disaster, and in response to greater understanding of risks to the public. The 1929 stock market crash led to a very detailed program of structured disclosure, in order to reduce financial risks to investors. After the Bhopal disaster in 1984 in India, the U.S. Congress required U.S. manufacturers to begin revealing the amounts of dangerous chemicals they released into the environment. The Toxics Release Inventory (TRI), supported by the Environmental Protection Agency (EPA), represents one of the most striking and now widely imitated examples of government regulation and private sector disclosure (see the chapter by Ramkumar and Petkova in this volume).

The Enron collapse in 2001 has led to a drastic overhaul and strengthening of disclosure requirements by the accounting sector, specifically the far-reaching Sarbanes-Oxley legislation in the United States.[10] Nutritional labeling, airline safety rankings, and reporting of workplace hazards are further examples. As Graham says, "Stated simply, *such strategies employ government authority to require the standardized disclosure of factual information from identified businesses or other organizations about products or practices to reduce risks to the public*" (her emphasis).[11]

There are four observations to be made in response to this background and to this proposition. First, valuable though these regulatory trends are, their piecemeal nature should not be ignored. They do not yet add up to a comprehensive system of transparency in relation to the for-profit world. Second, although the environmental protection disclosure regime is often described, at least in the United States, as a "right to know" system, the derivative history of these laws and regulations means that their philosophical grounding is at best uncertain. In other words, they have come about not because a new social norm, premised on the notion of a human right of access to information, has emerged and prevailed, but because corporations have been compelled to make limited disclosures in response to enunciated risks. Third, this sort of regulatory environment exists and is most likely to succeed in developed societies with relatively strong state authority and capacity. What about less developed societies and those with very weak state authority and capacity, where often for-profits, especially transnational corporations, exert huge influence over policy, markets, and social and economic conditions?

But there is no broad-based consensus for determining what corporations should disclose from the middle-ground, gray area of the spectrum identified above. This is a pivotal dispute. Are corporations "juristic persons" with "human rights" as the jurisprudential trend has held, with no responsibility to the public interest and with the predominant purpose of maximizing value for their shareholders? Or are corporations social actors, with quasi-governmental responsibilities to disclose information in the public interest? It is an irony of the logic of the argument in favor of transparency in the for-profit sector that in order to protect human dignity in wider society, it may be necessary to "dehumanize" corporations. This is to ensure that when balancing privacy and proprietary ownership with duties to disclose, we do not apply the same approach as we would with a human being. Corporations are not human beings. They have legitimate interests that deserve to be protected, including a responsibility to withhold information in some cases, but they are not *personal* interests—human rights are for people and not bureaucracies, whether governmental or for-profit. So it is to the relationship between people and for-profit corporations that this chapter now turns.

The (New) Arguments on Corporate Transparency

The Impact of Privatization on the Right of Access to Information

While privatization may take many forms, the philosophy that underpins it has a uniform quality: to remove from direct state control public services and to place them, to some degree, within private control or ownership. Throughout the world, privatization and related, variant policies such as the "contracting out" of public services and so-called "public-private partnerships" (PPPs) have radically altered the landscape of public power.

Local public services, such as waste collection, are now in the hands of private contractors. Major public works and systems are elaborate partnerships between government and large companies:

food services, repossession agencies, drug treatment facilities, road and rail maintenance, personnel record keeping. As has been noted, a "dizzying array of governmental agencies has engaged private entrepreneurs to perform government functions on a for-profit basis."[12] You name it, somewhere in the world it will have been privatized through contracting out. Even some prisons have been placed in the hands of the private sector. The notorious conduct of employees of private security contractors in the Abu Ghraib prison in Iraq in 2004 provides a potent example of both the range and the dangers of contracting out state functions. Private contractors working side by side with military intelligence officers were responsible for the abuse of prisoners by military police at Abu Ghraib, according to a fifty-three-page report prepared at the direction of the senior U.S. commander in Iraq, Maj. Gen. Ricardo Sanchez, and obtained by Seymour Hersh of *The New Yorker* magazine. The report, written by Maj. Gen. Antonio Taguba, found that there were numerous instances of "sadistic, blatant, and wanton criminal abuses" at Abu Ghraib, and recommended disciplinary action against two CACI International employees, according to the article. The use of private contractors in this role is called "insanity" by former CIA officer Robert Baer, who says, "These are rank amateurs, and there is no legally binding law on these guys as far as I could tell. Why did they let them in the prison?"[13]

Of all privatizations, water delivery has had the biggest impact on people's ordinary lives and has provoked the most controversy. Because water is so fundamental, some minimal level of access is a basic human right, but rules of privatizations to date have often removed accountability. In many cases, the privatization or contracting out provides the corporation with a monopoly. The user has no exit option. To him or her, the ownership of the service provider is immaterial; central concerns are access and cost. What matters to the individual is whether they and their family can access clean water and be able to afford it. From the green rolling mountains and valleys of the Cochabamba province in Bolivia to the dry, poverty-stricken townships of South Africa, citizens are resisting the increased costs of water that have sometimes followed fast on the heels of privatization.

Transparency in the operation of the service becomes even more important, potentially the main breakwater against abuse of the monopoly and protection of the rights of the users, as a South African case involving water privatization in Johannesburg, South Africa's largest city, attests. In 2000, the City of Johannesburg decided to privatize its water supplies and put in place a complicated train of corporations that ended with the giant transnational corporation, Suez.

This sort of legal arrangement is common in the sphere of public service privatization, including both the presence of a major multinational (Suez) and an attempt by the public authority to retain some element of control through its share ownership and the management contractual arrangement. An antiprivatization activist requested an array of records from the various entities, including items such as the bid for the management contract, the report of the evaluation committee on the winning bidder, evaluations by two entities established on behalf of the city, the water and wastewater master plans, and the minutes of various meetings. The requests were refused.

The applicant's evidence relies heavily on the history of Suez as a basis for the exercise of the right to access information, specifically with regard to its record of overcharging the citizens of Paris and Buenos Aires. Johannesburg appears to be heading in a similar direction. The latest tariff rates released by Johannesburg Water show that low-end users (i.e., poor communities) face a 30 percent tariff increase, versus a 10 percent increase for high-end users (i.e., rich communities and corporations), which is far above inflation. The applicant's founding affidavit concludes that in this context:

> the residents of Johannesburg cannot, if they are dissatisfied with the provision of water and wastewater services, democratically remove those who are responsible. The consequences of outsourcing the provision of these critical municipal services . . . is that this company will continue to perform vital public functions, for as long as the Management Agreement endures. It follows that other means must be found and fostered to ensure that [they] are in some measure accountable to the residents of Johannesburg. That will be achieved by ensuring that there is transparency . . . policies related to the disconnection of water services, including policies regarding pre-paid meters, directly implicate the right to water [contained within the South African constitution]. . . . Access will, furthermore, promote the ability of local communities to properly participate in the setting of key performance indicators and targets in relation to the provision of water and wastewater services.

Civil Society Activism: The Demand for Change and Corporate Social Responsibility

As *The Economist* noted in 2001, "In the next society, the biggest challenge for the large company—especially the multilateral—may be its social legitimacy, its values, its missions, its vision." In recent years, there has been increasing civil society activism campaigning for transparency in the corporate sector, often directed to ensure that transparency occupies a pivotal place in the development of the understanding and practice of CSR. Multilateral institutions, and some corporations, have responded positively. The UN Global Compact is an often-cited example of the new, multilateral, macro approach to corporate social responsibility. Principle One of the UN Global Compact states that "Businesses should support and respect the protection of internationally proclaimed human rights." A tenth principle on anticorruption practice, which reads "Businesses should work against corruption in all its forms, including extortion and bribery," was adopted in June 2004.

On August 13, 2003, after a four-year consultative and drafting process involving the private sector, academic institutions, human rights nongovernmental organizations, and intergovernmental bodies and states, the UN Sub-Commission on the Promotion of Human Rights adopted resolution 2003/16 (the Norms on the Responsibilities of Transnational Corporations and Other Business Enterprises with Regard to Human Rights).[14]

The Norms, together with their commentary, form the major product of the Sub-Commission's Working Group on the Working Methods and Activities of Transnational Corporations. The Norms help to clarify the assertion that business enterprises have human rights obligations. Yet curiously, the draft "Principles Relating to the Human Rights Conduct of Companies" fails to mention either transparency or any right to access information.[15] This shows that although thinking on the multilateral response to the power of the for-profit sector is growing, transparency is not yet a core part of the agenda.

Civil society, however, is further along the conceptual road toward transparency. Pressure from stakeholders for accountability on social and environmental issues is a major driver of companies' self-interested efforts to be good corporate citizens. Government, customers, community groups, or nongovernmental organizations (NGOs) can significantly impede a business plan if a company is not responsive. That is why citizenship reports are littered with terms like "license to operate," "license to grow," and "license to innovate." Being good corporate citizens gives companies a license to be successful. The report that accompanies the draft "Principles Relating to the Human Rights Conduct of Companies" refers to the voluntary approach adopted by some companies, often spurred by NGO pressure. The footnote to the section (note 25) refers to around fifty such codes, the majority of which are NGO-inspired. An excellent example of NGO activism on transparency is the work that has been done in recent years by the Publish-What-You-Pay coalition of more than 190 northern and southern NGOs. The coalition is calling for laws to require extractive companies to disclose their payments to all governments. As Global Witness, a key member, argues on its Web site, "This crucial first step would help citizens in resource-rich-but-poor countries to hold their governments to account over the management of revenues. In addition, by a level playing field through regulation, companies' reputational risks will be mitigated and they will be protected from the threat of having contracts cancelled by corrupt governments."[16]

The Global Witness report "Time for Transparency—Coming Clean on Oil, Mining and Gas Revenues" starkly illustrates how secrecy provides a perfect cloak to the unscrupulous, on both the host government and the corporations' side. Examining the cases of Kazakhstan, Congo Brazzaville, Angola, Equatorial Guinea, and Nauru, the report asserts that "In these countries, governments do not provide even basic information about their revenues from natural resources. Nor do oil, mining and gas companies publish any information about payments made to governments."[17] A theater of the absurd plays out under cover of the opacity: Kazakhstan President Nazarbayev receives US$78 million in kickbacks from Chevron and Mobil (as they then were). In Congo Brazzaville, Elf Aquitaine (now Total) treated the Congo as its colony, buying off the ruling elite, yet according to the IMF did not pay a single penny into the government's coffers. In Angola, as much as US$1 billion per year of the country's oil revenues—about a quarter of the yearly income—has gone unaccounted for since 1996. In the case of Equatorial Guinea, recent investigations show that major U.S. oil companies simply paid revenues directly into the personal account of the president at Riggs Bank in downtown Washington, DC in return for mining concessions. Finally, "the opaque and unaccountable management of phosphate reserves has transformed Nauru from the richest nation in the world (per capita) to a bankrupt wasteland."

Beyond the anticorruption initiatives, the international community has begun to see disclosure as a useful tool for dealing with what social scientists call externalities—the often negative but unintended social and environmental impacts of corporate behavior. There has been a substantial increase in corporate reporting on nonfinancial performance. Two best practice guidelines have emerged. One, the Global Reporting Initiative (GRI), established in 1997, provides guidance on the substantive issues to be included within a sustainability report, while the second, AccountAbility1000 (AA1000),[18] launched in 1999, provides a framework to guide the establishment of an inclusive engagement process. More than 270 companies and institutions are now using the GRI guidelines.[19]

More recently, the UK government initiated a new forum called the Extractive Industries Transparency Initiative (EITI) to promote action by governments and companies. The principal weakness of the EITI, according to its critics, is that it relies entirely on voluntary reporting. The Publish-What-You-Pay coalition of NGOs continues to call for mandatory reporting based on common norms and standards across home and host countries, and among the companies themselves. In 2004, the London-based NGO Save the Children: UK, a leading member of the Publish-What-You-Pay coalition, developed a set of indicators that attempt to measure transparency across all three actors.[20] By investigating information from each, a triangulation exercise can be performed to help verify information relating to revenue streams in particular. The intention is to assess levels of opacity, identify leaders and laggards, diagnose solutions, and set new standards of good practice. Phase I having conceptualized and piloted the Measuring Transparency Index, phase II of the project tested the transparency of companies in the oil and gas industries and the transparency standards and requirements set by home countries—that is to say, (generally First World or wealthier) countries where oil and gas companies are based.

The project coincides with the biggest reform of accounting standards in more than twenty-five years, following the Enron and

Anderson scandals, prompting significant reviews and reforms in other financial regulations, such as securities. Category A of the index measures transparency in relation to revenue payments, category B measures general corporate reporting ("supportive disclosure"), and category C measures policy, management, and performance of Access to Information laws. The index is two-dimensional, permitting a more diagnostic reading of the data based on an analysis of policy, management systems, and disclosure performance. Twenty-five companies with operations in six countries were assessed, with the Canadian companies Talisman and TransAtlantic Petroleum topping the table, and PetroChina and Petronas, the national petroleum corporations of China and Malaysia respectively, propping it up.

From the index and the data collected, the report makes clear recommendations for reform and lays out an extensive agenda for civil society advocacy. It concludes that, overall, transparency in the oil and gas sector is poor—23 of the 25 companies score less than 30 percent—showing the need for stronger measures, and that home government regulation of company reporting is vital as the "key driver" for disclosure performance. The three Canadian companies included in the study rank first (Talisman), second (TransAtlantic Petroleum), and fifth (Nexen, Inc.). As the report notes, "The strong results for Canadian companies indicate the role that home government regulations can play in increasing transparency in host countries. They demonstrate that at a global level, home government regulation is an efficient way to improve transparency."[21] In this context, it is noteworthy that in the sister report on home government transparency regulation of companies, Canada ranked first of the ten countries covered and was the only one to score more than 50 percent (58.1), thus inviting the conclusion that there is a compelling causal link between corporate transparency and mandatory regulation by government.

Voluntary Corporate Transparency

Nonetheless, some corporations are coming to believe that transparency is in their interests. Talisman's voluntary commitment to openness is evident in its comprehensive and extensive approach to both the scope and the manner and method of its transparency policy, ensuring, for example, that the disclosed information is presented in clear tables. Open—and accessible—disclosure promotes business confidence, among customers, shareholders, regulators, and investors.[22] It instills a sense of accountability throughout the company, from the most junior employee to the biggest shareholder. Organizations work best when their stakeholders—internal and external—know what is going on. Good communication requires a good information flow. An illuminating example is the British nuclear waste company Nirex, which provides advice on waste treatment and packaging relating to the disposal of nuclear waste—an important and controversial public health and safety issue. Mirroring government-led shifts toward openness, Nirex's own epiphany arose from a commercial and public relations disaster. In the mid-1990s the company aimed to get government permission to investigate whether the underground rock formations near Sellafield—a very beautiful part of the English countryside—were suitable for the safe disposal of nuclear waste. Local communities did not believe that the purpose was exploratory; they believed that Nirex had already made up its mind. In turn, the company was unable to persuade them otherwise and barely made the effort to do so. Just before the 1997 British General Election, the government refused the company's application.

Nirex realized that it was perceived as closed and secretive: it was slow to respond to public requests for information, it communicated badly, and it was unwilling to recognize the importance of social issues. It was seen as too close to the nuclear industry, as part of the problem and not the solution. From this analysis came the revelation that trust was the company's core business, and openness was identified as the means of achieving it. A transparency policy was drawn up, with five specific commitments: fostering openness as a core value, listening as well as talking to people who have an interest, making information readily available under a Publications Policy and responding to requests under a Code of Practice on Access to Information, making key decisions in a way that allows them to be traced so people can see and understand how they were arrived at, and enabling people to have access to and influence on [its] future program.[23] Moreover, the board of directors appointed a Transparency Panel chaired by a leading human rights activist, Jenny Watson, to oversee the operation of the policy and to scrutinize and assess the extent to which Nirex is meeting its five commitments.[24]

The notion of independent, external scrutiny is probably essential for the credibility of a voluntary initiative; otherwise, it may well be regarded as a mere public relations exercise. Where such voluntary initiatives exist and are complied with, they represent a very valuable contribution toward the necessary social consensus that must be found if transparency as a value is to flourish in the private sector. Leadership by champions such as Nirex will be very important in shifting the attitudes of CEOs and their boards. It will also allow the sector to lead the debate and to formulate an approach that takes its legitimate needs for secrecy into account. Nonetheless, there will always be policy advocates who are skeptical of the voluntary effort; they will argue that nothing short of a full legal, mandatory obligation will suffice. But how blunt or sharp can the law be?

The Challenge to Freedom of Information Regimes: The Governmental Response

The Legislative Response Around the World

Historically, freedom of information acts as they were originally generally termed provided for a "vertical" right of access—that is to say, from the citizens "upward" to the state. The earliest ATI laws tended to only cover "pure" state information, that is to say, the information to which the requester was entitled access was defined narrowly to limit requests to information owned, held, and controlled by the government.

The United States has one of the oldest freedom of information laws and arguably the most developed and effective system for facilitating citizen access to public documents, although it has been undermined by chronic delays in handling requests. The country also has extensive experience of a diverse range of privatization efforts. Its federal structure means that there have been an equally wide range of attempts to deal with the policy consequences, which provides some useful lessons. During the first main wave of privatization in the United States, little attention was paid to the freedom of information problems that might arise.[25] But later studies indicate an obvious difficulty: "Professors Matthew Bunker and Charles Davis have pointed out that by creating, maintaining, and controlling previously public records, private companies are controlling access, and that they are often 'at odds with the very purpose of public records laws.'"

As the media has argued, "once-public information has disappeared behind the curtain of corporate privacy";[26] Bunker and Davis note that corporations performing privatized governmental functions have attempted to deny the public access to a wide variety of records.[27] They cite a private contractor transporting pupils to and from public schools in Atlanta, the capital of the U.S. state of Georgia, unsuccessfully fighting a request for the personal driving records of its bus drivers (in terms of criminal convictions). In California, a waste disposal company contracted by a municipal government attempted to halt the release of financial records used to evaluate a rate increase that city officials granted it. In South Africa, a large, formerly publicly owned steel utility, ISCOR, attempted (albeit unsuccessfully[28]) to use its new, private legal status as a shield to avoid releasing documents relating to its environmental performance during the apartheid era.

Moreover, in the United States, the effect has been not only generally but also unequally negative; information flows depend on where exactly the person makes the request. Because of the failure of legislatures to meet the problem head-on—although all fifty U.S. states have right to know statutes, state legislatures have universally failed to amend their laws in the face of privatization—courts have had to interpret state openness laws and have done so in different ways in different states. "These decisions have ranged from flexible, access-favoring applications of freedom of information statutes to more restrictive, access-limited applications due to more explicit definitions found within the statutes themselves."[29]

The general failure of the (U.S.) courts to hold private entities accountable under the Freedom of Information Act means that government can frustrate the public disclosure purposes behind the act by delegating services to the private sector. This represents a major threat to transparency and to the exercise of the right of access to information. In terms of the traditional policy response, of the eight[30] countries to have passed laws prior to 1990, only one, New Zealand, passed a law that provided for a right of access to records other than "pure" public documents. In its interpretation chapter, the New Zealand Official Information Act 1982 offers a convoluted expansion of "pure" official information, to include state-owned corporations and public quangos (regulatory agencies organized outside the civil service but appointed and financed by the government, such as unincorporated advisory boards).

The explosion of access to information laws after 1990 was a part of the new "good governance" agenda and, in some cases, a response to citizen demands for openness. Of the new wave of ATI laws, two of the first batch—those of Italy and the Netherlands—contain provisions that offer at least some semblance of "partial" access to nonstate information. Article 23 of the 1990 Italian law states the right of access to information applies to "the administrative bodies of the state, including special and autonomous bodies, public entities and the providers of public services, as well as guarantee and supervisory bodies." This is far from clear or explicit in its intentions. Section 3(1) of the Dutch law is clearer. It states that "anyone may apply to an administrative authority or an agency, service, or company carrying out work for which it is accountable to an administrative authority for information contained in documents concerning an administrative matter."

This is the first reference in an ATI law that captures the concept of public accountability in the context of privately held information. Since then, a significant trend has emerged. Of the forty-six ATI laws surveyed for the purposes of this chapter, only seventeen have partial coverage of this sort, thirteen of them in laws passed since 1999. Eight of the thirteen are from the Central and Eastern European region, an area that has, of course, seen massive structural adjustments to the state and huge amounts of privatization of public services since the political changes of the post–Berlin Wall early 1990s.

The laws offering "partial coverage" do so in variety of ways, all variations on the core theme of public accountability. The Slovak law, for example, covers entities that "manage public funds or operate with state property or the property of municipalities."[31] The Finnish law covers private entities "appointed for the performance of a public task on the basis of an Act, a Decree or provision or order issued by virtue of an Act or Decree, when they exercise public authority."[32] The Bulgarian law goes further: article 2(1) defines public information as "any information of public significance, which relates to the public life in the Republic of Bulgaria"; article 2(3) states that the right to access extends to "public information relating to such public services, which are provided by either natural persons or legal entities, and are financed by the state budget or budget funds."

The Jamaican law offers a rather different approach. Section 5(3)(b) of its Access to Information Act 2002 gives the responsible minister the authority to declare that the act's right of access apply to "any other body or organization which provides services of a public nature which are essential to the welfare of the Jamaican society." The Jamaican law has only recently come into effect (January 5, 2004) and so there are no examples yet of the minister exercising his or her discretion in this way.

A Comprehensive Right of Access to Private Information: The South African Experiment

The South African law adopts a unique policy solution to the problem. It goes far further than any other ATI law, providing for a comprehensive right to all private information where access to the information is necessary for the protection or exercise of another right. Although it is still relatively early in the implementation of the law to draw detailed conclusions, the experience so far provides a glimpse into how a comprehensive legal right to access private information might transform requirements for disclosure by the profit-making sector and how such a regime would work in practice.

The first democratic election in South Africa in 1994 that swept Nelson Mandela into power marked the beginning of a halcyon age in constitutionalism and human rights. In the two years that followed, South Africa's entire political and governance structure was reformed and placed within the framework of a new Constitution, whose purpose is to drive a profound social and economic transformation away from the brutal iniquities of the apartheid era. Between 1994 and 1996, a special Constitutional Assembly met to write the new founding document. An interim Constitution, agreed upon during the all-party negotiations that led to the 1994 election, included a right to access public information where access was necessary to protect or exercise another right.

During the public participation process of the Constitutional Assembly, the Open Democracy Campaign Group argued for an open-ended right to public information and, moreover, the inclusion of a right to private information. This argument proved attractive to key members of the ruling African National Congress (ANC)'s representation in the Constitutional Assembly committees. They were alert to structural changes in state power around the world, cognizant of the fact that their own government was embarking on a course of privatization, and acutely aware of the immense wealth and power of both South African corporations and transnational companies. For one of the members of the campaign group, the umbrella trade union organization Congress of South African Trade Unions (COSATU), it was an issue of fundamental political and strategic importance. As its representative, Oupa Bodibe has argued: "Workers require information to exercise and protect their rights. If unions or workers could request information vital to the protection or exercise of the right to fair labour practices . . . this would strengthen the enforcement of human rights throughout South Africa. . . . Information is required to exercise and protect the right to equality, to ensure the absence of discrimination in hiring, promotion and salaries, and generally to promote democratization of the workplace."[33]

Thus, the version of the access to information right that emerged in the final Constitution represented a radical new path: section 32 provides for a right to access not only "any information held by the state" but also "any information that is held by another person and that is required for the exercise or protection of any rights." Elsewhere, "another person" is defined to include both natural and juristic persons, so section 32 unequivocally covers private companies. The Constitution required that national legislation be passed to give effect to the right; accordingly, in 2000, the Promotion of Access to Information Act was passed.

Despite its potential, usage of the South African act has been limited in relation to private records. Awareness of the legislation generally is poor, and understanding the potential in relation to private power, even more so. The Open Democracy Advice Centre (ODAC), a specialized NGO established in 2000 to help ensure effective implementation of the act, operates as a public interest law center and has been involved in a number of cases that test the "horizontal" reach of the act. In *Pretorius v. Nedcor Bank*, a former senior officer in the South African army sought the records relating to the bank's policy when evaluating loan applications. Pretorius had applied for a loan and had been turned down without any explanation. He wanted to know why. ODAC's interest was in testing the private information provisions of the law in order to establish a precedent that would be valuable for people who suspected they were subject to what is known as "redlining"—discrimination against particular communities or social groups. In South Africa, it is suspected that banks and other credit agencies discriminate against certain areas that they regard as high risk. Risk aversion is, of course, a perfectly legitimate commercial strategy. Blanket discrimination against people from a particular area or social group offends the South African Constitution's right to equal access, however, and the right to not be unfairly discriminated against. In the Pretorius case, the bank, having taken counsel's opinion, were anxious not to go to court and settled the case by providing the applicant with a range of papers setting out their policy and the reasons for the refusal in his case.

In another, more complicated case, on behalf of indigent fisherfolk, ODAC obtained the "transformation plans" of a number of fishing companies that had been set up to win contracts for fishing quotas, the main economic driver along the western and southern coasts of South Africa. In essence, a series of old, white-owned fish companies had executed a neat "legal fraud" by reconstituting through subsidiaries as "empowerment" companies—companies owned by blacks and/or with substantial black shareholding—in order to win quotas that had been earmarked for empowerment companies as a part of the new government's general strategy of economic transformation. Black fishermen and women had been duped into signing the shareholding forms and had received absolutely nothing in return. Accessing the "transformation plans" that set out the details of their black empowerment exposed the companies' fraud, revealed it to the fisherfolk so they could seek legal remedy, and reported it to Marine Coastal Management, the government's regulatory body. A national investigative television program, *Special Assignment*, reported on the fraud and the effort to unravel it. Transparency has compelled accountability for a series of local communities; without the right to access private information, it would not have been possible for ODAC to have prompted the exposé.

Secrecy is used to hide the hidden influence of big business over democratic politics. In a third case, ODAC is acting as attorney for one of its founder NGOs, the Institute for Democracy in South Africa (IDASA). IDASA is running a campaign calling for regulation of party political funding. At present, there is no regulation whatsoever; despite attempts to develop an anticorruption infrastructure, there is a lacuna in which a number of funding scandals have erupted. In one, the Italian millionaire industrialist Count Agusta entered into a plea bargain with the National Prosecutor, admitting in 2002 paying a R400,000 (about US$70,000) bribe to get planning permission for a golf estate. The bribe was paid into the coffers of the National Party, which was then in power in Western Cape provincial government. In a more serious scandal, a former ANC Member of Parliament (MP), Andrew Feinstein, told Swedish television and radio that a consortium between the Swedish company SAAB and the UK company British Aerospace, which in 1999 won a massive contract to supply fighter aircraft to South Africa, had paid the ruling ANC a US$35 million inducement.

In late 2002, IDASA made a series of requests under the Access to Information Act for records of private donations made by the biggest thirteen companies in South Africa to the thirteen political parties represented in the National Assembly. None of the political parties acceded to the request, but three of the companies accepted their duty to disclose and supplied records of donations that they had made since 1994. Another company, AngloGold Ashanti, has responded by compiling a voluntary code of disclosure. After that ground-breaking step, in the first quarter of 2004 in the run-up to the April general election, a further twelve major corporations followed suit, disclosing donations worth approximately R40 million ($5 million).

Very few cases have been heard in the High Court. As part of its campaign, in late 2003 IDASA launched proceedings under the Access to Information Act against the four biggest political parties—the ANC, the National Party, the Democratic Alliance, and the Inkatha Freedom Party—claiming the public's right to know about the private donations in order to be able to make an informed choice at election time and seeking a declaration of the principle of transparency in relation to substantial private donations and an order requiring disclosure of donations of R50,000 or more since January 1, 2003. A fifth party, the African Christian Democrat Party (ACDP), agreed shortly before the launch of the proceedings to open its books to public scrutiny and thereby declared the identity of all its recent substantial private donors. The case raised important, ground-breaking issues related to private transparency and attracted considerable international attention. In its April 2005 judgment, the Cape High

Court held that political bodies are private bodies but, applying the test very narrowly, found that access to the donations records was not necessary to protect and exercise the right to political freedom contained in section 19 of the South African Constitution. Nonetheless, as part of its submissions to the court, the ruling ANC introduced legislation to regulate private funding on the basis of the principle of transparency (in line with Article 10 of the African Union Anti-Corruption Convention, ratified by South Africa in November 2005). In the light of this undertaking, IDASA decided not to appeal the judgment, despite its restrictive interpretation of the right.

In another case, *Davis v. Clutcho (Pty) Ltd.*,[34] a minority shareholder requested access to certain company accounts for the purpose of determining the value of his shares. Although the case concerns a modest-sized car repair business, the principle involved has very far-reaching implications for businesses of any size: when majority and minority shareholders fall out, as they often do, what rights of access to information can the minority fall back on? In *Clutcho*, the applicant became concerned about the manner in which the respondent was being managed when he discovered that various companies had closed the respondent's credit facilities. Existing company law was of little use to the minority shareholder; in fact, it had been used against him: he had been lawfully removed as a director of the company by resolution of the majority shareholders, which cut off his main supply of information. At the hearing, the respondent argued that in order to fulfill the need to show that the information was "required for the exercise or protection of any rights," the applicant needed to show an antecedent legal right to such information. Carefully cataloguing the various company law provisions that might apply, the respondent's counsel concluded that there was no such statutory right to information. Judge Meer disagreed and ruled that:

> The Companies Act cannot . . . limit the right of access to information at section 32 of the Constitution . . . and nor can it be interpreted to exclude such right, which would thus be contrary to the spirit of the Bill of Rights. To the extent that the Companies Act does not provide for access to information, section 32 of the Constitution, and the Act, must be read into the Companies Act. It could never have been the intention of the legislature that a shareholder aggrieved by financial statements, as in this case, should be barred from access to the information

required to shed light on such statements in order to exercise his rights to sell shares or even prosecute a case against the company in terms of the remedies available to him in terms of either the Companies Act or the common law.[35]

Shifting the Legal and Human Rights Paradigm

This line of legal authority has potentially far-reaching implications for corporate transparency in South Africa and in other countries grappling with similar issues. In short, it is likely that the traditional approach of the law to the legal personality of a corporation will be tempered by the normative imperative of the Constitution. The application of the principle of the right to know in cases such as these articulates a potently different legal and political paradigm from the one that prevailed in the nineteenth century and that constituted the foundation upon which corporate secrecy was built. Then, in contrast to the traditional view of the vertical relationship between citizens and the state, relationships in the private sphere were regarded as being based on a degree of parity between free and autonomous parties. Politics and ideology contributed to the dominance of this paradigm, and legal theory mirrored these traditions.

A fresh look at the relationship between human rights instruments and protections and corporate legal identity is needed. It is important to take account of the nature of the right and the nature of the duty imposed. The right to dignity, to freedom of security and person (tort), to privacy, to a clean environment, to property, and children's rights all "infringe" upon the private sphere without any or much controversy.[36] The fact that legislation is commonly used to give effect to rights assists this inquiry, for example in the case of antidiscrimination rights, which intrude on labor relations and on the "private nature" of the employer-employee relationship.

The idea of universal human rights is premised on the notion of correcting inequalities of power so as to prevent harm and protect people from abuse, thus enabling them to sustain their human dignity. The concept of human rights has traditionally been applied to relations in the public sphere. The dominant view has been that the state/individual relationship involves unequal power dynamics between parties. A state's potential to abuse its position of authority to the detriment of an individual's interests was the basis for human rights to insulate the latter against state interference.[37] Muddying the waters, confusion between *personal* information and *private* information has served to constrain fresh approaches. There may be natural and appropriate concerns that rights of access to private information should not breach the right to privacy. But personal information is a legally defined category, generally exempt from right of access (whether in the public or private sphere). *Personal* information—such as an individual's HIV status or personal credit card details—must be carefully distinguished from private information where access is needed to protect or exercise a right—such as information about the side effects of an antiretroviral drug produced and sold by a multinational pharmaceutical company.

Conclusion: Crossing the Rubicon

Concepts of human rights first arose in an age of relative state omnipotence. Limiting the application of human rights to vertical relationships between the individual and the state is no longer sufficient to ensure their protection. The public sphere has changed dramatically in the past twenty-five years. Democratic control of public resources and goods and services became ideologically unfashionable. Much public power has, as a result of the policies of privatization and contracting out, been ceded to privately owned entities. The relative impact of the for-profit sector has grown, as has understanding of the harm as well as the good that the private sector can do to the lives of ordinary citizens everywhere and to their environment.

A great surge in access to information legislation around the world has largely failed to provide for granting access to information essential to citizens wanting to enforce accountability from the entities that affect their daily lives—through the provision of water and health services, transportation, waste collection and other local services, and telecommunications and financial services. Some laws have tried to adapt by defining "public records" in such a way as to cover entities fulfilling a public function. In the United States, state-level courts have applied a wide variety of tests to try to ensure that the public policy intentions of access to information laws are not defeated by structural changes in government.

An earlier trend in regulating private corporations in response to crisis and disaster has resulted in a plethora—at least in developed societies—of piecemeal law and regulation requiring disclosure of information controlled by for-profit entities in relation to specific identified social risks.

But these efforts approach the problem from the wrong angle. Even if the state could foresee all the possible risks that may arise and effectively require relevant disclosure in advance of disaster or crisis, few states and societies around the world could cope with the demands that such a regulatory responsibility would place on their capacity, resources, and weak authority. Equally, rather than attempting to extend coverage with convoluted legal gymnastics intended to cover the multitude of possible forms that "public, private information" may take, a more comprehensive approach is needed. As Alasdair Roberts argues, this requires a departure from the liberal framework that drives a wedge between public and private and insists on differential treatment of the two spheres.[38]

Once attention switches to the idea of unjustifiable harm and whether countervailing mechanisms such as disclosure and transparency requirements could prevent it, a paradigmatic evolution can gather pace. The South African experiment is a significant departure from the old paradigm. In essence, it says: why should private entities be ring-fenced from the same sort of responsibilities to which public entities are subjected, since they can have just as much, sometimes more, negative impact on the human dignity of citizens? When they pollute rivers, discriminate against social groups, fix prices in cartels, they undermine many human rights—the right to a clean environment, the right to equal treatment and equality, the right to water. This new thinking attaches the right to access information not to any evaluation of the functionality of the information or the entity that owns or control it, but instead to the need to protect or exercise a right.

Whatever the final, chosen formulation, the Rubicon must first be crossed. The psychological and legal barriers that have hitherto tended to encourage opacity deserve to be reconsidered in the light of corporate social responsibility trends and new global standards for disclosure and reporting. The arrangements society has made to encourage capital to multiply and create wealth—namely, the legal notion of the for-profit corporation—should not operate as a justification for continued secrecy. Corporate leaders are recognizing their responsibilities in this regard, sometimes as a result of NGO activist pressure and sometimes out of enlightened self-interest: there is growing understanding that trust is a precious commodity and that transparency can strengthen it and thereby protect or build reputation and brand. The voluntary approach of companies such as Nirex exemplifies this new thinking. In other words, there is also a strong business case for transparency.

Transparency has a profound instrumental value as a bridge to other rights. Accessing information so that social actors can play a full part in a vibrant society and economy is the underlying purpose. This is the case for extending the right to access information to information held not just by the state but also by the for-profit, private sector. Both activists and policy makers are finding that it is crucial to end what has become a false divide, increasingly irrelevant and confusing given the blurred lines between the two sectors and the transfer of power, functions, and responsibilities from one to the other.

NOTES

1. Richard Calland and A. Tilley, eds., *The Right to Know, The Right to Live: Access to Information and Socio-Economic Justice* (Cape Town: ODAC, 2002).

2. Thomas Blanton, "The World's Right to Know," *Foreign Policy* 131 (2002): 50; David Banisar, "Freedom of Information and Access to Government Records Around the World" (Washington, DC: freedominfo.org, 2004), http://www.freedominfo.org/survey/global_survey2004.pdf.

3. Alasdair Roberts, "Structural Pluralism and the Right to Information," in Richard Calland and A. Tilley, eds., *The Right to Know, The Right to Live: Access to Information and Socio-Economic Justice* (Cape Town: ODAC, 2002), 42.

4. Mark Nadel, "Corporate Secrecy and Political Accountability," *Public Administration Review* 35 (1975): 15.

5. Joel Bakan, *The Corporation* (New York: Free Press, 2004), 37.

6. R. Stevenson, "How Much Privacy Does Business Need?," *Business and Society Review* (2001):47.

7. See also Ann Florini's reference to the history of corporations in *The Coming Democracy: New Rules for Running the World* (Washington, DC: Island Press, 2003), 94–99.

8. Corporations are legal fictions that exist for the sole purpose of building wealth. They can live forever, change identity in a day when it suits

them, live without a real home, own others, cut off parts of themselves, and grow new parts (Thom Hartmann, *Unequal Protection: The Rise of Corporate Dominance and the Theft of Human Rights* [Emmaus, PA: Rodale Books, 2002]). But should they have the rights of the individual if they do not behave like individuals? Since the Supreme Court ruling, corporations have assumed the Bill of Rights for themselves, pushing in court for the right to free speech, which allows them to contribute money to politicians and political parties and effectively buy votes and rewrite laws for their benefit. They have won the right to privacy, which allows them to deny government agencies access to their papers and properties and, he says, hide crimes in the process. They have also secured the Fifth Amendment right against self-incrimination and the Fourteenth Amendment right of equal protection, allowing them to exist even in a community that objects to their presence on the grounds that they destroy small businesses.

9. Mary Graham, *Democracy by Disclosure: The Rise of Technopopulism* (Washington, DC: Brookings Institute Press, 2002), 147.

10. Sarbanes-Oxley Act of 2002, Pub. L. No. 107–204, 116 Stat. 745. Among other things, the act limits the extent to which an accountancy firm can serve as both an auditor of and consultant to the same corporation, due to the intense conflict-of-interests difficulties that arise.

11. Graham, *Democracy by Disclosure*, 138.

12. Matthew Bunker and C. Davis, "Privatized Government Functions and Freedom of Information: Public Accountability in an Age of Private Governance," *Journalism and Mass Communication Quarterly* 75 (3) (1998): 465.

13. Seymour Hersh, "Torture at Abu Ghraib," *The New Yorker*, May 10, 2004.

14. Sihaka Tsemo, speech on privatization of basic services, democracy, and human rights at Conference on Privatization and Human Rights, University of Western Cape, South Africa, December 2003.

On June 24, 2004, UN Secretary-General Kofi Annan added a tenth principle to the UN global compact not specific to transparency but nevertheless showing a commitment by the UN: "Businesses should work against corruption in all its forms, including extortion and bribery."

15. E/CN.4/Sub.2/2000.WG.2/WP.1.

16. "Time for Transparency—Coming Clean on Oil, Mining and Gas Revenues," *Global Witness* (March 2004):6, http://www.globalwitness.org/reports.

17. Ibid., 1.

18. http://www.accountability.org.uk.

19. Global Reporting Initiative (GRI), "Organisations Using the GRI Guidelines," http://www.globalreporting.org.

20. Save the Children UK, "Beyond the Rhetoric: Measuring Revenue Transparency: Company Performance in the Oil and Gas Industries," *Save the Children UK*, March 17, 2005. Published in tandem with a second report focusing on home government transparency: "Beyond the Rhetoric: Measuring Revenue Transparency: Home Government Requirements for Disclosure in the Oil and Gas Industries." Note: the Measuring Transparency Index was developed by the writer, with another consultant, Mohammed Ali, during an earlier phase of the project, and the Access to Information component of the home government report was undertaken by him and his colleague at the Institute for Democracy in South Africa (IDASA), Catherine Masuva.

21. Save the Children UK, "Beyond the Rhetoric: Measuring Revenue Transparency: Company Performance in the Oil and Gas Industries," 33.

22. As an example, see the first principle of ethical investment enunciated by Fraters Asset Management in South Africa: Communication and Disclosure: http://www.fraters.co.za/principles.

23. http://www.nirex.co.uk/index/ifoi.htm.

24. The panel is now chaired by Andrew Puddephatt, another prominent human rights activist and former Executive Director of the international freedom of information NGO, ARTICLE 19. Its other two members are Professor Patrick Birkenshaw, a freedom of information academic, and James Amos, who works for an NGO specializing in constitutional reform.

25. Craig Feiser, "Protecting the Public's Right to Know: The Debate Over Privatization and Access to Government Information Under State Law," *Florida State University Law Review* 27 (2000).

26. Don Noel, "Privatization Shouldn't Reduce Public Information," *Hartford Courant*, April 16, 1997, A11.

27. Bunker and Davis, "Privatized Government," 465.

29. In a judgment handed down by the Pretoria High Court in early 2005 (*Hlatshwayo v. Iscor Limited*), it was ruled that at the time that the documents were created, ISCOR was performing a public function by virtue of the extent of state control and that it could not use its new privatized status to keep the documents secret.

29. Feiser, "Protecting the Public's Right to Know," 836. Feiser's analysis of the response of U.S. state courts to the problem demonstrates the extent and depth of the confusion; seven different approaches have been taken by the courts of the thirty-four states in which cases have been decided. In

conclusion, Feiser lists the seven approaches thus, from the most favorable to public access to the least favorable (Feiser 2000:864):

> The nature of records approach (six states): allowing access to records as long as the records pertain to some aspect of government;
>
> The public function approach (ten states): allowing access when the private entity is performing a government function;
>
> The totality of factors approach (six states): allowing access as long as the presence of certain factors outweighs the absence of other factors (such as public funding, control, independence, etc.);
>
> The public funds approach (six states): limiting access to those cases where the requisite level of public funds is present;
>
> The public control approach (one state): limiting access to those cases where the requisite level of government control is present;
>
> The possession approach (one state): limiting access to those cases where the public entity is in possession of the documents;
>
> The prior legal determination approach (four states): limiting access to those cases where there has been a legal determination (statutory or constitutional) that the entity should be subject to access.

30. Sweden, USA, Norway, France, Australia, New Zealand, Canada, Denmark.

31. Section 2(3), Act on Free Access to Information and Amendments of Certain Acts, 2000.

32. Section 4(9), Act on the Openness of Government Authorities, 1999.

33. Calland and Tilley, *The Right to Know*, 109.

34. *Andrew Christopher Davis vs. Clutcho (Pty) Ltd.*, in the High Court of South Africa, Cape of Good Hope Provincial Division. Unreported; judgment June 10, 2003.

35. Ibid., at page 16 of the Judgment.

36. Halton Cheadle and D. Davis, "The Application of the 1996 Constitution in the Private Sphere," *South African Journal on Human Rights* 13 (1997): 44.

37. Danwood Chirwa, "Non-state Actors' Responsibility for Socio-economic Rights: The Nature of Their Obligations Under the South African Constitution," *ESR Review* 3 (3) (2002) (University of Western Cape, Community Law Centre), http://www.communitylawcentre.org.za/ser/esr2002/2002nov_nonstate.php#nonstate.

38. Roberts, "Structural Pluralism," 29.

Chapter Eight

The Struggle for Openness in the International Financial Institutions

Thomas Blanton

One of the greatest challenges to democratic governance in the globalized world lies in the growing gap—the "democratic deficit"—between the power of the international organizations to affect human lives throughout the planet and the power of the people so affected to exercise any control over those institutions. International organizations, from the World Bank to the International Monetary Fund (IMF) to the North Atlantic Treaty Organization (NATO), have grown dramatically in power and scope since they were designed decades ago. The World Bank has more than doubled its annual commitments since 1979 and now lends in more than 100 countries, including the previously off-limits territory of the former Soviet Union. The other development banks have emulated it in the growth of their own regional portfolios. The World Trade Organization (WTO) replaced the earlier General Agreement on Tariffs and Trade in 1995 with a more restrictive set of rules and binding dispute settlement procedures. The end of the fixed exchange rate system in the 1970s and the debt crisis of the 1980s changed the International Monetary Fund from the world's exchange rate fixer into a key provider of development assistance as well as ultimate arbiter for many countries of whether international capital will be available at all. After 1991, the North Atlantic Treaty Organization expanded to take in the former Warsaw Pact countries of Eastern and Central Europe, and now has troops on the ground in Afghanistan. But the governance structures of these international institutions have not changed to reflect their new size, power, and responsibilities.

At the root of the issue is the genealogy of the international financial and trade institutions (IFTIs) and the intergovernmental organizations (IGOs). The former descend directly from central banks, which even in the most democratic countries tend to be the least directly accountable governance institutions. The latter derive from alliances of nations with different governance systems, which tended to leave each IGO with a level of accountability equal to the lowest common denominator of its members. In both cases, diplomatic confidentiality served as the norm for communications among nations that established these institutions; such norms—although somewhat eroded—continue to shroud them today.

Discussion of the resulting "democratic deficit" is no longer limited to the protest movement that gave the place names Seattle and Genoa significance, both as a generic antiglobalization reaction and as a more sophisticated challenge to the legitimacy of international institutions.[1] In fact, these institutions face a legitimacy crisis, within which the problem of secrecy is the threshold issue and perhaps the most promising opportunity for change. One cannot underestimate the ameliorative effect of embarrassment, or as this book's editor has termed it, "regulation by revelation."[2] Such exposure has compelled the IFTIs in particular over the past fifteen years gradually to expand the documentation available to the public and to improve their communication with stakeholders and other target groups. In fact, the public relations and publications functions of international institutions may well be the fastest growing such bureaucracies in terms of budget and employee positions.

But critics allege that the new transparency more resembles a sophisticated publications scheme than an actual "revolution" in accountability. In general, IGOs find meaningful transparency a hard sell to their member states. At the World Bank, for example, some of the larger emerging-market countries have proved particularly resistant to calls for greater transparency about their World Bank–funded projects. Now that they are becoming major players in the world, they do not want international institutions in which they have relatively little voice to decide for them what information is to be disclosed.

Even so, there are at least four reasons to believe that more fundamental change may be possible—if civil society seizes the opportunity, and the institutions themselves internalize the need for change. First, what was once a marginalized, placard-expressed, protester critique of international institutions' secrecy and lack of accountability has risen to the level of conventional wisdom. When the dean of Harvard's Kennedy School of Government compares the IFTIs to "closed and secretive clubs," the European Union's commissioner for external affairs (the former chair of Britain's Tory party) pronounces in passing that international institutions "lack democratic legitimacy," and the World Bank's former chief economist describes increased openness as "short of a fundamental change in their governance, the most important way to ensure that the international economic institutions are more responsive to the poor, to the environment [and] to broader political and social concerns"—one sees the makings of an emerging elite consensus on the problem and the potential role of greater openness in addressing the "democratic deficit."[3] In this formulation, openness becomes the next best thing to democratic governance, and when it is unlikely because those in control are unlikely to give up power, transparency will serve as the most important alternative control mechanism.[4]

Second, as a result of outside pressure and the emerging conventional wisdom, international institutions themselves are acknowledging, at least rhetorically, the need for greater openness, and in some cases, have actually achieved significant progress toward more transparency. Each of the multilateral development banks, for example, has promulgated formal policies on access to their internal documentation, and a wide variety of records that were previously secret are now routinely provided to the public—although host government veto power and ingrained bureaucratic self-preservation instincts still prevent the routine publication of the most controversial information. Starting in 1999, the almost simultaneous emergence of the left-wing anti-neoliberalism critique featured in the Seattle and

Genoa demonstrations, among others, and the right-wing promarket critique offered by the Republican-dominated U.S. Congress and its Meltzer Commission about the banks and the IMF, pointed toward greater transparency as one of the few strategies that addressed both wings of the debate.[5] It certainly was not lost on the professional staff of the IFTIs that the IMF and World Bank's so-called "Washington consensus" model of market-driven economic development required free flows of information to make markets work—thus adding efficiency arguments to the moral and political critiques by activists. The real importance of these developments, however, is that the pro-openness rhetoric from inside the institutions and formal disclosure policies provide extensive leverage points for activists willing to test specific instances of secrecy and to pursue an "inside-outside" strategy of working with internal reformers and external watchdogs.[6]

Third, as many of the case studies in this book make clear, civil society organizations around the world have seized on openness as a threshold goal in struggles over the whole panoply of social issues, ranging from the environment to AIDS to poverty reduction to corruption. In India, for example, as Shekhar Singh's chapter describes in detail, the Mazdor Kisan Shakti Sanghatan (MKSS) grassroots movement based in Rajasthan began in 1990 with a focus on securing the legally required minimum wages for poor farmers and rural laborers, but soon realized that access to official records was key not only to that goal but also to preventing corruption and enforcing a connection between government expenditure and human need.[7] It was no coincidence that the leading international network trying to address corruption issues took as its name "Transparency International."

Fourth, the past decade witnessed an extraordinary international movement for freedom of information, including successful campaigns for national FOI laws in more than thirty countries. While there is enormous variation in the effectiveness of these laws and major difficulties remain in the implementation of such rights in transitional democracies with limited rule of law, one hallmark of the campaigns has been their attentiveness to other national models and their outreach for international connections and support. In the process, international FOI campaigners have identified the problem of IFTI and IGO secrecy as a major priority for future work, and have begun reaching out beyond the traditional FOI community to NGOs and civil society activists experienced in the various IFTI accountability efforts. Over time, these new networks are likely to develop even more dramatic reform proposals for openness and accountability in the international institutions, ranging from potential international treaties as an overarching framework based on human rights arguments to notice-and-comment requirements for projects and policy changes.[8]

This chapter provides a brief and necessarily selective history of the struggle for openness in the international institutions, a discussion of the founding secrecy norms and their erosion over time, summary descriptions of a few of the more important battles and campaigns in that struggle, an analysis of current transparency policies and institutional structures within the institutions, an overview of current issues and debates, and an outline of the two most likely areas for future transparency developments—the growing interest and role of parliamentarians, and the potential for restraining the power of international organizations through the development of global administrative procedures such as notice-and-comment. One major limitation derives from the limitations of the available scholarly and popular literature on transparency in the international institutions, that is, the preponderance of focus on the World Bank rather than on the regional development banks, the IMF, the WTO, NATO, or others. While the latter do feature in a number of significant studies, and the chapter draws on that material for illustrative purposes, it is the World Bank that has occupied the central place in the protest movements of the past twenty-five years as well as in the international openness reforms of the past decade.

The Roots of Secrecy in International Institutions

Diplomats, central bankers, generals, and corporate lawyers founded the international institutions that exercise power in the globalized world today. It is no wonder that the habits of confidentiality ingrained in these men (and they were almost all men) became the ethos of the institutions they started. Government-to-government discussions in those days were supposed to stay secret for fifty years or more after they took place, and freedom of information law existed only in Sweden and in the former Swedish province of Finland (for reasons peculiar to bourgeois-versus-noble competition in the late 1700s). Over the years since World War II and its immediate aftermath—the incubator period for the global order—those founding conventions of confidentiality eroded in the face of scandal, political challenge, and efficiency arguments.

The first to lose their luster were the diplomatic norms; central banker imperatives took longer, and both still persist in varying degrees of force. Diplomatic theorist Hans J. Morgenthau wrote in 1954 about the "vice of publicity" in diplomacy, and multiple other commentators have testified to the "ethos of confidentiality" in intergovernmental affairs.[9] The U.S. Supreme Court commented in 1936 that "The nature of transactions with foreign nations, moreover, requires caution and unity of design, and their success frequently depends on secrecy and dispatch."[10] Even Justice Stewart, in his concurring opinion in the Supreme Court's 1971 decision not to enjoin publication of the leaked Pentagon Papers, wrote, "It is elementary that the successful conduct of international diplomacy . . . require[s] both confidentiality and secrecy. Other nations can hardly deal with this Nation in an atmosphere of mutual trust unless they can be assured that their confidences will be kept."[11]

But the Pentagon Papers represented a turning point for diplomatic secrecy. Secretary of State William Rogers had entered an affidavit saying that foreign diplomats had specifically told him relations would be damaged by the disclosures in the papers, but then the government overreached. At a key appeals hearing, the government presented a sealed affidavit enclosed in three sealed manila envelopes, one inside the others, all three within a double-locked briefcase; the affidavit explained how certain cable intercepts in the papers showed that the United States had broken the North Vietnamese codes. One of the temporarily enjoined journalists sitting with the *Washington Post* legal team, reporter George Wilson, "stunned everyone by pulling out of his back pocket a verbatim record of the intercept, in an unclassified transcript of Senate Foreign Relations Committee hearings."[12] Years later, the Solicitor General who argued for the government in the Pentagon Papers case concluded that the arguments for diplomatic secrecy were vastly overstated: "I have never seen any trace of a threat to the national security from the publication. I have never even seen it suggested that there was such an actual threat."[13]

The U.S. executive branch continues to assert diplomatic secrecy and to take a maximalist position, but with mixed success. For example, in 1999, the Department of State opposed disclosure of a British consul's letter related to an extradition case, arguing that "it is a longstanding custom and accepted practice in international relations to treat as confidential and not subject to public disclosure information and documents exchanged between governments and their officials. . . . Diplomatic confidentiality obtains . . . even with respect to information that may appear to be innocuous."[14] The letter involved was so innocuous, however, that the consul had previously disclosed its contents to the plaintiff, unbeknownst to all involved, and the government, to its consternation, had to moot the case. As this case suggests, today there coexist uneasily both the proof of persistence of the secrecy norm (most prominently in the imposition by NATO of its information security policies onto new members, helping state secrecy trump new freedom of information laws)[15] and previously unthinkable expressions of the norm's erosion (the CIA's National Intelligence Council carried out its three most recent fifteen-year threat assessments in a series of unclassified workshops and a series of unclassified final reports posted on the Web).[16]

Similar erosion is under way for secrecy arising from the norm of central bank confidentiality. Perhaps the classic expression of the central banker attitude came from U.S. Federal Reserve Board chairman Arthur Burns Jr. in a 1976 speech reacting to the U.S. Freedom of Information Act and what he called a decade of "profound changes in the attitudes of Congress, the courts, and the public generally towards 'secrecy' in government." Under the title "The Proper Limits of Openness in Government," Burns said, "It has been my purpose to question the premise that disclosure is a desirable end in and of itself. I particularly question the premise that disclosure is the cure for bad government." He cited the tradition of "elaborate safeguards" in bank examination "to protect the privacy of bank customers and to preserve public confidence in individual banks and the banking system as a whole." He noted with approval that "Very few of the world's central banks regularly inform their national legislature of their plans for the future course of monetary policy" and argued that "premature disclosure" of Fed strategy would produce "greater short-run volatility in interest rates" and "exaggerated shifts in market expectations," thus making "speculators" the "chief beneficiaries of immediate disclosure." Most troubling to Burns was "the prospect that Board deliberations prior to decision may be opened to public scrutiny," since that would convert reasoned debate into "theater."[17]

Each of these arguments has been challenged in the years since, with nonsecretive policy alternatives put forward to accomplish the same ends, sometimes more effectively or efficiently. For example, the U.S. Congress decided that bank examination secrecy was less effective than deposit insurance in preventing runs on banks, and passed laws forcing transparency on bank practices such as "redlining" (discriminatory mortgage lending), money-laundering, and savings-and-loan accounting. The U.S. courts have reduced secrecy over bank customer data and taxpayer information by ordering disclosure in aggregate formats, stripped of personal identifiers, but allowing researchers to assess bank examiner and even IRS audit rates by income levels, geographic regions, job categories, and industries, and thus hold regulatory bodies far more accountable.[18] The most prominent claim by Burns—that releasing more information about deliberations of the Federal Reserve would benefit only the speculators, the insiders, and thus contribute to volatility in the markets—has largely been demolished by the school of information economics, with studies showing more information from regulatory bodies actually stabilizes the markets and creates more of a level playing field, and that information asymmetries are the real problem underlying bank runs, capital flights, and crashes.[19] As the Nobel Prize–winning economist Joseph Stiglitz has commented on the International Monetary Fund, "The IMF holds that transparency could undermine its effectiveness, a view it shares with the central bankers who play such a large role in its governance. With few exceptions, most of them are committed to the proposition that public discussions of monetary policy would not contribute to economic stability and believe that even public disclosure of the IMF's deliberations would be counterproductive. Remarkably, there is little empirical evidence in support of these strongly held views. On the contrary, few untoward consequences have resulted from the Bank of England's movement towards improved transparency and disclosure."[20]

Professor Stiglitz may be surprised to find that leaders of the IMF now agree with him on this point. Thomas Dawson, then the IMF's director of external relations, commented in 2003 that "information once guarded as closely as state secrets is now routinely published.

And fears in some quarters that the release of this information would shake the pillars of modern civilization seem to have been unfounded. Financial markets are happy getting a steady stream of information from us and from our member governments. And they like it better than the old system when a sudden deluge of information which had been bottled up would come out and destabilize markets and countries." Dawson described an IMF colleague who had come from a career in the British Treasury to work on the IMF's Code of Fiscal Transparency, and joked that he "spent the first 25 years of his career assisting ministers in hiding what was going on and the next five years trying to unveil what was actually happening."[21]

The Checkered History of Transparency at the World Bank

For many years, people affected by IFI programs and policies have raised questions about the legitimacy, efficiency, and accountability of these institutions. Such questions are particularly relevant at a time when several of these institutions are grappling with basic questions about their future, given the rise of Asian economies and long-standing resentments about what is widely seen as inadequate representation of developing countries in the governance structures of these institutions. But these issues are nothing new.

The World Bank's own authorized history of its first half century mentions that direct contact with the people affected by bank decisions "seemed to contradict two of the Bank's constitutional principles: that it would deal with citizens and legislators of member governments through the designated representatives of those governments on the Board of the Bank; and that it would maintain a fiduciary relationship with member governments, a relationship of confidentiality in which the responsibility for releasing information pertaining to a borrower lay with the borrowing government."[22] A leader of the Philippines-based Freedom from Debt Coalition stated the problem more directly and colorfully: "When we complain to the World Bank and the IMF, they tell us, 'So sorry, we don't talk to people. We only talk to governments. We only talk to your president. We only talk to your central bank governor. We only talk to your minister of finance.' This is a joint production of the international finance community with the cooperation of local elites and leaders in our own country. The majority of the people are shut out of the negotiations."[23]

But this opacity, insularity, and secrecy would change—not completely by any means, but markedly. Struggles over thirty years and in countries ranging from Brazil to India forced the change, and the struggle continues. Leadership came from nongovernmental organizations, the environmental movement, growing associations of indigenous peoples, and national parliaments, especially the U.S. Congress. The World Bank became the first international institution targeted and the first to change.

Activists targeted the bank for many reasons. It had global impact and tangible projects. It received contributions from the U.S. government over which taxpayers and the Congress had the right of oversight. It was handily based in Washington, DC, within walking distance of many U.S. and international NGO offices. It was not a foreign government that could exercise nationalist appeals in its defense. And it already had at least rhetorical commitments to the environment and to ameliorating the conditions of indigenous peoples. The bank was chosen not because its practices were worse than those of other development banks or institutions but because there were more handles with which to grip it.[24]

But the other institutions soon followed. After the financial crises in Mexico (1994), Asia (1997), and Russia (1998), IMF delegations found themselves surrounded by housewives beating tin cups and economists bearing hemlock. The IMF's Thomas Dawson summed up the lessons learned in a 2003 speech: "It was widely accepted that in reporting their financial positions some of the crisis countries had been, shall we say, 'economical with the truth.' . . . Not only were countries under pressure to come clean, but the IMF itself came in under unprecedented pressure to reveal its policy advice to countries, that is, to be less secretive."[25] Soon the IMF moved almost all of its documents onto the Web and began reaching out to parliamentarians and NGOs, although its decision-making process remained extremely problematic from an accountability perspective.[26]

In 1999, the WTO ministerial meeting in Seattle became the scene of violent and nonviolent street protest, so subsequent location choices for WTO meetings favored islands separated from demonstrators by causeways, barricades, and police. By 2002 the WTO was issuing press releases about its quicker release of restricted documents, sponsoring regular NGO seminars, and spending core budget funds to include lower-income countries in its Geneva proceedings.[27] In 2004, the former chairman of the WTO's Appellate Body called for opening "the proceedings of the panels and the oral hearings of the Appellate Body, both to press coverage and to overall public observation" and "the same for meetings of the General Council, the Dispute Settlement Body and all of the other major councils of the WTO," because otherwise "it's unlikely that members of the WTO will ever secure the public support needed to maximize the many gains to be made from trade through a rule-based world trading system."[28] The WTO has not yet adopted these suggestions, nor would they amount to a transparency revolution, only a "partial revolution," in Alasdair Roberts's phrase. But already the transparency changes have opened serious discussion of accountability and governance questions at the WTO and the other international organizations.

For the World Bank openness struggle, the start date that activists point to is 1966, when the General Assembly of the United Nations passed resolutions condemning the apartheid regime in South Africa and the continuing colonial subjugation of Angola and Mozambique by Portugal as violations of the UN charter. Despite its UN affiliation, the bank insisted that Article IV, Section 10 of its own charter, prohibiting interference in the political affairs of its members, required it to disregard the resolutions. It proceeded with a US$10 million loan to Portugal and a US$20 million loan to South Africa, even after a personal plea from UN Secretary-General U Thant to the bank's president, George Woods.[29] This was hardly the first, but certainly the most flagrant, of World Bank actions that raised the question of accountability. If the UN charter itself did not apply, then the bank had set itself up as an entity above national law but without international law. As activist David Hunter described it, because the bank was insulated from any legal responsibilities to the people directly affected by its actions, it was a "lawless institution."[30]

The first effective resistance by affected peoples came in the Philippines, only two years into the martial law imposed by Ferdinand Marcos in 1972. The World Bank had made the Philippines a priority, lending US$2.6 billion for 61 projects between 1973 and 1981. In particular, the Chico River dam project in the Cordillera would have provided hydroelectric power in the wake of the oil crisis, but only by flooding nearly 3,000 hectares of rice terraces belonging to the indigenous Kalinga and Bontoc peoples. They only found out about the dam a year after project approval, when survey teams came to the valley. Protests escalated, from petitions to the government that were ignored, to a regional pact among indigenous leaders against working in the construction, to incursions by the New Peoples' Army guerrilla forces, to direct protest at the IMF Manila conference in 1977, where bank president Robert McNamara felt compelled to say that "no funding of projects would take place in the face of continued opposition from the people." Ultimately, the bank withdrew, and the Philippine government postponed the dam indefinitely. "It was a silent retreat, but this did not detract from the fact that the Bontoc and Kalinga had accomplished something exceedingly rare in the Third World: the Bank's withdrawal in the face of popular resistance."[31] In partial response, the bank developed its first policies on indigenous peoples, but it would be years before those policies explicitly mandated informed consent and self-determination as core principles.[32]

In retrospect, the Polonoroeste road paving and forest colonization project in Brazil starting in 1982 may have been the paradigm case of controversial World Bank projects and of effective NGO opposition. Polonoroeste featured enormous environmental and social damage and no consultation with indigenous peoples, while internal bank warnings were ignored and government and extractive industry interests drove the process. The project's road paving, paid for with US$457 million from the World Bank, doubled the population of the region in a decade, while deforestation pulped the rain forest. The experience stirred up powerful emotions. Of the development fostered by the Polonoroeste road building, a professional forester wrote: "Visiting such areas it is hard to view without emotion the miles of devastated trees, of felled, broken and burned trunks, of branches, mud and bark crisscrossed with tractor trails—especially when one realizes that in most cases nothing of comparable value will grow again on the area. Such sights are reminiscent of photographs of Hiroshima, and Brazil and Indonesia might be regarded as waging the equivalent of thermonuclear war upon their own territories."[33]

But there's more to the Polonoroeste story. NGO protest, social networks of Brazilian and foreign anthropologists, and the first Washington-based international NGO campaign persuaded the U.S. Congress to intervene with hearings and an unprecedented meeting with the head of the World Bank. In March 1985, the bank suspended the loans. "It was an extraordinary double precedent: for the first time, the Bank was forced to account to outside NGOs and a legislator from a member country for the environmental and social impacts of a lending program; also for the first time, a public international financial institution had halted disbursements on a loan for environmental reasons."[34] Perhaps equally important for the future of openness struggles against the bank and the IFTIs, international activists forged close connections with the rubber tappers from Acre, Brazil, and their leader, Francisco "Chico" Mendes, whose subsequent assassination in 1988 by the hired guns of irate landowners put the rain forest issue on the front page of *The New York Times*. The connection transformed both activists and tappers, placing the human dimension of environmental change at the heart of the argument, adding sustainability proposals like Mendes's "extractive reserves" to the development debate, giving the tappers new access to international leverage, and giving the international activists new approaches to environmental debates that were grounded in social relations rather than technical expertise.[35]

More profound institutional change came about due to the Narmada dam project in India, which resulted in mass protest and ultimately catalyzed two major reforms at the bank—the new information disclosure policy and the Inspection Panel. Approved by the bank in 1985 with a loan of US$450 million, the Sardar Sarovar (Narmada) project was slated to displace more than 150,000 people—most of whom found out not from timetables or resettlement locations but from the markers placed in their villages indicating the submergence level of the prospective reservoir. NGOs and individuals such as Medha Patkar (a social worker originally from Bombay) insisted on access to information, and by 1988 the grassroots movement known as Narmada Bachao Andolan (NBA, or Save the Narmada Movement) had mobilized thousands of the "oustees" in opposition to the dam. A special U.S. congressional oversight hearing in 1989 featuring NBA testimony proved a turning point, when connections between the congressman who chaired the hearing and members of the Japanese Diet, plus media coverage of a subsequent NGO forum in Japan, persuaded the Japanese government to end its support for the project. Gradually, bank executive directors began questioning the version of events provided by their operations staff because it differed so strongly from the reports from the affected people themselves. The NBA launched a December 1990–January 1991 march to the dam site, but were stopped at the state border by police, which led to a 26-day fast by Patkar and other activists, and even more pressure on the bank.

Finally, the bank appointed an independent review team (the Morse Commission), but then voted to continue the project despite the Commission's findings that resettlement was "not possible under prevailing circumstances," that environmental impacts had "not been properly considered or adequately addressed," and that "progress will be impossible except as a result of unacceptable means," that is, police force. The bank's approval of continuing the dam, according to Patrick Coady, the U.S. executive director, at the October 1992 board meeting, signaled "that no matter how egregious the situation, no matter how flawed the project, no matter how many policies have been violated, and no matter how clear the remedies prescribed, the Bank will go forward on its own terms."[36] But Narmada catalyzed protests in Madrid at the 1994 World Bank–IMF annual meetings, multiple congressional inquiries, and a highly successful NGO campaign working with the U.S. Congress to hold back funding replenishment for the World Bank Group. Ultimately, the bank responded by creating the Inspection Panel and a new disclosure policy, and withdrew from Narmada. Reform at the bank, however, did not produce reform on the ground in India because the Indian government proceeded with the dam, which continues under construction today with reservoir levels rising and resettlement incomplete.

A similar episode of international campaign pressure occurred with the Bio-Bio River dam controversy in Chile—it produced major institutional reform, but too little and too late for the affected people at the local level. The case focused attention for the first time on the lack of accountability in the rapidly growing private sector side of the World Bank's operations, specifically the International Finance Corporation (IFC), while severely testing the nascent democratic processes in a country transitioning from the seventeen-year Pinochet dictatorship after 1990. The state-owned utility started planning for a series of dams on the Bio-Bio, a center of indigenous Mapuche/Pehuenche culture as well as a world-class whitewater-rafting destination, in the mid-1980s. But neither the IFC (which approved the first dam, Pangue, in 1992; it was finished in 1996) nor the power company carried out serious environmental or social impact studies.

A burgeoning protest movement brought together Chilean and international environmentalists and anthropologists with members of the indigenous groups and forced a series of significant reforms on the IFC, including its first compliance ombudsman, expanded environmental impact reviews, and a new disclosure policy. Remarkably, the Bio-Bio debates forced the IFC for the first time to release publicly an environmental assessment before the board's review, thus allowing debate about the assessment's deficiencies.[37] But secrecy habits die hard. The independent review ordered by the World Bank's president, James Wolfensohn, and carried out by the former head of the National Wildlife Federation, Dr. Jay Hair, ended up heavily censored by the bank, with almost a third never made public. According to the July 25, 1997 letter from Hair to Wolfensohn, "numerous deletions . . . appear to have been made for no other reason than to avoid embarrassing the individuals who made certain decisions regarding the Pangue project or how it was supervised by the IFC."[38] At the same time that the Bio-Bio campaign produced reforms at the IFC and even some significant success at the national level for the development of democratic institutions in Chile, it failed at the local level because the dams went forward, the power company succeeded in its divide-and-conquer tactics and dominated the local foundation set up to benefit the indigenous community, and only a handful of Pehuenche families were able to hold out for their original goal of stopping the dams.

Campaigners achieved more success against the Arun III dam project in Nepal, which became the poster child of the fiftieth-anniversary campaign against the World Bank and the first claim presented to the new Inspection Panel, in 1994–1995. The Arun case ultimately obliged the new bank president, Wolfensohn, to take a side in the preexisting internal debate over the project's viability and revealed how transnational advocacy networks can sometimes tip the balance. The claim and the Inspection Panel's report provoked Wolfensohn to withdraw the bank's support for Arun III (the Nepal government has not since been able to finance it) and established the Inspection Panel as a viable accountability institution. Even so, the bank attempted to prevent the release of the final panel report in August 1995, but its hand was forced because portions had leaked out, "causing distortion of the facts and embarrassment to the Bank."[39]

The China Western Poverty Reduction Project was perhaps the most recent "turning point" case in the transparency struggle at the World Bank. Starting in 1999, the bank sought to support the Chinese government's plan to resettle some 58,000 poor farmers onto lands traditionally roamed by nomadic Tibetan and Mongolian peoples. Local people sent letters seeking international support against the plan, and Tibet solidarity groups worked with the Bank Information Center and other bank watchdogs to generate skepticism in donor governments and intense media coverage—including television images of protesters scaling the façade of the bank building with their signs. The campaign led to high-level diplomatic tensions between the bank, its largest donor (the United States), and its largest borrower (China); an unusually intense level of board engagement; a scathing report by the Inspection Panel; and ultimately the cancellation of the project. The panel report not only documented the project's systematic violation of the bank's "safeguard" policies but went further to reveal weaknesses across the bank's entire system for avoiding and mitigating environmental and social risks. The bank responded with a new commitment to the safeguards and a series of checks and balances to ensure compliance.[40] Yet this victory for transparency did not ameliorate conditions for the Chinese and Tibetans affected by the project, because the Chinese government went ahead without the World Bank, whose president, James Wolfensohn, argued that "at the end of the day it would have been better if we were involved in the project than if we were not at all."[41] The Tibetan support groups disagreed, given the inadequacies of the bank's performance, the limitations imposed by China, and the legitimacy bestowed by bank sponsorship.

Crucially, these struggles over controversial projects from the Polonoroeste to Tibet catalyzed a remarkable pro-openness dynamic—directed internally rather than externally—among the professional staff of the bank and the other institutions. For example, in the authorized history of the bank's environmental dealings, based on almost complete access to its files, the author subtly denigrates what he terms the "extreme" rhetoric of the NGO activists, but reserves his deepest scorn for the internal deception and secrecy evident from the bank's own documents, and often deployed by its staff against management and even its board. For example, two years after the board had approved the first phase of the Amazon highway project, "some Board members expressed concern about Polonoroeste. To each the staff gave reassuring replies that concealed much contrary information. And the staff misled not only the Board but also the president. In a briefing paper on Polonoroeste to [A.W.] Clausen in December 1983, the staff wrote, '. . . Implementation of the Special Project [for Amerindian protection] is now satisfactory.' . . . Evidence from the files shows that the division chief was busy telling the Brazilian government that implementation was very unsatisfactory. Few of the thirty-seven Indian reserves had been demarcated and registered, and many had been invaded by squatters, loggers, and others."[42]

This critique suggests one significant component of a growing commitment by the World Bank to greater openness: its own realization that internal barriers to information sharing led to bad decisions and trapped the bank in bad projects. For example, after NGO critics had shown the myriad ways the Narmada dam project failed to meet stated bank policies, the bank staff began to fool itself. The authorized history described the situation this way, in a remarkable soliloquy: "Retrofitting is difficult. The effort to do so in Narmada as NGO pressure built up then began to produce apparently deceitful behavior on the part of the operational staff [of the World Bank]. Their logic went like this. 1. We know things are not going well in the project. 2. But do we want to pull out or suspend? 3. No, it is potentially a damn fine project, and things will go better if we are in. (Anyway, management will not allow a pullout, for "country relations" reasons.) 4. Therefore we need to justify staying in. We do so by sending up reports that things are going well or at least improving, making sure that if anything is said about things that are not going well the phrasing implies that they are minor or on the way to being fixed. The trick is to make the aroma of words do the work that the evidence cannot."[43]

One result of the openness battles at the World Bank has been an institutional commitment to encourage national and local freedom of information laws. The World Bank Group has produced a series of readings and training manuals for its country staff on government openness, organized seminars and video conferences in dozens of countries, included transparency in its governance recommendations and conditions for financing, and produced extensive research showing that "countries with better information flows also govern better."[44] Summarizing a host of papers and studies, the World Bank Institute's Daniel Kaufmann has concluded that transparency is "key to minimizing the risks of financial crises," "fundamental for enabling sustained development and growth" by encouraging competition and more efficient resource allocation, "a major deterrent to corruption" and state capture, and "a basic democratic right" that serves as a "major 'empowering' tool for the citizenry and, through it, for redistribution and poverty alleviation."[45] Of course, having made these arguments abroad, the bank has more difficulty resisting pressure for greater transparency within its own functions.

But the bank's pro-transparency proselytizing is not the only model for international institutions. In sharp contrast, the North Atlantic Treaty Organization has encouraged greater secrecy among its members. In 2002, NATO held its first-ever summit in the capital of a former Warsaw Pact nation—Prague—and formally announced the entry of seven new members from Eastern Europe and the Baltics. In the case of Romania, *The Times of London* commented that the invitation came "despite its endemic corruption, a systematic lack of government transparency and poor progress towards a Western-style civil society." Romanian president Ion Iliescu chose to emphasize that joining NATO would allow Romania "to be integrated into the civilized world, and to receive necessary support for internal reforms"; and NATO officials complimented the Romanian military for "satisfying its Membership Action Plan, a detailed set of changes in both the military and civilian sectors that NATO assigns applicant countries" including "promoting the rule of law."[46]

One of the most significant NATO assignments, however, has almost completely undercut Romania's halting progress toward greater freedom of information by forcing it to adopt a state secrets law that conforms to NATO's own information security system, which itself dates back to Cold War secrecy thinking. Romania's new secrecy law, enacted in 2002, creates a broad authority to withhold information that has been deemed sensitive by government officials and trumps its 2001 Law Regarding Free Access to Information of Public Interest. In fact, the NATO accession process has contributed to new state secrets laws in eleven Central and Eastern European countries that otherwise had been in the vanguard of the international freedom of information movement in the 1990s. Yet NATO has refused to make its standards publicly available and has instructed member countries to decline requests for its policy under national FOI laws.[47] New intergovernmental cooperation in the war on terrorism is likely to deepen and expand this emphasis on information security rather than openness on the part of NATO, other regional security alliances, and international governmental organizations (IGOs). As Alasdair Roberts's chapter in this volume demonstrates, that emphasis may undermine not just democracy but also the security that secrecy is intended to protect. The various investigations of the September 11, 2001 terrorist attacks indicate that excessive secrecy was part of the explanation why the intelligence community failed to prevent the attacks. Greater openness rather than reflexive secrecy may well make a better strategy against terrorism.[48]

Policies, Laws, and Institutional Structures

Unlike NATO's information policies, those of the international financial institutions are largely on the public record and susceptible of analysis. Each of the international financial and trade institutions has promulgated a formal disclosure policy, and several have gone through two or more revisions of their policies based on actual experience and input from outsiders.[49] Several have also included transparency procedures in their compliance requirements for host governments, yet those often fall far short of achieving openness— stated policy is one thing, actual practice is another. Likewise, experts based in Washington, DC or other financial centers enjoy levels of access to IFTI information far greater than that of indigenous people in the forests of Cambodia, to take only one recent example. Also, institutions that rank highly in one area may fail in others. The country of Singapore, for example, ranks at the top of the Transparency International index (measuring corruption perceptions) and serves as the baseline for the PricewaterhouseCoopers "Opacity Index" (which measures lost foreign investment in relation to perceived opacity in given countries), yet when journalists affiliated with the Southeast Asian Press Alliance asked 8 countries in the region for 45 specific items of government information, Singapore provided less than 50 percent, about equivalent to Cambodia.[50]

Despite the progress toward greater disclosure described above, none of the financial institutions qualifies as transparent when analysts examine institutional openness using the three most important criteria: *participatory disclosure, review mechanisms,* and *governance. Participatory disclosure* means openness that empowers participation in the decision-making process of the institution, rather than end-stage disclosure of decisions that have already been made. All of the international financial institutions are demonstrably better at the latter than at sharing detailed information early in the deliberative process. For example, at the World Trade Organization, trade negotiations and arbitrations that have the force of law take place behind closed doors. *Review mechanisms* involve process guarantees such as requirements that information refusals be made in writing, that refusals be subject to a "harm test" or "public interest test" as in many national freedom of information statutes, and that requesters have the right of appeal for independent review of the withholding. *Governance* means simply the level of meaningful public oversight for the governing bodies of the institutions. At the multilateral development banks, for example, almost total secrecy surrounds the operations of the boards of directors.

A comparative approach is essential to identify best and worst practices, to allow the institutions to learn from one another, and to raise the overall standards of openness. However, the core problem for comparative analysis along any dimension, not only openness, arises from the institutions' differences in form, function, governance, process, and financial instruments. For example, an IMF loan serves a very different function than does a World Bank loan; the Asian Development Bank has a very different decision-making process (dominated by Japan) than does the Inter-American Development Bank (dominated by the United States); and the World Trade Organization has no lending cycle at all.

To begin the process of measuring and comparing the international institutions, a team of analysts from the Bank Information Center, a leading NGO in the campaigns for greater accountability at the World Bank and other financial institutions, and freedominfo.org, a virtual network of international freedom of information advocates, created the IFI Transparency Resource, a "matrix" database compiling policy and practice information on openness. The initial versions of the database, released in draft form in April 2004 and revised for release in February 2005, focused on 10 key financial institutions: the World Bank, International Finance Corporation, Multilateral Investment Guarantee Agency, European Investment Bank, European Bank for Reconstruction and Development, Inter-American Development Bank, Inter-American Investment Corporation, African Development Bank, Asian Development Bank, and International Monetary Fund. This 255-item matrix made possible the most sophisticated comparison ever of IFI transparency policies and practices.[51] The matrix breaks down the banks' processes into categories such as "general institutional information," "the lending cycle," "bank-wide policies, guidelines, procedures and strategies," "evaluations and audits," "country-specific analysis and strategy papers," "governing bodies," "accountability mechanisms," "process guarantees," and "archives-websites-information centers." Within each category may be as many as 30 different information types. For example, "the lending cycle" includes social and environmental review procedures, early identification of potential loans, project preparation including feasibility and environmental assessments, preapproval notification and approval discussion, implementation and supervision reporting, and completion and evaluation reporting.

The findings of the IFI Transparency Resource indicate many common weaknesses that undermine both the operational efficiency and effectiveness of the organizations and render democratic accountability and participation difficult—few open meetings, the delayed release of many documents, the confidentiality of many documents, and no clear procedures for requesting information. The contrasts indicate that there are some areas where one or more institutions have moved ahead, such as the fact that the Asian Development Bank and the African Development Bank are the only institutions to release certain environmental information 120 days prior to project approval for both public and private sector lending, and the Inter-American Development Bank has become the first to release its board of directors meeting minutes. While none of the banks stands out across all the transparency categories, the matrix does show the World Bank with the highest disclosure standards generally—no small testament to the focused campaigns on the bank as well as to its internal forces for reform.

But the "presumption" of disclosure, claimed by many institutions as cornerstones of their policies, is seriously undercut by a plethora of exceptions that turn disclosure on its head and only allow those documents specifically listed as releasable to come out. Nor are there procedural avenues for those who feel access has been unfairly denied, or "process guarantees" such as clear standards on what should be disclosed, a promise of timely response, or a right of appeal. The policies are not tested on any scale for balancing the legitimate need for confidentiality with the public interest in transparency. The disclosure policies also appear to reflect substantial deference to private corporations. The matrix data reveal that there is little coherence in the transparency of institutionwide policy development, disclosure tends to come after decisions have been made, little information is released during project implementation, financial intermediary lending is generally exempt from disclosure rules, and some dissemination efforts lack procedures. The study indicates that basic institutional information is consistently released, but that the institutions are generally weak when it comes to giving the public specific information on how to contact directors or staff members. Meanwhile, the governing bodies are almost completely closed to public scrutiny, with no minutes, voting records, or transcripts available, except at the IADB. The meetings of the major decision-making bodies are uniformly held in private, and postmeeting announcements come in different forms and levels of specificity.

None of the ten IFIs included in the matrix study has clear procedures regarding the transparency of policy review and development processes. None of the institutions releases external comments made during a policy review. Drafts of proposed policies are not made available consistently before board action. Financial statements and audits are generally available, but more specific reporting on evaluations is often not disclosed. Most IFIs disclose the final economic reports or analyses for specific countries, but the preparation of them is largely opaque. As for project lending, none of the IFIs releases the draft board reports on potential projects, and background feasibility and technical studies are difficult to obtain. Policies on the release of environmental information vary widely. Project implementation and supervision is arguably the most secretive phase. Similarly, the lending activities of financial intermediaries are subject to a much lower standard of disclosure. Only a few institutions have accountability mechanisms—the systems that may allow IFI employees or outsiders to raise grievances—and few live up to the most transparent mechanism, the Inspection Panel found at the World Bank. None of the IFIs has an institutionwide, binding translation policy that would allow information to be disclosed to non-English-speaking people affected by their policies and programs. Many of the IFIs have archive policies with timelines for declassifying materials, among which the Asian Development Bank is the most progressive, with a five-year declassification period, but disclosure is still subject to government consent. In sum, the matrix study demonstrates that the highly touted disclosure policies of the international financial institutions are more akin to sophisticated publications schemes than they are to the new national freedom of information laws.

Contemporary Issues and Debates

Of late, a debate has emerged around the hangover of "business confidentiality" in the IFTIs. Before the campaigns and reforms of the 1980s and 1990s, this presumption of a fiduciary responsibility on the part of the IFTIs toward borrowers and contractors overrode all other considerations during decisions about transparency. This has changed somewhat, but the hangover continues, despite all the openness commitments. In November 2002, for example, it required no less than a Supreme Court decision in Uganda to break the World Bank's version of this barrier, with significant consequences. A Ugandan High Court justice overruled the Ugandan government and the World Bank to order the release of a key document defining the commercial arrangements relating to a controversial Nile River dam project supported by the bank. The US$550 million-dollar Bujagali dam project will commit the already heavily indebted country to pay billions of dollars to the private corporation that will own and operate the dam for the resulting electricity, whether or not Uganda can resell the power elsewhere in Africa. Yet the World Bank refused to require release of the Power Purchase Agreement between the corporation and Uganda. An internal World Bank ombudsman report in September 2001 noted that if the project's sponsor "wants to maintain a degree of secrecy consistent with a private sector project, perhaps public institutions should not be asked to provide guarantees for or subsidize the undertaking." Concerned citizens and civil society groups in Uganda went to court, citing Article 41 of the Ugandan Constitution as requiring release of the document, and

High Court justice Egonda-Ntende agreed with them. A subsequent NGO analysis of the document concluded that Ugandans "will pay hundreds of millions of dollars in excessive power payments" as a result of the project.[52] Yet the biographer of the World Bank's president was able to interview a number of Ugandan families who would receive cash compensation for their land from the dam builders and to conclude therefore that the story was a "tragedy for Uganda" because the protests were holding up electric power that would supply "clinics and factories"—never mentioning the excessive payments to the private corporation or the bank's own internal critiques.[53]

The blame game of shifting responsibility between international organizations and the host governments also provides cover for continued opacity. In Phnom Penh, about forty villagers from several Cambodian provinces showed up in front of the World Bank office on Monday, November 11, 2002, and vowed to sleep on the sidewalk until they received copies of the logging plans for the areas in which they lived. That Monday was the beginning of a nineteen-day public review period required by the World Bank for the plans, which indicate where and how cutting is to occur over the next twenty-five years. But the government's Department of Forestry and Wildlife apparently provided the World Bank—its biggest single funder—with only two copies of the plans, both in black and white, which obscured the color-coding that specifically outlined logging areas. Villagers demanded color copies to take back to their communities and told the bank that neither the logging companies nor the forestry department had consulted with them about which areas should be protected as community forest. Bank officials attempted to negotiate greater access but simultaneously affirmed the release of a US$15 million loan that had been held up while it pressed the government for the public review. An NGO observer called the review process "a farce," but a bank official told reporters, "it's a first, it's a start . . . not insignificant."[54]

The Cambodian villager confronting her own authoritarian government faces an even more difficult task. The links from citizens to international institutions remain tenuous even in robust democracies, where elected representatives form governments that appoint high officials who then select directors for the World Bank or the IMF. For undemocratic countries, there is no chain of accountability, and the attenuation of representation involved in arrangements like the IMF's, where a single executive director represents a whole group of countries, demolishes any notion of answerability.[55]

In response to the answerability problems in both directions (national and international), reformers inside and outside international institutions have welcomed the emergence of parliamentarians as a new source for dialogue, engagement, oversight, and even, to a limited but growing extent, participatory representation. For example, the World Bank hosted in 2000 the first-ever formal meeting of parliamentarians with top bank leaders, including 50 individuals from about 30 countries, and the Parliamentary Network on the World Bank subsequently separated itself from bank sponsorship, set up independent offices, and greatly expanded its reach. Its 2004 annual meeting attracted 183 parliamentarians from 70 countries, and the network has pressed the bank not to approve Poverty Reduction Strategy Papers unless governments have them reviewed by their legislatures.[56] The IMF has experienced a wide range of parliamentary interaction, ranging from the "very hard oversight" exercised by the U.S. Congress in making the release of approved funding conditional on certain IMF reforms, to "soft oversight" such as the U.K. House of Commons's questioning of IMF officials in 2002, to the rejectionist positions taken by several national parliaments against IMF agreements in which they had no voice (such as the Turkish parliament forcing the national government to break its promise to the IMF in 1998 about holding down public sector salaries).[57] Even the former director general of the WTO has called for greater national engagement with the international institutions, especially through parliamentarians: "A group of senior parliamentarians, serving in their national legislatures, should form a democratic caucus to provide systematic oversight of international institutions, focusing particularly on increasing the transparency of these organizations. . . . Not [to] replace national governments, but only strengthen their role in holding these agencies to account."[58]

National openness analogies also offer some interesting principled approaches that hold great promise for application to the international institutions. Many commentators have described the rise of the administrative state in the twentieth century as a major challenge to democratic governance in many of the same ways that analysts now criticize the international institutions, as secretive and capricious bureaucratic power unaccountable to those affected. The twentieth-century reform response to the administrative state was to limit, regulate, and legitimize that bureaucratic power through more open and participative rule-making procedures, appeal mechanisms, requirements for reasoned decision making, and substantive standards like proportionality, judicial review, and the expansion of citizen rights even more than legislative or executive responsibilities.[59] A classic example of this reform approach was the 1946 Administrative Procedures Act in the United States, which included in nascent form what became in 1966 the Freedom of Information Act. The APA compelled a notice-and-comment procedure by federal agencies for any regulation or policy change that would affect private parties or state and local governments. The procedure included litigation rights if the agency failed to provide notice or failed to take into account public comment, or otherwise flouted the participatory intent of the statute. Today, an entire section of the American Bar Association specializes in administrative law, and additional notice-and-comment-type provisions routinely show up in U.S. regulation and legislation (as the legal basis for environmental impact statements, for example). The experience has "not been a source of unmitigated joy in American rulemaking," since comment periods have "often taken on the look of an Internet poll where those interest groups with the most time and ambition can collectively submit thousands of replies about a proposed rule" and agencies spend "months and sometimes years responding in a substantive way to every individual comment no matter how trivial to pass judicial scrutiny."[60]

Yet the development of administrative law has dramatically restrained bureaucratic power and increased public participation in rule making and governance in the United States, so much so that debates over its application to international institutions have become central to the discourse about answerability and participation in the globalized world, both inside and outside those institutions.[61] For example, the first decision of the WTO's appellate body in the 1996 Shrimp/Turtle case criticized the United States for curtailing shrimp imports without giving any of the affected countries the "formal opportunity to be heard, or to respond to any arguments that may be made against it."[62] A recent set of recommendations for reform of the WTO capped its list of proposed changes with the idea of a global "Federal Register" where all international organizations, not only the WTO, would post notices of pending decisions, declarations, and agreements, and seek comment from the public.[63] Some of the international institutions themselves have taken such suggestions: for example, the Basel Committee of central bankers solicited comments from banks, industry groups, and other interested parties through a largely public process of establishing a new capital adequacy framework starting in 1999 (the final policy was issued in June 2004).[64]

Clearly, the international institutions have already built a global administrative space, populated with dense regulatory regimes such as the WTO, the Organization for Economic Cooperation and Development, the committees of the G-7 and G-8, the financial regulation carried out by the IMF or the Basel Committee, and the product and process rules adopted by the International Organization on Standardization (ISO), to name only a few. Even this short list gives a sense of the wide variety of global administration, which is carried out by formal international and treaty organizations, transnational networks of government officials taking collective action, private institutions with regulatory functions, hybrid private-intergovernmental arrangements, or national regulators under treaty regimes or cooperative standards. The logic of applying administrative procedures restraints to the growing regulatory power of the international bodies seems widely accepted, even by many of the institutions themselves, but the debate has moved to a more complicated level where many of the most important issues remain outstanding. For example, at the basic level of review, what new arrangements will be required to provide the equivalent of judicial review to the international organizations? After all, even the UN Security Council has failed so far to establish an independent body to scrutinize its sanctions decisions. At the normative level, what is the democratic basis for global administrative law in the absence of electoral or other models of direct representation at the global level, or put another way, through what mechanisms can global participation or deliberation actually occur? And would global administrative accountability actually aggravate the north–south cleavages and distributional issues already present in the globalized world, by empowering primarily northern populations, market actors, social interests, and states?[65]

Lessons Learned

The history of constant struggle for the past thirty years over issues of openness and accountability at the World Bank and the other international institutions holds significant lessons for activists, analysts, citizens, and the institutions themselves. The extraordinary pattern of grudging reforms preceded and enveloped by clouds of rhetorical commitments suggests that the eloquent abolitionist and former slave Frederick Douglass had it right: "Power concedes nothing without a struggle." The authorized history of the World Bank's interaction with environmental issues contains a constant refrain of pressure and reform: "governance reforms of the mid-1990s, intended to make the Bank more transparent and publicly accountable, reforms that were once again prompted mainly by environmental NGOs."[66] "Outside pressure was critical in getting the Bank to take action: 'There were a number of outside groups who were quite vociferous . . . in bringing this to our attention . . . groups like Amnesty International, the Harvard group of Cultural Survival . . . and others. They were quick to chastise us and rightly so.'"[67]

The lesson is that pressure works, and money pressure works especially well: the World Bank finally installed the Inspection Panel and issued its information disclosure policy after the U.S. Congress threatened to hold up refunding its capital accounts. Also important are rhetorical commitments, which provide leverage: it was the bank's successive and nearly continuous violations of its own stated policies that gave activists and affected populations the evidence to force accountability and openness. Such policy commitments may seem empty at first or subject to systemic flouting, yet they empower challenges to power in unexpected ways (as did the Helsinki agreements of 1975 and the impetus thus given to the dissent movements that brought down the Berlin Wall).[68] Today, the primary dynamic is that of keeping up with the neighbors: in openness consultations with IFTI staff, the constant refrain is not about "best practices," but about what other IFTIs are doing. In this regard, the focused pressure on the World Bank has had significant ripple effects on all the regional development banks, to the point that several have gotten ahead of the others on one or more measures of openness (such as the Inter-American Development Bank releasing its board meeting minutes). Now activists are producing report cards rating and comparing the banks as a key tool pushing toward openness reforms.

The biggest change occurs when external critics gain internal allies, who then change the organizational culture. This is what the World Bank leadership did when it set up the Inspection Panel in 1993–94. Similarly, the anticorruption unit within the bank has challenged the general counsel's office over continued secrecy around the contractors banned or penalized by the bank for corruption. In the European Union, the Scandinavian countries countered the initial lowest common denominator secrecy assumptions and moved the EU toward formal process guarantees on openness. This internalization process is vital to success. The Congressional Research Service analyst who has followed the transparency struggle most closely has commented: "The main problem with seeking transparency, in my experience, is finding a way of getting information without pushing the real decision process into another place where it is away from the window and only the cleaned-up results are transparent. The institutions have to want to be transparent because they believe it is in their best interest. A hard nut to crack."[69]

The most successful openness campaigns bring human faces to esoteric policies and projects, link activists and analysts across national borders, and apply the same demands for transparency and accountability at every level of governance, from the local project to the national government to the international institution. More and more often, this struggle is based on a rights discourse,[70] much to the dismay of the international institutions. The World Bank's James Wolfensohn, for example, commented to a 2004 meeting of Greenpeace activists in London, "If I talk about a rights-based approach, I get letters [from board members] saying I have exceeded my authority because we are a financial institution. Many countries on our board have signed the declaration of human rights but say this is not the job of a financial institution."[71] But the democratic deficit is compelling all the international institutions to take on the job of establishing legitimacy, while their critics and those affected by their decisions will continue to contest divergent notions of legitimacy and justice. The struggle for global transparency, like the history of administrative law reforms, demonstrates that all such change is the function of the power relations of various actors, who create new procedures and new openness as new actors gain power, particularly in moments of legitimacy crisis, like now.

1. See Joseph Nye Jr., "Globalization's Democratic Deficit: How to Make International Institutions More Accountable," *Foreign Affairs* 80 (4) (2001): 2–6; for a more stringent critique, see Graham Saul, "Transparency and Accountability in International Financial Institutions," in Richard Calland and A. Tilley, eds., *The Right to Know, The Right to Live: Access to Information and Socio-Economic Justice* (Cape Town: Open Democracy Advice Centre, 2002), 126–137.

2. Ann Florini, *The Coming Democracy: New Rules for Running a New World* (Washington, DC: Island Press, 2003), 34.

3. See Nye Jr., "Globalization's Democratic Deficit"; Chris Patten, "Jaw-Jaw, Not War-War: Military Success in Afghanistan Has Encouraged the US to Ignore European Doubts About Confronting the 'Axis of Evil,'" *Financial Times*, February 15, 2002, 16; Joseph Stiglitz, *Globalization and Its Discontents* (New York: Norton, 2002), 227; for additional evidence of the growing consensus, see Saul, "Transparency."

4. Joseph Stiglitz, "Democratizing the International Monetary Fund and the World Bank: Governance and Accountability," *Governance* 16 (1) (2003): 133.

5. A point made vividly by Marco Verweij and Timothy E. Josling in their introduction in the special issue of *Governance*. See Marco Verweij and Timothy Josling, "Deliberately Democratizing Multilateral Organization," *Governance* 16 (1) (2003): 3.

6. For the most extensive current reporting on disclosure policies, as well as specific links to actual texts at each of the IFTIs, see http://www.freedominfo.org/ifti.htm and the IFI Transparency Resource (February 2005 release) at http://www.ifitransparencyresource.org and the Bank Information Center at http://www.bicusa.org.

7. See the case study of the MKSS right to information campaign, including essays by Aruna Roy, Nikhil Dey, and Vivek Ramkumar, at http://www.freedominfo.org/case/mkss/mkss.htm.

8. For description and analysis of the international freedom of information movement, see Thomas Blanton, "The World's Right to Know," *Foreign Policy* 131 (2002): 50–58; and in an expanded version, "The Openness Revolution," *Development Dialogue* 1 (2002): 7–21.

9. See the discussion in Alasdair Roberts, "A Partial Revolution: The

Diplomatic Ethos and Transparency in Intergovernmental Organizations," *Public Administration Review* 64 (4) (2004): 411–412.

10. *United States v. Curtiss-Wright Export Corp.*, 299 U.S. 304 (1936).

11. *New York Times Co. v. United States*, 403 U.S. at 728 (1971) (J. Stewart, concurring).

12. Ben Bradlee, *A Good Life* (New York: Simon and Schuster, 1995), 320.

13. Erwin Griswold, "Secrets Not Worth Keeping," *The Washington Post*, February 15, 1989, A25.

14. Patrick Kennedy, Assistant Secretary for Administration, U.S. Department of State, Declaration in *U.S. v. Weatherhead* (cited in 9th Circuit Opinion, October 6, 1998, at http://www.fas.org/sgp/foia/weatherapp. html).

15. Alasdair Roberts, "Entangling Alliances: NATO's Security of Information Policy and the Entrenchment of State Secrecy," *Cornell International Law Journal* 36 (2) (2003): 329–360.

16. National Intelligence Council, "Mapping the Global Future: Report of the National Intelligence Council's 2020 Project" (2004), http://www.cia. gov/nic/NIC_2020_project.htm (accessed December 29, 2004).

17. Arthur Burns, "The Proper Limits of Openness in Government," presentation at International Monetary Conference, San Francisco, June 19, 1976.

18. Perhaps the leading example of recently won access to previously confidential data on matters like tax audits is the Transactional Records Access Clearinghouse at Syracuse University, which provides extensive databases and analyses of government law enforcement activities, much of it obtained through FOIA requests. See http://trac.syr/edu/aboutTRAC-general.html.

19. See, for example, Joseph Stiglitz and S. J. Grossman, "On the Impossibility of Informationally Efficient Markets," *American Economic Review* 70 (3) (1980): 393–408; see also Joseph Stiglitz, "On Liberty, the Right to Know, and Public Discourse: The Role of Transparency in Public Life," Oxford Amnesty Lecture, January 27, 1999, 20.

20. Stiglitz, "Democratizing," 115.

21. Thomas Dawson, "Transparency and the IMF: Toward Second Generation Reforms" (*Tallinn*, 2003), http://www.imf.org/external/np/speeches/2003/031703.htm (accessed June 28, 2004).

22. Robert Wade, "Greening the Bank: The Struggle Over the Environ-

ment, 1970–1995," in Devesh Kapur, John P. Lewis, and Richard Webb, eds., *The World Bank: Its First Half Century, Volume 2: Perspectives* (Washington DC: Brookings Institution Press, 1997), 657.

23. Leonor Briones quoted in Kevin Danaher, ed., *50 Years Is Enough: The Case Against the World Bank and the International Monetary Fund* (Boston: South End Press, 1994), 67.

24. From the activists' point of view, see the excellent collection by Jonathan Fox and L. David Brown, eds., *The Struggle for Accountability: The World Bank, NGOs, and Grassroots Movements* (Cambridge, MA: MIT Press, 1998); from the independent scholar contributing to the bank's authorized history, see Wade, "Greening the Bank," especially 658–659.

25. Dawson, "Transparency and the IMF."

26. Andrew Eggers, Ann Florini, and Ngaire Woods, "Chapter One: Accountability, Parliaments and the IMF Board," in Barry Carin and Angela Wood, eds., *Enhancing Accountability in the International Monetary Fund* (Victoria: Centre for Global Studies, University of Victoria, 2003 draft), 8–24.

27. World Trade Organization (WTO), "WTO Moves Towards a More Open Organization," *WTO*, May 16, 2002; with Document WT/L/452 of May 14, 2002 attached.

28. James Bacchus, "Open Up the WTO," *The Washington Post*, February 20, 2004, A25.

29. Graham Saul, personal communication, January 13, 2004. See also Bruce Rich, "World Bank/IMF: 50 Years Is Enough," in Kevin Danaher, ed., *50 Years Is Enough* (Boston, MA: South End Press), 8.

30. David Hunter quoted by Jonathan Fox, "Introduction: Framing the Inspection Panel," in Dana Clark, Jonathan Fox, and Kay Treakle, eds., *Demanding Accountability: Civil-Society Claims and the World Bank Inspection Panel* (Lanham, MD: Rowman & Littlefield, 2003), xiii.

31. Walden Bello, David Kinley, and Elaine Elinson, *Development Debacle: The World Bank in the Philippines* (San Francisco: Institute for Food and Development Policy/Philippine Solidarity Network, 1982), 57.

32. Andrew Gray, "Development Policy, Development Protest: The World Bank, Indigenous Peoples, and NGOs," in Fox and Brown, eds., *The Struggle for Accountability*, 269–270, 287–288.

33. Nicholas Guppy, "Tropical Deforestation: A Global View," *Foreign Affairs* 62 (4) (1984): 943.

34. Gray, "Development Policy," 279.

35. Margaret Keck and Kathryn Sikkink, *Activists Beyond Borders: Advo-*

cacy Networks in International Politics (Ithaca, NY: Cornell University Press, 1998), 135–141.

36. Lori Udall, "The World Bank and Public Accountability: Has Anything Changed?," in Fox and Brown, eds., *The Struggle for Accountability*, 400–401.

37. David Hunter, Cristian Opaso, and Marcos Orellana, "The Biobio's Legacy: Institutional Reforms and Unfulfilled Promises at the International Finance Corporation," in Clark, Fox, and Treakle, eds., *Demanding Accountability*, 115–143.

38. Ibid., 128–129.

39. Richard Bissell, "The Arun III Hydroelectric Project, Nepal," in Clark, Fox, and Treakle, eds., *Demanding Accountability*, 25–44, quote is on 42, from an internal bank memo.

40. Dana Clark and Kay Treakle, "The China Western Poverty Reduction Project," in Clark, Fox, and Treakle, eds., *Demanding Accountability*, 211–245.

41. Sathnam Sanghera and Stephen Fidler, "World Bank Chief Under Fire After Chinese Project," *Financial Times*, July 14, 2000, 5.

42. Wade, "Greening the Bank," 649–650, citing the summary of discussions at the meeting of the executive directors, October 25, 1983, the acting regional vice president's briefing paper dated December 28, 1983, and a bank telegram to the Brazilian Ministry of the Interior dated March 17, 1983.

43. Wade, "Greening the Bank," 708.

44. Roumeen Islam, "Do More Transparent Governments Govern Better?" (World Bank Policy Research Working Paper 3077), in *Sourcebook on Government Transparency Law: Background Readings for Making Government Accountable: An Introduction to Government Transparency Laws* (World Bank Workshop, 2003).

45. Daniel Kaufmann, "Transparency Matters: The 'Second Generation' of Institutional Reform" (2005), http://topics.developmentgateway.org/special/transparency/template2.do (accessed April 22, 2005). See also http://www.worldbank.org/wbi/governance for examples of the extensive research carried out by Kaufmann and his colleagues.

46. Adam LeBor, "Alliance Bends Its Rules for Strategic Romania," *The Times (London)*, November 20, 2002; for the Iliescu quote and the "Membership Action Plan," see Robert Kaiser, "Romania Sees NATO Membership as Remedy for Post-Communist Ills," *The Washington Post*, October 21, 2002, A18.

47. For a detailed analysis and critique of the NATO-imposed secrecy laws, see Alasdair Roberts, "NATO, Secrecy, and the Right to Information," *East European Constitutional Review* 11/12 (4/1) (2002/2003).

48. Thomas Blanton, "National Security and Open Government in the United States: Beyond the Balancing Test," in Alasdair Roberts, ed., *National Security and Open Government* (Syracuse, NY: Campbell Public Affairs Institute, 2003), 33–74.

49. Links to each of the IFTI disclosure policies are included at www. freedominfo.org/ifti.htm.

50. See "Open for Business," sidebar in Blanton, "The World's Right to Know," 54; also Sheila Coronel, ed., *The Right to Know: Access to Information in Southeast Asia* (Quezon City: Philippine Center for Investigative Journalism, 2001).

51. Bank Information Center and Freedominfo.org, *Opening the International Financial Institutions: The Complete Transparency Resource and Database* (Washington, DC: April 22, 2004 and February 7, 2005). Contributors included Abigail Parish, Toby McIntosh, Jen Kalafut, Graham Saul, and Thomas Blanton. Available at http://www.ifitransparencyresource.org.

52. Toby McIntosh, "Ugandan Judge Orders Release of Key Document on Bujagali Dam" (2002), with links to the judge's decision and the NGO analysis, http://www.freedominfo.org/ifti/worldbank/20021100.htm.

53. Sebastian Mallaby, "NGOs: Fighting Poverty, Hurting the Poor" (*Foreign Policy*, 2004), http://www.foreignpolicy.com/story/cms.php?story_id = 2672. The Wolfensohn profile by Mallaby is *The World's Banker: A Story of Failed States, Financial Crises, and the Wealth and Poverty of Nations* (New York: Penguin, 2004). The Mallaby article and book include a similarly one-sided treatment of the China Western Poverty Reduction Project.

54. Richard Sine and Nou Pohours, "Villagers Beg World Bank for Logging Plans," *Cambodia Daily*, November 12, 2002.

55. For an eloquent expression of this attenuation and the possibilities of enhanced parliamentary engagement in the IMF context, see Eggers, Florini, and Woods, "Chapter One," in Carin and Wood, eds., *Enhancing Accountability*.

56. Toby McIntosh, "Parliamentarians Seek Larger Role in IFI Decision-Making" (2004), http://www.freedominfo.org/ifti/worldbank/20040930a. htm.

57. Toby McIntosh, "Parliamentarians Flex Growing Organization, Make Request of Bank" (2004), http://www.freedominfo.org/ifti/worldbank/20040224.htm.

58. Norbert Mao, "Experiences with the Parliamentarians Network on the World Bank: A View from the Inside," in Carin and Wood, eds., *Enhancing Accountability*, 25–27.

59. A succinct expression of this analysis with extensive citations to the literature can be found in Alasdair Roberts, "A Partial Revolution: The Diplomatic Ethos and Transparency in Intergovernmental Organizations," *Public Administration Review* 64 (4) (2004): 410–411.

60. Rob Hennig, "Review of *Rulemaking, Participation and the Limits of Public Law in the USA and Europe* by Theodora Ziamou," 11 (11) (November 2001): 495–498, http://www.bsos.umd.edu/gvpt/lpbr/subpages/reviews/ziamou.htm. For original text see Theodora Ziamou, *Participation and the Limits of Public Law in the USA and Europe* (Burlington, VT: Ashgate, 2001).

61. For an excellent overview, from which much of this discussion is drawn, see Benedict Kingsbury, Nico Krisch, and Richard Stewart, "The Emergence of Global Administrative Law," New York University, Institute for International Law and Justice, Global Administrative Law Series, IILJ Working Paper 2004/1, http://www.iilj.org/global_adlaw/index.htm (accessed April 19, 2005).

62. See WT/DS58/RW, "United States—Import Prohibition of Shrimp and Shrimp Products," Panel Report, 3.180 *et seq.* (1996), quoted in Kingsbury, Krisch, and Stewart, "The Emergence of Global Administrative Law," 24.

63. Steve Charnovitz, "Economic and Social Actors in the World Trade Organization," *ILSA Journal of International and Comparative Law* 7 (2001): 274.

64. Bank for International Settlements, "The Basel Committee on Banking Supervision" (2004), http://www.bis.org/bcbs/aboutbcbs.htm (accessed April 20, 2005).

65. See discussion in Kingsbury, Krisch, and Stewart, "The Emergence of Global Administrative Law," 31–39.

66. Wade, "Greening the Bank," 613.

67. Ibid., 630.

68. Daniel Thomas, *The Helsinki Effect: International Norms, Human Rights, and the Demise of Communism* (Princeton: Princeton University Press, 2001).

69. Jonathan Sanford, Congressional Research Service, Washington, DC, e-mail communication to Sajit Gandhi of freedominfo.org, May 16, 2003.

70. Alasdair Roberts, "Structural Pluralism and the Right to Information," *University of Toronto Law Journal* 51 (2001): 243–271.

71. Bretton Woods Project, "Wolfensohn Discusses Human Rights, Environment at Greenpeace Lecture," (2004), http://www.brettonwoodsproject. org/article.shtml?cmd[126] = x-126-51253 (accessed June 28, 2004).

Chapter Nine

Transparency and Environmental Governance

Vivek Ramkumar and Elena Petkova

A New Paradigm in Environmental Governance

In December 1984, a factory explosion released a lethal toxic chemical among unsuspecting citizens in the north Indian city of Bhopal, killing some 2,000 people within hours and leaving several thousand others permanently handicapped. Another 15,000 died prematurely due in part to the aftereffects of their exposure. The explosion occurred in a local Union Carbide factory—a subsidiary of the American company Dow Chemicals. An investigation of the disaster revealed that the company's management had ignored warnings about the poor conditions of the Bhopal factory's infrastructure.[1]

The Bhopal gas tragedy provoked international condemnation.[2] Under the glare of public outrage, American legislators passed the Emergency Planning and Community Right to Know Act in 1986. Among other things, this law required industries to disclose the volume of certain chemicals released annually by them into the environment. As required by the law, the U.S. Environmental Protection Agency (EPA)—the agency in charge of environmental regulation in the United States—developed a matrix called the Toxic Release Inventory (TRI) to tabulate the various chemical releases reported by industries and made the data publicly available beginning in 1988. The results were dramatic: over the next 3 years, chemical releases fell 7 percent annually, even as production and manufacturing were rising. Since the enactment of the law, the total volume of chemical releases in the United States has been nearly halved.

The U.S. response to the Bhopal tragedy represented a paradigm shift in environmental regulation. Prior to Bhopal, environmental regulations set limits on environmental emissions, often requiring the use of specific technologies or equipment to ensure improved environmental performance. The Community Right to Know Act took a fundamentally different approach to environmental regulation. It set no limits on emissions. It simply required companies to report their emissions levels—data which most companies had not previously compiled, much less publicly revealed. The law significantly strengthened the role that citizens were able to play in environmental governance by empowering them to take more active roles in making and enforcing decisions about environmental governance. This new approach, now often referred to as "regulation by revelation," has been increasingly accepted by many countries around the world. It forms an essential part of environmental governance frameworks that are centered on expanding transparency to improve environmental outcomes.[3]

It is striking that such a law was needed in the United States as late as the mid-1980s, given the U.S. reputation as a leader in citizen access to information. The United States enacted its Freedom of Information Act (FOIA) in 1966;[4] the act was subsequently amended and strengthened in the 1970s and again in the 1980s. The FOIA required the U.S. government to publish several categories of information and ensured that citizens had the right to access it by filing information requests. Since this law made information about all aspects of environmental governance available upon request (including information collected by the U.S. government on tragedies like the Bhopal toxic chemical release), why was an additional law specifically treating environmental information deemed necessary?

Under the FOIA, citizens can request all types of information (subject to conditions) from public agencies; however, if requested information is not available or is not collected by public agencies, then this law is of little use to citizens. Thus, under the FOIA, the onus for initiating action is on the citizen—whose requests are necessarily limited by the availability of data. Prior to the enactment of the Community Right to Know Act, much environmental information of the kind required by the act was simply not collected.

Despite its apparent effectiveness in reducing toxic chemical releases, the Community Right to Know Act has come under criticism: that the information released under the law is difficult to understand; that the collection and publication of such information imposes significant financial burdens on industry (which are passed on to consumers); and that the release of such information may reveal sensitive business secrets among competitors (thus expanding the possibility that industrial sabotage may occur). Further, critics charge that while the TRI provides information on the total volume of chemicals released by industry, information is not provided on the toxicity of these releases and the specific risks they pose to human health; as a result, people may not be able to use this information to make choices that will protect their health. Finally, critics argue that the TRI discloses information only on emissions from point sources, which are only one among several types of emissions sources. Supporters of the disclosure-based regulatory approaches argue that nongovernmental organizations and other groups can assist citizens in understanding the information provided through TRIs, and that concerns regarding industrial espionage are greatly exaggerated, as most such espionage is conducted by industry insiders who have access to far more sensitive information than what is made available through the TRIs. Further, supporters argue that while TRIs are not comprehensive catalogues of all chemicals released into the environment, the information contained in them covers major polluting industries, and the TRIs are first steps in active disclosure processes that can eventually be expanded to cover other pollution sources.

Many governments have concluded that the strengths of the disclosure-based approach to environmental regulation outweigh its weaknesses. At the urging of the Organization for Economic Cooperation and Development (OECD), most of the world's wealthier countries have adopted TRI-like systems, commonly termed pollutant release and transfer registers (PRTRs). The results of the compilation of these PRTRs are beginning to help reduce toxic releases. In Britain, for example, the PRTR reportedly resulted in a 40 percent reduction in the release of carcinogenic chemicals across England and Wales between 1998 and 2001.[5]

The Community Right to Know Act's approach provides citizens with access to information. Information access alone, however, is only one part of the new paradigm of disclosure-based environmental governance. As the 1992 World Summit on Environment and Development held in Rio de Janeiro affirmed, for citizens to truly play a role in environmental governance, they must not only have access to environmental information but also be able to participate in the decision-making process and have public access to redress and remedy. This is especially key in developing countries where democracy has not been adopted as a governance structure or is still nascent. As the rest of this chapter will show, these three principles—information, participation, and access to justice—are increasingly being incorporated in regional agreements, national laws, and regulations promoting environmental transparency and participation. As we examine the development of these new governance paradigms, we will examine the crucial role played by nongovernmental actors. Finally, we will examine the issues and challenges that will likely confront a disclosure-based approach to environmental governance in the future.

The Principles of Good Environmental Governance

The new environmental governance paradigm requires that citizens be empowered to influence environmental outcomes. The governance framework must enable citizens to have access to environmental information; decision-making processes and the opportunity to participate in them; and redress and legal remedy to contest the denial of information and the denial of opportunities to participate in decision-making.[6]

These three types of access are defined in most international documents and decisions as essential "principles" of transparency in environmental governance. In any country—or any environmental governance framework—in which citizens are denied one or more of these principles of access (or in which one or more of the principles is sharply curtailed), the effectiveness and legitimacy of environmental governance is limited.

Access to Information

Access to information is the foundation that makes transparency in governance possible. Expanded information access can be justified on four grounds: equity, legitimacy, accountability, and self-protection. Each is examined in more detail below.

Transparency is essential to promoting *equity* and justice in environmental decision making. Poor communities in almost all developing countries rely heavily on natural resources for subsistence and income, and they are therefore especially vulnerable to any changes in the natural environment. One of the most effective ways of empowering citizens to make their voices heard in the political processes that govern projects with significant environmental impacts (such as mining projects or dam construction projects) is by providing them with information on the project or program that will enable them to defend their own interests.

Transparency also lends *legitimacy* to environmental decision-making processes. A government that operates behind the veneer of secrecy is often unable to win either the trust or the support of its citizens.[7] When people live in an environment in which information is closely guarded, it leads them to speculate on government action—and such speculation is usually predicated on the assumption of sinister motives. Rumor mongers and conspiracy theorists become the primary sources of information in such situations, and the "information" they provide may make citizens highly suspicious and combative.[8] It is in a government's interest to seek legitimacy and credibility for its decisions by building public support. Such support is particularly critical in the case of major environmental projects that entail significant trade-offs among "competing" constituencies, e.g., a major dam may affect some farmers positively by providing them with water for irrigation and with electricity but will affect other farmers and fisherman negatively by causing flooding, salination, and related effects. By providing timely and relevant information about their intentions in building and the costs and benefits of the projects, governments can anticipate and seek to manage serious conflicts.

Transparency makes government—and environmental polluters—directly *accountable* to citizens. The Community Right to Know

Act in the United States is a good example of how simply by releasing information, the government made corporations directly accountable to two sets of actors in addition to government regulatory agencies—viz., their customers (who exerted economic pressure on them) and voting citizens (who exerted political pressure on environmental policy makers). Similarly, in developing countries where fewer curbs have been put in place to slow environmental exploitation and where corruption in environmental management is common, citizens can be empowered to assist government in regulating environmental management by being given access to information.

Finally, when citizens have access to information, they can take action to protect themselves from some health risks and hazards. For example, the provision of information about the potential health effects of contaminants in drinking water can empower communities to make informed decisions about whether they should drink public water. In 2000, the LASKA Pure Water Plant in Hai Duong City, Vietnam, sold 217,000 bottles of "mineral water" nationally. These bottles were not, however, sold in Hai Duong. The people in Hai Duong refused to drink locally bottled water because they knew that when the LASKA mineral spring went dry in 1999, unused "mineral water" labels were subsequently affixed to bottles containing river water.[9]

Importantly, the effectiveness of an environmental governance framework based on transparency requires the full and accurate disclosure of information—rather than the selected release of incomplete (or, worse yet, inaccurate) data. The effective use of information also requires that parties acting on the information understand it, so that the possible outcomes of different responses can be weighed in a broad context. In 1991, local water officials in Lima, Peru, responded to an EPA study showing that some by-products of water chlorination could cause cancer by ending the chlorination of the city's drinking water supply. This action led to the outbreak of a cholera epidemic that is thought to have killed more than 3,500 people that year.[10]

If access to information is the foundation of a governance framework based on transparency, then the enactment of laws guaranteeing access—and prescribing the process through which information can be obtained—is the cornerstone of the foundation. Such laws must also provide citizens with recourse to justice when information is illegally withheld. Mere enactment of laws requiring transparency, however, is not sufficient to ensure that citizens will actually be able to access information. Procedural and administrative frameworks must be established to collect and disseminate information in a regular manner.

The strongest laws regarding information access are those—like the Community Right to Know Act—that explicitly require the release of environmental information. However, some countries that have not enacted such targeted laws have incorporated provisions regarding access to environmental information in their environmental protection laws. During the nearly fifteen years that have passed since the Earth Summit in Rio, national environmental protection laws that include provisions guaranteeing access to environmental information have been enacted in several countries; in some, the enactment of such laws has even preceded the enactment of wider information disclosure laws. For example, the Environmental Management Act passed in Indonesia in 1997 was the first legislation in that country to treat the issue of access to information on any subject. Two years after it was enacted, the Indonesian Constitution was amended to include general guarantees protecting the right to information. In Mexico, environmental protection legislation guaranteeing access to environmental information was enacted even before that country enacted an FOIA in 2002; provisions in environmental legislation explicitly protecting access to information also preceded the enactment of FOIA-like laws in Chile, Bulgaria, and Ukraine. Such cases show how transparency in environmental governance is often among the first steps leading to the introduction of transparency in all governance arenas.

In still other countries, provisions have been included in national constitutions guaranteeing the right to information. For example, recent amendments to the constitution of Thailand are the first laws in that country to contain a special provision on access to environmental information. Even in countries that lack specific constitutional guarantees of freedom of information or specific laws treating either freedom of information in general or access to environmental information in particular, other constitutional rights can sometimes support (albeit indirectly) citizens' demands for information. In India, for example, prior to the enactment of its access to information law, the constitutional guarantee to freedom of expression was interpreted by some courts to include an implied right to information.

Public Participation in Decision Making

The rationales cited to justify the provision of access to information can also be cited to justify the second principle of the new paradigm of environmental governance: access to the decision-making process. We have earlier discussed how citizens could use information on the environment to inform their decisions as voters and consumers. In countries where democracy is not developed—or in countries where there is significant poverty—people may not have the opportunity to vote and/or they may not have the wealth to affect policy through their consumption decisions. In these types of situations, it is essential that structures be created to provide citizens with formal access to decision-making processes.

The influence of formal community participation in decision making on environmental issues has been examined in several studies,[11] which have found that public participation in decision making frequently helps ensure that government decisions are informed by and responsive to citizen concerns. Citizens who are in direct contact with the environment bring firsthand knowledge of many of the issues that government seeks to address in environmental policies. By drawing on their knowledge and experience, government can reduce the risk that new projects, programs, and policies will fail to address actual needs and/or will create unintended environmental effects. For example, in early 2000, the Federal District Government of Mexico City organized extensive public hearings on a proposed land use plan and conservation program for the Valley of Mexico. As a result, the Mexico City government was able to incorporate citizen suggestions regarding such previously untreated issues as the conservation of areas that recharge groundwater aquifers.[12]

Public participation in environmental governance can legitimize and strengthen environmental ministries. In developing countries, the establishment of an independent environment ministry is often only the first step in providing political voice to environmental concerns. Many times, the newly constituted environment ministry competes with other ministries—like mining, chemicals, tourism, heavy industry, investment, etc.—that are more established and can bring the power of the revenues generated by their industries to bear in policy discussions (often placing the environment ministry at a distinct disadvantage). In such a scenario, increasing the awareness of environmental issues among citizens can provide a strong political base that the environmental ministry can draw on to strengthen its position vis-à-vis competing ministries.

While these arguments support increased public participation in environmental decision making, it is also true that such participation entails costs and benefits that must be weighed in determining how and to what degree the public is involved. Some types of environmental decisions cannot easily incorporate public participation. For example, decisions on the management of a river that runs across several countries necessarily involve decisions and negotiations among the governments of all affected countries. Each government will be responding to the demands and positions of the other governments, and it will therefore require a special effort on the part of these governments to inform the public about the (changing) provisions under consideration and to enable the public to voice their opinions. Even when there is active public participation in an environmental decision, the concerns of minorities may easily be overlooked—particularly in pluralistic societies in which the interests of minority communities frequently clash with those of the majority. Similarly, in some countries, certain sections of society (women, children, the poor) are constrained from freely voicing their opinions and participating in decision making by long-standing societal prejudices or even by legal restrictions. Further, the costs of facilitating public participation in time and money must also be considered. For example, if public participation takes the form of national referendums—which are generally regarded as the most direct form of democracy—this can place a heavy burden on the government. (At the same time, however, citizens must be vigilant when governments attempt to cite time and resource constraints as reasons for rejecting all public participation.)

On the other hand, excluding the public from environmental decision making also entails costs. The last few decades have witnessed a marked increase in the number of people's movements that have arisen to champion the cause of the environment—particularly when planned actions have threatened to disproportionately affect poor and marginalized communities. Movements like the Narmada Bachao Andalon (NBA) in India and the Amazon forest preservation movement in Latin America have developed precisely as responses to nonparticipatory decision-making processes. The popular dissent expressed and channeled by these groups has in several cases delayed project implementation schedules—which in turn has imposed huge costs on the affected projects (causing them to exceed their intended budgets by significant amounts). Thus, project sponsors—particularly governments—must weigh the costs of making decisions on environmental issues in nonparticipatory ways against the costs that can arise when citizens (who are increasingly aware of their rights) intervene in the implementation of projects in which they have had no say.

As with the issue of access to information, the existence of laws is not sufficient to ensure that citizens will be able to participate in decision making and/or that their opinions will inform decisions. Procedural and administrative frameworks must be established so that citizens are informed and consulted and their opinions and concerns are incorporated. These frameworks have to address such issues as 1) in what stage of the decision-making cycle public participation will occur; 2) which members of the public will participate and how their participation will be solicited; 3) what actions must be taken to respond to comments provided during public forums; and 4) whether and how the public will be informed of the outcomes of the decision-making processes in which they have participated. While such matters appear to be mundane, the determinations made by government regarding these critical procedural issues define the type and degree of access citizens have to decision making. Even if the principle of public participation is incorporated in official laws and policies, it is the procedural and administrative frameworks that put the laws and policies into practice.

Several formalized processes and procedures are used in different countries to give citizens the opportunity to participate in environmental decision making, including the holding of public hearings, provision of notice and comment periods, formation of advisory committees, and establishment of project information offices. Perhaps most central to ensuring effective participation, however, is the conduct of a thorough environmental assessment. A formal environmental assessment provides citizens with access to key information on a project, and specifies the legal procedures that will be followed to ensure that the environmental implications of decisions are available for public review and that the public has the opportunity to comment on them—and to participate in decision making.

To conduct an environmental assessment, government agencies (or other project/program sponsors as appropriate, including public contractors) analyze the likely effects of a proposed course of action on the environment and release findings to the public. Using this information, project sponsors are then often required by laws governing environmental assessments to organize public forums among affected communities to receive comments and suggestions on the proposed project/program and its environmental impacts. Since the 1992 Earth Summit, many countries have adopted national laws and/or policies to require that environmental assessments be conducted prior to the implementation of development, construction, planning activities, etc. Such laws or policies currently exist in fourteen Latin American and Caribbean countries; all include provisions requiring public participation, though they differ on such issues as the scope of participation required and the stages in the decision-making cycle during which the public consultation must be conducted.[13]

On May 21, 2003, the parties to the United Nations Economic Commission for Europe (UNECE) Espoo Convention, meeting in Kiev, signed the first protocol on strategic environmental assessments. Among other provisions, this protocol requires signatories to evaluate the environmental impacts of all official draft plans and programs and requires extensive public participation in government decision making in numerous development sectors. Thirty-seven UNECE countries had signed by the end of 2003.[14]

Redress and Remedy—Access to Justice

The third principle of transparency is the provision of access to justice, which enables citizens to seek redress when information is withheld or to challenge a decision that they consider to have been reached through illegal processes. In many countries, litigation involving environmental issues was rare as recently as a decade or two ago. However, the number of cases is increasing, and redress is now being sought not only on disputed decisions but also when there has been a failure on the part of government to provide either access to environmental information and/or to allow public participation in decision making as required by extant laws (particularly environmental assessment laws).

As with access to decision making, the extent of citizens' access to justice is defined both by legal provisions and by procedural matters; in the judicial arena, legal and procedural matters often intertwine. Forums through which adjudication is commonly sought on matters pertaining to transparency in environmental governance include administrative and appeals tribunals, judicial courts, offices of the ombudsman, and alternative dispute settlement tribunals.

Among the critical legal and procedural issues that determine the extent of access to justice are whether legal aid and advice is widely available and at what cost; whether class action suits are admissible; whether multiple types of dispute settlement options exist (such as alternative dispute resolution and small claims courts); whether claimants have to prove interest or harm; which types of courts can deal with environmental lawsuits (criminal, civil, and/or administrative); and how long it takes a case to be adjudicated (i.e., how efficient the legal system is in hearing and ruling on cases). An Access Initiative[15] report from Hungary argues that environmental cases may linger in that nation's court system for years; as a result, by the time decisions are handed down, they may no longer be relevant.[16] Similarly, in countries like India where the judicial system is confronting a backlog of more than 10 million cases, the opportunity for prompt redress of grievances is limited. Together, the legal and procedural decisions made on such issues determine whether a country's legal framework is fair and equitable across class and economic strata.

One of the most important issues regarding the extent of access to justice available to a country's citizens is legal standing. In the legal sense, if a person or group has standing, they have the right to appear in court or bring a legal suit on an issue. Standing is critical to determining the ability of concerned citizens as well as environmental associations, ad hoc groups, and NGOs to access justice on environmental issues. In countries that have enacted legislation guaranteeing citizens' rights to access information and participate in decision making, the issue of legal standing often remains inadequately addressed and thus is frequently a barrier that prevents citizens from effectively claiming their rights. In countries like Mexico, standing is limited by law to "affected" people; the vagueness of this term gives courts and other administrative officials wide discretion in limiting who actually has access to the court system regarding an environmental matter.[17] Similarly, in other countries, a person is "affected" only when she or he can show proof that she or he has been harmed by the environmental action addressed in a proposed suit; often, however, it is unclear what level of "harm" is sufficient to bestow standing on a party.

Equally important to the guarantee of standing to individuals is the establishment of legal standing for NGOs and other associations and ad hoc groups. Such groups frequently have the resources to pursue cases that individuals lack—particularly class action suits that demand redress for an entire group of people affected by an environmental issue. In addition, NGOs can use lawsuits as part of ongoing campaigns to raise awareness of environmental issues and/ or to prevent actions that they believe might violate environmental regulations.

The State of Environmental Transparency

The rise of the new disclosure-based approach to environmental governance has both causes and consequences for broader political developments around the world. The Ecoglasnost movement in Bulgaria, for example, began as a demand for information on environmental issues and eventually contributed to the changeover from the communist to a more democratic, accountable government.

The Ecoglasnost movement was initiated in 1985 by the Committee for the Ecological Protection of Ruse. Located on the Danube River near Bulgaria's border with Romania, Ruse was exposed to pollutants released by a chemical plant just inside the Romanian border. By the late 1980s, the members of Ecoglasnost had organized public demonstrations and petitions demanding "glasnost" or openness regarding environmental information—particularly about pollution that threatened public health. The communist government of Bulgaria cracked down and arrested several of the movement's leading members merely for asking for information and leading efforts to mobilize public opinion.[18]

Following the crackdown, the activists began to leverage their demand for environmental information to demand broader access to government information as well as increased accountability from all levels of government; ultimately, the environmental activists joined with those throughout Bulgaria who were demanding a democratic government. In this way, the movement for increased transparency in environmental governance contributed to the general anticommunist movement in the country. After the fall of communism, this movement participated in demanding from the postcommunist government new procedures that would give citizens access to government-held information.

As this example makes clear, the success of a disclosure-based system of environmental governance depends heavily on the performance of citizens. Citizens must actively use the laws, demand information, participate in the public fora provided, and make use of the existing systems for redress. If they do not engage in decision-making processes, government officials who prefer a more centralized approach can claim that the new paradigm simply does not work. Indeed, officials have been known to make such claims even when citizens are being active.

A public opinion poll recently conducted in 47 countries revealed the extent and nature of the demand for each of the 3 principles of transparency. The poll found that demand for both information and participation is high worldwide, with more than half of respondents—and in some countries more than 80 percent—expressing willingness to spend time and effort to obtain and use relevant environmental information and participate in decision making.[19] The poll also found, however, that governments are not satisfying their citizens' demands for information and participation—only 40 percent of the respondents were happy with their governments' efforts.

The Access Initiative examined legal and policy trends in the development of laws and policies guaranteeing the principles of access in nine countries—Chile, Hungary, India, Indonesia, Uganda, Mexico, South Africa, Thailand, and the United States. The initiative found that these governments have made broad strides in the establishment of legal and policy frameworks that guarantee access to information, but have been less willing to provide people with the opportunity to use the information and/or to seek redress when information is withheld. Although most of the nine have freedom of information laws and specific legal provisions on access to environmental information, only a few recently adopted or amended their constitutions to guarantee the right of the public to participate in decisions made by public authorities. Thailand's constitution, for example, guarantees the right of the public to participate in the policies and decisions made by public authorities. The majority of the national legal frameworks of these countries, however, were found to "exclude or restrict groups from participating," to "exclude some sectors of the economy from public participation," and to "lack adequate provisions for participation at different stages of the decision making cycle."[20]

Such exclusion of the public seriously undermines the effectiveness of environmental governance. Although access to information is the foundation on which participation rests, it is public participation that is instrumental in integrating different perspectives, knowledge, and interests into government policies. In Mexico City, for example, citizens proposed tax incentives and other economically viable measures to preserve wildlife and undeveloped land that shaped the wildlife management plan ultimately adopted. Broad consultation with citizens in the development of Uganda's forest policy ensured that issues such as biodiversity and the water generation capacity of forests were taken into account despite opposition from strong vested interests.

The researchers found that access to justice among the nine countries studied is even more circumscribed. Less than half the countries enabled the public to use administrative and judicial review to contest the way national or provincial policies were made.[21] Further, even when access to justice is provided by the legal framework, practical considerations often limit people's access to the court system. Thus, the researchers found that the efficiency, accountability, and independence of judicial systems were very poor in some countries, which hampered the people's ability to seek enforcement of their access rights.

The Role of NGOs

Governments usually adopt a framework of transparency in environmental governance only in response to demands made—and sustained—by citizens. However, individual citizens acting alone generally have only limited influence on a country's environmental governance scheme.[22] NGOs play critical roles in leveraging and focusing public demands for transparency into campaigns that can influence public policies. These groups have become critical in providing forums in which a number of groups and interests can effectively demand transparency in environmental governance. Although there is limited data on NGOs active in the environmental sector, it was estimated that there were more than 100,000 groups working on environmental protection worldwide by 1990.[23] NGOs now participate effectively in all stages of environmental governance, including agenda setting, negotiation, implementation, and monitoring.

NGOs often work to place overlooked issues on national or international agendas. For example, in the 1980s, forestry concerns were included on the agenda of intergovernmental deliberations as a result of pressure exerted by NGOs. In the 1990s, NGOs highlighted the issue of global warming at a variety of international policy-making fora. NGOs working with the United Nations Environment Programme and the Food and Agricultural Organization have successfully utilized the international media to raise awareness of the dangers posed by the use of specific chemical pesticides.[24] Similarly, at the national level, NGOs have succeeded in channeling the concerns, viewpoints, and values of minority or under-represented groups to policy makers.

Sometimes NGOs go to quite dramatic lengths to draw attention to issues. In the summer of 1975, a Soviet whaling ship came within 50 miles of the California coast. Armed with a 90-millimeter cannon that was loaded with a 160-pound grenade harpoon, the ship was hunting sperm whales. A group of Greenpeace activists began pursuing the Soviet vessel in small rubber dinghies (known as Zodiacs). The activists intended to stop the ship from hunting whales, and one group of activists succeeded in positioning their Zodiac between the whaling ship and a whale. The activists believed that the crew of the whaling ship would not attempt to shoot the whales for fear of hitting the Zodiac. Undeterred by the activists, however, the whaling ship fired its harpoon toward the whale, missing the Zodiac by less than 5 feet.[25]

Though Greenpeace's direct action failed in its immediate goal of saving the whale, it succeeded in generating extensive publicity about international whaling. Greenpeace caught its confrontation with the Soviet vessel on film, and these images, broadcast around the world, raised awareness among the general public about whaling. This and similar events helped engender an international movement to ban whaling.

As policy makers try to determine how to address environmental issues, NGOs have much to offer in information collection, dissemination, and analysis capacity.[26] During international meetings held to formulate and/or revise multilateral environmental agreements, such as the United Nations Convention on Biological Diversity and the United Nations Framework Convention on Climate Change, NGOs produced research and policy documents that shed new light on the costs of inaction and the appropriateness of specific options for change.[27] At the Earth Conference in Rio in 1992, some 17,000 NGO representatives participated in the NGO parallel forum, and 1,400 were directly involved in the intergovernmental negotiations. NGOs helped make the conference a success, claimed an important place in the conference declaration, and played a key role in developing postconference institutions, like the Commission on Sustainable Development.[28]

NGOs can also mobilize public opinion to support political reform efforts and can even organize constituencies to support politicians who advocate for what are frequently controversial reforms in environmental governance policies. Once policies have been formulated and adopted, NGOs can then also assist in implementation by drawing on their knowledge of operational contexts to guide the formulation of regulations and by mobilizing their members—many of whom are frequently drawn from local communities—to assist in stewarding local resources.

Finally, NGOs can act as guardians or "watchdogs" of the public interest by monitoring and assessing the performance of political and economic players and the state of environmental resources. Thus, for example, the Chesapeake Bay Foundation in the U.S. state of Maryland publishes an annual "State of the Bay" report that details the current level of pollutants in the Chesapeake Bay as well as the overall health of aquatic animals there. Similarly, in the international arena, NGOs can help "give teeth" to agreements by monitoring governmental compliance. They have been extremely effective in highlighting disparities between those who bear the burdens of environmental management programs and those who reap the benefits.

For example, in India, the Centre for Science and Environment publishes ratings that compare companies within a given industry on their environmental performance.[29] Environmental Defense, a U.S. NGO, has developed a Web-based "scorecard" that has done much to enhance the effectiveness of the Community Right to Know Act. The Scorecard (http://scorecard.org) presents data from the TRI and other sources in a very user-friendly form, enabling U.S. residents to obtain information on air pollution and toxic releases in their local neighborhood simply by entering their zip code.

These multiple and often powerful roles for NGOs have raised concerns. Many government officials—particularly elected officials—argue that because NGOs are not elected (and are sometimes not membership-based or democratic in their own structures), they cannot legitimately claim to represent the "will of the people." National government officials frequently argue that only they have the right to represent the people, and therefore only they are entitled to participate in the international political arena on behalf of their countries. While there is some truth to this criticism, NGOs respond by arguing that the legitimacy of their actions and positions is based on their unique expertise or moral imperatives, or upon popular support for specific issues (even if this support does not necessarily translate into direct support for the organization). Further, NGOs argue that as governments are increasingly soliciting (and even relying on) advice and counsel from "experts" and other nonelected persons, their reluctance to admit NGOs to political discussions is based on unsupportable bias against organized groups of citizens whom they may consider threatening to the frameworks and groups from which they draw their power.

At the international level, the location of multilateral institutions and other transnational bodies sometimes presents high barriers to the participation of southern NGOs; frequently, then, northern NGOs dominate the limited space allotted for civil society representatives. The absence of significant numbers of southern voices legitimizes the claims of critics who argue that NGOs mirror the inequality observed in the participation of marginalized groups in national governments and other political processes. Such barriers require that efforts be redoubled to involve southern NGOs, and recent trends confirm that their participation in international fora has been increasing.

The Example of Aarhus

To date, the best example of the new paradigm of environmental governance is the Convention on Access to Information, Public Participation in Decision Making, and Access to Justice in Environmental Matters (commonly referred to as the Aarhus Convention), adopted by country members of the United Nations Economic Commission for Europe (UNECE) and the European Union on June 25, 1998, at the Fourth "Environment for Europe" Ministerial Conference. The convention aims to provide the public and NGOs with common tools and standards they can use to monitor compliance with environmental laws and engage in all decisions affecting regional environments. In October 2001, the convention entered into force. Less than two years later, it adopted its first protocol and established a compliance mechanism. Currently, it has forty signatories and twenty-seven parties.

Most multilateral environmental agreements (MEAs) establish specific environmental policies with the intention of achieving measurable improvements in selected areas of environmental management. A good example of the typical MEA is the Kyoto Protocol to the United Nations Framework Convention on Climate Change, which sets specific targets for the reduction of greenhouse gas emissions and establishes a deadline by which countries are expected to achieve them. By contrast, the Aarhus Convention follows a different paradigm in multilateral environmental regime formation. Rather than set targets that must be achieved through the environmental management decisions made by countries, it prescribes the types of decision-making processes that governments must employ. With this model, Aarhus takes the first steps toward extending the principles of transparency and accountability in environmental governance beyond the level of the nation-state by establishing common regional standards for good environmental governance. Aarhus also demands what could be termed "horizontal accountability" from governments and corporations toward stakeholders, including NGOs and citizens, irrespective of their citizenship, nationality, or domicile.[30] Finally, the convention endeavors to integrate the environmental interests of the public and NGOs in national economic and development goals by establishing rules and processes for public participation in decision making in nonenvironmental sectors that have significant impacts on the environment.

The Aarhus Convention seeks to introduce the new paradigm in environmental regime formulation by embracing the three principles of public involvement in environmental management: access to information, participation in decision making, and access to justice. Its specific provisions treating each of these three principles are discussed in more detail below.

Public Access to Environmental Information

The convention requires governments at all levels to disclose environmental information to the public (Articles 4 and 5). Its first section specifies the types of information that should be made public as well as the channels through which it should be disclosed and the frequency with which disclosures should be made. The convention requires that information be made public not only on levels of pollution releases but also about the specific sources of the pollution, the impact of the pollutants on the environment and on human health and planned and operational measures taken to reduce the release of pollutants and mitigate their impact. The convention's first section also stipulates that governments should institute PRTRs or other registries and inventories documenting performance by industry and other polluting groups.

Public Participation in Decision Making

The second pillar of the Aarhus Convention defines the rules for public involvement in three kinds of environmental decisions. First, decisions regarding specific development activities as described in Annex I must be subjected to public review and consultation (Article 6). Second, in formulating plans, programs, and policies, governments at all levels must provide forums for public participation if the plans involve environmental issues (Article 7); examples of plans and policies subject to this requirement include environmental action programs and waste management policies. Third, Aarhus establishes a limited right to public and NGO involvement in the formulation of regulations promulgated by executive agencies and in legislation and legally binding agreements (Article 8). In essence, this section of the convention establishes a framework that requires governments at regional, national, and subnational levels to ensure that competing interests are represented in decision-making processes. Underlying this requirement is the assumption that participation provides the best opportunity for the formulation of policies, plans, and projects that are fair to all parties.

Access to Justice

The third pillar of the Aarhus Convention guarantees to individuals and NGOs the ability to access institutions of justice when public authorities or corporations do not comply with the rules established in the convention (Article 9). Specifically, Aarhus defines who has the standing to seek justice in a court of law or other impartial body and in what types of cases. NGOs are explicitly included under the definitions of "the public" and "the public concerned" set out in Article 2, Sections 4 and 5, though their standing is subject to the criteria, if any, laid down in national law. In an effort to ensure that justice is timely and fair, Aarhus also mandates the establishment of equitable, affordable, and efficient judicial procedures.

The Role of NGOs in Developing the Aarhus Convention

Even though voting rights in the Aarhus Convention remained formally confined to governments, NGOs played a central role in drafting and negotiating the convention. Environmental NGOs participated in the intergovernmental working groups set up to conduct negotiations, and their representatives were present on the Committee on Environmental Policy, which approved the draft text before it was transmitted to country ministers for final adoption. NGOs also participated in smaller drafting and advisory groups established on an ad hoc basis during the negotiations to resolve contested issues. Thus, departing from the norms of most prior international convention negotiations, much of the Aarhus negotiation process included NGOs as full and equal partners for all practical purposes.

NGO representatives now participate as experts on the Compliance Committee established by the Parties, and have formal standing to submit complaints directly to that committee regarding alleged non-compliance on the part of national governments.

Although NGOs and other nonstate stakeholders have been full participants in several other international fora for environmental policy making—including the World Commission on Dams and the Forestry Stewardship Council—the Aarhus process was the first time NGOs played a central role in creating a legally binding international treaty and in ensuring governments' compliance with it. The Aarhus process therefore presents a new model for the formation of multilateral public policy—one that affords to public interest groups the opportunity to actively draft and negotiate international law.

Looking Toward the Future

As we have seen, the trend toward more transparent and participatory environmental governance has made real progress. In the future, advances in technology and the increased acceptance of citizen participation in governance may combine to expand transparency and thus regulation by disclosure in environmental governance. But expanded transparency may present both the public and governments with increasingly complex questions regarding the trade-offs between competing goals that a commitment to transparency raises but alone cannot resolve.

Transparency may be supported—and expanded—by a variety of new technological innovations. Satellite imagery, for example, provides real-time information that people can use to press for changes in environmental management; to monitor compliance with new agreements, laws, and paradigms; and even to generate plans for ecosystem revitalization.[31] Several large NGOs have actively embraced the use of this technology as part of their environmental campaigns. In 1998, a major paper producer in Russia, the Svetogorsk Pulp and Paper Mill, announced that it would phase out the use of ancient forest wood in its production entirely. Russia has more ancient forests than any other country in the world and they are especially threatened by industrial logging; it is estimated that 80 percent of the large ancient forest areas in Russia have already been destroyed by commercial exploitation.

Maps produced by Greenpeace and the Biodiversity Conservation Centre documenting the decline in ancient forests served as major sources of information on the impact of logging on forests in Russia. Greenpeace used satellite technology and on-the-ground verification to produce detailed maps showing forest areas down to 20,000 hectares in size. The maps provided information to companies involved in the production and use of wood products in Russia and in Europe that showed exactly which areas should be protected. The maps can now also be used to ensure that products supplied by wood companies do not contain old-growth wood.[32] Such data are now readily available: Global Forest Watch maintains a Web site that allows users to download more than 35 gigabytes of up-to-date map data free of charge.[33]

But technology is not a panacea. Citizens must often continue to rely on highly trained specialists (who are frequently members of NGOs) to interpret the data (e.g., to interpret satellite imagery), and such specialists can often be uncertain—or disagree among themselves—about the meaning of what they are seeing. Further, there are often significant capital costs involved in the utilization of technology to gather and publicize information—satellite imagery, for example, requires the development, launch, and operation of very expensive satellites—that limit the ability of some environmental organizations to make full use of the technology and/or ensure that richer organizations have access to better and more detailed information. In many cases, such technology is so prohibitively expensive that NGOs must continue to rely on data gathered by governments (primary users), which are focused on collecting information to serve their own ends rather than those of NGOs or other groups that are incidentally relying on this data.

Another issue reveals just how complex disclosure-based regulation can be. One of the most controversial issues in world trade currently is the use of genetically modified organism (GMO) technology to enhance food plants. Specifically, GMOs are foods that have been created or modified by the use of genetic engineering techniques in which deoxyribonucleic acid (DNA)— the molecules that carry the genetic information necessary for the organization and functioning of most living cells and that control the inheritance of characteristics—has been introduced, deleted, or inhibited.

The opponents of GMO products argue that the long-term effects are unknown and that such products may potentially be harmful to consumers' health. They argue that intellectual property rights and monopoly control of seeds by multinationals will not enable farmers in poor countries to obtain all the benefits from GMOs that proponents argue are possible. The proponents of GMO products counter by pointing to the rapid growth and acceptance of such products among farmers around the world—including farmers in developing countries. They claim that biotechnology is actually helping increase yields, lower pesticide use, and improve soil conservation and prevent water pollution, and that biotechnology is therefore helping reduce hunger and poverty around the world.

Whatever the technical merits of GMO products, efforts to deal with the GMO controversy underline important points about transparency and environmental regulation—particularly about the potential limits of transparency in enabling consumers to make truly informed decisions. In a controversial move, the European Commission unveiled a regulation in 2001 requiring that GMO products be tracked through the food chain "from farm to table"[34] and that all GMO food products be labeled as such. In the United States (where consumer sentiment has not taken an aggressive stance against GMOs), labeling GMO products is not mandatory—though firms can choose to do so. Following the EU decision, several other countries, including Indonesia, Brazil, Chile, the Czech Republic, Malaysia, Russia, and Saudi Arabia, have introduced (or have announced that they plan to introduce) similar regulations to require the labeling of GMO products. These countries argue that labeling will enable consumers to decide whether or not to buy GM food and thus ensure that their right to know about their foods is protected by law.

However, while the issue of GMO food labeling is often presented as a simple matter of defending consumers' right to know, it involves more than questions about policy choices for or against information disclosure. GMO labeling requirements—particularly the onerous requirements imposed by the EU—add significant new costs and can have profound effects on the international trade of such products, and thus on the very future of biotechnology in food production.

The high penetration of different types of GMO products in the food chain in some countries makes it difficult for manufacturers to certify the presence or absence of individual GM items among their products. The issue of labeling—and in fact the identification of what is a GMO product—is further complicated by the lack of consistency in labeling laws; thus, the EU allows only a 1 percent threshold for GMO content in any product while Japan, for example, has set a 5 percent threshold.[35] Further, for such thresholds to be meaningfully enforced, regulators must have the capacity and the equipment to identify the precise GMO content of food products, while exporting countries must have similar capacities for measurement (and similar definitions of GMOs); exporting countries must also have the capacity to keep GMO and non-GMO products separated throughout the entire production and exporting process—which only adds to the production costs of both types of products.

Not surprisingly, labeling requirements are viewed by the proponents of GMO products as "technical barriers to trade" not actually intended to enshrine the right to know but instead intended to replace (illegal) bans by playing on consumers' fears (which may be unjustified) to slow the sale of GMO products. Proponents advocate for voluntary labeling of GMO-free goods and of specific GMO attributes in other goods. They argue that this will allow firms incurring additional costs for including such labels on their products to charge a premium or rent on their products specifically because of their GMO content. They also argue that the level of scientific sophistication associated with the production of GMOs makes it difficult for consumers to know or completely understand the scientific techniques that have been utilized; the impact of consumption on human health and safety, both in the short term and over the long term; or the impact of production and consumption upon broader consumer concerns such as animal welfare, environmental protection, or moral, ethical, and religious issues. They also point out that there is a lack of universal definitions of what constitutes a risk to human safety, animal and plant welfare, or the environment, and that this lack of universal agreement leads to the differences in the types of information that countries are requiring to be provided on food labels.

The end result of this type of disagreement among countries may be that a product is denied access to foreign markets. It is for this reason that one country's labeling requirements may be viewed by another country as trade protectionism. Such disagreements—conducted as they are in the absence of perfect information—emphasize that even when all available information is disclosed, consumers may still be unable to make rational consumption decisions, and the disclosure of certain pieces of information may in fact be producing unintended negative consequences for the food supply and future food production options. Such complex issues force policy makers to weigh the costs and resource requirements of disclosure policies against their potential benefits.

This chapter has examined the structures that underpin disclosure-based environmental regulation by creating transparency in environmental governance. We have argued that the term "transparency" must be broadly defined to encompass three essential principles that must be present if citizens are to have a meaningful role in environmental governance. Access to information is the foundation of transparency—but it is not in all cases sufficient by itself to empower citizens to meaningfully influence environmental decisions. Access to information must be coupled with access to decision-making processes and access to justice.

We have also examined how transparency can be institutionalized as an essential component of environmental governance through the constant vigilance of intermediaries, like civil society groups. In the past few decades, civil society organizations—including grass-roots environmental movements and transnational nongovernmental organizations—have come to play very important roles in shaping domestic and international environmental governance policies and confronting these vested interests. Such groups frequently spearhead the demand for increased transparency in governance, and, gradually, governments have begun to accede space to them. The development of the Aarhus Convention represents one of the biggest achievements of NGOs to date in influencing the development of environmental governance frameworks. In many ways, Aarhus also provides a road map for the development of future regional and international environmental treaties.

Looking toward the future, we have argued that disclosure-based environmental regulation is likely to become an even more effective part of environmental governance throughout the world as technological innovations continue to be made and as basic norms of transparency and citizen participation are integrated into governance frameworks.

Ultimately, policy making is essentially a power struggle among competing interests—governments, citizens, corporations, nongovernmental organizations, and multilateral organizations. In the creation of institutional frameworks in which the principles of transparency are enshrined as rights, a more level playing field may be established upon which citizens can protect their interests against those of more powerful actors.

NOTES

1. Mary Graham, *Democracy by Disclosure: The Rise of Technopopulism* (Washington, DC: Brookings Institution Press, 2002), 25.

2. The Bhopal gas tragedy was one of many accidental chemical releases that occurred in the 1970s and 1980s. A dioxin leak in Seveso in northern Italy in 1976 affected more than 37,000 people and rendered farmland unusable for agricultural production. A nuclear radiation leak in Chernobyl, Ukraine, in 1986 killed more than 30 people immediately and resulted in a 64 percent increase in the cancer rate among people who received the greatest exposure; the leak also contaminated land and food products in large areas of land near Chernobyl. The Seveso, Chernobyl, and Bhopal accidents provoked strong condemnation of industrial safety protocols from the international community and mobilized national movements demanding increased transparency in environmental governance.

3. The phrase "regulation by revelation" was coined by Environmental Defense attorney Karen Florini and first appeared in print in Ann Florini, "The End of Secrecy," *Foreign Policy* 111 (1998).

4. The first steps toward empowering citizens through the provision of information were taken in 1946, when the Administrative Procedures Act was enacted. Among other things, this legislation required that citizens be given both notice of proposed government regulations and an opportunity to comment on them.

5. Friends of the Earth, "Safer Chemicals: Factory Watch" (2004), http://www.foe.co.uk/campaigns/safer_chemicals/resource/factory_watch/index.html.

6. World Resources 2002–2004, *Decisions for the Earth: Balance, Voice, and Power* (Washington, DC: World Resources Institute, 2003), 20.

7. Against the background of the attacks in the United States in September 2001, concerns that terrorists might use publicly available information to plan future attacks have led many to question whether sensitive environmental information should be made widely available. The rollback of some disclosure policies has been a setback to the expansion of transparency and access to information.

8. Richard Calland and Alison Tilley, eds., *The Right to Know, the Right to Live: Access to Information and Socio-Economic Justice* (Cape Town: Open Democracy Advice Center, 2002), xi.

9. Elena Petkova et al., *Closing the Gap, Information, Participation, and Justice in Decision-Making for the Environment* (Washington, DC: World Resources Institute, 2002), 45. Available from: http://pdf.wri.org/closing_gap_cho3.pdf (accessed June 24, 2005).

10. Susan Dudley, "'It's Time to Reevaluate the Toxic Release Inventory,' Testimony Before the Subcommittee on Regulatory Reform and Oversight, Committee on Small Business, United States House of Representatives" (2002), http://www.mercatus.org/pdf/materials/426.pdf (accessed July 29, 2004).

11. Lamont Hempel, *Environmental Governance: The Global Challenge* (Washington, DC: Island Press, 1996), 6.

12. Petkova et al., *Closing the Gap*, 65.

13. Lina Ibara, *Public Participation Provisions in Environmental Impact Assessment: Law and Policies of Latin American and Caribbean Countries* (Washington, DC: World Resources Institute, 2002).

14. United Nations Economic Commission for Europe, "Protocol on Strategic Environmental Assessment" (Kiev: UNECE, 2003), http://www.unece.org/env/eia/sea_protocol.htm (accessed August 11, 2004).

15. The Access Initiative is a network of civil society groups formed in 2002. Members include the World Resources Institute and nongovernmental organizations active in Chile, Hungary, India, Indonesia, Mexico, South Africa, Thailand, Uganda, and the United States.

16. World Resources Institute, "Closing the Gap, Information, Participation, and Justice in Decision Making for the Environment," (Washington, DC: World Resources Institute), http://www.accessinitiative.org.

17. World Resources 2002–2004, *Decisions for the Earth*, 60.

18. Green Party in Bulgaria, "Ecological Movements in Bulgaria," http://www.greenparty.bg/in%20Engish/non-formal%20movements.htm (accessed September 10, 2004).

19. Gallup International's 2002 *Voice of the People* survey, designed in

collaboration with Environics International and conducted from July to September 2002, included face-to-face or telephone interviews with 36,000 citizens across 47 countries on s6ix continents. With this sample, results are statistically representative of the views of 1.4 billion citizens.

20. World Resources 2002–2004, *Decisions for the Earth*, 57.

21. Ibid., 53.

22. Barbara Gemmill and Abimbola Bamidele-Izu, "The Role of NGOs and Civil Society in Global Environmental Governance" (2002), http://www.yale.edu/environment/publications/geg/gemmill.pdf (accessed July 15, 2004).

23. World Resources 2002–2004, *Decisions for the Earth*, 69.

24. Peter Haas, Robert Keohane, and Marc Levy, eds., *Institutions for the Earth: Sources of Effective International Environmental Protection* (Cambridge, MA: MIT Press, 1993), 24.

25. Kevin DeLuca, *Image Politics: The New Rhetoric of Environmental Activism* (New York: Guilford Press, 1999), 1.

26. Abraham Chayes and Antonia Handler Chayes, *The New Sovereignty: Compliance with International Regulatory Agreements* (Cambridge, MA: Harvard University Press, 1995), 251.

27. Gemmill and Bamidele-Izu, *The Role of NGOs*.

28. James Paul, "NGOs and Global Policy-Making" (2000), http://www.globalpolicy.org/ngos/analysis/analoo.htm (accessed August 10, 2004).

29. Ann Florini, *The Coming Democracy: New Rules for Running a New World* (Washington, DC: Brookings Institution Press, 2005), 189.

30. UNECE, 1998. "Convention on Access to Information, Public Participation in Decision-Making and Access to Justice in Environmental Matters" (Aarhus Convention) (Aarhus: UNECE, 1998), http://www.unece.org/env/pp/documents/cep43e.pdf (accessed August 10, 2004).

31. Ann Florini and Yahya Dehqanzada, "Secrets for Sale: How Commercial Satellite Imagery Will Change the World" (Washington, DC: Carnegie Endowment for International Peace, 2000), http://www.ceip.org/programs/transparency/FINALreport.pdf (accessed August 10, 2004).

32. Alexey Yaroshenko, "Greenpeace Satellite Mapping Moves the First Major Producer to Phase Out Ancient Forest Use" (1998), http://archive.greenpeace.org/pressreleases/forests/1998dec17.html (accessed July 29, 2004).

33. Global Forest Watch (GFW), "GFW Data Warehouse," http://www.globalforestwatch.org/english/datawarehouse/index.asp (accessed July 20, 2004).

34. Organic Consumers Association, "Detailed Description on New GMO Labeling Rules" (EU European Report, 2001), http://www.organicconsumers.org/gefood/gmolabeling080101.cfm (accessed July 24, 2004).

35. Hera Diani and Maria Endah Hulupi, "Indonesians Demand GMO Labeling," *The Jakarta Post*, 2001, http://www.organicconsumers.org/gefood/indonesia110801.cfm (accessed July 25, 2004).

Chapter Ten

Transparency in the
Security Sector

Alasdair Roberts

A Decade of Revelations

The 1990s were a decade of horrible revelation. Around the world, walls of secrecy that had been built in the name of national security collapsed, giving proof of the terrible abuses done by military, intelligence, and police forces in the decades of the Cold War.

In 1992, a dissident KGB archivist, Vasili Mitrokhin, seized the opportunity created by the collapse of the Soviet Union to smuggle out thousands of documents that revealed how Soviet leaders had wielded power over seven decades. The "Mitrokin Archive" provided evidence of Moscow's attempt to liquidate "enemies of the people," its disinformation campaigns against Western leaders and its own dissidents, and infiltration of Western governments, political parties, and media.[1]

The collapse of military regimes throughout South America also unveiled evidence of systematic terror. In Paraguay, activists discovered tons of documents—dubbed an "Archive of Terror"—that traced the torture and execution of dissidents. Proof of collaboration among national intelligence agencies in "disappearances" was found in a court archive in Buenos Aires.[2] In Chile and Argentina, truth and reconciliation commissions provided more evidence of human rights abuses by military and police forces.

In the Soviet bloc, the end of the Cold War led to the opening of the archives of the state security services. One million Germans applied within five years to read surveillance files of the Stasi, the East German secret police—sometimes discovering that friends or co-workers had betrayed them as Stasi informers.[3] The collapse of other authoritarian regimes led to further revelations of secrets once hidden in the name of public security. South Africa's apartheid regime had relied on emergency laws that prevented the distribution of information about activity of the police and defense forces; the postapartheid regime established a Truth and Reconciliation Commission that laid bare the cruelties of apartheid and adopted a new constitution that guaranteed a right to government information.[4] In June 2002, Mexican President Vicente Fox Quesada released 60,000 files that documented the government's long "dirty war" against its left-wing opponents, and signed the country's first right to information (RTI) law.[5]

The United States itself tore down walls of secrecy throughout the decade, revealing many cases of governmental misconduct. Special projects were undertaken to declassify documents that revealed the government's complicity in the Chilean coup of 1973, and its knowledge of human rights abuses by Chilean and other South American security forces.[6] Other declassification efforts uncovered the support given by U.S. officials to former Nazi officials in the earliest years of the Cold War,[7] as well as radiation experiments undertaken by government scientists on unwitting American citizens.[8]

These exercises in disclosure might have taught us something about the perils of allowing state actors to insist on absolute secrecy in the name of national security. Unfortunately, the lesson was not taken to heart. Even as right to information laws spread around the globe, the national security establishments within most governments remained enclaves in which the presumption of secrecy held fast. In fact, there is evidence that for a combination of reasons, the problem of undue secrecy is becoming more severe. Such secrecy is indefensible in principle, because it undermines political participation rights and other basic human rights. It may also be imprudent: as we shall see, secrecy actually corrodes the capacity of government agencies to perform their mission of promoting better security. A sound policy is one that allows for open deliberation about the boundaries of secrecy and effective independent review of government decisions to deny access to information.

The Security Sector as a Protected Enclave

Throughout the Cold War, the security sector of government—comprising agencies responsible for defense, intelligence, and internal security[9]—was regarded as a special enclave of secrecy, even in countries that professed a general commitment to open government. Security imperatives seemed to overwhelm any possible case for transparency in this sector. But the first decade of the post–Cold War period provided grounds for challenging the wisdom of this policy. Secrecy, justified in the name of national security, had provided cover for serious abuses of power. The rapid diffusion of right to information laws—throughout Central and Eastern Europe, South America, and South Africa—seemed to suggest that in many places the old practice of blanket secrecy would no longer be followed.

But for a combination of reasons, the security sector of government remained a protected enclave in which transparency norms held little or no sway. In many countries—Russia, China, and Indonesia, to name a few major cases—there was little success in establishing a statutory right to government information at all. Elsewhere, the right to information was carefully bounded to preserve secrecy norms.

One difficulty was the limited scope of the many new RTI laws. The United Kingdom's Freedom of Information Act, adopted in 2000, explicitly acknowledged that a portion of the country's security sector would continue to be protected. Some security agencies—such as the intelligence service (MI6) and counterintelligence service (MI5)—are not subject to the law at all.[10] There is also a strict prohibition on disclosure of information sent by security agencies to other government departments, or relating to security agencies. India's Right to Information Act, adopted in 2002, took a similar approach: it did not apply to sixteen of the country's security and intelligence organizations. (In 2005, the Indian government responded to criticism of this rule by promising a limited right to information from security and intelligence agencies in cases of alleged human rights abuses.) South Africa's National Intelligence Agency has lobbied for a similar exclusion from the South African law.[11]

Other techniques were also used to protect an enclave of secrecy. In the United States, four intelligence agencies have successfully lobbied to have their "operational files" completely excluded from the country's Freedom of Information Act.[12] Several countries give elected officials the right to issue "conclusive certificates" that can block any attempt to apply an RTI law to national security information.[13]

Elsewhere, more liberal RTI laws have been confounded by the judiciary's unwillingness to challenge official claims that disclosure of information would compromise national security. In the United States, the Supreme Court said in a 1974 decision that the national RTI law gave it "no means to question any Executive decision to stamp a document 'secret,' however cynical, myopic, or even corrupt that decision might have been."[14] The U.S. Congress amended the law to expand the court's power, but judges still proved reluctant to challenge executive claims that disclosure of information would jeopardize national security.[15]

In the United States, and in many other countries, the field of national security is still protected by a distinctive aura of impenetrability. Its influence is evident in the tendency of officials to deny categorically that there is a right to information relating to the work of institutions in the security sector. "The right to classified information is not a human right," the head of Slovakia's security bureau said in 2002.[16] The Latvian Supreme Court reached the same conclusion in 2003.[17]

Other forces have also compromised recently adopted RTI laws. One of these has been the diffusion of new state secrecy laws, which set rules for the handling of information classified as secret by government officials. The trend was most obvious in Central and Eastern Europe (CEE), where the spread of RTI laws in the early 1990s was followed, a few years later, by the spread of new state secrecy laws. These statutes affected access to information in two ways. Some—such as those in Belgium and Spain—simply deny any right to information that has been classified as secret by officials.[18] The grounds on which information can be classified may be very broad. In addition, these laws may impose severe penalties for the unauthorized disclosure of classified information by officials, or its subsequent publication by journalists.[19]

The diffusion of state secrecy laws was one result of the reconstruction of political and military alliances in the post–Cold War era. In the early 1990s, CEE countries abandoned secrecy rules that had been imposed to preserve security within the Soviet bloc. By the end of the decade, however, many countries in the region were striving to join the North Atlantic Treaty Organization (NATO)—and NATO expected that its members would adopt laws that ensured the security of information shared within the alliance. Precisely what NATO required in the way of new secrecy laws has never been made clear: NATO itself has refused to publish its standards. Nevertheless, many CEE countries said that their new state secrecy laws were tailored to meet the organization's requirements. The European Union also tightened its secrecy rules as it began collaborating more closely with NATO. In several countries, the new laws prompted protests or constitutional challenges from civil liberties groups.[20]

The decade also saw more intergovernmental agreements on defense and intelligence cooperation that restricted the capacity of governments to respond to citizens' pressure for increased openness. In 2003, for example, the United States and the United Kingdom negotiated an agreement on the sharing of information relating to British participation in the development of the United States' controversial ballistic missile defense (BMD) system. The agreement prevents the United Kingdom from releasing any information received from the United States without its permission. The agreement itself, although unclassified, has been withheld by the British government, which relied on the national security exemption in its code on access to government documents.[21]

Secrecy within the security sector has also been bolstered by the increased reliance on private contractors. As Peter Singer has shown, private firms have taken on a larger role in defense, police, and intelligence work, often fulfilling functions once thought to be the exclusive responsibility of government employees.[22] Although the security work undertaken by private firms can have a profound effect on human rights—as controversies over the role of contractors in Iraq, Kosovo, and Colombia have recently shown—contractors are rarely required to comply with RTI laws.[23] "Company contracts are protected under propriety law," says Singer, "often making their activities completely deniable."[24]

The terrorist attacks of September 2001 also led to a consolidation of the rule of secrecy within the security sector, particularly in the United States. Government agencies withdrew much published information about vulnerable facilities and systems. Federal agencies also developed new policies for the sharing of unclassified information that threatened to undermine federal and state RTI laws. The Bush administration resisted demands for disclosure of information about individuals detained by the immigration service, about combatants or civilians held within a chain of secret prisons run by the Department of Defense, and about its motivation and plans for the invasion of Iraq. Other countries also restricted transparency following September 2001. Canada amended its RTI law to restrict access to national security information and adopted special review procedures for information requests that appeared to have security implications.[25]

Consequences of Excessive Secrecy

The case for greater openness in the security sector does not rest on a challenge to the importance of public security itself. As Thomas Powers has recently argued, public order is a prerequisite for the construction of a viable liberal democracy. A society cannot honor the civil and political rights of its citizens if it has not already obtained a reasonable level of security.[26] A widespread sense of insecurity can also compromise the legitimacy of a democratic state.[27] And a certain level of secrecy is essential for public order to be maintained. Complete openness would compromise efforts to collect intelligence about looming threats and to plan for national defense or investigate criminal behavior.

There is a need for secrecy within the security sector. But this does not imply that the security sector should be a protected enclave, in which a national security claims always trump demands for openness. Officials often argue that national security claims *should* take precedence, and that officials themselves can be trusted to exercise power responsibly behind that wall of complete secrecy. However, experience has shown that a policy of total secrecy can create an environment in which power is abused, and civil and political rights undermined.

In the early years of the United States' Freedom of Information Act, public officials made a determined effort to preserve the absolute secrecy of the security sector, arguing that any increased transparency would jeopardize vital national interests. Responding to President Johnson's concern about greater openness in the sector, Congress included a broad exclusion for national security information in the first Freedom of Information Act, adopted in 1966. That law, a Supreme Court justice later said, "ordained unquestioning deference to the Executive's use of the 'secret' stamp."[28] In the Pentagon Papers case (1971), the Nixon administration again warned about the dangers of interfering in "difficult and complex judgments" about the disclosure of national security information.[29] In 1974, President Ford made an unsuccessful attempt to block statutory changes that improved access to national security and law enforcement information, arguing that the proposals would endanger vital interests of the United States.[30]

Throughout the 1970s, a succession of leaks and special investigations revealed how the United States' police, intelligence, and defense forces had wielded power behind this wall of complete secrecy. The Pentagon Papers revealed how several administrations had escalated U.S. involvement in the Vietnam War while publicly exaggerating the threat to the United States and the effectiveness of the American intervention.[31] The Federal Bureau of Investigation had twisted legitimate counterintelligence efforts into a program aimed at monitoring and crushing legitimate political dissent. The Central Intelligence Agency had engaged in domestic spying, sponsored experiments with LSD on unwitting patients, and plotted efforts to assassinate foreign leaders and overthrow unfriendly governments.[32]

The same cycle—demands for deference, followed by revelations of abuse—has been repeated more recently. Senior officials in the Bush administration have criticized legislative controls such as the Freedom of Information Act as "unwise compromises" that "undermine the ability of the President to do his job."[33] As the administration's "global war on terrorism" has expanded, officials have become more forceful in asserting the need for greater deference to executive branch judgments about the balance to be struck between security concerns and civil liberties. In January 2004, White House counsel Alberto

Gonzales deployed this argument to rebuff calls for greater scrutiny of the administration's handling of detainees. Congress and the public, Gonzales said, needed to rely on the administration's assurance that it was doing its best to reconcile security needs with detainees' rights.[34]

Unfortunately, revelations of abuse within American prisons and interrogation centers have provided new proof of the foolhardiness of a policy of blind trust. The U.S. government resisted scrutiny of its detention systems through the Freedom of Information Act, by the courts or by nongovernmental organizations, such as the International Committee of the Red Cross, in the name of national security. But its practice of complete secrecy created an environment that resulted in unjustified detention and torture, and ultimately in a collapse in the legitimacy and effectiveness of U.S. security forces.

In general, the power to obtain information held by government is important as a tool for protecting a range of basic human rights.[35] Obviously there may be circumstances in which basic rights have to be weighed against more fundamental security needs. But the danger, now demonstrated by much experience, is that governments that are able to operate in secrecy will give little or no weight to basic rights. The Abu Ghraib prison scandal has showed how easily highly trained military and intelligence forces, operating with no expectation of public accountability, could descend to grievous abuses, including violations of the right to protection against arbitrary detention (Article 9 of the Universal Declaration of Human Rights) and the right to protection against torture or cruel, inhuman, or degrading treatment (Article 5 of the declaration). Of course, the decade of revelations that followed the end of the Cold War revealed more widespread abuses of these rights by governments operating under the mantle of secrecy.

Political Participation Rights

A policy of strict secrecy can also undermine the right to participate effectively in political affairs. The Universal Declaration of Human Rights says that individuals have the right to take part in the government of their country, and that government should exercise its authority on the basis of the will of the people (Article 21). Political participation is obviously compromised if citizens lack access to the information they need to make informed decisions about national policy. Secrecy compels the public to defer to the judgment of a narrow elite.[36]

This has been illustrated by the debate over the process by which the American and British governments decided to invade Iraq. A decision to go to war is arguably one of the most important choices that a nation can be expected to make because it involves an explicit gamble with human lives. Citizens are entitled to expect that they will be given an opportunity to make an informed judgment about the need for war. In the case of preventative rather than defensive war, this expectation cannot be dismissed on the grounds of urgency.

There is good evidence that citizens in the United States did not make an informed judgment about the Bush administration's proposed war with Iraq. In the months before the start of the war, opinion polling showed that a large majority of Americans believed that the Iraqi regime had weapons of mass destruction, and that it had played an important role in the September 2001 terrorist attacks. On the eve of war, almost half of Americans believed that Saddam Hussein had been "personally involved" in the attacks, and that some or most of the attackers had been Iraqis.[37]

In fact, the evidence available to U.S. government agencies did not establish that there was an immediate threat that the Iraqi regime would develop or use weapons of mass destruction. Nor was there good evidence that the regime had involvement with the September 2001 attacks.[38] Nevertheless, senior policy makers in the Bush administration succeeded in contorting the available evidence to bolster the case for war with Iraq. National security concerns were invoked to justify the suppression of dissenting views held by officials within the intelligence community.[39] In the United Kingdom, the Blair government made similar efforts to bend the available evidence to make the strongest case for war—a project made easier by the secrecy that habitually covers the British intelligence community and that hid internal disagreements about the meaning that should be put on the evidence at hand.[40]

Citizens of the United States and the United Kingdom had a right to participate in the decision to go to war that was undercut by overreaching secrecy. Much of the information withheld did not relate to pieces of intelligence or sources of intelligence, which if released would compromise security. Instead, much of it related to the conflicting interpretations of available intelligence by specialists within each government. The widespread disclosure of information in both countries as a result of inquiries following the war now show the extent to which the withholding of information was driven by political and not security concerns.

Transparency During Emergencies

Many well-established democratic states, facing uncertain but potentially fundamental threats to their security, resort to the use of emergency powers. Security agencies insist on a loosening of rules that restrict search and surveillance, arrest, detention, and deportation. Policy makers insist that extraordinary circumstances demand immediate action, and that the usual processes for law making must be circumvented. In moments of crisis, it is difficult for citizens to resist these calls for stronger state powers. Nevertheless, the resort to extraordinary powers is perilous. Under conditions of uncertainty, it is unclear how far the state should go, and there is the risk that it will overreact.

There is an understandable tendency for governments to insist on greater secrecy during emergencies. However, this is the moment at which openness actually plays an especially important role. Openness allows citizens to understand precisely what a grant of emergency authority means in practice—how it is used, and how far it appears to compromise basic rights. Openness helps electorates to debate policy and correct overreactions, and can maintain the accountability of entire electorates by subjecting them to scrutiny by citizens in neighboring democracies. And openness also limits the capacity of security agencies to abuse new powers.[41]

In sum, openness is a critical safeguard against abuse or overextension of emergency powers. This point has been affirmed in the United States since the terrorist attacks of September 11. The existence of a free press and unrestricted rights to free expression have allowed journalists and civil liberties groups to protest government policies on the detention of aliens who are alleged to pose a national security risk. (The new policies allow detention of aliens based on minor violations of immigration law, or detention without charges "in times of emergency.") Such scrutiny—and the risk of embarrassment in world opinion—have probably discouraged more dramatic steps against suspect aliens.

On the other hand, the capacity of civil liberties groups to monitor government has been compromised by excesses of secrecy regarding these detention programs. As David Cole has observed, many of the details about the Bush administration's preventative detention program have been "shrouded in mystery."[42] The U.S. justice department has refused to disclose the names of detainees or the place of their detention. In November 2001 the department also stopped providing a weekly statement on the number of detainees, already more than 1,000, and subsequently refused requests for information about the detainees made under the Freedom of Information Act.[43]

By May 2002, more than 600 of these detainees had been subjected to deportation hearings that were closed to family members, journalists, and any other member of the public. The justice department did not rely routinely on classified information in these hearings, or impose nondisclosure requirements on the detainees or their lawyers—actions that might explain or reflect a serious worry over national security. "The real concern," says Cole, "may not have been that Al Qaeda would find out what was going on, but that the American public would find out."[44]

The secrecy that surrounded the 660 foreign nationals held at the U.S. military base at Guantánamo Bay, Cuba was more profound. The government did not identify all of the detainees or acknowledged their right of habeas corpus, which would compel the presentation of reasons for their detention. Although the International Committee of the Red Cross was permitted to visit the prisoners, it attempted to preserve its neutrality by providing opinions in confidence to U.S. officials. Remoteness and military restrictions limited media coverage. The government said that the Guanatánamo detainees could be tried in secret proceedings, using secret evidence, and with proscriptions imposed on defense lawyers against consultation with outside experts or public disclosure of information about the trials.[45]

The wisdom of this emphasis on secrecy could be questioned on purely tactical grounds. The government's treatment of aliens within the United States following September 11 had the effect of discouraging cooperation within immigrant communities, thereby undermining security efforts in the long run.[46] Its excesses also stoked popular protests in allied nations and soured diplomatic relations with countries that should be partners in the war on terror.

More importantly, this secrecy also undermines the capacity of citizens to determine whether a new balance of security concerns and basic rights has been struck. Secrecy denies citizens the ability to understand the real impact of new policies—such as the accuracy of the government's suspicions about detainees or the psychological effect of prolonged and indeterminate detention. Secrecy makes it easier to forget the individuals who have borne the burden of extraordinary measures, and in this way abets the process of normalizing emergency measures.

How Openness Promotes Security

Secrecy has been justified in the name of national security for so long that we naturally assume that the two ideas are perfect correlates, and that any limitation on secrecy necessarily implies some weakening of security. In many respects this is incorrect. For at least three reasons, improved openness may actually improve the capacity of societies to preserve security.

Better Policy Decisions

In April 1968, Professor James C. Thomson Jr. wrote a widely acclaimed article in *The Atlantic* magazine that attempted to explain the weaknesses in the United States government's policy toward Vietnam. Thomson, who had served in the Kennedy and Johnson administrations, predicted that historians would look back at the Vietnam years and wonder how "men of superior ability, sound training, and high ideals" could have made decisions that were "regularly and repeatedly wrong." The answer, thought Thomson, could be found largely in the process of decision making itself. The concentration of responsibility at the top led to executive fatigue and an inability to respond to new and dissonant information. This was compounded by a lack of expertise within key agencies and "closed politics" of policy making on sensitive issues.[47]

Defense Secretary Robert McNamara understood the weaknesses of the process by which decisions on Vietnam were being made. Unknown to Thomson, McNamara had taken the unusual step a few months earlier of commissioning a large study of American decision making on Vietnam. Unfortunately the resulting Pentagon Papers—as they were eventually known—did little to improve the quality of government policy. Classified as "TOP SECRET," the papers were largely inaccessible inside government until leaked by Daniel Ellsberg in 1971.

The problems identified by Thomson were not unique to the Vietnam controversy. On the contrary, they are typical of large public bureaucracies. The concentration of authority at the top of the bureaucratic pyramid means that leaders and their advisors are overwhelmed with information, juggling problems that are often outside their area of expertise. Fatigue, confusion, and ignorance about key facts are commonplace, and the damage that can be done by flawed decision making can be substantial. The price that America paid for the series of missteps on Vietnam was incalculable. An intervention begun with the aim of promoting the United States' own security turned into a "calamity," Thomson concluded—a brutal, unwinnable, and immoral war.

Increased openness can help to solve problems such as these. By granting access to internal documents, governments give nongovernmental organizations the capacity to spot bad analysis or contribute data not already collected by public agencies. Nongovernmental organizations can also share the burden of synthesizing analysis and reaching conclusions about policy. The public sphere is a more powerful analytic engine than even the largest public bureaucracy, but it cannot be harnessed to serve the decision-making needs of government leaders without transparency. Of course, this policy may require the disclosure of information that would otherwise be protected in the name of national security. But the important point is that disclosure improves security in the long run—by avoiding the tremendous costs that can be associated with poor bureaucratic decision making.

Openness certainly would have improved the U.S. government's policy on the administration of postwar Iraq. There are strong similarities between the Bush administration's approach to postwar planning and the problems observed by Thomson thirty years earlier. The Bush administration carefully avoided a public presentation of its estimate of the cost of postwar reconstruction in Iraq and likely troop requirements,[48] as well as other elements of its occupation plan. This precluded effective public scrutiny and allowed decision makers to act on assumptions about the nation's long-term obligations in Iraq that have since proved to be grossly inaccurate.

Moreover, it stretched the administration's internal resources to the limit. James Fallows, writing in *The Atlantic* magazine in 2004, provides a description of postoccupation planning that is similar to Thomson's 1968 summary. "Everyone had that 'Stalingrad stare,'" a senior administrator told Fallows. "People had been doing stuff under pressure for too long and hadn't had enough sleep."[49]

Improved Agency Coordination

Citizens outside government may not recognize that their complaints about lack of access to government information are often shared by officials who work inside public agencies. Rules designed to protect sensitive information can also impede the flow of information within government agencies, sometimes with disastrous consequences for national security. The United States' Congressional Joint Inquiry into September 11 concluded that such impediments contributed to the country's inability to prevent the terror attacks in New York and Washington.[50]

This problem is not unique to the United States. In the southern Chinese province of Guangdong, a similar obsession with secrecy in the name of national security also imposed a terrible cost. In the early weeks of 2003, the province's health department received a warning from a government health committee about the emergence of a dangerous new pneumonialike illness—later identified as severe acute respiratory syndrome, or SARS. Unfortunately, the warning came in a document classified "TOP SECRET," and for several days there was no employee in the health department with the security clearance to read it.

Guangdong's health officials, fearful of criminal penalties for disclosure of state secrets, later failed to share the information with colleagues who had begun to encounter the mysterious new disease in Hong Kong.[51] At the same time, China's government-controlled media were restrained from publishing information about the epidemic.[52] This chokehold on information produced the disruption that secrecy had been intended to avoid: needless deaths, broad damage to the Chinese economy, and further corrosion of the credibility of government officials.

The weaknesses of conventional approaches to information security are now widely recognized, even within government. The rules on management of classified information that were designed in the early years of the Cold War are now seen to encourage the overproduction of "classified information" and impose excessively strict limitations on its circulation to other officials.[53] As a consequence, this is an area in which internal pressure for reform of information controls coincides with external pressure. For government agencies to do a better job of protecting national security, they will need to reduce the incentives for overproduction of classified information and liberalize rules on the distribution of classified information within government. Incidentally, this will make it easier for nongovernmental organizations to argue that the benefits of public disclosure of information outweigh the potential harm to national security.

Public disclosure of information can also be an effective way of circumventing information blockages within large bureaucracies. Frontline officials in government agencies do not rely exclusively on internal sources for information on how to do their jobs effectively; they rely on public sources—the print and electronic media—as well. The sheath of publicly accessible information that surrounds every government organization plays an important but unacknowledged part in maintaining the organization's effectiveness. As Tom Blanton points out, it was publicly accessible information, not internal communications, that provided a U.S. Customs official with the clues needed to detain a suspicious visitor to the United States—and thereby thwart a terrorist attack apparently planned for Los Angeles or Seattle on the eve of the millennium.[54] Improved transparency enriches the informational environment in which frontline officials do their work.

Fighting Bureaucratic Inertia

National security is a function that stretches the capacities of public organizations to their limits. It requires that intelligence and defense bureaucracies stay on alert for events that rarely occur. Unfortunately, we know that bureaucracies find it hard to maintain vigilance and readiness at a high level for prolonged periods of time. Human and organizational factors can conspire to make security agencies inattentive and sluggish.

Oversight by political leaders and legislators is one way of ensuring that security agencies maintain their vigilance and readiness. But this kind of oversight has its own limitations. Top decision makers have limited time and are distracted by multiple problems, many of which can seem more urgent than the hypothetical dangers posed by inadequate readiness.

Oversight by nongovernmental organizations—made possible by access to information held by security agencies—can compensate for inadequate supervision within the political process. However, the ability of these organizations to exercise oversight is often constrained precisely because access to information is denied on the grounds of national security. This is, of course, another irony: long-term risks to security created by weak oversight are allowed to fester because of a short-term concern with risks posed by openness.

This has become a common problem since the September 2001 terrorist attacks. For instance, Canada's transport ministry stopped releasing the results of its routine airport security screening tests, previously made available through its RTI law. Government officials justify the decision by arguing that the data would provide a road map to terrorists looking for vulnerable points in the Canadian airport system. But the Canadian government could have released summary data for the entire system that would have showed whether efforts to improve security were making headway. A legislative committee later complained about "unreasonable secrecy" surrounding the test results. The committee's chair argued that secrecy "hides incompetence [and] inefficiencies" and warned that the refusal to release information could endanger lives.[55]

Secretiveness has also compromised efforts to monitor progress in securing ports. In June 2004, a spokesman for the International Maritime Organization complained that the agency had little information about national efforts to comply with new security requirements, because of governments' reluctance to alert terrorists to vulnerabilities.[56] The United States Department of Homeland Security has denied Freedom of Information Act requests for information about inspection practices at U.S. seaports, as well as information about grants given to seaport operators for security improvements, on similar grounds.[57]

New rules developed by the Department of Homeland Security to protect "critical infrastructure information," contained in the U.S. Homeland Security Act of 2002, create similar difficulties of accountability. The rules absolutely prohibit the public disclosure of information about the vulnerabilities of privately owned infrastructure, such as communication or water systems. Obviously this sort of information needs some protection. But critics have complained that the complete ban on disclosure will actually increase the danger in the long run, by reducing the capacity of citizens to exert pressure for improvements.[58] As Joseph Jacobson says, efforts to restrict information about vulnerabilities in critical infrastructure will easily be overcome by determined terrorists—so the restrictions will do no good, and serve only to compromise public monitoring of government efforts to fix vulnerabilities.[59]

Defining the Limits to Secrecy

There have been at least two efforts by nongovernmental bodies to draft general principles about openness and national security. In 1995, a group of leading experts on freedom of expression and transparency met in Johannesburg and prepared a declaration—the Johannesburg Principles—that sought to define the limits to secrecy in the security sector.[60] The declaration included four key propositions:

- That the public's right to information held by the security sector must be recognized;
- That agencies within the security sector should permitted to withhold only "specific and narrow" categories of information, enumerated in law, to protect national security;
- That these justifications for withholding information must be put aside if some larger public interest would be better served by disclosure; and
- That there should be independent review of a government decision to deny access to information on the grounds of national security.[61]

In 2001, the freedom of expression group ARTICLE 19 proposed a model RTI law that would allow government agencies to withhold information if disclosure would be likely to cause "serious prejudice to defense or national security," unless there is a broader public interest in disclosure, and subject to the requirement of review by an independent tribunal.[62]

There is an important distinction between the Johannesburg Principles and ARTICLE 19's Model Law. The two documents share an interest in keeping the bar for nondisclosure high. But the 1995 Principles attempt to achieve this goal by enumerating the "specific and narrow" categories of information that could be withheld for national security reasons, while the 2001 Model Law proposes a rigorous but general test of serious prejudice to national security. Which approach is more appropriate? This question has often provoked spirited debate—as it has recently during the revision of the Czech Republic's Classified Information Protection Act.[63]

The rationale for insisting on a precise enumeration of the categories of information that might be protected on national security grounds is clear enough. The expectation is that this will check the temptation of governments to invoke national security considerations indiscriminately, thereby withholding information that properly belongs in the public domain. However, the effectiveness of this check should not be overestimated. American law defines six circumstances in which information can be withheld on national security grounds,[64] but complaints about the indiscriminate withholding of information in the name of national security have persisted in any case.[65]

There are, in addition, potential dangers associated with a too-detailed enumeration of the categories of information that can be withheld for national security reasons. Any such enumeration may be inflexible and incapable of adapting to shifts in perceptions about threats to national security and the degree of secrecy needed to counter those threats. It is arguable, for example, that rules of thumb about secrecy and openness that were developed in the Cold War era are no longer suited to a world in which security threats are posed by loose networks of nonstate actors. The practice of withholding information about intelligence agency budgets may have had some justification in a world dominated by superpower rivalries, but seems to have little justification today. By contrast, our calculus about the risk of disclosing information about private chemical facilities—which during the Cold War would have faced a low risk of sabotage from other governments outside a state of war—has clearly changed. As noted earlier, a shift in threats might also lead to greater openness, by prodding a reassessment of the practice of holding information about homeland security threats closely within a small group of senior decision makers.[66]

There are two truly critical elements in a policy within the security sector. The first is an insistence that the standard for withholding information should be rigorous. A law that requires a mere apprehension of possible harm is likely to be abused, resulting in the denial of access to information that properly ought to be in the public domain. (In Vietnam, the ordinance on state secrets is so broadly drawn that economic data routinely published elsewhere is classified, its disclosure punishable by death.)[67] It ought to be necessary for officials to substantiate that disclosure of information would pose a serious threat to public security.

The second critical element is that decisions to withhold information on security grounds should be subject to effective review by an independent office. Independent review accomplishes several goals. In general, the threat of independent review encourages officials to make their initial decisions about disclosure more carefully. It also provides a remedy in cases where agencies have attempted to use national security as a pretext for avoiding embarrassment or accountability for misconduct. Finally, the process of independent review encourages public discussion about where the line should be drawn between secrecy and openness.

The extent to which government agencies may abuse the discretion given to them by the absence of effective independent review has been illustrated in two high-profile cases in Europe and the United States. The first case arose in 1979 after a Swedish carpenter, Torsten Leander, was denied work at the Swedish Naval Museum, following an unfavorable decision in the security vetting process. Leander suspected that he had been denied a security clearance because of his earlier and lawful involvement with radical organizations—an outcome that was explicitly barred by Swedish law. Leander asked to see the information that had been used to reach the decision, and was denied on national security grounds. The case was appealed to the European Court of Human Rights, which decided in 1987 that the Swedish government was justified in denying access to the information. Although the court did not itself inspect the information, it was satisfied with the safeguards imposed on the security clearance system, such as the statutory restriction on collection or use of information about lawful activities and the oversight role played by the Minister of Justice, legislators, and special officers, such as the Swedish Chancellor of Justice.[68] The *Leander* decision became a leading case in European human rights jurisprudence.

A decade later, after the end of the Cold War, Leander finally received his file, which showed that the Swedish government had lied to the European Court of Human Rights. Leander had in fact been denied work because of his political affiliations. Other documents showed a spectacular corruption of the security clearance system. The Swedish Security Police, operating under secret instructions that flatly contradicted national law, had routinely collected information about the lawful political activities of Swedish citizens. A succession of government ministers had sanctioned the practice. Legislators and other overseers had either neglected to monitor the Security Police or quietly approved of their work. In 1990, the Chancellor of Justice had issued a public report clearing the government of wrongdoing—and at the same time prepared a secret report to the government that documented systematic abuses of national law. In 1997, Leander received a public apology from the Swedish government, while the Security Police—in the understated words of his lawyer—"suffered certain legitimacy problems."[69]

A comparable controversy has recently arisen in the United States. In 1952 the United States Supreme Court heard arguments in a case that arose following the death of three civilians in the crash of an Air Force B-29 Superfortress. The widows of the three men had asked for the Air Force's investigation report, and the Air Force refused, arguing that release of the information would seriously hamper national security by revealing details about the test of highly secret electronic equipment. The U.S. Supreme Court, without inspecting the report itself, acceded to the Air Force's position and ruled that the report need not be released to the widows. Relying in part on the *Reynolds* decision, the federal government made comparable arguments against disclosure in a growing number of cases in succeeding years.[70]

In 2000, a daughter of one of the three victims finally obtained the investigation report, which had become publicly available as part of routine declassification effort a few years earlier. The report contained no information about experiments with secret electronic equipment. On the contrary, it showed that the B-29 had crashed because of the Air Force's repeated failure to deal with mechanical problems that ultimately caused the plane's engines to catch fire. The Secretary of the Air Force and other senior officials had misled the Supreme Court when they said in 1952 that the threat to national security was so dire that even the court could not see the documents. "In other words," as Tom Blanton says, "the *Reynolds* precedent— cited in more than 600 subsequent cases . . . rose directly from government fraud and lies."[71]

Most of the devices used to preserve the security sector as an enclave of secrecy—such as the wholesale exclusion of security organizations or security files, a demand for unqualified deference to classification decisions, or ministerial certificates that trump access laws—are designed to thwart effective independent review of government judgments about the weighing of security and transparency claims. They are problematic precisely because they deny an opportunity for independent review. Experience has showed that discretion given to government officials is easily misused to prevent accountability for abuses of authority and block public participation in critical decisions about government policy.

Governments sometimes resist the principle of third-party review out of concern that this may lead to unauthorized disclosure of sensitive information. However, steps can be taken to minimize this risk. Ombudsmen or commissioners and their staff can be subjected to the same security clearance procedures that are applied to other public officials, and equally strong rules on the physical protection of sensitive information that has been delivered for review can also be maintained. The office of the Canadian Information Commissioner has operated under such rules for two decades without any instance of unauthorized disclosure of sensitive information sent for review.[72]

The Broader Context

Despite important advances in the last decade, the security sectors of many governments remain enclaves of secrecy, largely unaffected by transparency norms. A combination of factors—deeper networking among security agencies, privatization of security functions, and new concerns about security against terrorist attacks—may actually be deepening the commitment to secrecy.

For several reasons, excessive secrecy within the security sector is troubling. Experience has shown that secrecy corrodes accountability and increases the likelihood that basic rights will be abused. During periods of emergency, secrecy also compromises citizens' ability to monitor and control the use of extraordinary powers. Secrecy can also restrict the ability of nongovernmental actors to sort out complex questions of national policy and monitor bureaucratic performance in preparing for threats.

The principles that should govern transparency in the security sector are essentially the same as those that operate in any other sector of government. Agencies should be subject to a justifiable right of access to information. National security claims can be invoked to defend decisions to withhold information, but the bar should be high. The possibility that reasons for withholding information might be outweighed by broader public interest considerations should be anticipated. The decision to withhold should be subject to independent review, not left to government officials.

These rules, codified in an RTI law, are a necessary condition for greater openness in the security sector. However, other laws may also play an important role in discouraging the outflow of information. In some British Commonwealth countries, the ability to obtain government information is compromised by Official Secrets Acts that impose severe sanctions on public servants for the unauthorized disclosure of information. These laws are often said to perpetuate a culture of secrecy that undermines the influence of new RTI laws.

Restrictions on free expression could also dampen the effect of RTI laws. In Israel, censorship laws allow the government to block the publication of information regarded as sensitive on national security grounds. Felipe González has documented the chilling effect of Latin America's *desacato* laws, which may be used to impose criminal penalties on writers whose work shows contempt for public figures.[73] Governments may also resort to cruder measures—such as the expulsion of individuals whose reports are critical of security agencies. In June 2004, the Indonesian government attempted to expel the Jakarta-based representative of the International Crisis Group. The decision was said to be dictated by security forces that had been stung by the group's complaints of human rights abuses.[74]

Finally—and perhaps most critically—the effectiveness of an RTI law hinges on the capacity of journalists and nongovernmental organizations to exploit the potential it creates. If media outlets cannot invest the resources needed for thorough investigative work, the value of an RTI law is less likely to be realized. Independent oversight groups—such as the United States' National Security Archive, the South African History Archive, or the United Kingdom's LIBERTY—also play a critical role.

In short, transparency in the security sector requires a combination of steps that improve the right to information, eliminate barriers to free expression, and build up civil society's capacity to exercise these rights.

NOTES

1. Christopher Andrew and Vasili Mitrokhin, *The Sword and the Shield* (New York: Basic Books, 1999).

2. John Dinges, *The Condor Years* (New York: New Press, 2004), 233–241.

3. Timothy Garton Ash, *The File: A Personal History* (New York: Vintage, 1998).

4. Benita de Giorgi, "The Open Democracy Bill," *Politeia*, 18/2 (1999), web edn.

5. Kate Doyle, "'Forgetting Is Not Justice': Mexico Bares Its Secret Past," *World Policy Journal* 20 (2) (2003): 61–72.

6. Peter Kornbluh, *The Pinochet File* (New York: New Press, 2003); Dinges, *The Condor Years*.

7. Richard Breitman, Norman Goda, Timothy Naftali, and Robert Wolfe, *U.S. Intelligence and the Nazis* (Washington, DC: National Archives and Records Administration, 2004).

8. Advisory Committee on Human Radiation Experiments, *Final Report* (Washington, DC: Advisory Committee on Human Radiation Experiments, 1995); S. I. Schwartz, *Atomic Audit* (Washington, DC: Brookings Institution Press, 1998).

9. The term is defined in more detail by Nicole Ball, "Governance in the Security Sector," in Nicolas van de Walle and Nicole Ball, eds., *Beyond Structural Adjustment: The Institutional Context of African Development* (New York: Palgrave Macmillan, 2003), 263–304.

10. John Wadham and Kavita Modi, "National Security and Open Government in the United Kingdom," in Campbell Public Affairs Institute, *National Security and Open Government: Striking the Right Balance* (Syracuse, NY: Campbell Public Affairs Institute, 2003).

11. Christelle Terreblanche, "Intelligence Agency Wants Permanent Secrecy on Classified Documents," *The Mercury*, June 18, 2003.

12. The Central Intelligence Agency, National Reconnaissance Office, National Imagery and Mapping Agency, and National Security Agency.

13. Such as Australia, New Zealand, the United Kingdom, and Ireland.

14. Statement of Justice Stewart in *EPA v. Mink*, 410 U.S. 73 (1973).

15. "The courts," a panel of federal judges later explained, "are unschooled in diplomacy and military affairs." Louis Fisher, *The Politics of Executive Privilege* (Durham, NC: Carolina Academic Press, 2004).

16. SITA, "NBU Says Revision to Classified Information Law Is Necessary," *SITA Slovak News Agency* (Bratislava, 2002).

17. A Latvian citizen, the court said, "has no right of requiring access to state secrets." Judgment of the Constitutional Court of the Republic of Latvia in Case 2002–20–0103, April 23, 2003.

18. David Banisar, "Freedom of Information and Access to Government Records Around the World" (Washington, DC: freedominfo.org, 2004), http://www.freedominfo.org/survey/global_survey2004.pdf.

19. As was the case with the Bulgarian government's proposed amendments to the Penal Code provisions on unauthorized disclosure of state secrets. This controversy has been reported on by the Bulgarian Access to Information Programme, http://www.aip-bg.org.

20. Alasdair Roberts, "Entangling Alliances: NATO's Security Policy and the Entrenchment of State Secrecy," *Cornell International Law Journal* 36 (2) (2003): 329–360.

21. BASIC, "BASIC Acquires 'Confidential' Document on Missile Defence," press release (London, 2003).

22. P. W. Singer, *Corporate Warriors* (Ithaca, NY: Cornell University Press, 2003).

23. Alasdair Roberts, "Structural Pluralism and the Right to Information," *University of Toronto Law Journal* 51 (3) (2001): 243–271.

24. Singer, *Corporate Warriors*, x.

25. Alasdair Roberts, "Spin Control and Freedom of Information," *Public Administration* 83 (1) (2005).

26. Thomas Powers, "Can We Be Secure and Free?," *The Public Interest* 151 (2003): 3–24.

27. Orlando Perez, "Democratic Legitimacy and Public Insecurity," *Political Science Quarterly* 118 (4) (2004): 642.

28. Statement of Justice Stewart in *EPA v. Mink*, 410 U.S. 73 (1973).

29. Brief for the United States in *New York Times v. United States*, June 1974, 18, 25.

30. Veto Message from the President on the Freedom of Information Act, *Congressional Records*, November 18, 1974, 36243.

31. Daniel Ellsberg, *Secrets* (New York: Penguin Group, 2002).

32. Kathryn Olmsted, *Challenging the Secret Government* (Chapel Hill: University of North Carolina Press, 1996), 97–108.

33. Dana Milbank, "Cheney Refuses Records' Release," *Washington Post*, January 28, 2002, A1.

34. Alberto Gonzales, "Remarks to the ABA Standing Committee on Law and National Security" (Washington, DC: Executive Office of the President, 2004).

35. This argument is developed at greater length in Roberts, "Structural Pluralism."

36. Eric Alterman, *Who Speaks for America? Why Democracy Matters in Foreign Policy* (Ithaca, NY: Cornell University Press, 1998).

37. Linda Feldmann, "The Impact of Bush Linking 9/11 and Iraq," *Christian Science Monitor*, March 14, 2003; Steven Kull, C. Ramsay, and E. Lewis, "Misperceptions, the Media, and the Iraq War," *Political Science Quarterly* 118 (4) (2004): 572.

38. James Bamford, *A Pretext for War: 9/11, Iraq, and the Abuse of America's Intelligence Agencies* (New York: Doubleday, 2004).

39. John Prados, *Hoodwinked* (New York: The New Press, 2004), 33, 113.

40. Simon Rogers, ed., *The Hutton Inquiry and Its Impact* (London: Politico's Publishing, 2004), 358.

41. The critical importance of openness as a discipline on the use of emergency powers is emphasized by Michael Ignatieff, *Lesser Evil: Political Ethics in an Age of Terror* (Princeton: Princeton University Press, 2004). A similar argument is made by Jody Freeman, "Private Parties, Public Functions and the New Administrative Law," in D. Dyzenhaus, *Recrafting the Rule of Law* (Portland, OR: Hart Publishing, 1999), 331–369.

42. David Cole, *Enemy Aliens: Double Standards and Constitutional Freedoms in the War on Terrorism* (New York: The New Press, 2003), 25.

43. The United States Court of Appeals for the D.C. Circuit upheld the justice department's refusal to provide the information. See *Center for*

National Security Studies v. Department of Justice, D.C.C.A., June 17, 2003. Leave to appeal was denied by the United States Supreme Court.

44. Cole, *Enemy Aliens*, 27–30.

45. Lawyers Committee, "Assessing the New Normal: Liberty and Security for the Post-September 11 United States" (Washington, DC: Lawyers Committee for Human Rights, 2003), 56–58.

46. Cole, *Enemy Aliens*, 189.

47. Thomson Jr., James, "How Could Vietnam Happen?," *The Atlantic* 221 (1968): 47–53.

48. Peter Slevin, "U.S. Military Lays Out Postwar Iraq Plan," *Washington Post*, February 12, 2003, A21; Patrick Tyler, "Panel Faults Bush on War Costs and Risks," *New York Times*, March 12, 2003, A15.

49. James Fallows, "Blind Into Baghdad," *The Atlantic Monthly* 293 (2004): 53–74.

50. Congressional Joint Inquiry, "Findings and Conclusions of the Congressional Joint Inquiry Into September 11" (Washington, DC: Government Printing Office, 2002).

51. John Pomfret, "China's Slow Reaction to Fast-Moving Illness," *Washington Post*, April 3, 2003, A18.

52. Congressional-Executive Commission on China, "Annual Report" (Washington, DC: Government Printing Office, 2003), 36–38.

53. Bruce Berkowitz, "Secrecy and Security," *Hoover Digest*, 2001, http://www.hooverdigest.org/011/berkowitz.html.

54. Thomas Blanton, "Beyond the Balancing Test: National Security and Open Government in the United States," in Campbell Public Affairs Institute, *National Security and Open Government* (Syracuse, NY: Campbell Public Affairs Institute, 2003), 65–66.

55. Jim Bronskill, "Transport Won't Release Airport Security Results," *Ottawa Citizen*, February 5, 2003, A1.

56. "Ports Withholding Security Data Over Terrorism Fears," *Shipping Times*, June 4, 2004.

57. *Coastal Delivery Corp. v. United States Customs Serv.*, No. CV 02–3838 (C.D. Cal. Mar. 17, 2003). See also Jennifer Lin, "Big Grant to Oil Firm Shrouded in Secrecy," *Philadelphia Inquirer*, June 19, 2003.

58. Rena Steinzor, "'Democracies Die Behind Closed Doors': The Homeland Security Act and Corporate Accountability," *Kansas Journal of Law & Public Policy* 12 (2) (2003): 664. Some critics have already complained that the Department of Homeland Security lacks the authority and resources to monitor security precautions for critical infrastructure in the chemical

industry, while the industry itself appears to have little new investment in security since September 11. Margaret Kriz, 2003. "Bush Not Doing Enough to Protect Chemical Plant, Critics Contend" (2003), http://www.govexec. com/dailyfed/0803/080703nj3.htm.

59. Joseph Jacobson, "Safeguarding National Security Through Public Release of Environmental Information" (Washington, DC: George Washington University Law School, 2002).

60. Thomas Mendel, "National Security vs. Openness: An Overview and Status Report on the Johannesburg Principles," in Campbell Public Affairs Institute, *National Security and Open Government: Striking the Right Balance* (Syracuse, NY: Campbell Public Affairs Institute, 2003).

61. Principles 11 to 14 of the Johannesburg Principles. Sandra Coliver, *Secrecy and Liberty: National Security, Freedom of Expression, and Access to Information* (The Hague: M. Nijhoff Publishers, 1999).

62. Sections 22, 30, 35 and 44(2) of the Article 19 Model Law. The Model Law is published at http://www.article19.org/docimages/1112.htm.

63. Helena Svatošová, "Analysis of the Draft Bill on Classified Intelligence and Security Vetting" (Prague: Transparency International Czech Republic, 2003).

64. See Section 1.4 of Executive Order 12958, as amended by Executive Order 13292.

65. J. W. Leonard, "Remarks to the National Classification Management Society's Annual Training Seminar" (Washington, DC: Information Security Oversight Office, 2004).

66. There is also a risk of assuming that a similar list of legitimate national security concerns will be suited to different countries. Social and political differences may mean that information that seems harmless in one country could pose a serious threat to order if disclosed in another country.

67. Amy Kazmin, "Hanoi's Culture of Secrecy Thwarts IMF," *Financial Times*, October 1, 2003.

68. *Leander v. Sweden*, European Court of Human Rights, Application No. 9248/81, Decision March 26, 1987.

69. Dennis Töllborg, "Sweden," in David Greenwood and S. Huisman, eds., *Transparency and Accountability of Police Forces, Security Services and Intelligence Agencies* (Geneva: Geneva Centre for the Democratic Control of Armed Forces, 2003), 117–138.

70. William Weaver and R. M. Pallitto, "State Secrets and Executive Power," *Political Science Quarterly* (forthcoming).

71. Blanton, "Beyond the Balancing Test," 45–46.

72. Information Commissioner of Canada, "Annual Report 2001–2002" (Ottawa: Office of the Information Commissioner, 2002), 16.

73. Felipe Gonzalez, "Access to Information and National Security in Chile," in Campbell Public Affairs Institute, *National Security and Open Government: Striking the Right Balance* (Syracuse, NY: Campbell Public Affairs Institute, 2003), 167–188.

74. Tim Johnston, "Indonesia Orders Crisis Group's Leader to Leave Over Work Permit," *Financial Times*, June 3, 2004, 7.

Conclusion

Whither Transparency?

Ann Florini

No single chapter can weave together all the threads spun in this book. Information flow—its causes and its consequences—is too enormous a topic for all its ramifications to fit within a few pages. Moreover, as the case studies make clear, information is a fundamental component of power and governance, inherently subject to the idiosyncracies of specific national or organizational histories and cultures. There can be no single "how-to" primer on making the best use of what transparency tools can offer for governance. Nonetheless, several broad themes cut across nations and issues. What this chapter *can* do, therefore, is to highlight some of the most significant issues that emerge from the book's case studies. These key lessons are intended to help policy makers, executives, activists, and the public think through how this wide range of experience might apply to them.

What Disclosure Can Do

Decision makers need to understand why they are now so often besieged with demands to disclose. To design good transparency systems, they need to understand why those systems are wanted and what they are expected to accomplish. Only then is it possible to assess whether the disclosure systems in place are achieving those goals, or how the systems might need to be changed.

From the cases in this book, we see that disclosure is demanded because people believe it will improve governance in a variety of ways—by enabling people to enjoy a wide array of basic rights, deterring corruption, improving decision making, enabling actors to coordinate their actions, building public support for needed policies, and even serving as a direct regulatory tool.

The Effectiveness and Efficiency of Government

As was noted in this book's Introduction, the discourse around disclosure has shifted substantially over the decades. Freedom of information had long been seen primarily as a political right, both inherent in and essential to democratic forms of government. But in the twentieth century, transparency began to be viewed as an administrative tool, a way of making increasingly large and complex government agencies work more efficiently and effectively, as well as with greater accountability to the citizenry. By the end of the century, and in large part due to some of the experiences described in this book, the thinking on transparency had broadened.

Now, disclosure is seen not only as a right in and of itself but also as a crucial and necessary tool for the achievement of all other rights. As the Indian campaign for the right to know has long argued, very often "the right to know [is] the right to live."

That slogan is no mere exaggeration for campaign purposes. As Shekhar Singh's description of the struggle for information in India and Richard Calland's account of the South African experience both exemplify, the corruption that becomes endemic under conditions of secrecy frequently deprives the most vulnerable members of a society of the basic necessities of life—food, water, employment. And as Calland's chapter argues, the need for disclosure to prevent such corruption extends not only to the government itself but also to its surrogates in the private sector who are providing public goods.

But transparency can improve governance even when financial corruption is not an issue. As Alasdair Roberts argues in this volume's chapter on security, excessive secrecy has a negative impact on the quality of decision making. Although his chapter focuses on the problem in the security realm, the arguments often apply to other complex policy issues. Secrecy closes down the process of decision making, with predictable and often negative effects. There is never enough time for a small group of decision makers to consider all potentially relevant information. Transparency gives more people "the capacity to spot bad analysis or contribute data not already collected by public agencies," as Roberts argues. He also contends that transparency helps to overcome the difficulty of coordinating action across the many agencies and other actors that often must be involved in complex public policy. In cases ranging from the 2001 terrorist attacks on the United States to the outbreak of SARS in southern China, secrecy has prevented government agencies from putting together the pieces of the puzzle in time to take effective action.

Moreover, as Vivek Ramkumar and Elena Petkova point out in their study of environmental transparency, disclosure has become a powerful signal of trustworthiness. Because secrecy is perceived to indicate bad intentions, building public support for a public policy requires a degree of openness. Governments often keep problems secret because they do not trust the public to handle information about them in a responsible matter. But when the problems eventually becomes widely known—as often happens in this information age—the previous secrecy may come back to haunt the government in the form of public distrust.

Regulation by Revelation

In addition to making government work better as a provider of services and maker of policy, disclosure can also serve as a direct regulatory tool, in some cases as a more efficient and effective regulatory approach than traditional command and control mechanisms. As noted in the introduction, disclosure requirements for corporate financial information, for all their recent travails, have long served to make the U.S. stock market relatively open and efficient. The Ramkumar/Petkova chapter describes in great detail how disclosure is sweeping the field of environmental regulation, with some success. But as they show, disclosure-based regulation requires more than a general information-access law, even if such a law applies to the public portion of privately held information. Such regulation must include specific disclosure requirements. And even then, it will not always work.

A group of Harvard scholars has recently assessed a wide range of disclosure-based regulatory systems to evaluate how well they work and why, looking at everything from nutritional labeling systems to the Toxic Releases Inventory discussed by Ramkumar and Petkova to corporate financial reporting.[1] They found that although disclosure-based regulation is increasingly being used, it is often not done well. In the area of nutritional labeling, for example, they found that the U.S. system was only partly effective in reaching its goals. That system requires manufacturers to list on their food products such information as the calorie content of the item, grams of fat, sugar, and protein, percentage of recommended daily allowances of particular vitamins, etc. The policy aim is to improve public health by giving consumers the information needed to make healthier choices about their food purchases. But the system assumes a substantial degree of consumer knowledge about what makes up a desirable diet. Moreover, the system does not provide good feedback to the producers, in that they have no way of knowing whether declining or rising sales are related to the nutritional information. As the Harvard researchers note, "food manufacturers may believe that declines in sales of high-sugar cereals indicate that a competitor's advertising is more effective, whereas shoppers may actually be responding to nutritional data."[2] Thus, like the TRI, the system is only moderately effective in achieving its regulatory goals because it fails to match the needs of users and disclosers with the specifics of the information-provision system.

The Harvard study argues that disclosure-based regulation works well when 1) potential information recipients are making less than ideal choices about a matter of public concern because they lack information; 2) the potential recipients could and would change their behavior if they had the appropriate information; 3) that changed behavior would cause the disclosers, in turn, to act in ways more desired by the regulators. When any of these pieces is missing, government may have to do more than order disclosure to bring about desired changes in behavior.[3] And even if all the pieces are present, regulatory systems need to carefully design exactly what information is to be provided, to whom, in what format, and when, if they are to have a significant impact on behavior.

Indeed, that need for good design applies to all transparency systems, not just regulatory ones. Demands for transparency are at root efforts to use disclosure to change the behavior of the discloser, even without a specific regulatory outcome in mind. So like all transparency systems, regulation by revelation *can* work—but not always or automatically. Success depends on what information is provided, in what form, to what audience, and on what options that audience has to induce the discloser to behave differently—a point made strongly in the Ramkumar/Petkova chapter's discussion of the need for "access to justice" to accompany "access to information."

Transparency as a Principle of Democratic Government

In addition to the growing number of instrumental arguments for transparency, the long-standing claim that disclosure is an inherent principle of democracy remains robust. Yet even here, the nature of the debate is changing. No longer is disclosure primarily seen as an instrument for enabling the public to hold decision makers accountable, although it still serves the vital purpose of allowing "we the people" to determine if "you the government" is doing its job the way the citizens want it to. Increasingly, transparency is demanded to enable people affected by decisions to participate in making those decisions. Thomas Blanton's chapter on intergovernmental organizations (IGOs), for example, describes numerous cases of public protest against projects funded by such entities as the World Bank leading to demands for disclosure as a necessary step to enabling a stronger public voice in decision making over projects. Ramkumar and Petkova describe a growing trend toward participatory, rather than purely representative, democracy, based on principles that include equity and the legitimacy of decision-making processes.

Achieving Transparency

The authors in this volume are all too aware that despite its potential utility, transparency is hard to come by. Effective and sustained demand for information is essential, given the nature of bureaucracies that almost instinctively horde information, whether or not they have something to hide. As the introduction notes, demands for information are needed to overcome resistance due to corruption, fear of being held accountable for decisions that may prove unpopular or unwise, distrust of the public, and simple competing demands for resources. As Neuman and Calland point out in their extensive discussion of the challenges of implementing information access laws, transparency costs money—money to develop or improve archives, train and pay civil servants, purchase needed equipment such as photocopiers, and make public the large categories of information that should be disclosed even in the absence of a specific law—such as the existence of a transparency law itself.

Many analysts, including Neuman and Calland, argue that the single most important source of demand for disclosure comes from civil society. Civil society groups can excel at creating political pressures by mobilizing political coalitions. They often do so for reasons that originally seem far removed from traditional ways of thinking about freedom of information as a political liberty. In the case of India, Shekhar Singh's chapter describes how the extraordinary national movement that succeeded in 2005 in getting a sweeping freedom of information law adopted originated in the early 1990s as a grassroots uprising to demand payment of wages due to some of the poorest of the poor. The trend toward regulation by disclosure on environmental issues took off after the 1984 Bhopal disaster that poisoned thousands, as Ramkumar and Petkova show. In Nigeria, the efforts of civil libertarians to redress horrendous human rights abuses in prisons proved the spark for that country's continuing struggle for a freedom of information law. Wages, toxins, and prison reform would seem to have little in common, but in all these cases citizens found transparency to be a needed part of the solution.

Pressure for increased disclosure can also come from outside. As Ivan Szekely shows in his description of the emergence of new transparency laws in Central and Eastern Europe following the fall of communism, demand for transparency within those societies largely focused on information about the previous regimes. Although indigenous civil society groups played important roles, outside pressure in the form of European Union membership requirements and support from U.S. and other donors significantly shaped the laws that emerged in the region. Jamie Horsley's chapter on China points out that part of the shift toward greater openness in that nondemocratic country reflected the desire of the Chinese leadership to take full part in the global economy, including meeting the membership requirements of the World Trade Organization. Nigeria may now start to find itself under external pressures, according to Ayo Obe, as frustrated activists turn to outside sources of pressure such as the New Economic Plan for Africa to push their country's leadership to adopt a more open government. Yet outside pressures do not necessarily push in the direction of enhanced transparency. As Roberts shows in his discussion of NATO secrecy requirements, outside pressures can also push countries toward greater secrecy.

Two other sources of demand, however, play a surprisingly minor role in this book's cases: market forces and the media. Although scholarly research has indicated both theoretically and empirically that greater economic transparency can make countries more attractive to investors and less subject to market volatility,[4] by and large those concrete advantages have not induced governments to change their economic policies in favor of greater transparency. (China, as Horsley's and Zhou's chapters show, is something of an exception.) This may be because the economic advantages of an open and transparent government and market system accrue to society as a whole, creating a significant free-rider problem. No one within the country has sufficient incentive to pay the costs of demanding economic disclosure, while a handful of actors who benefit from information asymmetries have every reason to maintain secretive systems. Obe's compelling account of the distorting effect of oil revenues shows just how difficult the politics of transparency become when the few find the advantages of secrecy to be extremely remunerative.

The other plausible source of demand for greater transparency that is noticeably absent from the stories described in this book is the media. One might assume that journalists of all types, whether print, on-air, or online, would be at the forefront of demands for greater public disclosure. But the media show up only occasionally in these accounts—and not always on the side of the transparency angels. As Szekely points out, in Slovakia the press have helped both bring about the information law and ensure that it is effectively implemented, but in Romania the media "did not support the campaign for free-dom of information because they have become complicit in a range of largely dishonest information-related activities," including black-mail. More broadly, although the media benefit greatly from rules requiring proactive government disclosure, the systems in place for requesting specific information generally work too slowly to be of use to journalists facing deadlines.

The Motives of Disclosers

Whether information gets supplied depends not only on the actions of demanders but also on the incentives facing disclosers. One con-dition that can be extremely helpful to the original passage of a law is to have top political leadership committed to transparency. In several of the cases described in this book, individuals or political parties adopted pro-transparency platforms to distinguish themselves from political opponents or discredited predecessors, as was the case in South Africa, India, several Central and Eastern European countries, and (in a case not covered in this volume) Mexico, whose first freely elected non-PRI President, Vicente Fox, made governmental infor-mation disclosure a centerpiece of his political agenda.

But leadership from the top is not enough to make for sustained open government. In the case of Mexico, for example, where none of his potential successors has indicated much interested in Fox's push for transparency, the future of the Mexican information access law is in doubt. Ultimately, countries achieve significant sustained governmental openness when a culture of transparency becomes widespread within the governmental bureaucracy. As Laura Neuman and Richard Calland say in their discussion of the politics of imple-mentation, "The notion of transparency is invariably far beyond the range of experience and mindset of most public bureaucrats. There-fore, a fundamental mind shift is necessary."

Such changes in political culture are difficult, but achievable. In the United States, for example, staff positions in charge of com-pliance with Freedom of Information Act requests have become a separate professional track, whose standards frequently—although not always—favor compliance with the law over bureaucratic ob-structionism. Blanton's discussion of the transparency struggle at the World Bank reveals the development of "its own realization that internal barriers to information-sharing led to bad decisions and trapped the bank in bad projects."

Practical Considerations

However, even if these various sources of demand prove sufficient to bring about information access laws, and even if disclosers are willing in principle to disclose, considerable practical problems still have to be overcome to create an effective transparency system that can achieve the governance and/or regulatory goals described above.

One key issue is what, if any, agencies and types of information should remain immune to disclosure requirements. Most laws carve out substantial areas of exemption, most notably in the national security area. As Roberts discusses, even through the recent explosion of right to information laws around the globe, "the national security establishments within most governments remained enclaves in which the presumption of secrecy held fast." Yet Roberts points to mounting evidence that very often such secrecy serves no security purpose, and often actually "corrodes the capacity of government agencies to perform their mission of promoting better security."[5]

Information disclosure laws vary widely in terms of how far outside the national government their coverage extends. Mexico's law, for example, covers only federal agencies, not states or localities, while India's applies to all levels of government. A growing number step outside government altogether to address information in private hands. Calland's chapter raises the two crucial questions that apply to transparency in the private sector: "Should corporations that are playing quasi-public roles and providing public goods and services be held to the same standards of public transparency and accountability as their public sector brethren? Does voluntary disclosure of environmental and other social impact information adequately fill the existing regulatory gap, or should such disclosures be standardized and made mandatory?" His chapter, and particularly his analysis of the South African law that has gone farther than any other in addressing the private sector, provides guidance on an increasingly urgent set of issues related to private sector disclosure.

International organizations—and their member states—are similarly grappling with issues of how far the organizations' disclosure policies should extend. Blanton's discussion of a recent comparative study of ten key international financial institutions such as the World Bank and the International Monetary Fund shows the range of information policies and practices now prevalent. The study found that overall, both the policies and the procedures remain seriously constrained, in particular by "a plethora of exceptions that turn disclosure on its head and only allow those documents specifically listed as releasable to come out." Moreover, the organizations have failed to develop procedures for appeals when information is denied. Although most of the organizations studied are far more open than was the case as recently as the early 1990s, their disclosure policies still reflect considerable deference to norms of diplomatic secrecy. The question is whether such deference is appropriate now that the organizations have so much more direct power over the lives of millions around the world.

As the Neuman/Calland chapter notes, however, far too often policy makers spend an excessive amount of time and energy considering what agencies and categories of information a disclosure law should cover and much too little on designing a law that will work effectively for whatever categories are covered. That is why their chapter goes into great detail about the difficulties of implementing even the best-intentioned information disclosure laws and edicts. Frequently, laws are drafted with inadequate attention to the feasibility of implementing their provisions. Their chapter gives detailed practical advice on the provisions needed if laws are to work (the Ramkumar/Petkova chapter similarly provides guidance for disclosure-based regulation).

As many of the chapters indicate, a key challenge is how to get information provided at reasonable cost. Any potential discloser, whether governments or intergovernmental organizations or the private sector, must make records of the information that is to be disclosed; keep those records in some kind of organized fashion; establish systems for disseminating information; and train and pay people to do all the above.

The costs are coming down to some degree, thanks to advances in information technology, but they remain substantial. However, as described throughout this volume, secrecy can also impose substantial costs: corruption, poor decision making, and public distrust.

Issues for the Future

Transparency is a spreading, but far from universal, norm. Some 70 countries now have freedom of information laws—but the majority of the world's roughly 200 sovereign nations lack any such law. And even where transparency is nominally embedded, rhetoric frequently outstrips reality. Despite the rapid spread of freedom of information laws around the world, the new disclosure policies at a wide array of intergovernmental organizations, and the growing number of both voluntary and mandatory disclosure systems covering the private sector, many of the fundamental issues about transparency remain far from consensus, both within countries and across borders.

In particular, as globalization and privatization shift ever more information of public concern into the hands of the private sector, questions of who has the right to have access to that information will become ever more significant. The private sector often depends on information asymmetries for its profits, so the answer cannot be simply to require the private sector to disclose everything to anyone who asks. In the absence of any systematic debate on, much less consensus about, what constitutes a public function the public is entitled to know about even if the function is being handled by a private entity, we are making do with a hodgepodge of voluntary standards and occasional disclosure requirements. A few national laws, notably those of India and South Africa, do address the private sector, but most do not. That more systematic debate, within and across countries, is long overdue.

But even were that issue to be settled, the future of transparency would remain open to question. Until recently open government, or more broadly open governance, was a Western and particularly American ideal. Yet a glance at the headlines makes clear that power is shifting. With the rise of Asia, a key question becomes what road Asian governance will take. The two Asian giants have to date taken very different paths, as the chapters on China and India make clear. China's approach to transparency is driven largely by the leadership's desire to "informationize" the Chinese economy, part of a larger effort to transform China into an economic great power. India's new laws and policies arose from a grassroots movement of impressive staying power. Will either, or both, prove a successful model for Asia, and for the world as a whole? What policies will these countries advocate and adopt toward information disclosure in the intergovernmental organizations of which they are increasingly powerful members? What, if any, information disclosure requirements will, and should, they impose on corporations or civil society groups within their borders?

Moreover, the transparency revolution is taking place within the context of rapidly changing technologies. In the twentieth century, the pendulum swung between fears of information technology leading to a "big brother" police state that would watch everyone everywhere to assertions about the technological inevitability of a fully transparent world where secrecy would become impossible. Clearly, neither has (yet) come to pass, and information technology remains an arms race between efforts to ferret out information and efforts to protect that information. It is not at all clear which side will win—if, indeed, either ever does.

For there are few, if any, inevitabilities in the struggle for greater transparency. Because the fight for information is so often a struggle for power, the battle for transparency will continue as long as human beings contend for power.

NOTES

1. David Weil, Archon Fung, Mary Graham, and Elena Fagotto, "The Effectiveness of Regulatory Disclosure Policies," *Journal of Policy Analysis and Management* 25 (1) (2006): 155–181.

2. Ibid., 164.

3. Ibid., 175.

4. For a brief overview, see Shang-Jin Wei and Heather Milkiewicz, "A Case of 'Enronitis'? Opaque Self-Dealing and the Global Financial Effect," Policy Brief #188 (Washington, DC: The Brookings Institution, 2003).

5. For an extended discussion of the connection between transparency and security, see Campbell Public Affairs Institute, *National Security and Open Government* (Syracuse, NY: Campbell Public Affairs Institute, 2003).

Contributors

ANN FLORINI is visiting professor and director, Centre on Asia and Globalization, Lee Kuan Yew School of Public Policy, National University of Singapore, and Senior Fellow at the Brookings Institution in Washington, DC. She is the author of numerous publications on information policy and global governance, including *The Coming Democracy: New Rules for Running a New World* (Island Press 2003/Brookings Press 2005).

THOMAS S. BLANTON is Director of the National Security Archive at George Washington University in Washington, DC. He filed his first Freedom of Information Act request in 1976 as a weekly newspaper reporter in Minnesota. His books include *White House E-Mail: The Top Secret Computer Messages the Reagan-Bush White House Tried to Destroy* (The New Press, 1995). His articles have appeared in *The International Herald-Tribune, The New York Times, The Washington Post, Los Angeles Times, The Wall Street Journal, The Boston Globe, Slate,* the *Wilson Quarterly,* and many other publications. He is a graduate of Harvard University, and a founding editorial board member of freedominfo. org, a virtual network on international freedom of information.

RICHARD CALLAND is the Executive Director of the Open Democracy Advice Centre (ODAC) in Cape Town and a founding member of the law center, formed in 2000. He is also head of the Right to Know program at the democracy think tank Idasa. Prior to joining Idasa in 1995, he practiced law at the London Bar for seven years, specializing in human rights law. He holds postgraduate degrees in world politics and comparative constitutional law (LLM) from the London School of Economics and the University of Cape Town respectively. He has published extensively on the politics of the South African transition and is a political columnist for the *Mail & Guardian* newspaper. His most recent book, *Anatomy of South Africa: Who Holds the Power?* was published in October 2006.

JAMIE P. HORSLEY is Deputy Director of The China Law Center and lecturer in law at Yale Law School. She has been the managing partner of the China offices of Paul, Weiss, Rifkind, Wharton & Garrison; commercial attaché in the U.S. embassies in Beijing and Manila; Vice President of Motorola International, Inc. and Director of Government Relations for China for Motorola, Inc.; and a consultant to The Carter Center on village elections in China. She is a graduate of Harvard Law School and has an M.A. in Chinese studies from the University of Michigan and a B.A. from Stanford University.

LAURA NEUMAN is Assistant Director for the Americas Program at the Carter Center in Atlanta, Georgia. She is the Access to Information Project Manager and directs and implements Carter Center transparency projects in countries ranging from Mali to Bolivia. Her publications include: *Access to Information, A Key to Democracy*; *Using Freedom of Information Laws to Enforce Welfare Benefits Rights in the United States*; and editor and author of *Access to Information: Building a Culture of Transparency*, *The Promotion of Democracy Through Access to Information*, and *The Path to the Right to Access to Information*. She is a graduate of the University of Wisconsin Law School.

ELENA PETKOVA was formerly with the World Resources Institute. She has led a global effort in developing and applying an indicator-based methodology to assess national-level law and practice of access to information, participation, and justice in environmental decision making. Her publications of the last ten years focus on issues of transparency and participation in the environment and climate change. She has also convened and led various international multistakeholder dialogues around these issues.

AYO OBE is a legal practitioner and former president of the Civil Liberties Organisation, the pioneer human rights organization in Nigeria. From 2001 to 2006 she was a member of the Police Service Commission, the civilian oversight body on policing in Nigeria, representing human rights nongovernmental organizations.

VIVEK RAMKUMAR is Program Officer at the International Budget Project, Center on Budget and Policy Priorities, where his time is divided between IBP's training projects and budget transparency research. He previously worked with the MKSS, an organization that pioneered the right to know movement in India and is best known for its innovative public hearing forums in which village communities track local budget expenditures. He has also worked with a Mumbai based NGO, SPARC, that is part of the Shack/Slum Dwellers International. Ramkumar is a qualified Chartered Accountant and holds a master's degree from the London School of Economics.

ALASDAIR ROBERTS is associate professor of public administration at the Maxwell School of Citizenship and Public Affairs, Syracuse University.

SHEKHAR SINGH is founding member and former convenor, National Campaign for People's Right to Information in India, and former director of the Centre for Equity Studies, New Delhi. He has taught at the Indian Institute of Public Administration, New Delhi, the North-Eastern Hill University, Shillong, and St. Stephen's College, University of Delhi. He has been advisor to the Planning Commission of India and has been associated with a variety of nongovernmental organizations and popular movements. His publications include: *Large Dams in India: Environmental, Social and Economic Impacts* (2002); *Setting Biodiversity Conservation Priorities for India* (2000); and *Strengthening Conservation Cultures* (2000).

IVAN SZEKELY is Counsellor, Open Society Archives at Central European University and associate professor at the Budapest University of Technology and Economics (BUTE). He has written some thirty major studies on the theoretical and practical aspects of openness and secrecy, including conducting the first Hungarian research on data protection and information privacy (1989–1990) and coauthoring both the Hungarian National Information Strategy (1995) and the government's theses on the information society (2000). He has helped to create numerous institutions in Central and Eastern Europe on data protection, freedom of information, and archives. In 1994, he prepared a multidisciplinary doctoral thesis at the Faculty of Natural and Social Sciences of BUTE (information management); he defended his second thesis for candidacy (sociology) in 1998.

HANHUA ZHOU is a Professor of Law and the Director for Constitutional and Administrative Law Division in the Institute of Law, Chinese Academy of Social Sciences. He was also one of the founders and serves as vice chairman in the China Information Law Society. As a member of the Advisory Committee for State Informatization and the State Advisory Committee for Cutting the Red Tape, and as advisory expert for several other governmental agencies, Dr. Zhou has been involving in cutting-edge research and decision-making process in connection with freedom of information and regulatory reform for some time, including leading the first task force on freedom of information research in China, drafting the Freedom of Information Regulations for the government, and taking part in drafting the Administrative License Law organized by the State Council Legal Affairs Office. Dr. Zhou was a senior visiting scholar at Yale Law School from September to December 2000, a visiting scholar in the Norwegian Institute of Human Rights from July to December 1998, and a visiting scholar at University of Michigan Law School from 1993 to 1995. From 1997 to 1999, Dr. Zhou practiced law in the Beijing Jun He Law Offices.

Index

CEE. *See* Central and Eastern Europe

China's Tenth Five-Year Economic Plan (2002–07), 63
Chinese Academy of Social Sciences (CASS), 69
chlorination, 284
cholera, 284
CIA. *See* Central Intelligence Agency
Citizen Democracy Association—Slovakia (CDF), 130, 136
Citizen's Shopping (Slovakia), 129
civil liberties groups, 319
Civil Liberties Organisation—Nigeria (CLO), 151–52, 154, 173n26
civil servant sanctions/incentives, 206–8
civil society activism, 223–26, 304, 342
class action suits, 290
classified information, 312, 323
Classified Information Protection Act (Czech Republic), 326
CLO. *See* Civil Liberties Organisation—Nigeria
"closed politics," 320
CM. *See* Chief Minister—India
CMP. *See* Common Minimum Programme
Coady, Patrick, 256
Coca-Cola, 218
Cold War, 7, 260, 310–11, 316, 323, 326–27
Cole, David, 319
Colombia, 313
"commercial secret," 73, 89n50
Commission on Sustainable Development, 295
Committee for the Ecological Protection of Ruse (Bulgaria), 291
Committee to Protect Journalists (China), 79
Common Minimum Programme (CMP), 44
Communist Party of China (the Party), 55–56, 60, 83; elections and, 57–58; leadership in, 58
competition, 216
Congress of South Africa Trade Unions (COSATU), 185, 232

consensus building, 203–4
Constitutional Affairs Committee (United Kingdom), 191
Copyright Law (China), 114n9
corporate disclosure, 8–9
corporate law, 216
corporate secrecy, 215, 216–20
corporate social responsibility (CSR), 12, 216; change and, 223–26; human rights and, 223; practice of, 223
corporate transparency, 215; new arguments for, 220–28; voluntary, 226–28
corporations: dehumanizing, 220; rights of, 239n8
corruption, 2, 149, 155, 161, 168, 172n19, 172n22, 197, 271; in China, 58, 65, 105; in India, 29, 49; in Nigeria, 149–50, 154–55, 160, 163
COSATU. *See* Congress of South Africa Trade Unions
cost of information, 6, 102, 112, 131, 173n35, 192–93, 301, 342, 346
counterintelligence service (MI5), 311
Criminal Law (China), 110, 115n11
"critical infrastructure information," 325
CSR. *See* corporate social responsibility
Cuba, 10
culture of secrecy, 180
Czech Republic, 302, 326

Data Protection and Freedom of Information—Hungary (DP-FOI), 122–23, 125, 128, 136
Davis, Carlton, 179, 194
Davis, Charles, 228–29
Davis v. Clutcho (Pty) Ltd., 235
Dawson, Thomas, 250–52
Declaration of Principles on Freedom and Expression, 10
defense, 311
Delhi High Court, 50
Delhi RTI, 35, 42
democracy, 1, 3, 82; in CEE, 137–39; China Constitution and, 104–5; in

Federal Register, 269
Feinstein, Andrew, 234
Financial Management and Accountability Act (1997), 200
Finland, 247
Florini, Ann, 1, 13, 337
FOI. See freedom of information
FOI compliance, 191
FOI laws, 2, 246; "gold standard" of, 12; in India, 9; for Nigeria transparency, 154–60
FOIA. See Freedom of Information Act
FOIA laws, 285
Ford Foundation, 162, 188
forestry concerns, 294
Forestry Stewardship Council, 300
forums, 97, 290
Fourth Plenum of 16th Party Central Committee (China), 64
Fox, Vincente, 344
Frankel, Maurice, 207
fraud, 28
free expression, 330
Freedom from Debt Coalition (Philippines), 251
freedom of information (FOI), 2
Freedom of Information Act (China), 74
Freedom of Information Act (FOIA), 8, 13, 158, 191, 200, 229, 249, 268, 324; amending, 44–46; citizens and, 281; compliance with, 344; detainees under, 319; early years of, 315; enactment of, 280; exceptions to, 312
Freedom of Information Act (Trinidad and Tobago), 205
Freedom of Information Act (United Kingdom), 311
Freedom of Information Advocates Network and Web site, 135
Freedom of Information Bill (India), 44
Freedom of Information Law (Belize), 185
Fujimori, Alberto, 185

Galbraith, J. K., 216

Gandhi Peace Foundation, 43
Gandhi, Shailesh, 39–40
GDP. See Gross Domestic Product
General Agreement on Tariffs and Trade, 67, 243
genetically modified organisms (GMOs), 301; labeling for, 302–3; opponents of, 301–2; proponents of, 302; tracking of, 302
"ghost employees," 193
"ghost works," 28
Global Forest Watch, 301
Global Reporting Initiative (GRI), 225
Global Witness, 224
globalization, 2, 12, 347
GMOs. See genetically modified organisms
Gonzales, Alberto, 315–16
Gonzáles, Felipe, 330
governance, 1, 33, 39–41; see also environmental governance
government, 152, 197; Blair, 317; effectiveness/efficiency, 338–39; E-government, 61, 100; of Nigeria, 172n21; secrecy, 218; transparency as principle of democratic, 341; see also Bush administration; intergovernmental organizations; Johnson administration; Nixon administration; nongovernment organizations; open government information
Gowon, Yakubu, 146, 149
Graham, Mary, 217, 218, 219
Great Britain, 7, 207; see also United Kingdom
Great Proletarian Cultural Revolution—China (1966–76), 54, 58
Greenpeace, 271, 294–95, 301
GRI. See Global Reporting Initiative
Gross Domestic Product (GDP), 99
Guangdong, China, 322
Guangzhou Office of Legislative Affairs, 70
Guangzhou OGI Provisions, 70–71, 74, 89n48
Guantánamo Bay, Cuba, 319
Gulf War, 146, 156, 157

Hair, Jay, 257
"hamara paisa-hamara hisaab," 25
harm test, 262
Harvard group of Cultural Survival, 270
Hazare, Anna, 24
health system, 29
hearings, 97
Hersh, Seymour, 221
Highly Indebted Poor Countries Program, 181
HIV status, 218, 237
horizontal accountability, 297
Horsley, Jamie, 54, 343
Hu Jintao, 79
human rights, 3, 78, 217, 220, 223–24, 316, 327; abuses, 330; classified information and, 312; corporate obligations for, 223; CSR and, 223; legal rights and, 236–37; limiting application of, 237; in Nigeria, 150–52, 162; universal, 236; violations, 29; *see also* European Court of Human Rights; Kharkiv Group for Human Rights Protection
Human Rights Violations Investigation Commission (Nigeria), 162
Hungary, 116–17, 117, 121, 125, 128, 290, 292; Constitution of, 122–23; ombudsman in, 132; Parliament of, 132; penal code in, 123; secrecy in, 123, 130; transparency model in, 122; *see also* Data Protection and Freedom of Information—Hungary
hunger strikes, 25

IADB. *See* Inter-American Development Bank
ICPC. *See* Independent Corrupt Practices Commission—Nigeria
IDASA. *See* Institute for Democracy in South Africa
IFC. *See* International Finance Corporation
IFI Transparency Resource, 262–64
IFTIs. *See* international financial and trade institutions

IGOs. *See* intergovernmental organizations
Iliescu, Ion, 260
IMF. *See* International Monetary Fund
IMF Code of Fiscal Transparency, 251
IMF Manila conference, 254
independent appeals, 44
Independent Corrupt Practices Commission—Nigeria (ICPC), 155, 168
India, 4, 34, 37, 40, 52n4, 52n7, 184, 285, 292, 296, 311, 347; China's invasion of, 22; corruption in, 29, 49; democracy in, 19; electrification of, 22; FOI laws in, 9; governance in, 33; information in, 19; justice system of, 290; language in, 22; media in, 22; "model district" in, 188; population displacement in, 33; public interest litigation in, 52n4; RTI in, 19–20, 34; women's movement in, 19–20, 33; *see also* Narmada Bachao Andolan; Narmada dam project
India Congress Party, 21, 22, 23, 44
India Constitution, 23, 31
India Election Commission, 33–34
India Supreme Court, 10, 23, 30–31, 32, 34, 44
India transparency: arbitrary governance and, 39–41; contemporary issues in, 46–48; development projects and, 32–33; elections and, 33–34; environmental movement and, 30–31; evolution of, 21–24; future directions for, 51–52; people's movements for, 24–26; policies/laws/institutional structures in, 43–44; right to food and, 41–42; urban municipal governance and, 34–35
Indonesia, 285, 292, 302
information: asymmetries, 6; control of, 216; cost of, 6, 102, 112, 131, 173n35, 192–93, 301, 342, 346; "critical infrastructure," 325; demystifying, 52; in India, 19; officers, 202–3; personal, 237; power

law(s), 2; of Bolivia, 210*n*6; for CEE transparency, 122–24; of China, 62, 66, 68, 72–73, 78, 82, 93–94, 97, 98, 103, 107–11, 114*n*9, 114*n*10, 115*n*11; corporate, 216; *desacato*, 330; disclosure in U.S., 7; drafting for transparency implementation, 188–90; of Ecuador, 210*n*6; India transparency, 43–44; RTK, 229, 241*n*29; of Sweden, 110; in Ukraine, 125; *see also* ATI laws; disclosure laws; FOI laws; RTI laws; transparency law

Law Against Unfair Competition (China), 108

Law of Administrative Litigation (China), 103

Law of Administrative Review (China), 103

law on access to information—Bulgaria (APIA), 124

Law on Administrative Punishment (China), 97

Law on Environmental Impact Assessment (China), 68

Law on Guarding State Secrets (China), 66

Law on Organization of Villagers' Commissions (China), 93–94, 97

Law on Protecting State Secrets (China), 73, 108

Law on the Freedom to Publish (Sweden), 110

Leading Group on National Informatization—China, 60–61, 100, 101

Leander, Torsten, 327–28

legal rights, 236–37

legitimacy, 283

LIBERTY, 331

literacy, 22

Macedonia, 129

Madison, James, 7

Maduna, Penual, 195

Maharashtra, 24; activists in, 20; RTI activism in, 39–41

Maharashtra Right to Information Act (MRTI), 39

Malaysia, 226, 302

Mali, 192, 193

Mandela, Nelson, 231

Marcos, Ferdinand, 253

Marriage Law (China), 97, 98

Marwa, Buba, 174*n*47

Mazdoor Kisan Shakti Sangathan (MKSS), 23–24, 34, 49, 167, 246; *dharna* and, 26; formation of, 24–26

Mbeki, Thabo, 195

MCD. *See* Municipal Corporation of Delhi

McNamara, Robert, 254, 320

MEAs. *See* multilateral environmental agreements

Measuring Transparency Index, 225–26, 241*n*20

media, 8, 72, 187, 258, 294, 323, 331, 343–44; in CEE transparency, 119, 123, 135, 138; in China, 79, 89*n*48; in India, 22; in Nigeria, 167; in U.S., 74; *see also* Press Council of India; Southeast Asian Press Alliance

Media Rights Agenda—Nigeria (MRA), 152–55, 158

Mehta, M. C., 30

Member of the Legislative Assembly—India (MLA), 37

Mendes, Francisco "Chico," 255

mentalidad, 209

Mexican Federal Institute for Access to Information (IFAI), 205

Mexico, 180, 184, 193, 285, 292, 344; affected people in, 290–91; ATI laws in, 190; conservation in, 286

miniaturization, 5

minimum exclusions, 44

minimum wages, 25, 27

Mitrokhin, Vasili, 309

"Mitrokin Archive," 309

MKSS. *See* Mazdoor Kisan Shakti Sangathan

MLA. *See* Member of the Legislative Assembly—India

mohalla samiti (local area committee), 36

moral claims, 3
Morgenthau, Hans J., 248
Mozambique, 253
MRA. *See* Media Rights Agenda—Nigeria
MRTI. *See* Maharashtra Right to Information Act
Muhammed, Murtala, 169
multilateral environmental agreements (MEAs), 297
multilateral institutions, 296
Multilateral Investment Guarantee Agency, 262–63
Mungiu-Pippidi, A., 136
Municipal Corporation of Delhi (MCD), 35, 36, 37–38, 50
Municipal Corporation of Thane, 40

NAC. *See* National Advisory Council—India
Nagrik Chetna Manch, 39
NAO. *See* National Auditing Office—China
Narmada Bachao Andolan (NBA), 33, 255–56, 287
Narmada dam project, 33, 255–56, 259
National Advisory Council—India (NAC), 44–45
National Auditing Office—China (NAO), 65–66
National Campaign for People's Right to Information (NCPRI), 24, 34, 35, 43–44
National Intelligence Agency (South Africa), 312
national openness, 267
National Party Congress—China (November, 2002), 63
National Party of Nigeria (NPN), 171*n*10
National People's Congress—China (NPC), 56, 63
national security, 1, 331; secrecy *v.*, 9; in U.S., 13, 312
NATO. *See* North Atlantic Treaty Organization
Nazarbayev, Nursultan, 224
Nazis, 310

NBA. *See* Narmada Bachao Andolan
NCPRI. *See* National Campaign for People's Right to Information
Nehru, Jawaharlal, 21
NEITI. *See* Nigerian Extractive Industries Transparency Initiative
NEPAD. *See* New Economic Partnership for African Development
Nepal, 257
Netherlands, 230
Neuman, Laura, 11, 179, 342, 344, 346
New Economic Partnership for African Development (NEPAD), 161
New Economic Plan for Africa, 343
New South Wales, 198
New Zealand, 198, 229
New Zealand Official Information Act (1982), 229
NGO. *See* nongovernment organizations
Nicaragua, 192, 198
Nigeria, 11; accountability in, 154; Constitution of, 145, 147–48, 151, 165, 174*n*45; corruption in, 149–50, 154–55, 160, 163; ethnic diversity in, 147; government of, 172*n*21; human rights in, 150–52, 162; media in, 167; military/civilian rule in, 144–46; resource curse in, 146–47; secrecy in, 147; *see also* Civil Liberties Organisation—Nigeria; Economic and Financial Crimes Commission—Nigeria; Media Rights Agenda—Nigeria; Official Secrets Acts (Nigeria); People's Democratic Party—Nigeria; Secretary to the Federal Military Government—Nigeria; Structural Adjustment Program (Nigeria)
Nigeria Police Force, 150
Nigeria transparency, 342; attitudes/habits of, 165–68; background for, 144–50; challenges to future, 169–70; challenging secrecy, 150; FOI laws for, 154–60; introduction, 143–44; lessons learned for, 161; military-civilian continuum

and, 168–69; prospects for future, 161–65

Nigeria Union of Journalists (NUJ), 152, 154, 173n26

Nigerian Extractive Industries Transparency Initiative (NEITI), 162, 164, 167, 168

Nigerian National Petroleum Corporation (NNPC), 165

Nirex, 227–28

Nixon administration, 315

NNPC. *See* Nigerian National Petroleum Corporation

nongovernment organizations (NGOs), 4, 6, 30, 31, 50, 125–27, 133–35, 152, 185, 290–91; achievements of, 304; activism by, 224; impediments from, 224; oversight by, 324; pressure from, 239; Publish-What-You-Pay coalition, 225; role in environmental transparency, 293–300; role of in Aarhus Convention, 299–300; as watchdogs, 295

North Atlantic Treaty Organization (NATO), 119, 124, 243, 249, 260–61, 313, 343

Not My Will (Obasanjo), 169

NPC. *See* National People's Congress—China

NPN. *See* National Party of Nigeria

NUJ. *See* Nigeria Union of Journalists

OAS. *See* Organization of American States

Obasanjo, Olusegun, 145, 149, 153–54, 157, 160–61, 163–65, 168–69; as African Union Chairperson, 161; control by, 155–57

Obe, Ayo, 11, 143, 343

ODAC. *See* Open Democracy Advice Centre

OECD. *See* Organization for Economic Cooperation and Development

Official Secrets Acts, 330

Official Secrets Acts (Nigeria), 147–48, 151, 165, 171n17, 174n45

OGI. *See* open government information

Okigbo Panel Report, 157

Okigbo, Pius, 156

ombudsman, 132, 257

Onagoruwa, Olu, 153

Onitsha-Owerri road, 175n48

opacity, 14, 191, 252

Open Democracy Advice Centre (ODAC), 202, 209, 232–33

Open Democracy Campaign Group—South Africa, 185, 231

"open door" policy, 55

open government information (OGI), 55, 63, 64–65, 78–83

Open Society Institute (OSI), 134, 182

Open Society Justice Initiative, 129

openness, 4, 318; information in China, 64–66, 101–4; national, 267; promoting security, 320–25; secrecy and, 327; *see also* Principle of Openness

Oputa Panel, 162

Organic Law on Villagers' Committees—China (the VC Law), 59

Organization for Economic Cooperation and Development (OECD), 281

Organization of American States (OAS), 16n16

Oroh, Abdul, 153, 159, 173n27

OSI. *See* Open Society Institute

oversight groups, 331

oversight/coordination units, 204–6

Panchal, Balu, 48

panchayat, 28, 52n3

Paniagua, Valentine, 186

Paraguay, 185, 309

Parivartan, 50; meetings held by, 36; story of, 34–35; workers of, 38, 48

Parliamentary Network on the World Bank, 267

participatory disclosure, 262

the Party. *See* Communist Party of China

PATIA. *See* Promotion of Access to Information Act

Patkar, Medha, 255

84; achieving, 341–47; activism, 224; arguments for, 2–3; battle for, 348; in Bulgaria, 124; debate over, 1; definitions of, 14n5, 304; in economics, 5; during emergencies, 318–20; equity promoting, 283; future of, 14; history/current state of, 7–10; IMF and, 250–51; issues for future of, 347–48; legitimacy lending, 283; meaning/purposes of, 4–7; model in Hungary, 122; as norm for democratic state, 214; in politics, 5, 343; as principle of democratic government, 341; revolution, 348; rights and, 239; in Romania, 123–24; rules of IGOs, 12; selling by IGOs, 244–45; in Slovakia, 124; technology and, 5; as transformative tool, 14; in Ukraine, 123; U.S. as proponent of, 9; at World Bank, 251–61; WTO and, 105; *see also* CEE transparency; China transparency; corporate transparency; environmental transparency; India transparency; Nigeria transparency
"transparency champions," 180
transparency implementation: automatic publication and, 200–201; conclusion about, 209; demand side of, 208–9; diagnosing challenge of, 182–83; drafting law for, 188–90; implementing law for, 190; internal systems for, 201–6; introduction to, 180–82; politics of, 191–96; prologue for, 179–80; public servants for, 195–96; record keeping/archiving, 196–99; record making and, 199–200; setting stage for, 184–90; supply side for, 196–206; vanguard steps toward, 186–88
Transparency International, 2, 246
Transparency International Corruption Perception Index, 149, 161, 172n22
Transparency International index, 261
transparency law, 11; drafting, 188–

90; in India, 43–44; indications of strong, 44
"transparency line," 218
transparency principles, 282, 292, 304; access to information, 283–85, 298; access to justice, 289–91, 299; public participation in decision making, 286–89, 298–99
"transparency triangle," 183
transparent society, 5
Treatment Action Campaign (TAC), 209
TRI. *See* Toxics Release Inventory
Trinidad and Tobago, 195, 205
Triveni, 42–43
Truth and Reconciliation Commission, 310

Uganda, 194, 265–66, 292, 293
Ugokwe, Jerry, 158
Ukraine, 116, 117, 128, 133; Constitution of, 123; laws in, 125; public servants in, 130; transparency in, 123
Ukrainian Law on Information, 125
Ukrainian Secrecy Act, 123
UN. *See* United Nations
UN Global Compact, 223
UN Security Council, 269
UN Sub-Commission on Promotion of Human Rights, 223
UNECE. *See* United Nations Economic Commission for Europe
Union Carbide, 23, 279
United Kingdom, 182, 188, 191
United Nations (UN), 223
United Nations Convention on Biological Diversity, 295
United Nations Economic Commission for Europe (UNECE), 289, 297
United Nations Environment Programme, 294
United Nations Food and Agricultural Organization, 294
United Nations Framework Convention on Climate Change, 295
United Progressive Alliance (UPA), 44

GPSR Authorized Representative: Easy Access System Europe, Mustamäe tee
50, 10621 Tallinn, Estonia, gpsr.requests@easproject.com